All in One®

Recommended by **Teachers** Trusted by **Toppers**

INFORMATICS PRACTICES

Class 11

AF819586

EVERYTHING YOU NEED TO SCORE

- Simplified Theory
- Topic & Chapter Exercises
- Solved NCERT Exercise
- All Types of Exam Pattern Questions
- CBQs; MCQs, A-R, Case Based
- Sample Question Papers

CBSE Exams 2026

All in One

Recommended by Teachers Trusted by Toppers

INFORMATICS PRACTICES

Class 11

EVERYTHING YOU NEED TO SCORE

- Simplified Theory
- Topic & Chapter Exercises
- Solved NCERT Exercise
- All Types of Exam Pattern Questions
- CBQs; MCQs, A-R, Case Based
- Sample Question Papers

CBSE Exams 2026

Authors
Sanjib Pal, Lalita Kaler,
Abhishek

arihant
SUCCESS AND NOTHING LESS

arihant
SUCCESS AND NOTHING LESS

ARIHANT PRAKASHAN
(School Division Series)

卐 ADMINISTRATIVE & PRODUCTION OFFICES

Regd. Office

'Ramchhaya' 4577/15, Agarwal Road, Darya Ganj, New Delhi -110002
Tele: 011- 47630600, 43518550; Fax: 011- 23280316

卐 *Head Office*

Kalindi, TP Nagar, Meerut (UP) - 250002, Tel: 0121-7156203, 7156204

卐 SALES & SUPPORT OFFICES

Agra, Ahmedabad, Bengaluru, Bareilly, Chennai, Delhi, Guwahati, Hyderabad, Jaipur, Jhansi, Kolkata, Lucknow, Nagpur & Pune.

PO No : TXT-XX-XXXXXXX-X-XX

Published By Arihant Publications (India) Ltd.

For further information about the books published by Arihant, log on to www.arihantbooks.com or e-mail at info@arihantbooks.com

Follow us on

卐 PRICE ₹300.00

PRODUCTION TEAM

Publishing Managers	*Cover Designer*	*Inner Designer*
Mahendra Singh Rawat & Keshav Mohan	Rakesh Rawat	Ankit Tyagi
Project Head	*Page Layouting*	*Proof Reader*
Shruti Aggarwal	Ravinder Kumar	Sumit Rawat

Index *cum* Study Planner

One Book- Endless Features

to Help you Succeed

01

CHAPTER

Computer Overview

Computers are an integral part of our daily lives, shaping how we communicate, work, learn, and solve problems. This chapter provides a foundational understanding of computers, their evolution, components, and the role they play in the digital world.

YOUR STUDY GOALS

1.1 Evolution of Computer
1.2 Functional Units of Computer
1.3 Basic Units of Measurement
1.4 Data and Information

YOUR PRACTICE GOAL

- Objective Type Questions (30 Qs ; MCQs, True or False, Fill in the Blanks, Assertion and Reason)
- Subjective Type Questions (45 Qs ; VSA, SA, LA)
- Case Study Based Questions-4

A computer is an electronic device that can be programmed to accept data (input), process it according to a set of instructions, and generate meaningful results (output).

It performs complex calculations, stores information, and automates various tasks efficiently. A computer, along with additional hardware components such as a monitor, keyboard, mouse, printer, and storage devices, as well as software like operating systems and application programs, together form a complete computer system. Computer systems are used in various fields, including education, healthcare, business, research, and entertainment, making them an essential part of modern life.

In this Chapter

At the start of each chapter, all the chapter topics have been listed , so that students may know what they are going to study.

Basic Computer Operations

Basic computer operations are as follows:

1. **Input** This is the process of entering data and instructions into the computer. For example, typing on a keyboard or clicking with a mouse.
2. **Store** The computer stores the data and instructions for easy access during processing. This includes saving information in memory (e.g., RAM or hard drive).
3. **Process** The computer performs arithmetic (e.g., addition, subtraction) or logical operations (e.g., comparing values) on the input data to transform it into useful information.
4. **Output** After processing, the computer produces results or information for the user, such as displaying on the screen or printing a report.
5. **Control** The control operation manages the order in which all the above operations are carried out, ensuring everything happens in the correct sequence.

TEACHER TIP

Relate the concept of memory to real-life examples like human memory. For example, short-term memory can be compared to RAM, and long-term memory can be compared to secondary storage.

Teacher Tips

Important Points related to given concept to bring students focus on important points.

Simplified Theory

Each chapter contains the necessary study material well supported by Definitions, Facts, Figures, Flow Charts, etc.

Quick Test 1

1. What is computer? What are the basic operations of a computer?
2. What is the difference between input and output devices?
3. What is the role of the control unit in a computer?
4. What are the four functional units of a computer system?
5. What is the primary function of the arithmetic logic unit (ALU)?

Quick Tests

To make students understand the chapter in a smooth part-by-part manner, Quick Tests have been given in each chapter. These Exercises help students to assess the understanding of related concepts at regular interval.

One Book- Endless Features
to Help you Succeed

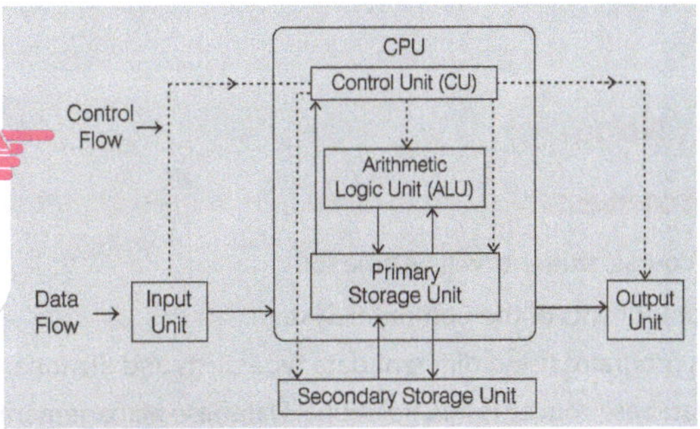

Illustrative Figures

To make the concepts completely visible, illustrative diagrams have been given at various place.

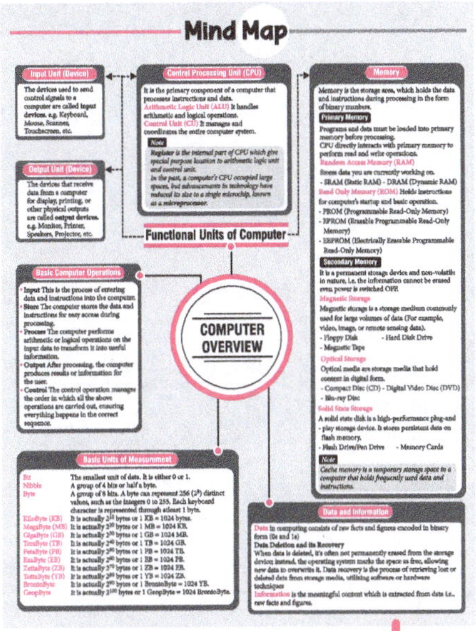

NCERT Questions

To make students completely understand NCERT books, answers of selected NCERT questions have been given in each chapter.

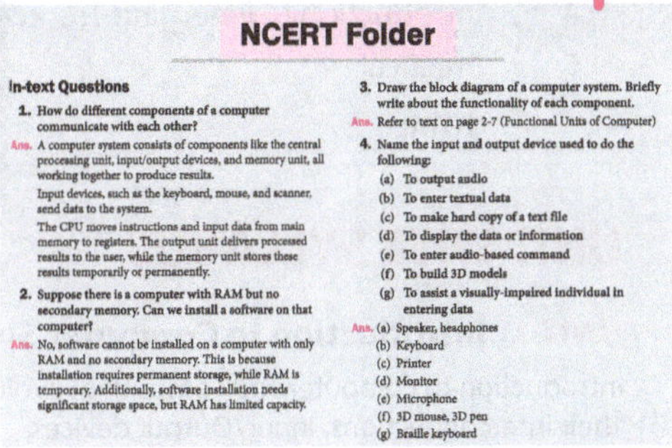

NCERT Folder

In-text Questions

1. **How do different components of a computer communicate with each other?**

Ans. A computer system consists of components like the central processing unit, input/output devices, and memory unit, all working together to produce results.

Input devices, such as the keyboard, mouse, and scanner, send data to the system.

The CPU moves instructions and input data from main memory to registers. The output unit delivers processed results to the user, while the memory unit stores these results temporarily or permanently.

2. **Suppose there is a computer with RAM but no secondary memory. Can we install a software on that computer?**

Ans. No, software cannot be installed on a computer with only RAM and no secondary memory. This is because installation requires permanent storage, while RAM is temporary. Additionally, software installation needs significant storage space, but RAM has limited capacity.

3. **Draw the block diagram of a computer system. Briefly write about the functionality of each component.**

Ans. Refer to text on page 2-7 (Functional Units of Computer)

4. **Name the input and output device used to do the following:**
   - (a) To output audio
   - (b) To enter textual data
   - (c) To make hard copy of a text file
   - (d) To display the data or information
   - (e) To enter audio-based command
   - (f) To build 3D models
   - (g) To assist a visually-impaired individual in entering data

Ans. (a) Speaker, headphones
(b) Keyboard
(c) Printer
(d) Monitor
(e) Microphone
(f) 3D mouse, 3D pen
(g) Braille keyboard

Mind Map

A quick revision visual tool for the complete chapter.

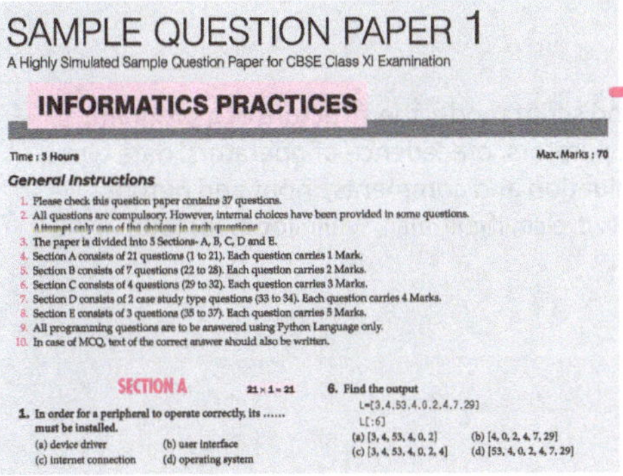

SAMPLE QUESTION PAPER 1

A Highly Simulated Sample Question Paper for CBSE Class XI Examination

INFORMATICS PRACTICES

Time : 3 Hours | Max. Marks : 70

General Instructions

1. Please check this question paper contains 37 questions.
2. All questions are compulsory. However, internal choices have been provided in some questions. Attempt only one of the choices in such questions.
3. The paper is divided into 5 Sections- A, B, C, D and E.
4. Section A consists of 21 questions (1 to 21). Each question carries 1 Mark.
5. Section B consists of 7 questions (22 to 28). Each question carries 2 Marks.
6. Section C consists of 4 questions (29 to 32). Each question carries 3 Marks.
7. Section D consists of 2 case study type questions (33 to 34). Each question carries 4 Marks.
8. Section E consists of 3 questions (35 to 37). Each question carries 5 Marks.
9. All programming questions are to be answered using Python Language only.
10. In case of MCQ, text of the correct answer should also be written.

SECTION A $21 \times 1 = 21$

1. In order for a peripheral to operate correctly, its ...... must be installed.
   (a) device driver (b) user interface
   (c) internet connection (d) operating system

6. Find the output

```
L=[3,4,53,4,0,2,4,7,29]
L[:6]
```

(a) [3, 4, 53, 4, 0, 2] (b) [4, 0, 2, 4, 7, 29]
(c) [3, 4, 53, 4, 0, 2, 4] (d) [53, 4, 0, 2, 4, 7, 29]

Sample Question Papers

To make students practice of examination in real sense, there are 3 Sample Question Papers at the end. All these Sample Questions Papers are exactly prepared on the latest syllabus & pattern of examination.

Latest Course *Structure*

Prerequisite : None

Learning Outcomes:

At the end of this course, students will be able to:

- Identify the components of the Computer System.
- Create Python programs using different data types, lists and dictionaries.
- Understand database concepts and Relational Database Management Systems.
- Retrieve and manipulate data in RDBMS using Structured Query Language.
- Identify the Emerging trends in the fields of Information Technology.

Distribution of Marks and Periods:

Unit No.	Unit Name	Marks
1	Introduction to Computer System	10
2	Introduction to Python	25
3	Database Concepts and the Structured Query Language	30
4	Introduction to Emerging Trends	5
5	Practical	30
	TOTAL	100

UNIT WISE SYLLABUS

UNIT 1 Introduction to Computer System

Introduction to computer and computing: evolution of computing devices, components of a computer system and their interconnections, Input/Output devices.

Computer Memory: Units of memory, types of memory – primary and secondary, data deletion, its recovery and related security concerns.

Software: purpose and types – system and application software, generic and specific purpose software.

UNIT 2 Introduction to Python

Basics of Python programming, Python interpreter - interactive and script mode, the structure of a program, indentation, identifiers, keywords, constants, variables, types of operators, precedence of operators, data types, mutable and immutable data types, statements, expressions, evaluation and comments, input and output statements, data type conversion, debugging, control statements: if-else, if-elif-else, while loop, for loop

Lists: list operations - creating, initialising, traversing and manipulating lists, list methods and built-in functions len (), list (), append (), insert (), count (), index (), remove (), pop (), reverse (), sort (), min (), max (), sum ().

Dictionary: concept of key-value pair, creating, initialising, traversing, updating and deleting elements, dictionary methods and built-in functions dict (), len (), keys, () values (), items(), update (), del (), clear ().

Introduction to NumPy : Introduction, Creation of NumPy Arrays From List.

UNIT 3 Database Concepts and the Structured Query Language

Database Concepts: Introduction to database concepts and its need, Database Management System. Relational data model: concept of domain, tuple, relation, candidate key, primary key, alternate key.

Advantages of using Structured Query Language: Data Definition Language, Data Query Language and Data Manipulation Language, Introduction to MySQL: Creating a database using MySQL, Data Types.

Data Definition : CREATE DATABASE, CREATE Table, DROP, ALTER.

Data Query : SELECT, FROM, WHERE with relational operators, BETWEEN, logical operators, IS NULL, IS NOT NULL

Data Manipulation : INSERT, DELETE, UPDATE.

UNIT 4 Introduction to the Emerging Trends

Artificial Intelligence, Machine Learning, Natural Language Processing, Immersive experience (AR, VR), Robotics, Big data and its characteristics, Internet of Things (IoT), Sensors, Smart Cities, Cloud Computing and Cloud Services (SaaS, IaaS, PaaS); Grid Computing, Block chain technology.

Practical Marks Distribution

S. No.	Unit Name	Marks
1	Problem solving using Python programming language	11
3	Creating database using MySQL and performing Queries	7
4	Practical file (minimum of 14 Python programs and 14 SQL queries)	7
5	Viva-Voce	5
	TOTAL	**30**

SUGGESTED PRACTICAL LIST

(a) Programming in Python

1. To find average and grade for given marks.
2. To find sale price of an item with given cost and discount (%).
3. To calculate perimeter/circumference and area of shapes such as triangle, rectangle, square and circle.
4. To calculate Simple and Compound Interest.
5. To calculate profit-loss for a given Cost and Sell Price.
6. To calculate EMI for Amount, Period and Interest.
7. To calculate tax - GST / Income Tax.
8. To find the largest and smallest numbers in a list.
9. To find the third largest/smallest number in a list.
10. To find the sum of squares of the first 100 natural numbers.
11. To print the first 'n' multiples of given number.
12. To count the number of vowels in a user entered string.
13. To print the words starting with a alphabet in a user entered string.
14. To print number of occurrences of a given alphabet in each string.
15. Create a dictionary to store names of states and their capitals.
16. Create a dictionary of students to store names and marks obtained in 5 subjects.
17. To print the highest and lowest values in the dictionary.

(b) Data Management: SQL Commands

18. To create a database.
19. To create a student table with the student id, class, section, gender, name, dob and marks as attributes where the student id is the primary key.
20. To insert the details of at least 10 students in the above table.
21. To display the entire content of the table.
22. To display Rno, Name and Marks of those students who are scoring marks more than 50.
23. To display Rno, Name, DOB of those students who are born between '2005- 01-01' and '2005-12-31'.

01

CHAPTER

Computer Overview

Computers are an integral part of our daily lives, shaping how we communicate, work, learn, and solve problems. This chapter provides a foundational understanding of computers, their evolution, components, and the role they play in the digital world.

YOUR STUDY GOALS

YOUR PRACTICE GOAL

- Objective Type Questions (30 Qs ; MCQs, True or False, Fill in the Blanks, Assertion and Reason)
- Subjective Type Questions (46 Qs ; VSA, SA, LA)
- Case Study Based Questions-4

A computer is an electronic device that can be programmed to accept data (input), process it according to a set of instructions, and generate meaningful results (output).

It performs complex calculations, stores information, and automates various tasks efficiently. A computer, along with additional hardware components such as a monitor, keyboard, mouse, printer, and storage devices, as well as software like operating systems and application programs, together form a complete computer system. Computer systems are used in various fields, including education, healthcare, business, research, and entertainment, making them an essential part of modern life.

Basic Computer Operations

Basic computer operations are as follows:

1. **Input** This is the process of entering data and instructions into the computer. For example, typing on a keyboard or clicking with a mouse.
2. **Store** The computer stores the data and instructions for easy access during processing. This includes saving information in memory (e.g., RAM or hard drive).
3. **Process** The computer performs arithmetic (e.g., addition, subtraction) or logical operations (e.g., comparing values) on the input data to transform it into useful information.
4. **Output** After processing, the computer produces results or information for the user, such as displaying on the screen or printing a report.
5. **Control** The control operation manages the order in which all the above operations are carried out, ensuring everything happens in the correct sequence.

1.1 Evolution of Computer

Computing devices have come a long way, from simple calculators to powerful computers. This rapid evolution is shown in the below timeline figure

500 BC — Abacus
Computing is attributed to the invention of ABACUS almost 3000 years ago. It was a mechanical device capable of doing simple arithmetic calculations only.

1642 — Pascaline
Blaize Pascal invented a mechanical calculator known as Pascal calculator or Pascaline to do addition and subtraction of two numbers directly and multiplication and division through repeated addition and subtraction.

1834 — Analytic Engine
Charles Babbage invented analytical engine, a mechanical computing device for inputting, processing, storing and displaying the output, which is considered to form the basis of modern computers.

1890 — Tabulating Machine
Herman Hollerith designed a tabulating machine for summarising the data stored on the punched card. It is considered to be the first step towards programming.

1937 — Turing Machine
The Turing machine concept was a general purpose programmable machine that was capable of solving any problem by executing the program stored on the punched cards.

1945 — EDVAC/ENIAC
John Von Neumann introduced the concept of stored program computer which was capable of storing data as well as program in the memory. The EDVAC and then the ENIAC computers were developed based on this concept.

1947 — Transistor
Vacuum tubes were replaced by transistors developed at Bell Labs, using semiconductor materials.

1970 — Integrated Circuit
An Integrated Circuit (IC) is a silicon chip which contains entire electronic circuit on a very small area. The size of computer drastically reduced because of ICs.

- In the **1970s**, Large Scale Integration (LSI) enabled entire CPUs on single chips, known as microprocessors. Moore's Law predicted exponential growth in transistor density.
- By the **1980s**, Very Large Scale Integration (VLSI) allowed around 3 million components on a chip, advancing to Super Large Scale Integration (SLSI) with over 1 million components per IC.
- IBM introduced its first PC in **1981**, and Apple launched Macintosh in **1984**. Graphical User Interfaces (GUI) replaced command-line systems, boosting PC popularity. The **1990s** saw the rise of the World Wide Web (WWW), making computers essential.
- Laptops, smartphones, and tablets enhanced portability and accessibility, driven by processor miniaturization and high-speed connectivity. Wearable gadgets like smartwatches and IoT-enabled smart appliances now utilize Artificial Intelligence (AI), shaping the next wave of computing.

1.2 Functional Units of Computer

The basic organization of computer system includes four major functional units; Input unit, Output unit, CPU and computer memory/memory unit. The block diagram of basic computer system is shown below

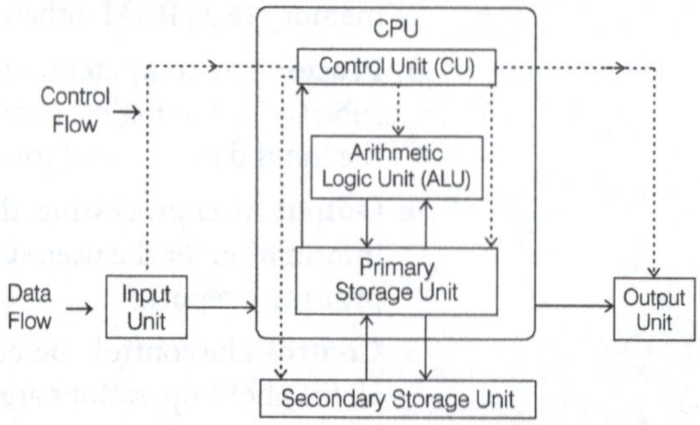

Input Unit (Device)

The devices used to send control signals to a computer are called **input devices**.

The following functions are performed by an input unit

(i) It accepts (or reads) the instructions and data from the outside world.

(ii) It converts these instructions and data in computer acceptable form (i.e., binary form) because a computer can understand only binary symbols (i.e., 0 and 1).

(iii) It supplies the converted instructions and data to the computer system for further processing.

Some of the commonly used input devices:

- **Keyboard** Keyboard is used for typing text and entering commands.
- **Mouse** Mouse is used for navigating the screen and selecting options.
- **Scanner** Scanner is used for digitizing physical documents.
- **Touchscreen** It is used for direct interaction with the screen.

Note *Specially designed braille keyboards are also available to help the visually impaired for entering data into a computer.Besides, we can now enter data through voice, for example, we can use Google voice search to search the web where we can input the search string through our voice.*

Output Unit (Device)

The devices that receive data from a computer for display, printing, or other physical outputs are called **output devices.**

The following functions are performed by an output unit

(i) It accepts the results produced by the computer, which are in coded form (i.e., in binary form), and hence, can't be easily understood by us.

(ii) It converts these coded results to human acceptable (readable) form.

(iii) It supplies the converted result to the outside world.

Some of the commonly used output devices:

- **Monitor** Monitor is used for displaying visual information to the user.
- **Printer** Printer produce hard copies of documents.
- **Speakers** It is used for producing sounds.
- **Projector** Projector display images on a large screen.

3D Printers

Now-a-days 3D printers are widely accessible, used across various industries for prototyping, creating custom parts, and even producing finished products. Advancements allowing for higher print quality, faster speeds, and a wider range of materials, have made them valuable tools in fields like engineering, healthcare, manufacturing, education, and even consumer markets, where people can print items at home for personal use.

Central Processing Unit (CPU)

Sometimes CPU is only referred as the central processor, but more commonly called only processor, the CPU is the brain of the computer where all or most of the calculations take place. In terms of computing power, the CPU is most important element of a computer system.

Two typical components of a CPU are the following

(i) The **Arithmetic Logic Unit (ALU)**, performs arithmetic and logical operations.

(ii) The **Control Unit (CU)**, extracts instructions from memory and decodes it, then executes them.

Arithmetic Logic Unit (ALU)

The Arithmetic Logic Unit (ALU) is a key component of a computer's CPU, It is responsible for performing arithmetic operations like (+, -, ×, /) as well as logical operations such as comparisons and Boolean operations.

It processes binary data, taking input from CPU registers and generating output that is stored back in registers or memory. The ALU is the processing unit that carries out instructions and calculations necessary for different tasks.

Control Unit (CU)

The CU manages communication between input and output devices. It directs the execution of stored instructions by coordinating with the ALU and registers, ensuring proper data and instruction processing.

The primary function of the CU is to fetch instructions from memory, decode operations, identify involved devices, and generate necessary control signals.

Register

It is the internal part of CPU which give special purpose location to arithmetic logic unit and control unit. These are used to store intermediate results obtained during the execution of instructions.

Quick Test 1

1. What is computer? What are the basic operations of a computer?
2. What is the difference between input and output devices?
3. What is the role of the control unit in a computer?
4. What are the four functional units of a computer system?
5. What is the primary function of the arithmetic logic unit (ALU)?

Memory

Memory is the storage area (internal or external), which holds the data and instructions during processing in the form of binary numbers.

Memory Hierarchy

Memory hierarchy is a system of arranging memory components based on their speed and cost.

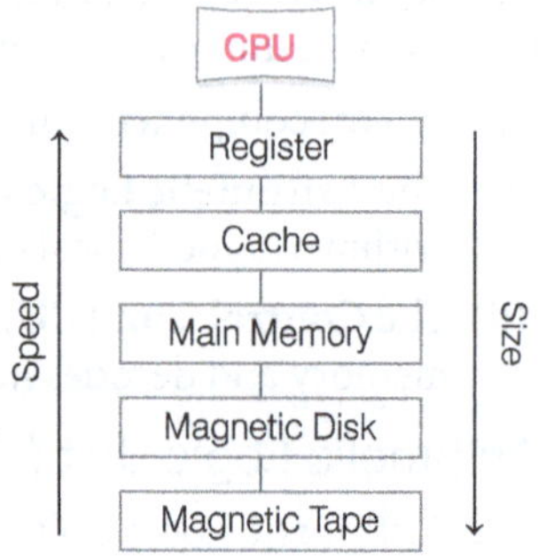

The faster memory components, like registers and cache, are smaller and more expensive, while slower but larger memory components, like main memory and secondary storage, are cheaper.

This hierarchy structure allows computers to balance performance and cost-effectiveness.

The memory is characterised on the basis of two key factors: capacity and access time.

Classification of Computer Memory

Computer memory mainly classified into two categories shown below

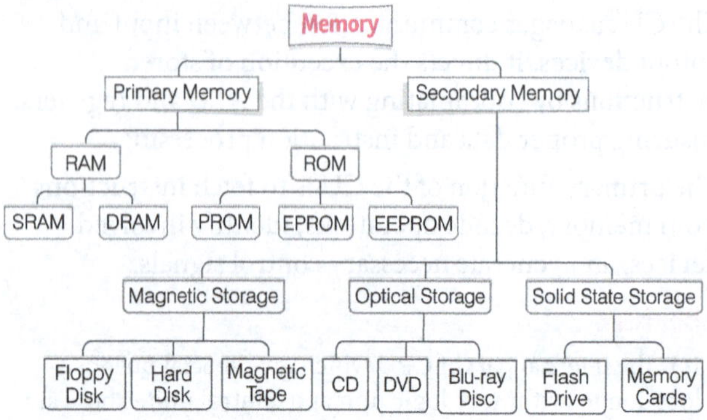

Primary Memory

Primary memory is a essential part of a computer system. Programs and data must be loaded into it before processing. The CPU directly interacts with primary memory to perform read and write operations.

There are two types of primary memory

Random Access Memory (RAM)

RAM (Random Access Memory) is a type of computer memory that allows for both **reading** and **writing** of data. It is faster than other types of memory, such as hard drives, and is used to store data that the computer is actively working with. However, RAM is volatile, meaning that its contents are lost when the power is turned off.

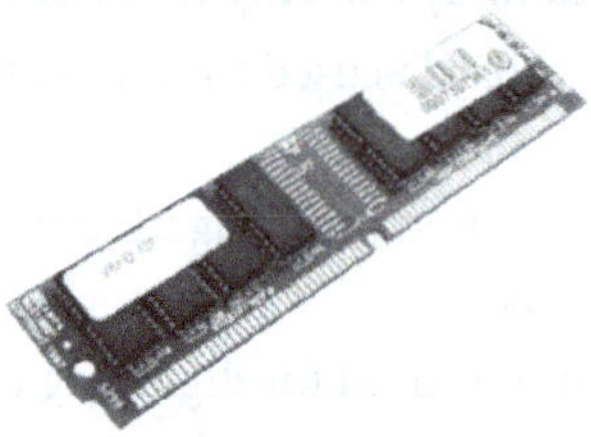

There are two main types of RAM:

(i) **SRAM (Static RAM)** is a type of memory that requires a constant power supply in order to hold the data and information. SRAM is faster but more expensive and is often used for cache memory.

(ii) **DRAM (Dynamic RAM)** stores the information and data in a cell containing a capacitor and transistor, these cells may be refreshed with electric pulses in few milliseconds. DRAM is slower but cheaper, and the most common type of RAM used in computers.

Read Only Memory (ROM)

ROM (Read Only Memory) is a type of computer memory that stores permanent information. It's a non-volatile memory means once data is written to ROM, it cannot be changed. It holds essential instructions for the computer's startup and basic operations.

ROM is further sub divided into following categories

(i) **PROM (Programmable Read-Only Memory)**
- Data is written to PROM once, typically during manufacturing.
- After programming, the data cannot be changed.
- It is used for storing firmware, device drivers, and other essential system software.

(ii) **EPROM (Erasable Programmable Read-Only Memory)**
- Data can be erased using ultraviolet light.
- Once erased, the EPROM can be reprogrammed.
- It is less flexible than EEPROM but more cost-effective.

(iii) **EEPROM (Electrically Erasable Programmable Read-Only Memory)**
- Data can be erased and reprogrammed electrically.
- This one is more flexible than EPROM but slower.
- It is used for storing configuration settings and firmware that may need updates.

Cache Memory

It is the type of memory which is very nearest to the CPU and all the recent instructions are stored in it. The cache memory stores the program (or its part) currently being executed or which may be executed within a short period of time. The cache memory also stores temporary data that the CPU may recently require for manipulation.

The capacity of the cache memory is too low in compare to memory and hard disk.

Importance of Cache Memory

Cache memory is a high-speed memory that sits between the processor and main memory. It stores frequently accessed data, reducing the need to fetch data from the slower main memory.

A cache memory has an access time of 100ns (100 nano seconds) while the main memory may have an access time of 700ns. This significantly improves the overall performance of the computer by bridging the speed gap between the processor and main memory.

Secondary Memory

Secondary memory/storage, also known as **auxiliary memory**, is a slower and cheaper form of memory compared to primary memory. It is a permanent storage device and **non-volatile** in nature, i.e. the information cannot be erased even power is switched OFF. CPU does not access the secondary memory directly.

Some secondary memories are described below

Magnetic Storage

Magnetic storage is a storage medium commonly used for large volumes of data (**For example**, video, image, or remote sensing data). Some points related to magnetic storage medium are given below:

(i) It uses magnetic head to read and write the data.

(ii) It gets the data from a magnetisable medium. The medium may be a plastic tape coated with fine particles of a metal.

(iii) It can store lots of data, but this data is slower to access.

This storage device includes floppy disk drives, tape drives and hard drives. Some of them are described below:

- **Floppy Disk** A floppy disk is a removable storage device used to save data on computers. Floppy disks are round in shape and a thin plastic disk is coated with iron oxides. The data inside is stored in tracks and sectors. Floppy disks are available in three sizes: 8 inches, 5.25 inches, and 3.5 inches.

The entire floppy is divided into circular segments called **tracks**. Each track is given a unique number. The outermost track is referred as 0 and the track inner to that is 1 and so on.

Each track is further divided into segments called **sectors**. The number of segments in each track has the same capacity. The outer plastic cover has read/write hole covered by a metal sheet. This metal cover automatically opens when the floppy is inserted inside the floppy disk drive.

Floppy disks are commonly used to move files between different computers. The first widely used floppy disk drives were the 8 inch, $5\frac{1}{4}$ inch, which were later replaced with $3\frac{1}{2}$inch.

Note *Floppy disks were a popular storage medium from the 1970 s to the early 2000s but their use has declined significantly since then.*

- **Hard Disk Drive** Hard Disk Drive or HDD is a non-volatile, random access digital storage device. It is a data storage device used for storing and retrieving information using rotating disks (platters) coated with magnetic material.

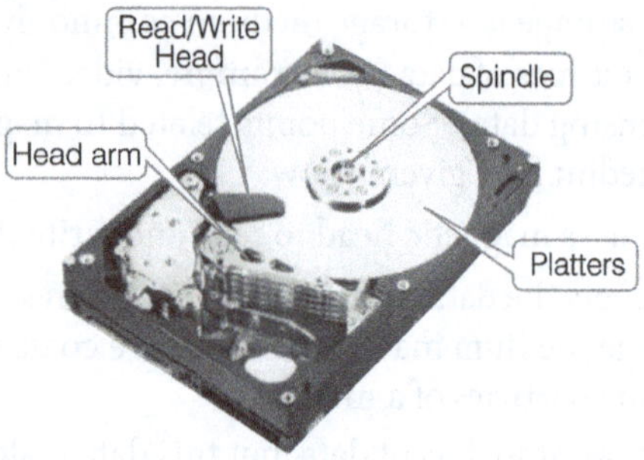

It consists of a spindle that holds non-magnetic flat circular disks, called **platters**, which hold the recorded data. Each platter requires two read/write heads, that are used to read and write the information from a platter. The information is stored in bands; each band of information is called a **track**. Each platter has the same number of tracks, and a track location that cuts across all platters is called a **cylinder**. The tracks are divided into pie-shaped sections known as **sectors**.

- **Magnetic Tape** Magnetic tape is a storage medium made of magnetic material, often found in large open reels or smaller cartridges/cassettes. It is usually 12.5mm to 25mm wide and 500m to 1200m long. It's a plastic ribbon coated with a magnetic recording medium where data is stored as magnetized and non-magnetized spots.

Magnetic tapes are cheaper than other storage media, but they are sequential access devices, meaning the tape must be rewound or moved forward to access specific data. This makes them unsuitable for frequently updated files but ideal for backups and data transfer.

Optical Storage

Optical media are storage media that holds content in digital form. Some point related to optical storage are as follows

(i) It uses a laser to read and write data.

(ii) In optical storage media, the data is stored in the form of pits that are prepared by using a laser beam. This process is known as **burning** data onto a disk.

(iii) The data on the storage media is read by bouncing the laser beam off the surface of the media. If the beam hits a dot, it is reflected back, then records the pit as a 1, otherwise records the pit as 0.

(iv) Optical disc capacity ranges up to 8GB.

(v) It tends to be slower than typical hard drive speeds.

(vi) Examples of optical storage devices include CDs, DVDs etc.

Some of the optical storage are described below

(i) **Compact Disc** (CD) CD is an optical media that is used to store digital data.

It consists of a circular disc, which is coated with a thin metal that is highly reflective. Laser beam technology is used for recording/reading of data on the disk. It is also known as **laser disc** or **optical laser disc**, due to the use of laser beam technology.

The diameter of the CD ranges from 10 cms to 30 cms. One CD can store 600 MB to 750 MB.

Compact discs are categorized into three parts

(a) Compact Disc-Read Only Memory (CD-ROM)

(b) Compact Disc-Recordable (CD-R)

(c) Compact Disc-Rewritable (CD-RW)

(ii) **Digital Video Disc** (DVD) DVD is also known as **Super Density Disc** (SDD) or **Digital Versatile Disc** (DVD). DVDs offer higher storage capacity than compact disc while having the same dimensions. It has capacity of 4.7 GB to 9.4 GB.

DVDs come in three varieties

(a) DVD ROM (DVD-Read Only Memory).

(b) DVD-R (DVD-Recordable).

(c) DVD-RW (DVD-Rewritable).

(iii) **Blu-ray Disc** It is an optical disc storage medium designed to re-capture the data normally in DVD format. Blu-ray disc (BD) contains 25 GB (23.31 GB) per layer space.

The name Blu-ray disc refers to the blue laser used to read the disc, which allows information to be stored at a greater density than the longer- wavelength red laser used in DVDs.

Blu-ray can hold almost 5 times more data than a single layer DVD.

The variations in the formats are as follows

(a) BD-ROM (Read only)

(b) BD-R (Recordable)

(c) BD-RW (Rewritable)

(d) BD-RE (Rewritable) erasable

Solid State Storage

The term solid state essentially means **no moving parts.** Solid- state storage devices are based on electronic circuits with no moving parts.

It stores persistent data on flash memory. A solid state disk is a high-performance plug-and-play storage device. Examples of solid-state storage include pen drive, memory card etc.

Some of solid state storage are described below

(i) **Flash Drive/Pen Drive** A flash drive is a portable data storage device that includes flash memory with an integrated Universal Serial Bus (USB) interface.

Flash drives are typically removable, rewritable and physically much smaller than a floppy disk (as same as the size of your thumb).

Today flash drives are available in various storage capacities, 256 MB, 512 MB, 1 GB, 2 GB, 4 GB, 8 GB, 16 GB, 64 GB upto.

(ii) **Memory Cards** These are the data storage devices in a chip shaped which can store the data in it. They are commonly used in many electronic devices, including digital cameras, mobile phones, laptop computers. They are small, re-recordable, easily portable and very light weighted.

TEACHER TIP

Relate the concept of memory to real-life examples like human memory. For example, short-term memory can be compared to RAM, and long-term memory can be compared to secondary storage.

1.3 Basic Units of Measurement

When you use a RAM, ROM, floppy disk or hard disk, the data is measured using some unit. In computer terminology, they are called Nibble, Bit, Byte, Kilobyte, Megabyte, Gigabyte etc.

Units of computer memory measurements

Bit The smallest unit of data. It is either 0 or 1.

Nibble A group of 4 bits or half a byte.

Byte A group of 8 bits. A byte can represent 256 (2^8) distinct values, such as the integers 0 to 255. Each keyboard character is represented through atleast 1 byte.

KiloByte (KB) It is actually 2^{10} bytes or 1 KB = 1024 bytes.

MegaByte (MB) It is actually 2^{20} bytes or 1 MB = 1024 KB.

GigaByte (GB) It is actually 2^{30} bytes or 1 GB = 1024 MB.

TeraByte (TB) It is actually 2^{40} bytes or 1 TB = 1024 GB.

PetaByte (PB) It is actually 2^{50} bytes or 1 PB = 1024 TB.

ExaByte (EB) It is actually 2^{60} bytes or 1 EB = 1024 PB.

ZettaByte (ZB) It is actually 2^{70} bytes or 1 ZB = 1024 EB.

YottaByte (YB) It is actually 2^{80} bytes or 1 YB = 1024 ZB.

BrontoByte It is actually 2^{90} bytes or 1 BrontoByte = 1024 YB.

GeopByte It is actually 2^{100} bytes or 1 GeopByte = 1024 BrontoByte.

Here, GeopByte is the highest memory measurement unit.

Hardware

Hardware refers to the physical components of a computer system that can be seen and touched. It includes input devices (keyboard, mouse), output devices (monitor, printer), storage devices (HDD, SSD), and processing units (CPU, RAM). Hardware is essential for running software and performing computing tasks. It is broadly classified into:

- **Input Devices** Devices like a keyboard, mouse, or scanner used to enter data into a computer.
- **Processing Unit** The CPU (Central Processing Unit) is the brain of the computer, responsible for executing instructions.
- **Memory** Includes Primary Memory (RAM, Cache) for temporary storage and Secondary Memory (HDD, SSD) for permanent storage.
- **Output Devices** Devices like a monitor, printer, and speakers that display or output processed data.

Hardware and software work together to make a computer functional.

1.4 Data and Information

Data

Data in computing consists of raw facts and figures encoded in binary form (0s and 1s)

For example, +, 3, 8, 11, =, etc.

Data can be classified into three types

1. **Structured Data** Organized in a defined format, such as tables. Examples include attendance records or sales transactions.
2. **Unstructured Data** Data without a specific format, like audio, video, and social media posts.
3. **Semi-structured Data** Data with internal tags for separating elements, such as emails or CSV files.

Data Deletion and its Recovery

When data is deleted, it's often not permanently erased from the storage device; instead, the operating system marks the space as free, allowing new data to overwrite it. Data recovery is the process of retrieving lost or deleted data from storage media, utilizing software or hardware techniques

Types of Data Recovery

- **Logical Data Recovery** Focuses on restoring data when the physical storage device is functional but data has been lost due to accidental deletion, formatting, or software corruption.
- **Physical Data Recovery** Addresses situations involving physical damage to storage devices, requiring specialized hardware and expertise.

Related Security Concerns

There are usually two security concerns associated with data. One is its deletion by some unauthorised person or software. These concerns can be avoided by limiting access to the computer system and using passwords for user accounts and files, wherever possible.

There is also an option of encrypting files to protect them from unwanted modification.

There other concern is related to unwanted recovery of data by unauthorised user/software. Many a times, we discard our old, broken or malfunctioning storage devices without taking care to delete data.

Information

Information is the meaningful content which is extracted from data i.e., raw facts and figures.

For example, 3 + 8 = 11 is the information.

The process of converting data into information is known as **Information Processing Cycle** or **Input Process Output Cycle.**

Quick Test 2

1. Which memory is the fastest?
   (a) RAM (b) Cache
   (c) Hard disk (d) SSD
2. What is primary memory and how is it different from secondary memory?
3. What is the difference between SRAM and DRAM?
4. Define cache memory.
5. What is the smallest unit of data in a computer?
   (a) Byte (b) Bit
   (c) Nibble (d) Word
6. Can you give some more examples of unstructured data?

Mind Map

COMPUTER OVERVIEW

Functional Units of Computer

Input Unit (Device)

The devices used to send control signals to a computer are called **input devices**. e.g. Keyboard, Mouse, Scanner, Touchscreen, etc.

Output Unit (Device)

The devices that receive data from a computer for display, printing, or other physical outputs are called **output devices.** e.g. Monitor, Printer, Speakers, Projector, etc.

Central Processing Unit (CPU)

It is the primary component of a computer that processes instructions and data.

Arithmetic Logic Unit (ALU) It handles arithmetic and logical operations.

Control Unit (CU) It manages and coordinates the entire computer system.

Note

__Register__ is the internal part of CPU which give special purpose location to arithmetic logic unit and control unit.

In the past, a computer's CPU occupied large spaces, but advancements in technology have reduced its size to a single microchip, known as a __microprocessor__.

Memory

Memory is the storage area, which holds the data and instructions during processing in the form of binary numbers.

Primary Memory

Programs and data must be loaded into primary memory before processing.

CPU directly interacts with primary memory to perform read and write operations.

Random Access Memory (RAM)

Stores data you are currently working on.

- SRAM (Static RAM) - DRAM (Dynamic RAM)

Read Only Memory (ROM) Holds instructions for computer's startup and basic operation.

- PROM (Programmable Read-Only Memory)
- EPROM (Erasable Programmable Read-Only Memory)
- EEPROM (Electrically Erasable Programmable Read-Only Memory)

Secondary Memory

It is a permanent storage device and non-volatile in nature, i.e. the information cannot be erased even power is switched OFF.

Magnetic Storage

Magnetic storage is a storage medium commonly used for large volumes of data (For example, video, image, or remote sensing data).

- Floppy Disk - Hard Disk Drive
- Magnetic Tape

Optical Storage

Optical media are storage media that hold content in digital form.

- Compact Disc (CD) - Digital Video Disc (DVD)
- Blu-ray Disc

Solid State Storage

A solid state disk is a high-performance plug-and - play storage device. It stores persistent data on flash memory.

- Flash Drive/Pen Drive - Memory Cards

Note

Cache memory is a temporary storage space in a computer that holds frequently used data and instructions.

Basic Computer Operations

- **Input** This is the process of entering data and instructions into the computer.
- **Store** The computer stores the data and instructions for easy access during processing.
- **Process** The computer performs arithmetic or logical operations on the input data to transform it into useful information.
- **Output** After processing, the computer produces results or information for the user.
- **Control** The control operation manages the order in which all the above operations are carried out, ensuring everything happens in the correct sequence.

Basic Units of Measurement

Bit	The smallest unit of data. It is either 0 or 1.
Nibble	A group of 4 bits or half a byte.
Byte	A group of 8 bits. A byte can represent 256 (2^8) distinct values, such as the integers 0 to 255. Each keyboard character is represented through atleast 1 byte.
KiloByte (KB)	It is actually 2^{10} bytes or 1 KB = 1024 bytes.
MegaByte (MB)	It is actually 2^{20} bytes or 1 MB = 1024 KB.
GigaByte (GB)	It is actually 2^{30} bytes or 1 GB = 1024 MB.
TeraByte (TB)	It is actually 2^{40} bytes or 1 TB = 1024 GB.
PetaByte (PB)	It is actually 2^{50} bytes or 1 PB = 1024 TB.
ExaByte (EB)	It is actually 2^{60} bytes or 1 EB = 1024 PB.
ZettaByte (ZB)	It is actually 2^{70} bytes or 1 ZB = 1024 EB.
YottaByte (YB)	It is actually 2^{80} bytes or 1 YB = 1024 ZB.
BrontoByte	It is actually 2^{90} bytes or 1 BrontoByte = 1024 YB.
GeopByte	It is actually 2^{100} bytes or 1 GeopByte = 1024 BrontoByte.

Data and Information

Data in computing consists of raw facts and figures encoded in binary form (0s and 1s)

Data Deletion and its Recovery

When data is deleted, it's often not permanently erased from the storage device; instead, the operating system marks the space as free, allowing new data to overwrite it. Data recovery is the process of retrieving lost or deleted data from storage media, utilizing software or hardware techniques

Information is the meaningful content which is extracted from data i.e., raw facts and figures.

NCERT Folder

In-text Questions

1. How do different components of a computer communicate with each other?

Ans. A computer system consists of components like the central processing unit, input/output devices, and memory unit, all working together to produce results.

Input devices, such as the keyboard, mouse, and scanner, send data to the system.

The CPU moves instructions and input data from main memory to registers. The output unit delivers processed results to the user, while the memory unit stores these results temporarily or permanently.

2. Suppose there is a computer with RAM but no secondary memory. Can we install a software on that computer?

Ans. No, software cannot be installed on a computer with only RAM and no secondary memory. This is because installation requires permanent storage, while RAM is temporary. Additionally, software installation needs significant storage space, but RAM has limited capacity.

3. Explore possible ways of recovering deleted data or data from a corrupted device.

Ans.
- **Using Data Recovery Software** Programs like Recuva, EaseUS, or Stellar can scan storage and restore deleted or damaged files if not overwritten.
- **Restoring from Backups** – Data can be easily recovered from cloud storage, external drives, or system backups if available.
- **Professional Data Recovery Services** Experts use special methods to recover data from damaged or corrupted storage devices.

Exercise Questions

1. What is the need of RAM? How does it differ from ROM?

Ans. RAM is used for quickly accessing a data.

RAM is temporary and volatile memory, used for active programs and data whereas ROM is permanent and non-volatile memory, storing essential system instructions.

2. What is the need for secondary memory?

Ans. Secondary memory (like hard drives, SSDs) provides non-volatile storage for programs and data when the computer is OFF.

3. Draw the block diagram of a computer system. Briefly write about the functionality of each component.

Ans. Refer to text on page 2-7 (Functional Units of Computer)

4. Name the input and output device used to do the following:

(a) To output audio

(b) To enter textual data

(c) To make hard copy of a text file

(d) To display the data or information

(e) To enter audio-based command

(f) To build 3D models

(g) To assist a visually-impaired individual in entering data

Ans. (a) Speaker, headphones

(b) Keyboard

(c) Printer

(d) Monitor

(e) Microphone

(f) 3D mouse, 3D pen

(g) Braille keyboard

5. Convert the following into bytes:

(a) 2 MB **(b) 3.7 GB**

(c) 1.2 TB

Ans. (a) $1\text{ MB} = 2^{10} \times 2^{10}\text{ bytes} = 2^{20}\text{ bytes}$

$2\text{ MB} = 2 \times 2^{20}\text{ bytes} = 2^{21}\text{ bytes}$

(b) $1\text{ GB} = 2^{10} \times 2^{10} \times 2^{10}\text{ bytes} = 2^{30}\text{ bytes}$

$3.7\text{ GB} = 3.7 \times 2^{30}\text{ bytes}$

(c) $1\text{ TB} = 2^{10} \times 2^{10} \times 2^{10} \times 2^{10}\text{ bytes} = 2^{40}\text{ bytes}$

$1.2\text{ TB} = 1.2 \times 2^{40}\text{ bytes}$

6. Write down the type of memory needed to do the following:

(a) To store data permanently

(b) To execute the program

(c) To store the instructions which cannot be overwritten.

Ans. (a) Secondary memory (e.g., Hard Disk Drive (HDD), Solid State Drive (SSD), Flash Memory)

(b) Random Access Memory (RAM)

(c) Read-Only Memory (ROM)

EXAM PATTERN QUESTIONS

Objective Type Questions

Multiple Choice Questions

1. **The set of instructions given to a computer is called:**
(a) Program (b) ALU (c) CU (d) Storage

2. **A computer takes ____ then ____ it and returns ____.**
(a) Process, input, output (b) Input, output, process
(c) Input, process, output (d) None of these

3. **User communicates with a computer with the help of which device?**
(a) Input device (b) Output device
(c) Software device (d) Both (a) and (b)

4. **The device that used to give single or multiple colored image and drawings are______**
(a) Monitors (b) Printers (c) Plotters (d) VDUs

5. **Which among the following is an important circuitry in a computer system that directs the operation of the processor?**
(a) Memory (b) Address Bus
(c) Accumulator (d) Control unit

6. **A computer science student is analyzing the factors affecting the speed of program execution. They observe that a specific component within the CPU temporarily holds data and instructions, allowing faster access compared to other storage types. Which component is responsible for this function?** **Competency Based Que.**
(a) Register (b) Cache
(c) Control Unit (d) ALU

7. **During a system startup, a technician notices that the computer loads essential firmware before the operating system begins. This firmware is stored in a type of non-volatile memory that retains data even when the system is powered off. Which type of memory is used for this purpose?** **Competency Based Que.**
(a) DRAM (b) SRAM
(c) ROM (d) Cache memory

8. **Which of the following statements about DRAM is true?**
(a) It is faster than SRAM.
(b) It retains data as long as power is supplied.
(c) It needs to be refreshed periodically.
(d) It is used in specialized applications.

9. **......... acts as temporary high speed holding area between the memory and the CPU thereby improving processing capabilities.**
(a) ROM
(b) RAM
(c) Temporary memory
(d) Cache memory

10. **Which of the following is not a characteristic of secondary memory?**
(a) It is volatile.
(b) It is used to store data permanently.
(c) It is slower than main memory.
(d) It can transfer data between devices.

11. **A disc's content that is recorded at the time of manufacture and that cannot be changed or erased by the user is**
(a) memory only (b) write only
(b) once only (d) read only

12. **Which of these is not optical media?**
(a) CDs (b) Blue ray Disc
(c) DVDs (d) Flash memory

13. **1 TB is equivalent to ______ bytes.**
(a) 1024 (b) $(1024)^2$
(c) $(1024)^3$ (d) $(1024)^4$

Fill in the Blanks

14. The devices through which control signals are sent to a computer are termed as ______ devices. These devices convert the input data into a digital form that is acceptable by the computer system.

15. Data entered through input devices is temporarily stored in the ______ (also called RAM) of the computer system. For permanent storage, data is stored in ______ memory.

16. During the 1970s, Large Scale Integration (LSI) of electronic circuits allowed integration of complete ______ on a single chip, called microprocessor.

17. Cache memory helps bridge the speed gap between the ______ and ______, providing faster data access than RAM.

18. Secondary memory is ______ and has a larger storage capacity than primary memory, but it is ______ and cannot be directly accessed by the CPU.

State Whether True or False

19. The timeline indicates that the development of the Integrated Circuit was a crucial step in making computers smaller and more powerful.

20. The Central Processing Unit (CPU) uses its local memory, called registers, to temporarily store data, instructions, or intermediate results during processing.

21. The Arithmetic Logic Unit (ALU) is responsible for both fetching instructions from memory and carrying out the arithmetic and logical operations on the data.

22. EEPROM is more flexible than EPROM because it can be erased and reprogrammed electrically.

23. Cache memory is faster than main memory and has a limited capacity compared to main memory.

24. A Kilobyte (KB) is equivalent to 2^{10} bytes, which is exactly 1000 bytes.

Assertion and Reason Based Questions

Assertion (A) and Reason (R) Type questions. Choose the correct option as:

(a) Both Assertion (A) and Reason (R) are true, and Reason (R) is the correct explanation of Assertion (A).

(b) Both Assertion (A) and Reason (R) are true, but Reason (R) is not the correct explanation of Assertion (A).

(c) Assertion (A) is true, but Reason (R) is false.

(d) Assertion (A) is false, but Reason (R) is true.

25. Assertion (A) A computer converts raw data into meaningful information through the Information Processing Cycle (IPC).

Reason (R) The Input Process Output (IPO) cycle involves processing data using the Arithmetic Logic Unit (ALU) of the CPU.

26. Assertion (A) Computers are highly accurate and reliable because they can perform operations without errors.

Reason (R) Computers depend on human input and programming to perform tasks accurately.

27. Assertion (A) A CPU's Control Unit manages the flow of data between the CPU and other components.

Reason (R) The Arithmetic Logic Unit (ALU) of the CPU is responsible for controlling the sequence of operations.

28. Assertion (A) Cache memory is faster than main memory.

Reason (R) Cache memory stores programs or data that the CPU is likely to access soon, reducing the need to fetch data from main memory.

29. Assertion (A) ROM is a type of volatile memory.

Reason (R) ROM retains data even when the power is turned OFF.

30. Assertion (A) Solid-state drives (SSDs) are slower than traditional hard disk drives (HDDs).

Reason (R) SSDs use flash memory, which has no moving parts, making them faster and more reliable than HDDs.

Answers

1. (a) Program **2.** (c) Input, process, output
3. (a) Input device **4.** (c) Plotters
5. (d) Control unit **6.** (a) Register
7. (c) ROM
8. (c) It needs to be refreshed periodically.
9. (d) Cache memory **10.** (a) It is volatile.
11. (d) read only **12.** (d) Flash memory
13. (d) $(1024)^4$ **14.** input
15. main, secondary **16.** CPU
17. CPU, Main memory **18.** non-volatile, slower
19. True **20.** True **21.** False
22. True **23.** True **24.** False
25. (a) Both Assertion (A) and Reason (R) are true, but Reason (R) is the correct explanation of Assertion (A).
26. (b) Both Assertion (A) and Reason (R) are true, but Reason (R) is not the correct explanation of Assertion (A).
27. (c) Assertion (A) is true, but Reason (R) is false.
28. (a) Both Assertion (A) and Reason (R) are true, and Reason (R) is the correct explanation of Assertion (A).
29. (d) Assertion (A) is false, but Reason (R) is true.
30. (d) Assertion (A) is false, but Reason (R) is true.

Subjective Type Questions

Very Short Answer Type Questions

1. What is computer?

Ans. Computer is an electronic device, which manipulates the data according to the list of instructions.

2. (a) What was the first mechanical computing device?

(b) Which invention led to the miniaturization of computers?

Ans. (a) The first mechanical computing device was Abacus.

(b) Integrated Circuit (IC)

3. Which unit in a computer is responsible for decoding and executing instructions?

Ans. Control unit is responsible for decoding and executing instructions.

4. Give the name of the basic functional unit of a digital computer system.

Ans. Computer organisation displays the four major building blocks of a digital computer system.

- Input Unit
- Output Unit
- Central Processing Unit
- Memory

5. What is input unit?

Ans. The unit that takes input from the users and converts it into computer understandable form is called input unit.

6. Write about the most commonly used input device.

Ans. Keyboard is used to enter text information into the computer. It is the most commonly used input device which can also be used to type commands directing the computer to perform certain actions.

7. What is the use of output unit?

Ans. Output unit converts the coded results to human acceptable form.

8. What role does the control unit play in the instruction cycle?

Ans. The control unit initiates and coordinates the fetch-decode-execute cycle.

9. Name the three components of the central processing unit.

Ans. Control unit (CU), Arithmetic logic unit (ALU) and the main/primary memory are the three components of the CPU.

10. What is register?

Ans. Register is the internal part of the CPU which is used to store intermediate results obtained during the execution of instructions.

11. A software developer is optimizing a computer system for faster data access. They need to understand how memory is structured to efficiently manage data storage and retrieval. Based on this, how is the main memory organized, and why is this organization important for system performance?

Competency Based Que.

Ans. The main memory is organized into memory locations, each with a unique address. It consists of RAM (for temporary data storage and quick access) and ROM (for permanent instructions). This organization ensures efficient data retrieval and processing, improving system performance.

12. List the two basic types of RAM.

Ans. (i) Static RAM (SRAM) (ii) Dynamic RAM (DRAM).

13. Can RAM retain data when computer is switched OFF?

Ans. No, RAM cannot retain data when computer is switched OFF because it is temporary storage.

14. Define static RAM.

Ans. Static RAM or SRAM is a type of RAM that holds the data and information in static form, i.e., as long as the power supply is ON.

15. A technician is troubleshooting a computer that is failing to boot properly. They suspect an issue with the system firmware stored in ROM. Can they modify the data stored in ROM? If not, what alternatives are available for updating system firmware?

Competency Based Que.

Ans. No, data in ROM (Read-Only Memory) cannot be directly modified. However, firmware updates can be made using Flash ROM or EEPROM, which allow rewriting data under special conditions.

16. (a) What is the primary function of cache memory?

(b) Name the types of ROM used in a computer system.

Ans. (a) The primary function of cache memory is to speed up data access by storing frequently used data from the main memory.

(b) (i) PROM (Programmable ROM)

(ii) EPROM (Erasable Programmable ROM)

(iii) EEPROM (Electrically Erasable programmable ROM).

17. (a) Name four secondary storage devices.

(b) Give one difference between primary and secondary memory.

Ans. (a) (i) Floppy disk (ii) Hard disk

(iii) Compact disc (iv) Magnetic tape.

(b) Primary memory is volatile in nature and has limited storage capacity, whereas secondary memory is non-volatile in nature and store huge amount of data.

18. What are the two advantages of using floppy disks?

Ans. (i) They are quite cheap.

(ii) They allow to copy files from one computer to another.

19. (a) What are tracks?

(b) What are sectors?

Ans. (a) A magnetic disk is divided into concentric circles known as tracks.

(b) The track on the disk surface is divided into invisible segments known as sectors.

20. What component is responsible for reading and writing data on a magnetic disk?

Ans. Read/Write heads are the components that facilitate the process of reading and writing data on a magnetic disk.

21. Which unit is used to store information on optical disc?

Ans. In optical disc, information is stored in bits that are prepared by using a laser beam.

22. Name the varieties of DVD.

Ans. (i) DVD ROM (ii) DVD-R (iii) DVD-RW

23. How can we read the content of memory card?

Ans. Content of memory card can read by connecting the device having the card to your computer or by using a USB card reader.

24. What is the difference between a bit and byte?

Ans. A bit is the smallest unit of data in computing, representing a single binary digit (0 and 1), while a byte is a group of 8 bits.

25. How can deleted data be recovered?

Ans. Data can be restored using recovery tools or backups if its storage space has not been overwritten.

Short Answer Type I Questions

26. Describe the types of inputs are given to the computer.

Ans. Two types of inputs are given to the computer, data and instructions.

- Data may be in the form of numbers, characters, pictures, graphics, etc.
- Instructions can be in the form of a computer program/software or it may be just a single instruction.

27. Distinguish between input unit and output unit.

Ans.

Input Unit	Output Unit
It accepts the data and instructions from the outside world.	It accepts the result produced by the computer.
It converts the accepted instruction and data in computer acceptable form.	It converts the results, which are in coded form to human readable form.
It supplies the converted instruction and data to the computer system for further processing.	It supplies the converted results to the user.

28. What is the purpose of input and output devices in a computer system?

Ans. Input and output devices enable communication between the computer and the user. Input devices allow users to provide data and instructions to the computer, while output devices display the results of computations or other information to the user.

29. What are the functions of Arithmetic Logic Unit (ALU)?

Ans. Arithmetic logic unit performs all the arithmetic and the logical operations. i.e. all the calculations take place in this unit. Arithmetic instructions include addition, subtraction, multiplication and division operations, while logic instructions include Boolean comparisons, such as AND, OR, XOR and NOT operations. The numbers on which the operations have to be done are taken from the memory and after operation is done then the result is again sent to the memory.

30. Imagine you are using a video editing software on your computer. While editing a high-resolution video, the software processes multiple frames, applies effects, and temporarily stores data before saving the final video. How does the computer's memory contribute to the smooth functioning of such tasks, and why is it essential for real-time processing?

Competency Based Que.

Ans. The computer's memory acts as a temporary storage area, holding data, intermediate results, and final outputs to ensure smooth and efficient performance. It allows quick access to frequently used data, which is crucial for processing-intensive tasks like video editing.

31. What is the primary function of RAM, and how does it differ from ROM?

Ans. RAM, or Random Access Memory, is a volatile memory used for temporary storage of data and instructions that are currently being used by the CPU. It allows for rapid access to data. ROM, or Read-Only Memory, is a non-volatile memory that stores permanent data and instructions. Unlike RAM, ROM retains its data even when the power is turned OFF.

32. How does SRAM store data?

Ans. SRAM stores data using flip-flops, which are electronic circuits that can store a single bit of information. As long as the device has power, the flip-flops retain the stored data.

33. How does DRAM maintain data over time?

Ans. DRAM uses a technique called refreshing to maintain data. Since DRAM cells lose their charge over time, the memory controller periodically recharges these cells to prevent data loss.

34. Why we use cache memory in a computer system.

Ans. Cache memory is the reserved section of main memory (RAM) that is used to enhance performance of a CPU. It is located between the main memory and the CPU. Cache memory is used to hold data and instructions that are transferred to and from main memory.

35. Which memory is slower among the following memories:

(i) Primary Memory

(ii) Secondary Memory.

Explain the slower memory.

Ans. Secondary memory is the slower memory. It is the memory which is not directly accessible by the central processing unit of a computer system. It is non-volatile in nature and is used to store large amount of data on permanent basis.

36. Differentiate between volatile and non-volatile memory.

Ans.

Volatile Memory	Non-Volatile Memory
Volatile memory needs power to work and to keep the data in it.	Non-volatile memory does not needs power to keep data in it.
Once the power is OFF, the volatile memory loss the data in it.	Once the power is OFF, the non-volatile memory does not loss the data in it.
Volatile storage affects system performance.	Non-volatile storage affects storage capacity.
For example, RAM	For example, ROM

37. Secondary storage is also known as auxiliary memory. Explain it.

Ans. Secondary storage is also known as auxiliary memory because it is a part of external memory and used to store a large amount of data at less cost per-byte than primary memory. The secondary storage devices were used to overcome the problems with primary memory.

38. A small business owner needs to store large amounts of customer data, financial records, and software applications on their computer. They are looking for a cost-effective and reliable storage solution.

Why would a hard disk drive (HDD) be a suitable choice for their storage needs compared to other storage options? **Competency Based Que.**

Ans. A hard disk drive (HDD) is suitable because it offers large storage capacity, fast access to files, and is cost-effective compared to other storage media. This makes it ideal for storing extensive business data while keeping expenses low.

Short Answers Type II Questions

39. A school is planning to set up a digital learning system where students can access online study materials, submit assignments, and interact with teachers through video conferencing. To ensure smooth operation, the school administrator needs to understand how computers process data, execute instructions, and manage storage.

How do the basic operations of a computer (input, processing, storage, and output) help in managing the digital learning system efficiently? Explain with examples. **Competency Based Que.**

Ans. Refer to text on page no. 1. (Basic Computer Operations)

40. What role does central processing unit play in the computer system?

Ans. A Central Processing Unit (CPU) plays a vital role in the functioning of a computer system. It is termed as 'brain of a computer' because its primary function is to execute programs. In terms of computing power, the CPU is the most important element of a computer system.

Two typical components of a CPU are the following

(i) **Arithmetic Logic Unit (ALU)** ALU performs all the arithmetic (+, -, *, /) and logical (<, >, =, < =, > =, <>) operations. It is the place, where the actual execution takes place, during the processing operation. The data and instructions, stored in memory before processing are transferred as and when needed to the ALU, where processing takes place.

(ii) **Control Unit (CU)** A control unit guides the flow of work or procedure which takes place in CPU. Control unit is just like a circuitry that directs operations within the computer's processor by directing the input and output of a computer system.

Control unit co-ordinates various operations of the computer like,

(i) It directs the sequence of operations.

(ii) It interprets the instructions of a program in storage unit and produces signals to execute the instructions. It directs the flow of data and instructions in the computer system.

41. Explain main memory and its types.

Ans. Main memory, also known as primary memory, is a crucial component of a computer system. It serves as a temporary storage area for data and instructions that the CPU needs to access quickly.

There are two primary types of main memory:

1. **Random Access Memory (RAM)**
   - **Volatile Memory** It is volatile in nature means data stored in RAM is lost when the power is turned OFF.

- **Fast Access:** RAM allows for rapid access to data, making it ideal for storing currently running programs and data.
- **Types of RAM**
  - **DRAM (Dynamic RAM)** The most common type of RAM, it requires periodic refreshing to retain data. It's relatively cheap but slower than SRAM.
  - **SRAM (Static RAM)** Faster and more expensive than DRAM. It doesn't require constant refreshing, making it suitable for cache memory.

2. **Read-Only Memory (ROM)**
- **Non-Volatile Memory** It is non-volatile in nature means data stored in ROM persists even when the power is turned OFF.
- **Read-Only** Data can only be read from ROM, not written to.
- **Types of ROM**
  - **PROM (Programmable ROM)** Can be programmed once, typically during manufacturing.
  - **EPROM (Erasable Programmable ROM)** Can be erased and reprogrammed using ultraviolet light.
  - **EEPROM (Electrically Erasable Programmable ROM)** Can be erased and reprogrammed electrically.

42. What do you mean by secondary memory and give a brief note on any of its two types?

Ans. Secondary memory is the memory which is not installed inside the computer system. These memories are used to store the data, so that the internal memory could be made free and the speed of the computer system could be enhanced. This secondary memory uses many memory devices known as secondary storage devices.

Two of them are described below

(i) **Hard Disk Drive** Hard Disk Drive or HDD is a non-volatile, random access digital storage device. It is a data storage device used for storing and retrieving information using rotating disks (platters) coated with magnetic material.

It consists of a spindle that holds non-magnetic flat circular disks, called **platters**, which hold the recorded data. Each platter requires two read/write heads, that are used to read and write the information from a platter. The information is stored in bands; each band of information is called a **track**. Each platter has the same number of tracks, and a track location that cuts across all platters is called a **cylinder**. The tracks are divided into pie-shaped sections known as **sectors**.

(ii) **Compact Disc** (CD) CD is an optical media that is used to store digital data.

It consists of a circular disc, which is coated with a thin metal that is highly reflective. Laser beam technology is used for recording/reading of data on the disk. It is also known as **laser disc** or **optical laser disc**, due to the use of laser beam technology. It provides random access medium for high capacity secondary storage. The diameter of the CD ranges from 10 cms to 30 cms. One CD can store 600 MB to 750 MB.

43. Discuss the security concerns related to data deletion and recovery, and suggest measures to mitigate these risks.

Ans. Data deletion and recovery can lead to security risks

1. **Unauthorized Deletion** Important data may be deleted accidentally or on purpose, causing disruptions and losses.
2. **Unauthorized Recovery** Deleted sensitive data can be recovered from discarded devices or backups, leading to privacy and security issues.

Ways to Prevent These Risks:

1. Limit who can access sensitive data based on their roles.
2. Encrypt data to protect it from unauthorized access, both when it's stored and when it's being transferred.
3. Use special tools to fully erase data before discarding storage devices.
4. Keep regular backups to recover data if it gets lost or damaged.

Long Answer Type Questions

44. What is keyboard? Also, write types of keys on keyboard.

Ans. It is one of the most common input devices. The user can type text and command using this device. The layout of the keyboard was borrowed from the regular typewriter with some additional keys.

Keyboard is used to enter data or information in a computer system, which may be in numeric form or alphabetic form. When key is pressed, keyboard interacts with a keyboard controller and keyboard buffer.

Keyboard controller stores the code of pressed key in keyboard buffer. There are different types of keyboard such as QWERTY, DVORAK and AZERTY.

The keys are categorised under the following groups

1. **Alphanumeric Keys** include the alphabet keys (A, B, C, ..., Z) and number keys (0, 1, 2, 3, ..., 9).
2. **Numeric Keys** are located at the right hand side of the keyboard. They consist of digits and mathematical operators.
3. **Function Keys** are the programmable keys, i.e. the programs can assign some specific actions. They are numbered from F1 to F12.
4. **Cursor Control Keys** include four directional (left, right, up, down) arrow keys that are arranged in a inverted T formation between the alphanumeric and numeric keypad. Above the arrow keys there are four more keys to control the cursor. *These are as follows*

(i) Home (ii) End
(iii) Page Up (iv) Page Down

5. **Other Keys** A keyboard contains some other keys such as follows
   (i) **Control Key** It performs a special operation with the combination of other keys.
   (ii) **Enter Key** It is used to finish an entry and begin the new entry in a document. Enter key is an alternative to press ok button.
   (iii) **Shift Key** Some keys on the keyboard like numeric keys have a symbol printed on their upper portion. Shift key is used to print these symbols. This key is also called combination key.
   (iv) **Escape Key (Esc)** It allows a user to cancel or abort operations, which are executing at present. It opens Start menu with the combination of Ctrl key.
   (v) **Backspace Key** It is used to erase anything typed.
   (vi) **Delete Key** It is used to erase information from the computer's memory and characters on the screen.
   (vii) **Caps Lock Key** It is used to type the alphabet in capital letters. It enables or disables all the letters from being typed in capital letters. When this key is enable, the alphabet would be in capital letters and when it is disabled, the alphabet would be in small letters.
   (viii) **Num Lock Key** It is used to enable and disable the numeric keypad.
   (ix) **Windows Key** It is used to open the Start menu.
   (x) **Spacebar Key** It provides a space between two words. It is the longest key on the keyboard.
   (xi) **Tab Key** It is used to move the cursor over to the right to a pre-set point. In Word document, tab is used to indent a paragraph.

45. What is monitor? Also, explain its popular types in detail.

Ans. It is also known as Visual Display Unit (VDU). The monitor is provided along with the computer to view the display result. A monitor is of two kinds; monochrome display monitor and colour display monitor.

A monochrome display monitor uses only one colour to display text and colour display monitor can display 256 colours at a time. An image on the monitor is created by a configuration of dots, also known as pixels. The refresh rate of monitor is measured in Hertz (Hz).

The popular types of monitor are as follows

1. **Cathode Ray Tube** (CRT) It is a typical rectangular shaped monitor that you see on a desktop computer. The CRT works in a same way as a television. CRT has a vacuum tube. CRT works by moving an electron beam back and forth across the back of the screen. A screen covered with a fine layer of phosphorescent elements, called phosphores.
2. **Liquid Crystal Display** (LCD) These screens are used in laptops and notebook sized PCs. A special type of liquid is sandwiched between two plates. It is a thin, flat and light weight screen made up of any number of colour or monochrome pixels arranged in front of a light source.
3. **Liquid/Light Emitting Diode** (LED) It is an electronic device that emits light when electrical current is passed through it. LEDs usually produce red light, but today's LEDs can produce RGB (Red, Green and Blue) light, and white light as well.
4. **3-D Monitor** It is a television that conveys depth perception to the viewer. 3-D describes an image that provides the perception of length. When 3-D images are made interactive then user feels involved with the scene and this experience is called **virtual reality**.
5. **Thin Film Transistor** (TFT) TFT and Active-Matrix LCD (AMLCD) is a Liquid Crystal Display (LCD). With active-matrix displays, each pixel is controlled by one to four transistors that can make the screen faster, brighter, more colorful than passive-matrix and capable of being viewed at different angles.
   Because of this improved technology, active-matrix screens are often more expensive.

46. Which memory allows only to read the data? Explain that memory with its types?

Ans. ROM is a type of memory that normally can only be read.

The two main reasons why the read-only memory is used for certain functions within the PC are

Permanent The values stored in ROM are always there, whether the power is ON or not.

A ROM can be removed from the PC, stored for an indefinite period of time, and then replaced, and the data it contains will still be there. For this reason, it is called non-volatile storage. A hard disk is also non-volatile, for the same reason, but regular RAM is not.

Security The fact that ROM cannot easily be modified, provides a measure of security against accidental (or malicious) changes to its contents. There are no possible ways that the virus can affect the true ROMs. Read only memory is most commonly used to store system-level programs that we want to make available to the PC at all times. It contains the programs that are used to start up the computer and bring the operating system into main memory. This memory is set at the factory and usually never changed.

ROMs are of three types namely

(i) **PROM (Programmable Read-Only Memory)**
- Data is written to PROM once, typically during manufacturing.
- After programming, the data cannot be changed.
- It is used for storing firmware, device drivers, and other essential system software.

(ii) **EPROM (Erasable Programmable Read-Only Memory)**
- Data can be erased using ultraviolet light.
- Once erased, the EPROM can be reprogrammed.
- It is less flexible than EEPROM but more cost-effective.

(iii) **EEPROM (Electrically Erasable Programmable Read-Only Memory)**
- Data can be erased and reprogrammed electrically.
- This one is more flexible than EPROM but slower.
- It is used for storing configuration settings and firmware that may need updates.

Case Study Based Questions

Case Study 1

Shreya got an assignment from her teacher for a school project. She has written the following lines on a chart paper.

A computer is a versatile and powerful machine that can perform a wide range of tasks. It consists of various components working together to process information. The central processing unit (CPU) is the brain of the computer, responsible for executing instructions and performing calculations. The memory unit stores data and instructions, while the input and output units allow communication with the user.

But her younger sister has some doubts on the concepts of computer system.

(i) **Which of the following is the brain of the computer?**
(a) Memory (b) Input unit
(c) Output unit (d) Central Processing Unit

(ii) **Which component is responsible for storing data and instructions?**
(a) CPU (b) Memory unit
(c) Input unit (d) Output unit

(iii) **Which of the following is not a core component of a computer system?**
(a) Central Processing Unit (CPU)
(b) Input/Output Devices
(c) Memory
(d) Power supply unit

(iv) **What is the primary function of the CPU?**
(a) Store data (b) Display information
(c) Execute instructions (d) Input data

(v) **Which of the following is an example of an output device?**
(a) Keyboard (b) Mouse
(c) Monitor (d) Joystick

(vi) **What is the role of input device in a computer system?**
(a) Process data
(b) Store data
(c) Display information
(d) Enter data into the computer

Ans. (i) (d) Central Processing Unit
(ii) (b) Memory unit (iii) (d) Power supply unit
(iv) (c) Execute instructions (v) (c) Monitor
(vi) (d) Enter data into the computer

Case Study 2

Input and output devices facilitate interaction with the computer. Input devices, such as keyboards and mice, allow users to enter data and commands. Output devices, like monitors and printers, display information and generate tangible results.

(i) **Which of the following is an input device?**
(a) Monitor (b) Printer
(c) Keyboard (d) Speaker

(ii) **Which of the following is not an output device?**
(a) Monitor (b) Printer
(c) Keyboard (d) Speaker

(iii) **Which input device is used to control the movement of a cursor on a computer screen?**
(a) Keyboard (b) Mouse
(c) Scanner (d) Microphone

(iv) **Which output device is used to produce hard copies of documents?**
(a) Monitor (b) Printer
(c) Speaker (d) Projector

(v) **What is the function of a scanner?**
(a) To input audio data
(b) To input video data
(c) To input printed text and images
(d) To output sound

Ans. (i) (c) Keyboard (ii) (c) Keyboard
(iii) (b) Mouse (iv) (b) Printer
(v) (c) To input printed text and images

Case Study 3

Memory is the electronic holding place for the instructions and data that a computer needs to access quickly. It is where information is stored for immediate use. Memory is one of the fundamental components of a computer because, without it, the system would not function properly. Additionally, memory is utilized by a computer's operating system, hardware, and software.

There are two main types of computer memory: primary memory and secondary memory. The term memory is often used as a synonym for primary memory or as an abbreviation for a specific type of primary memory called random access memory (RAM). This type of memory is located on microchips that are physically close to a computer's microprocessor.

Answer the following questions:

(i) **The boot sector files of the system are stored in which type of computer memory?**
(a) RAM (b) ROM (c) Cache (d) Register

(ii) **Which memory acts as a buffer between the CPU and main memory?**
(a) RAM (b) ROM (c) Cache (d) Storage

(iii) **Which of the following is the smallest unit of data in a computer?**
(a) Bit (b) KB (c) Nibble (d) Byte

(iv) **Where does your PC store your programs when the power is off?**
(a) DRAM (b) Cache
(c) ROM (d) Hard Disk Drive

(v) **What is the name of the storage device used to compensate for the difference in data transfer rates between two devices?**
(a) Cache (b) Concentrator
(c) Buffer (d) I/O device

Ans. (i) (b) ROM (ii) (c) Cache
(iii) (a) Bit (iv) (d) Hard Disk Drive
(v) (c) Buffer

Case Study 4

Computing devices have come a long way from simple counting tools to powerful digital processors. The journey started with early mechanical devices like the Abacus, followed by Pascaline, and later Charles Babbage's Analytical Engine, which introduced the concept of a general-purpose computing machine. The invention of the Turing Machine provided a theoretical model for modern computers. The Von Neumann Architecture, used in ENIAC, laid the foundation for binary-programmed computers.

The development of transistors (1947) and integrated circuits (1970s) led to the creation of microprocessors, allowing complete CPUs to be built on a single chip. With the introduction of personal computers (IBM PC in 1981, Apple Macintosh in 1984) and Graphical User Interfaces (GUI), computers became more user-friendly and accessible to the masses. The growth of the World Wide Web (WWW) in the 1990s further accelerated the widespread use of computers.

Today, computing devices have evolved into portable gadgets like laptops, tablets, and smartphones. The rise of Artificial Intelligence (AI) and the Internet of Things (IoT) has paved the way for smart appliances and wearable technology, making computing more integrated into daily life.

Based on the above information, answer the following questions:

(i) **Which of the following was one of the earliest computing devices used for arithmetic calculations?**
(a) ENIAC (b) Pascaline
(c) Transistor (d) Turing Machine

(ii) **Which computing model introduced the concept of storing a program in memory for execution?**
(a) Abacus (b) Von Neumann Architecture
(c) Turing Machine (d) Analytical Engine

(iii) **What was the key technological advancement in the 1970s that allowed complete CPUs to be built on a single chip?**
(a) Vacuum Tubes
(b) Super Large Scale Integration (SLSI)
(c) Large Scale Integration (LSI)
(d) Artificial Intelligence (AI)

(iv) **Which company introduced the first personal computer (PC) for home users in 1981?**
(a) Microsoft (b) IBM
(c) Apple (d) Intel

(v) **Which of the following best describes the latest trend in computing technology?**
(a) Command-line interface
(b) Use of vacuum tubes
(c) Wearable gadgets and IoT devices
(d) Only desktop computing

Ans. (i) (b) Pascaline
(ii) (b) Von Neumann Architecture
(iii) (c) Large Scale Integration (LSI)
(iv) (b) IBM
(v) (c) Wearable gadgets and IoT devices

SELF ASSESSMENT TEST

Multiple Choice Questions

1. **Which unit of computer helps in communication between the memory and the arithmetic logical unit?**

(a) CMU (b) CCU

(c) UPS (d) CPU

2. **A device, which is used for making drawings, graphics and for menu selection.**

(a) Keyboard (b) Mouse

(c) Touch screen (d) Light Pen

Fill in the Blanks

3. The CPU (Central Processing Unit) is known as the _______ of the computer.

4. RAM (Random Access Memory) is an example of _______ memory, which provides fast access to data but is volatile.

5. 1 Byte consists of _______ bits.

State Whether True or False

6. The CPU is responsible for processing data and instructions in a computer system.

7. Secondary memory is faster than primary memory and is used to store temporary data.

Assertion and Reason Based Questions

Assertion (A) and Reason (R) Type questions. Choose the correct option as:

(a) Both Assertion (A) and Reason (R) are true, and Reason (R) is the correct explanation of Assertion (A).

(b) Both Assertion (A) and Reason (R) are true, but Reason (R) is not the correct explanation of Assertion (A).

(c) Assertion (A) is true, but Reason (R) is false.

(d) Assertion (A) is false, but Reason (R) is true.

8. **Assertion (A)** The Central Processing Unit (CPU) is known as the brain of the computer.

Reason (R) The CPU controls all operations of a computer, processes data, and executes instructions.

9. **Assertion (A)** Secondary memory is faster than cache memory.

Reason (R) Cache memory is located closer to the CPU and stores frequently accessed data for quick retrieval.

Very Short Answer Type Questions

10. The word computer has been derived from which of the language?

11. What do you mean by function keys of the keyboard?

12. Give relation between byte and gigabyte.

Short Answer Type Questions

13. What is the hardware ?

14. A company is planning to have a video conference. In its video conferencing area, there are some microphones, speakers and webcams. Describe the purpose of each of the devices.

15. Can a damaged, missing or encryped file be recovered? If yes, how? If no, why?

Long Answer Type Questions

16. Explain hard disk drive with its advantages and disadvantages.

17. Describe the functioning of a computer.

Case Study Based Questions

18. Ravi is a high school student who recently bought a new computer for his studies. He is curious about how different components work together in a computer system. His teacher explains that a computer has hardware and software components.

The hardware includes the CPU, memory, and input/output devices, while software enables users to perform tasks. Ravi also learns about different types of memory, such as primary, cache, and secondary storage, and the various units of memory measurement.

Answer the following given questions

(i) Which of the following is NOT a type of computer memory?

(a) Primary memory (b) Cache memory

(c) Virtual memory (d) Mechanical memory

(ii) Ravi wants to store large files, such as movies and software programs, on his computer. Which type of memory should he use?

(a) Cache memory (b) Primary memory

(c) Secondary memory (d) Register memory

(iii) The CPU is often referred to as the "brain" of the computer. Which of the following is NOT a function of the CPU?
(a) Processing data
(b) Storing long-term files
(c) Controlling input and output devices
(d) Executing instructions

(iv) Ravi notices that his computer's speed slows down when he runs multiple applications at once. His teacher explains that an essential component of the CPU helps in faster data access. Which component is responsible for this?
(a) Cache memory (b) Hard disk
(c) USB storage (d) DVD-ROM

19. XYZ Bank, a major financial institution, processes large volumes of customer data daily. The bank collects data from multiple sources, such as online transactions, ATMs, and customer service interactions. This information is securely stored in cloud databases and local servers.

One day, a system failure led to the accidental deletion of recent transaction records. The IT team attempted data recovery using specialized tools, but some records had already been overwritten. To prevent such issues in the future, the bank introduced stronger data security measures, including encrypted storage, restricted access, and regular backups.

Now, answer the following questions based on the case study:

(i) Why couldn't the IT team recover all deleted records?
(a) The data was stored in a cloud database
(b) Some of the deleted data had been overwritten
(c) The system lacked recovery tools
(d) The bank had no backup system in place

(ii) What is an effective way to prevent unauthorized access to stored data?
(a) Using public cloud storage without encryption
(b) Disabling data encryption
(c) Restricting access and enabling password protection
(d) Keeping data in multiple unprotected locations

(iii) Which measure can help XYZ Bank enhance data security in the future?
(a) Ignoring backup procedures
(b) Implementing encryption and scheduled backups
(c) Allowing unrestricted access to customer data
(d) Storing all data on a single local server

(iv) What is the biggest risk of disposing of old storage devices without secure erasure?
(a) Faster data retrieval
(b) Unauthorized recovery of sensitive data
(c) More efficient use of storage space
(d) Reduced reliance on data backups

Answers

1. (d) 2. (d) 3. Brain 4. Primary
5. 8 6. True 7. False 8. (a) 9. (d)
18. (i) → (d), (ii) → (c), (iii) → (b), (iv) → (a)
19. (i) → (b), (ii) → (c), (iii) → (b), (iv) → (b)

02 CHAPTER

Software

Software is a generic term for programs, scripts and applications that run on a device.

YOUR STUDY GOALS

2.1 System Software
2.2 Programming Tools
2.3 Application Software

YOUR PRACTICE GOAL

- Objective Type Questions (36 Qs ; MCQs, True or False, Fill in the Blanks, Assertion and Reason)
- Subjective Type Questions (42 Qs ; VSA, SA, LA)
- Case Study Based Questions-3

The concept of software is essential to modern computing, acting as the bridge between hardware and user interaction. It includes a diverse array of programs, applications, and systems that enable a computer to perform various tasks, ranging from basic calculations to complex data processing activities such as video editing, online shopping, and document creation and editing.

Classification of Software

Depending on the mode of interaction with hardware and functions to be performed, the software can be broadly classified into three categories.

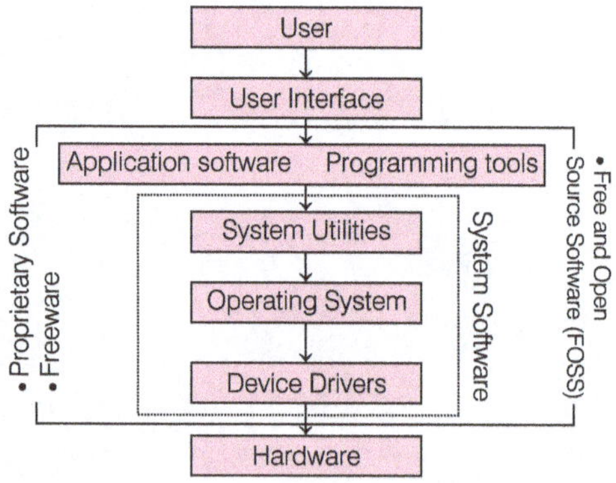

2.1 System Software

It is a program that manages and supports the computer resources and operations of a computer system while the computer executes its various tasks such as processing data and information, controlling hardware components, and allowing users to use application software.

System software is the invisible backbone of a computer system. It's the software that manages all the internal operations, making it possible for us to interact with the computer and run our favorite applications.

Without system software, our computers would be useless.

Examples of system software include:

Operating system, Device drivers, Utility software

1. Operating System

An Operating System (OS) is the fundamental software that controls your computer. It's like the brain of your computer, managing everything from **hardware** resources to **software applications**.

The OS ensures smooth operation, handles tasks like memory allocation, input/output operations, and file management. It creates a user-friendly interface, allowing you to interact with your computer effortlessly.

An operating system is a collection of softwares or a series of programs which performs various types of functions in order to manage and organize files.

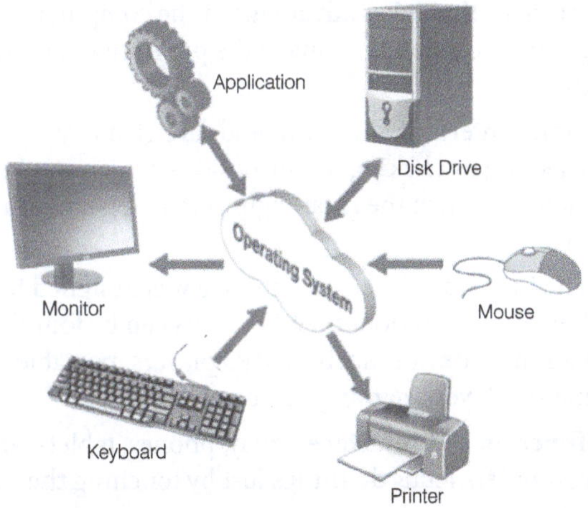

Needs of Operating System

An operating system (OS) is essential for a computer to function. It acts as an intermediary between the hardware and software, making it possible for us to interact with the computer and use various applications.

The OS performs crucial tasks such as:

- **Managing hardware resources** An operating system efficiently manages a computer's hardware resources, including memory, CPU, and input/output devices. It allocates memory to running processes, schedules CPU time for different tasks, and controls the flow of data between the computer and external devices.
- **Providing a user-friendly interface** The OS provides a user-friendly interface, such as a graphical user interface (GUI) or a command-line interface, allowing users to interact with the computer easily. It simplifies complex tasks and makes the computing experience more simple.
- **Executing user commands** The OS translates user commands into machine-understandable instructions, enabling the computer to execute tasks. It interprets user input, whether it's a mouse click, keyboard input, or voice command, and converts it into a sequence of instructions that the CPU can process.
- **Coordinating system activities** The OS manages all the processes running on the computer, ensuring smooth and efficient operation. It manages the scheduling of tasks, handles resource allocation, and coordinates the interaction between different software components.

> **TEACHER TIP**
> An Operating System (OS) is the first program that is loaded into the computer's main memory, when a computer is switched ON.

Types of Operating System

At present, operating systems come in various types, each designed for specific purposes.

1. **Batch Processing OS** Batch processing OS groups jobs submitted on punch cards into batches based on similar requirements. The processor executes these batches together, improving efficiency and ensuring smooth task execution. Users don't need to interact with the computer directly as the system manages the job execution automatically
2. **Multi-Programing Operating Systems** Multi-Programing OSs allow multiple users to access and utilize a computer's resources simultaneously. They are commonly used in server environments and large organizations. These systems manage user accounts, allocate resources, and ensure that multiple users can work efficiently without interfering with each other. Examples include Unix and Linux.
3. **Time-Sharing Operating System** Time-sharing OSs allow multiple users to share a single computer

system. Each user gets a specific time slot to use the CPU and other resources. This enables efficient resource utilization and cost-effective computing in large organizations.

4. **Multi-tasking Operating Systems (Multitasking OS)** The OS that allows you to run multiple programs at once, even though the processor can only handle one at a time. They efficiently switch between tasks, creating the illusion of simultaneous operation. Examples include Windows and macOS.

   Multi-tasking OS can be classified as

   (i) **Preemptive Multitasking** It is a type of multitasking that allows computer programs to share operating system and underlying hardware resources.

   It divides the overall operating and computing time between processes, and the switching of resources between different processes occurs through predefined criteria. OS/2, Windows 95, Window NT, Amiga operating system and UNIX use preemptive multitasking.

   (ii) **Cooperative Multitasking** It is the simplest form of multi-tasking. In it, each program can control the CPU for as long as it need it. If a program is not using the CPU, however it can allow another program to use it temporarily.

   For example Mac OS, MS Window 3-x etc.

5. **Real-Time Operating Systems (RTOS)** RTOS are designed for systems that require strict timing constraints.

   They prioritize tasks and ensure timely responses to events. This makes them suitable for applications like industrial control systems, medical devices, and robotics. Linux OS is an example of real-time operating system.

   Real-time operating system can be classified as

   (i) **Hard Real-Time OS** An OS that can absolutely guarantee a maximum time for the operations it performs, is referred to as hard real-time OS.

   (ii) **Soft Real-Time OS** An OS that cannot absolutely guarantee a maximum time for operations it performs, is referred to as soft real-time OS.

6. **Single-User Operating Systems** As the name suggests a Single-user OSs are designed for individual use on personal computers. They provide a user-friendly interface and are commonly used for tasks like browsing the internet, word processing, and playing games. Examples include Windows, macOS, and Linux distributions like Ubuntu.

7. **Distributed Operating System** Distributed OSs distribute computing tasks across multiple interconnected computers. This allows for increased processing power, improved reliability, and scalability. By sharing resources and workload, distributed systems can handle complex tasks and large datasets efficiently.

User Interface

The user interface is one of the most important parts of any operating system. It allows users to easily access and communicate with the applications and the hardware.

The user can interact with the computer by using these kinds of interfaces:

1. **Command-based or Character User Interface (CUI)** It is a means of interacting with computer program where the user issues commands to the program in the form of successive lines of text (command lines). It was used by DOS. It is also known as command line interface.

2. **Graphical User Interface (GUI)** It is a program interface that takes advantage of the computer's graphics capability to make the program easier to use.

   In this interface, the commands are given by selecting or clicking on the options, which can be identified with the small figures that appear with them.

   The first graphical user interface was designed by Xerox Corporation in 1970s. GUIs can be found in handheld devices such as MP3 players, portable media players, gaming devices, etc.

3. **Touch-based Interface** Today, phones, tablets, and computers let us do things just by touching the screen.

   When we touch the screen, the computer understands what we want, like opening an app, closing it, calling someone, or scrolling through apps. Popular systems like Android, iOS, Windows 8.1, and Windows 10 work well with touchscreens.

4. **Voice-based Interface** Today's computers are made to work for everyone, even people who need special help or want to use their computer or phone while doing other things. For people who can't use a

mouse, keyboard, or touchscreen, modern computers let you use your voice to control them. Some operating systems, like iOS (with Siri), Android (with Google Now or "OK Google"), and Windows 10 (with Cortana), let you do this.

5. **Gesture-based Interface** Some phones and computers, like those using Android and iOS, let you control them with gestures, like waving, tilting, moving your eyes, or shaking the device. This technology is getting better and could be really useful for games, medicine, and other things.

Booting

Booting is starting up a computer or computer appliance until it can be used. It can be initiated by hardware such as a Start button or by software command. There are two types of booting:

- **Cold Booting** When a computer is turned ON after it has been completely shutdown.
- **Warm Booting** When a computer is restarted by pressing the combination of Ctrl + Alt + Del keys or by restart button.

Quick Test 1

1. What are the main examples of system software?
2. Explain the concept of multitasking and multiprogramming in operating systems.
3. Differentiate between a GUI and a CUI.
4. What are the key differences between batch operating systems, time-sharing operating systems, and real-time operating systems?

2. Device Drivers

Device drivers are specific programs that enable the computer to communicate with hardware devices. They act as intermediaries, translating data between the device and the operating system.

Without device drivers, a computer would be unable to recognize and utilize connected hardware devices, such as printers, scanners, sound cards, or even input devices like keyboards and mouse.

Key Functions of Device Drivers

- **Hardware Initialization** Device drivers initialize hardware devices upon system startup, ensuring they are ready to operate.
- **Input/Output Operations** They manage the transfer of data between the device and the system's memory.
- **Error Handling** Device drivers detect and handle errors that may occur during device operations, such as paper jams in printers or disk read/write errors.
- **Resource Allocation** They allocate system resources, such as memory and interrupt requests, to the device.
- **Configuration** Device drivers allow users to configure device settings, such as printer resolution or sound card volume.
- **Power Management** They can help manage power consumption by devices, especially in laptops and mobile devices.

TEACHER TIP

Consider device drivers as the language translators between the Operating system and hardware devices.

3. Utility Software

Utility software is a category of system software designed to enhance the performance, security, and maintenance of a computer system. Unlike application software, which is used to perform specific tasks, utility software works behind the scenes to optimize system performance, protect data, and troubleshoot issues.

Here are some of the most common types of utility software:

Antivirus Software

Antivirus software is essential for protecting computers from malicious software, such as viruses, worms, and malware. It scans the system for threats, removes existing infections, and prevents future attacks.

Disk Defragmenter

Disk defragmentation is a process that reorganizes fragmented files on a hard drive, improving access time and overall system performance. By bringing scattered file fragments together, the disk defragmenter reduces the time it takes for the computer to access data. To start disk defragmenter tool, follow the following steps

Click Start → All Programs → Accessories → System Tools → Disk Defragmenter.

Backup Utility

Backup utilities create copies of important data, allowing for data recovery in case of hardware failures, accidental deletions, or malicious attacks. Regular backups are crucial for data protection and business continuity.

You can run backup option to backup or restore files from settings of your computer system as follows

Click Start → All Programs → Accessories → System Tools → Backup. After that, you will be guided to Backup or Restore Wizard. Press two times Next button.

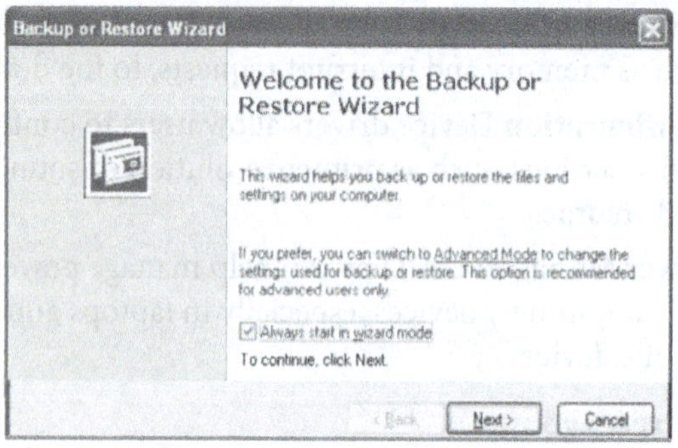

Backup or Restore Wizard Window

Select a place and press Next button again. Click Finish to take backup.

Compression Utility

Compression utilities reduce the size of files, making them easier to store, transmit, and download. This is particularly useful for large files, such as videos and images. It is a technique used to reduce the size of data by eliminating redundancy. This process results in compressed data, which can be significantly smaller than the original data.

Decompression is the reverse process, restoring the compressed data to its original form. Compression can be applied to both data content and transmission units, leading to substantial reductions, especially in text files, which can be compressed by up to 50%.

Popular compression tools include Disk double, Superstar Pro, Double Disk Gold, Xtra Drive, and WinZip.

Disk Cleaner

Disk cleaner utilities identify and remove unnecessary files, such as temporary files, system logs, and old downloads, freeing up disk space and improving system performance.

You can start disk cleanup tool as

Click Start → All Programs → Accessories → Systems Tools → Disk Cleanup.

File Management Tools

File management tools help users organize and manage files and folders on their computer. They provide features like searching, sorting, and copying files, making it easier to find and access data.

Files are collections of information stored on a disk and accessed by a name. A file manager organizes and maintains these files within directories. The most common operations performed on files or group of files are create, open, edit, view, print, delete, copy, paste, etc.

Mistake Alert!

Student can ignore utility software but it plays a crucial role in system maintenance.

Quick Test 2

1. Explain the concept of utility software and provide examples of common utility programs.
2. How do system utilities like disk defragmenters and antivirus software contribute to system performance and security?
3. Discuss the role of compression utilities in efficient data storage and transmission.

2.2 Programming Tools

To make a computer perform tasks, we provide instructions in the form of programs. These instructions are written using computer languages. Since computers understand machine language, human-written programs in high-level languages must be converted to machine language using translators.

Language Translators (Language Processor)

Language translators bridge the gap between human-readable programming languages and machine code.

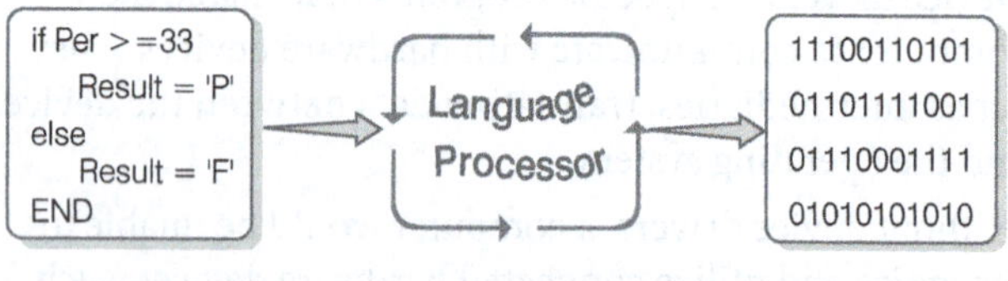

Program Translator

This language is extremely difficult to learn for a general programmer and thus there is a need for some special language which is easy to learn and understand for the programmer in order to interact with the computer system. These special languages or set of commands are collectively known as programming languages or High Level Languages (HLL).

In other words, **'Language processor is a program that performs tasks, such as translating and interpreting,**

required for processing a specified programming language.'

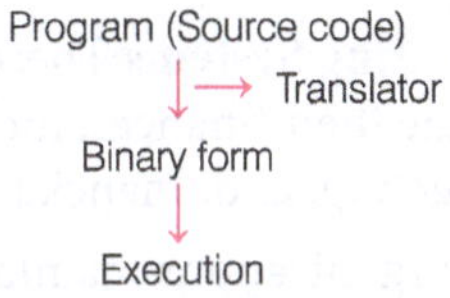

The language translator is of three types as shown below

- **Compilers** These programs translate entire high-level language programs into machine code before execution. This pre-compilation process results in faster execution.

- **Interpreters** These programs translate and execute high-level language programs line by line, without creating an executable file.

  This provides flexibility but can be slower than compiled programs.

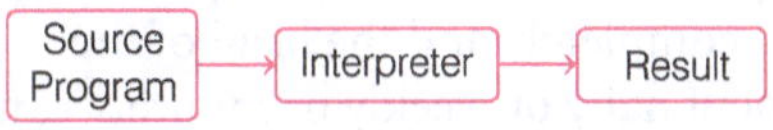

- **Assemblers** These programs translate assembly language, a low-level language, into machine code. Assembly language is closer to machine code and is often used for performance-critical tasks.

Mistake Alert!

Student can misunderstand the difference between compilers and interpreters.

Specifically regarding which one translates the code completely & which one translates it line-by-line.

2.3 Application Software

Application software is a category of software designed to perform specific tasks for users.

It can be broadly categorized into two types:

1. Generic/General-Purpose Application Software

General-purpose application software refers to software that can be used for a wide range of tasks and is not specific to a particular industry or job function. It often provides essential tools for productivity, creativity, and communication.

There are several good reasons for using general purpose software and some of them are given below

- These are relatively cheap.
- Easily available.
- Thoroughly tested.
- Easily handleable.

Some of the general purpose softwares are:

- **Word Processors** These applications are used to create, edit, and format text documents. Today, the Word processor is one of the most frequently used programs or online services used on a computer system.

  Examples include Microsoft Word and LibreOffice Writer.

- **Presentation Tools** These tools help create visually appealing presentations with slides, images, text, and multimedia elements.

  It has three major functions

  (i) An editor that allows text to be inserted or formatted.

  (ii) A method for inserting and manipulating graphic images.

  (iii) A slide-show system to display the content.

  Popular examples are Microsoft PowerPoint and LibreOffice Impress.

- **Spreadsheet Software** These applications allow users to organize data in rows and columns, perform calculations, and generate charts and graphs.

  In a spreadsheet application, each value exists in a cell, and user can define what type of data is in each cell and how different cells depend upon one another.

  The relationships between the cells are called **'Formulas'** and the names of the cells are called **'Labels'**. Each cell is labeled according to its placement.

  Some basic functions of a spreadsheet package are as follows

  - It creates and manipulates simple databases.
  - Establishes a relationship between numerical data.
  - Represents datasets in graphical or chart form.

- It create simple lists and tables of alphabetic or numerical data.

Microsoft Excel and LibreOffice Calc are widely used spreadsheet software.

- **Database Management Systems (DBMS)** DBMS software helps manage and organize large amounts of data. It enables a user to define, create and maintain the database and provide controlled access on it.

  Database management system provides several additional features as
  - Remove data redundancy
  - Elimination of data inconsistency
  - Data sharing
  - Data integration
  - Data security.

  Examples include Microsoft Access and LibreOffice Base.

- **Desktop Publishing Package (DTP)** is a digital process that involves creating documents using page layout software on a computer.

  It combines text and graphics to produce high-quality printed materials. Before DTP, printing was a manual and time-consuming process. With the introduction of DTP software, the process has become significantly more efficient and accessible.

  Popular DTP software includes Adobe PageMaker, CorelDraw, and iStudio Publisher.

2. Special-Purpose Application Software

These software applications are personalized to specific needs and industries. They are often developed to automate tasks or solve particular problems. Some examples include:

- **Inventory Management Systems** These systems help businesses track and manage their inventory, including stock levels, purchase orders, and sales.

  The transactions possible in an inventory management system are
  (a) Receipts/Purchase of items
  (b) Issues an item
  (c) Purchase return
  (d) Issue return

- **Payroll System** Payroll software helps streamline the payroll process by automating tasks like calculating pay, deducting taxes, and generating paychecks. This reduces errors and saves time compared to manual methods.

- **Financial Accounting Systems** These systems help businesses manage their finances, including accounting, budgeting, and financial reporting.

  All the business organizations maintain the following books of accounting
  (a) Sales book
  (b) Journal
  (c) Creditors ledger
  (d) Advance to staff
  (e) Purchases book
  (f) Cash book
  (g) Debtor's ledger
  (h) General ledger.

- **Hotel Management Systems** These systems help hotels manage reservations, room assignments, billing, and other operations. In hotel management there is another system of restaurant billing. The reports can be viewed completely and the head of the management daily or weekly or monthly can review it. The proposed system will be interactive, faster and user friendly for the end users.

- **Reservation Systems** These systems are used to book various services, such as airline tickets, hotel rooms, and restaurant tables.

  There are different types of reservation systems running in various organizations as follows
  (a) Railway reservation system
  (b) Hotel reservation system
  (c) Central reservation system.

- **Weather Forecasting Systems** These systems use complex algorithms and data to predict weather patterns. Numerical Weather Prediction (NWP) is a scientific method that uses computer models to forecast future weather conditions. It involves collecting current weather data, processing it through complex models, and generating predictions for various meteorological elements.

Advantages of Special-Purpose Software

- Special-purpose software can be designed to fit the exact needs of an organization, improving efficiency and productivity.
- By automating tasks and streamlining workflows, special-purpose software can significantly improve operational efficiency.

- Unique software solutions can give businesses a competitive edge by providing features and capabilities that competitors may lack.
- Special-purpose software can be designed with strong security measures to protect sensitive data.
- Special-purpose software can be easily scaled to accommodate future growth and changing business needs.

Note *A computer system can work without application software, but it cannot work without system software. For example, we can use a computer even if no word processing software is installed, but if no operating system is installed, we cannot work on the computer. In other words, the use of computer is possible in the absence of application software.*

Open Source Concepts

Open source based software refers to those categories of software/programs whose licenses do not impose much conditions.

The term 'open source' has been derived from the fact that the software's source code is atleast available and in fact usually distributed with the executable code. The software developers who support the open source concept believe that the application will be more useful and error free over the long term by allowing anyone who is interested in modifying the source code.

Some of the softwares related to this concept are given below

Open Source Software

It is a computer software with its source code made available and licensed with a licence in which the copyright holder provides the rights to study, change and distribute the software to anyone for any purpose. *For example,* Linux , Unix, MySQL etc.

To be considered as open source software by the software development industry, certain criteria must be met

- *Software must be available free or at a low cost.*
- Source code must be included.
- Anyone must be allowed to modify the source code.
- Modified versions can be redistributed.

Freeware

It generally refers to the softwares which are available for use at no cost or for an optional fee. The user has no restriction on copying and distribution of the software. But the user cannot modify such software because the source code is not available. Usually, the copyright holder allows people to use the software, but not sell it. Notepad, WordPad, Internet Explorer etc., are examples of freeware.

Shareware

It refers to the software which is made available with a right to redistribute copies. The objective of shareware is to make the availability of the software to as many its users as possible.

But often after a certain period, a license fee is to be paid, otherwise it may stop running. It does not provide any source code and no modifications are allowed. It is also known as 'Try before you buy'. Kaspersky Antivirus, Wondershare are examples of shareware.

Proprietary Software

It is a software that is owned by an individual or a company (usually the one that developed it). There are almost always major restrictions on its use, and its source code is always kept secret. This software is licensed under exclusive legal right of the copyright holder with the intent that the license has given the right to use the software only under certain conditions, and restricted from other uses, such as modification, sharing, studying, or redistribution. This software is also called as **close source software.**

For examples, Microsoft Windows, Adobe Flash Player etc.

Quick Test 3

1. What is the main difference between a compiler and an interpreter?
2. What is the difference between general-purpose and special-purpose application software?
3. Which of the following is an example of general-purpose application software?
   (a) Word processor
   (b) Spreadsheet
   (c) Web browser
   (d) All of the above
4. Which of the following is an example of special-purpose application software?
   (a) Accounting software (b) CAD software
   (c) Medical software (d) All of these

Mind Map

SOFTWARE

System Software

It is a set of programs that manage a computer's hardware and resources. It also provides a platform for running application software.

Operating System (OS)

It allows users to interact with their computer's hardware. It performs basic tasks like memory management, file management, and controlling devices like printers and disk drives.

Device Driver

It allows computer to communicate with hardware devices. Device drivers act as a bridge between the operating system and hardware, allowing the two to interact.

Utility Software

It helps maintain and analyze a computer's performance. It can help with tasks like disk space management, file organization, and backup.

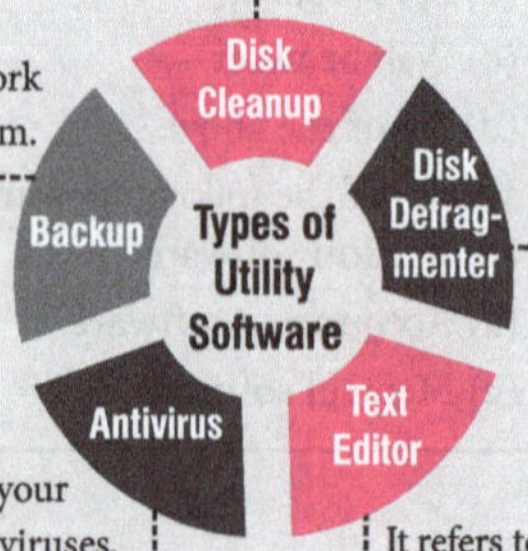

- **Disk Cleanup:** Removes unused files to free up disk space
- **Disk Defragmenter:** Rearranges scattered files into contiguous spaces to improve disk performance
- **Text Editor:** It refers to a computer program that allows users to create, edit, and manipulate plain text files
- **Antivirus:** It helps protect your computer from viruses, malware, and other threats. It can also help prevent identity theft and phishing.
- **Backup:** It is a software that copies data from a computer or network to a storage medium.

Application Software

It is a computer program that helps users perform tasks on their computer. It can be used for personal, professional, or educational purposes.

General Purpose Application Software

It can perform a variety of tasks. It's often used at home and school. e.g., Word processors, Spreadsheets, Web browsers , Multimedia software ,Accounting and finance software,etc.

Special Purpose Software

It is designed to perform a specific task or set of tasks. It is often created to meet the needs of a specific business, organization, or user. e.g., Camera application, Chess game ,Scientific calculator , Accounting software ,Medical billing software , Engineering design tools , Airline reservation systems, etc.

Language Processor

It is a software program that translates programming languages into machine language so that computers can understand and execute them.

Compilers

Read entire source codes and translate them into machine code object files

Assemblers

Translate assembly language into machine code

Interpreters

Read and translate source code line by line before executing each line

NCERT Folder

1. Name the software required to make a computer functional. Write down its two primary functions.

Ans. **Operating System (OS)** OS manages the hardware and the software resources, It provides a user interface.

Primary services include Process management, Input/Output management.

System Software System Software includes device drivers, utilities, and compilers/interpreters which requires to make any computer functional.

Primary services include Language processors, System tools.

2. Differentiate between proprietary software and freeware software. Name two software for each type.

Ans.

Proprietary Software	Freeware Software
These software is commercially licensed.	No licensing fees are required for these software tools.
In proprietary software we often requires purchase.	Freeware software is distributed free of charge
Example include Microsoft Office, Adobe Photoshop.	**Example include** VLC Media player, Notepad++.

3. Mention any browsers used for browsing the internet.

Ans. Internet explorer, Firefox.

4. Identify the category (system, application, programming tool) of the following software:

(a) Compiler (b) Assembler
(c) Ubuntu (d) Text editor

Ans. (a) Programming tool
(b) Programming tool
(c) System software
(d) Application software

EXAM PATTERN QUESTIONS

Objective Type Questions

Multiple Choice Questions

1. Which of the following is not a type of software?

(a) System software
(b) Application software
(c) Utility software
(d) Hardware software

2. System software

(a) allows the user to diagnose and troubleshoot the device
(b) is a programming language
(c) is a part of productivity suite
(d) helps the computer manage internal resources

3. What type of software is used to manage computer hardware and software resources?

(a) Application software (b) System software
(c) Utility software (d) Firmware

4. It is the set of programs that enables your computer's hardware device and application software to work together.

(a) Management (b) Processing
(c) Utility (d) System software

5. A company is setting up a new office and needs to install software that manages hardware resources and provides a platform for running other software. Which type of software should they install first? Competency Based Que.

(a) Application Software (b) System Software
(c) Programming Tools (d) Language Translators

6. Which of the following is the type of software that controls the internal operations in the computer and controls how the computer works well all its parts?

(a) Shareware (b) Public domain software
(c) Application software (d) Operating system software

7. What is the primary function of an operating system?
(a) To run application software
(b) To manage hardware and software resources
(c) To create documents
(d) To play games

8. A mobile phone requires special software to allow the operating system to communicate with its touchscreen and camera hardware. Which type of software performs this function? **Competency Based Que.**
(a) Assembler
(b) Device Driver
(c) Programming Language
(d) Compiler

9. Which of the following is not an example of a device driver?
(a) Printer driver (b) Keyboard driver
(c) Mouse driver (d) Web browser

10. A user installs an antivirus program to scan and remove malware from their computer. This type of software falls under which category? **Competency Based Que.**
(a) Application Software (b) System Utility
(c) Language Translator (d) Operating System

11. What is the purpose of disk defragmentation?
(a) To remove viruses from the computer
(b) To compress files to save space
(c) To reorganize files on the hard drive
(d) To translate code into machine language

12. …….. helps in converting programming language to machine language.
(a) Operating system (b) Device driver
(c) Language translator (d) Linker

13. A software developer writes a program in a high-level language. To convert this code into machine language for execution, which of the following software tools is required? **Competency Based Que.**
(a) Device Driver (b) Operating System
(c) Compiler (d) System Utility

14. Software designed for a specific purpose/ application such as pay calculations, processing of examination result etc., are known as
(a) utility software (b) system software
(c) application software (d) customized software

Fill in the Blanks

15. ______ represents set of programs that govern operations of a computer system.

16. A set of instructions given to a computer is called ____.

17. ______ is the collection of programs that. coordinates the operation of computer hardware and software.

18. ______ are the graphical representations of the programs on the desktop.

19. CLI stands for ________.

20. ________ programs perform specific tasks, usually related to managing a computer, its devices or its programs.

21. ______ utility is used to create copy of complete data on a disk.

22. ____ converts one line of a high level language program to machine code at a time.

State Whether True or False

23. A Real-Time Operating System (RTOS) is designed for systems where strict timing constraints are not critical, such as desktop computers.

24. A Multitasking Operating System allows a computer to execute multiple programs or tasks concurrently.

25. The first graphical user interface (GUI) was developed by Apple in the 1970s.

26. Device drivers are responsible for allocating system resources such as memory and interrupt requests to the device they manage.

27. Anti-virus software can only detect and remove existing malware infections, and cannot prevent future attacks.

28. Application software, like Microsoft Word, is considered general-purpose software because it can be used for a wide range of tasks.

29. An interpreter translates the entire high-level language program into machine code before execution, resulting in faster execution compared to compilers.

30. Open-source software is freely available to use, modify, and distribute, even for commercial purposes.

Assertion and Reason Based Questions

Assertion (A) and Reason (R) Type questions. Choose the correct option as
(a) Both Assertion (A) and Reason (R) are true, and Reason (R) is the correct explanation of Assertion (A).
(b) Both Assertion (A) and Reason (R) are true, but Reason (R) is not the correct explanation of Assertion (A).
(c) Assertion (A) is true, but Reason (R) is false.
(d) Assertion (A) is false, but Reason (R) is true.

31. Assertion (A) System software manages the hardware and software resources of a computer system.
Reason (R) System software directly interacts with the user to perform specific tasks.

32. **Assertion (A)** An operating system is a type of system software.
Reason (R) An operating system manages the hardware and software resources of a computer system.

33. **Assertion (A)** An operating system provides a user interface for interacting with the computer.
Reason (R) The command-line interface is a type of user interface.

34. **Assertion (A)** Device drivers are software programs that enable communication between hardware devices and the operating system.
Reason (R) Device drivers are a type of application software.

35. **Assertion (A)** An interpreter translates and executes each line of code one at a time.
Reason (R) Interpreted programs generally run faster than compiled programs.

36. **Assertion (A)** Application software is designed to perform specific tasks for users.
Reason (R) Word processors, spreadsheets, and web browsers are examples of application software.

Answers

1. (d) Hardware software
2. (d) helps the computer manage internal resources
3. (b) System software
4. (d) System software
5. (b) System Software
6. (d) Operating system software
7. (b) To manage hardware and software resources
8. (b) Device Driver
9. (d) Web browser
10. (b) System Utility
11. (c) To reorganize files on the hard drive
12. (c) Language translator
13. (c) Compiler
14. (c) application software
15. Software
16. Program
17. Operating System
18. Icons
19. Command Line Interface
20. Utility
21. Backup
22. Interpreter
23. False
24. True
25. False
26. True
27. False
28. True
29. False
30. True
31. (c) Assertion (A) is true, but Reason (R) is false.
32. (a) Both Assertion (A) and Reason (R) are true, and Reason (R) is the correct explanation of Assertion (A).
33. (a) Both Assertion (A) and Reason (R) are true, and Reason (R) is the correct explanation of Assertion (A).
34. (c) Assertion (A) is true, but Reason (R) is false.
35. (c) Assertion (A) is true, but Reason (R) is false.
36. (a) Both Assertion (A) and Reason (R) are true, and Reason (R) is the correct explanation of Assertion (A).

Subjective Type Questions

Very Short Answer Type Questions

1. Name the set of instructions that directs the computer to process the information.

Ans. Software

2. How many types of softwares are there? Name them.

Ans. There are three types of software
(i) System Software (ii) Application Software
(iii) Programming tools

3. What is the difference between system software and application software?

Ans. System software manages the computer's hardware and software resources, while application software performs specific tasks for users.

4. What are the main components of system software?

Ans. Operating system, device drivers, system utilities.

5. What purpose does the operating system serve to the computer and the user?

Ans. The operating system reduces the gap between the user and computer by receiving and interpreting user's request and then get this work done with the help of hardware.

6. A computer technician is setting up a new system. When the computer is switched ON, a specific program is loaded first into memory to manage hardware and software resources. Identify this program.

Competency Based Que.

Ans. Operating System.

7. Write the example of Android operating system.

Ans. Android operating system is basically designed for touch screen mobile devices like tablets, smart phone etc.

8. What is the difference between command-line interface and a graphical user interface?

Ans. A command-line interface requires users to type commands, while a graphical user interface uses icons and menus for interaction.

9. How are device drivers installed in a computer system?

Ans. Device drivers are usually installed from a CD or downloaded from the manufacturer's website.

10. Define a utility software.

Ans. A utility software is a kind of software designed to help analyze, configure, optimize and maintain a computer system.

11. Which program carries out some of the common tasks needed when using a computer?

Ans. A utility program carries out some of the common tasks needed when using a computer.

12. Name three utility softwares.

Ans. Text editor, Antivirus program and Compression tool.

13. Which utility software is used to free the disk space?

Ans. Disk cleanup.

14. Why is it important to regularly update antivirus software?

Ans. Regular updates protect against new viruses and threats.

15. Why is backup utility used in the computer system?

Ans. Backup utility is used to keep the backup of stored data in computer.

If the original files are lost or damaged, this data can be used. This backup can be used after the event of a disaster also.

16. A travel company wants to automate its railway ticket booking process. They are considering different types of software. Would a utility software be suitable for this task? Justify your answer. Competency Based Que.

Ans. No, a railway reservation system is not a utility software because it does not analyze, configure, or maintain a computer system.

It is an application software designed for booking and managing reservations.

17. Write the method, which is used to remove viruses?

Ans. Antivirus software is the method which is used to remove viruses.

18. Why application software is required in computer system?

Ans. Application software is required because system software cannot carry out the routine jobs performed by the user which application software can easily do.

19. Write the name of three application softwares.

Ans. Word processor, DBMS and railway reservation system.

20. A recent graduate wants to create a professional and visually appealing resume. Which application software should they use, and why? Competency Based Que.

Ans. A word processor (e.g., MS Word, Google Docs) is the best choice as it allows formatting, text editing, and adding design elements to make the resume attractive.

21. Which records are maintained by the financial accounting software?

Ans. Budget, General Ledger, Balance sheet, Profit & Loss statement.

22. Explain hotel management system.

Ans. Hotel management system refers to the management techniques used in the hotel sector. These can include hotel administration accounts, billing, marketing, housekeeping etc.

Short Answer Type I Questions

23. Name the types of software with examples for each.

Ans. There are three types of software, i.e., system software, application software and programming tool. Operating systems, etc., are system softwares. Payroll system, financial accounting etc., are application softwares. Translators, program development tools etc., are programming tools.

24. Which type of operating system is used in palmtop computers? Explain that operating system.

Ans. In palmtop computers, single user (with single task) operating system is used. This type of operating system is designed for use by a single user for a stand-alone single computer for performing a single task. Operating systems for personal computers are single user operating systems.

25. A company is developing a new range of compact handheld devices for business professionals. Which type of operating system should they integrate to ensure smooth functioning? Justify your answer. Competency Based Que.

Ans. The company should use a mobile operating system (like android or IOS) because these systems are designed for portability touch interaction, and have a wide range of bussiness applications available.

26. Which activities are performed by an operating system as a resource manager?

Ans. As a resource manager operating system performs the following activities.

(i) Monitors the different resources.

(ii) Allocates the resources.

(iii) Reclaims the resources.

(iv) Decides which resource get what, when and for how much time.

27. When a disk is said to be fragmented and also write one disadvantage of a fragmented disk.

Ans. A disk is said to be fragmented when some of the files are divided into pieces and are scattered around the disk. Fragmentation occurs naturally when you use a disk frequently, creating, deleting, and modifying files.

Disadvantage At some point, the operating system needs to store parts of a file in non-contiguous clusters. This is entirely invisible to users, but can slow down the speed at which data is accessed. This is the main disadvantage of disk fragmentation.

28. What is application software? Why it is required?

Ans. Application software is a type of software designed to perform specific tasks for users, such as word processing, web browsing, or data management.

Application software are required for such reasons

- It helps users accomplish specific tasks efficiently.
- Enhances productivity in various fields like business, education, and entertainment.
- Provides a user-friendly interface to interact with computer hardware.

Examples: MS Word, Google Chrome, Tally, Photoshop.

29. A travel agency wants to automate its booking process to improve efficiency and customer experience. What system should they use, and how will it benefit their business? **Competency Based Que.**

Ans. The travel agency should implement a reservation system (Central Reservation System - CRS). This computerized system helps store and retrieve booking information for air travel, hotels, car rentals, and other activities. By using CRS, businesses can streamline transactions, provide real-time availability, and offer customers easy online booking options through platforms like www.yatra.com and www.makemytrip.com.

Short Answer Type II Questions

30. What are operating systems and utility software, and how do they contribute to computer functionality?

Ans. An operating system (OS) serves as the fundamental software layer that bridges the gap between a computer's hardware components and the user. It handles essential tasks such as managing files, allocating memory, executing processes, and controlling input/output devices like printers and disk drives.

Utility software, often integrated into the OS, complements the core functions of the operating system. These tools are designed to optimize, maintain, and troubleshoot computer systems. They encompass a wide range of functions, including disk defragmentation, virus scanning, data backup, system optimization, and network configuration.

31. Differentiate between system software and application software? Give examples of each type of software.

Ans. Differences between system software and application software are

System Software	Application Software
Enables the computer to function properly.	Enables users to work efficiently with documentation such as letters, accounting reports and presentation.
Compulsory-each computer must have a system software to function.	Optional-depends on usage and needs. Without an application software, the computer is still able to function.
Independent system software can function without an application software.	Dependent-application software cannot work without system software.
Provides the environment in which the applications run.	Provides the environment to enable users to accomplish specific tasks.
e.g. Operating system, compiler, interpreter, etc.	e.g. Payroll system, word processor, database management system, etc.

32. What are the different types of software that can be used to convert human-readable code into machine-executable instructions?

Ans. Language translators are specialized software programs designed to bridge the gap between human-readable programming languages and machine code. They fall into three primary categories:

Assembler Translate assembly language to machine code. This process involves a one-to-one mapping between assembly instructions and machine instructions.

Interpreter An interpreter executes source code line by line, translating and executing each instruction before proceeding to the next.

Compiler A compiler translates entire source code programs into machine code in a single process.

Long Answer Type Questions

33. Define application software with its types.

Ans. Refer to text on page no. 27-29 (Application software).

34. A school is setting up a computer lab, and the administrator needs to ensure that all computers function efficiently. They must install a system that manages hardware, provides a user-friendly interface, and coordinates all activities.

Based on this scenario, explain why an operating system is necessary and how it helps in managing computer resources effectively. **Competency Based Que.**

Ans. An Operating System (OS) is essential for a computer to function as it acts as a bridge between hardware and software, ensuring smooth operation.

1. **Managing Hardware Resources** The OS efficiently allocates memory, schedules CPU tasks, and controls input/output operations, optimizing system performance.
2. **Providing a User-Friendly Interface** It offers interfaces like GUI or CLI, making it easier for users to interact with the computer.
3. **Executing User Commands** The OS translates user inputs (mouse clicks, keyboard strokes, or voice commands) into machine-readable instructions for execution.
4. **Coordinating System Activities** It manages multiple processes, ensuring smooth execution of tasks and efficient resource utilization.

35. Operating system is an important component of computer system. Various types of operating systems are available.

(i) What kind of software is an operating system?

(ii) Why operating system is important?

Ans. (i) An operating system is a type of system software. This means it's a program that controls the inner workings of the computer. It makes sure that the hardware (like the processor and memory) works together properly and allows other software (like games or word processors) to run.

(ii) The operating system is like the brain of the computer. It makes the computer work effectively and allows you to use it easily.

36. Reena got an assignment on the topic Word processing software. Help her to solve the assignment. **Competency Based Que.**

(i) What is Word processing software?

(ii) Which type of software is Word processor?

(iii) Give some examples equivalent to type of Word processing software.

Ans. (i) Word processing software is a type of computer program that allows you to create, edit, and format text documents. It makes writing and manipulating text easier and more efficient than using a typewriter.

(ii) Word processors belong to the category of application software. Application software is designed to perform specific tasks for users, such as creating documents, browsing the web, or editing images.

(iii) Here are some other examples of application software:

- Spreadsheets (like Excel)
- Presentation software (like PowerPoint)
- Image editing software (like Photoshop)
- Media players (like VLC)
- Web browsers (like Chrome)
- Email clients (like Outlook)

37. Name a software that can be used to display the information in the form of a slide show. Explain that software.

Ans. Presentation tool is the general-purpose application software which is used to display the information in the form of a slide show. Presentation is the practice of showing and explaining the content of a topic to audience or learner visually. A presentation tool involves graphics and animation packages.

It has three major functions

(i) An editor that allows text to be inserted or formatted.

(ii) A method for inserting and manipulating graphic images.

(iii) A slide-show system to display the content.

Presentation tool is used by users to create professional looking visual aids for an audience to make the information easily understandable.

For example, marketing managers use presentation tool to present new marketing strategies to their superiors, and students use it to create high quality class presentations.

Some of the examples of presentation tool include Microsoft PowerPoint, Corel presentations, Lotus Freelance Graphics etc.

38. Explain Open source concept in detail.

Ans. Refer to text on page no. 29 (Open source concepts).

39. Explain system software in detail along with its types.

Ans. System software is a program that manages and supports the computer resources and operations of a computer system while it executes various tasks such as processing data and information, controlling hardware components, and allowing users to use application software, i.e., system software functions as a bridge between computer system hardware and the application software.

The system software is made up of many control programs, including the operating system. There are many kinds of computers these days. Some of them are easier to learn than others.

Some of them perform better than others. The system software contains those programs that control and support the computer system and its data processing applications. It includes

(i) **Operating System** An Operating System (OS), is a software program that enables the computer hardware to communicate and operate with the computer software. Without an operating system, a computer would be useless.

(ii) **Device Drivers** It ensure the proper functioning of hardware by acting as an interface between the device and the operating system.

(iii) **Utility Software** Software used for maintaining and configuring the computer system, such as disk defragmentation, antivirus and disk cleaner tools.

40. Differentiate between GUI and CUI.

Ans.

GUI (Graphical User Interface)	CUI (Character User Interface)
Uses graphical elements like icons, menus, and windows	Uses text-based commands and prompts
Generally easier to learn and use	Requires more technical knowledge and command-line syntax
More intuitive and user-friendly	Can be more efficient for experienced users
Often requires more system resources (CPU, memory)	Less resource-intensive
Offers more flexibility for customization	Less customization options
Can be slower due to graphical elements	Generally faster due to direct command execution
Less precise for complex tasks	More precise for specific tasks
Windows, macOS, Linux desktop environments	Command prompt, terminal, DOS

41. Discuss the features of electronic spreadsheets that make it useful?

Ans. (i) It provides facilities of cutting, pasting, moving, copying data values of formulae or formats etc.

(ii) Spreadsheets cannot represent only data values but their relationship also.

(iii) Data can be represented graphically.

(iv) The relationships between cells are called 'Formulae' and the names of the cells are called 'Labels'.

(v) Spreadsheet accepts data in a tabular form.

(vi) Numerous built-in functions are available in spreadsheets.

(vii) The user of the spreadsheet can make changes in any stored value and observe the effects on calculated values.

(viii) We can sort data to find individual data easily.

(ix) Spreadsheets replaced paper-based systems throughout the business world.

(x) Calculations such as net present value or standard deviation can be applied to tabular data with a pre-programmed function in a formula.

42. What is utility software, and what are some common types of utility software?

Ans. Utility software is a category of system software designed to optimize, maintain, and troubleshoot computer systems. These tools are essential for ensuring efficient and reliable computer operation.

Common types of utility software include:

(i) **Disk Compression Utilities** These tools reduce the size of files and directories on a hard drive, freeing up valuable storage space. By compressing data, these utilities can significantly increase the effective storage capacity of a drive.

(ii) **Backup Utilities** Backup utilities create copies of important data, protecting it from accidental deletion, hardware failures, or natural disasters. These tools allow users to restore files and entire systems to their previous state in case of data loss.

(iii) **Disk Defragmentation Utilities** Over time, file fragments can become scattered across a hard drive, leading to slower performance.

Disk defragmentation utilities reorganize these fragments, improving access times and overall system responsiveness.

(iv) **Virus Scanning and Removal Utilities** Antivirus software protects computers from malicious software, such as viruses, worms, and malware. These utilities scan files and systems for threats, remove infections, and provide real-time protection.

(v) **Data Recovery Utilities** Data recovery software can recover lost or deleted files from hard drives, USB drives, and other storage devices. These tools can be invaluable in recovering important data after accidental deletion or system failures.

Case Study Based Questions

Case Study 1

Software is the intangible set of instructions, data, and programs that tell a computer how to function. It acts as the brain of the computer, dictating its actions and guiding its operations. Unlike hardware, which refers to the physical components of a computer, software is a collection of digital instructions that enable the hardware to perform specific tasks.

There are two main types of software:

1. **System Software** This category forms the foundation for all computer operations. It includes core functions like operating systems (e.g., Windows, macOS, Android), disk management tools, utilities (e.g., antivirus software, disk defragmenters), and hardware management tools. System software acts as the intermediary between the user and the hardware, providing the essential services needed to run applications and manage resources.
2. **Application Software** As the name suggests, application software (often called apps) helps users accomplish specific tasks. This broad category encompasses a wide range of programs, including office productivity suites (e.g., Microsoft Office, Google Workspace), data management software (e.g., databases), media players (e.g., VLC Media Player), and security programs (e.g., firewalls). Applications also extend to the web and mobile world, with tools for shopping (e.g., Amazon), social networking (e.g., Facebook), and photo sharing (e.g., Instagram).

(i) **What refers to the set of instructions that tell a computer how to function?**
(a) Hardware
(b) Software
(c) Data
(d) User Interface

(ii) **Which of the following is an example of application software?**
(a) Operating System
(b) Word Processing Software (e.g., Microsoft Word)
(c) Device Drivers
(d) Memory Management Tools

(iii) **What type of software provides core functions like managing files and memory?**
(a) User Interface Software
(b) System Software
(c) Development Tools
(d) Entertainment Software

(iv) **Which software acts as the intermediary between the user and the computer hardware?**
(a) Operating System
(b) Application Software
(c) Hardware Drivers
(d) Programming Languages

(v) **What software helps protect your computer from viruses and malware?**
(a) Operating System (b) System Utilities
(c) Security Software (d) Productivity Tools

(vi) **Which type of software allows users to create and edit digital images?**
(a) Multimedia Software
(b) System Management Tools
(c) Communication Software
(d) Web Browsers

Ans. (i) (b) Software
(ii) (b) Word Processing Software (e.g., Microsoft Word)
(iii) (b) System Software
(iv) (a) Operating system
(v) (c) Security Software
(vi) (a) Multimedia Software

Case Study 2

Operating system is a program that acts as an interface between the user and the hardware (i.e. for all computer resources). An operating system is an important component of a computer system, which controls and co-ordinates all other components of it. It activates all devices that make them ready for work. It also performs all internal management functions and ensures systematic functioning of a computer system.

The operating system performs the following functions:

- **It recognises input from keyboard and sends output to the display screen.**
- **It makes sure that the programs running simultaneously do not interfere with each other.**
- **It is also responsible for security and ensuring that unauthorised users cannot access the System e.g. MS-DOS, Windows 95, Windows XP, Windows Vista etc.**

Based on the above information, answer the following questions.

(i) What is the primary role of an operating system?

(a) To develop software applications
(b) To act as an interface between the user and hardware
(c) To provide internet access
(d) To create and edit documents

(ii) Which of the following is NOT a function of an operating system?

(a) Managing hardware resources
(b) Controlling and coordinating system components
(c) Developing new programming languages
(d) Ensuring security from unauthorized access

(iii) How does an operating system handle multiple programs running at the same time?

(a) By shutting down the computer
(b) By ensuring programs do not interfere with each other
(c) By deleting unnecessary programs
(d) By allowing only one program to run at a time

(iv) Which of the following is an example of an operating system?

(a) MS Word
(b) Windows XP
(c) Google Chrome
(d) Python

(v) What function of an OS ensures that unauthorized users cannot access the system?

(a) Memory management
(b) Device activation
(c) Security management
(d) File editing

Ans. (i) (b) To act as an interface between the user and hardware
(ii) (c) Developing new programming languages
(iii) (b) By ensuring programs do not interfere with each other
(iv) (b) Windows XP
(v) (c) Security management

Case Study 3

Software is a set of computer programs, procedures and associated documentation concerned with the operation of a data processing system. Software commonly known as programs, consists of all required instructions that tell the hardware how to perform a task. It is not basic requirement of a computer system, but it makes a computer more powerful and useful.

Software can be broadly classified into two major categories as follows:

1. **System software** 2. **Application software**

Based on the above information, answer the following questions.

(i) What is the term used to describe intangible instructions that tell the computer what to do?

(a) Hardware (b) Software
(c) Database (d) Network

(ii) What is software?

(a) A set of physical computer components
(b) A type of hardware device
(c) A collection of programs, data and instructions
(d) A storage device for data

(iii) Which of the following are examples of software?

(a) CPU and RAM (b) MS Word and Windows
(c) Monitor and Keyboard
(d) Printer and Scanner

(iv) The primary purpose of software is to turn data into what?

(a) Hardware (b) Programs
(c) Information (d) Network

(v) A set of instructions that tell the computer how to perform a task is called?

(a) Algorithm (b) Software
(c) Database (d) Hardware

Ans. (i) (b) Software
(ii) (c) A collection of programs, data and instructions
(iii) (b) MS Word and Windows
(iv) (c) Information (v) (b) Software

SELF ASSESSMENT TEST

Multiple Choice Questions

1. **This type of software works with end-users, application software and computer hardware to handle the majority of technical details.**
(a) Communications software
(b) Application software
(c) Utility software
(d) System software

2. **It is the program that manages the hardware of the computer system including the CPU, memory storage devices and input/output devices.**
(a) Software
(b) Operating system
(c) Hardware
(d) System software

3. **The primary purpose of the Windows operating system is**
(a) to make the most efficient use of the computer hardware
(b) to allow people to use the computer
(c) to keep systems programmer's employed
(d) to make computers easier to use

Fill in the Blanks

4. Since computers understand __________ language, human-written programs in high-level languages must be converted using translators.

5. __________ translate entire high-level language programs into machine code before execution, making them faster than interpreters.

6. High-level languages like C++, Java, and Python are __________ and require translators to convert code into machine language.

State Whether True or False

7. The device driver acts as an interface between the device and the operating system.

8. Compression utilities reduce the size of files to make storage and transmission more efficient.

9. A disk defragmenter deletes unnecessary files from the system to free up storage space.

Assertion and Reason Based Questions

Assertion (A) and Reason (R) Type questions. Choose the correct option as
(a) Both Assertion (A) and Reason (R) are true, and Reason (R) is the correct explanation of Assertion (A).
(b) Both Assertion (A) and Reason (R) are true, but Reason (R) is not the correct explanation of Assertion (A).
(c) Assertion (A) is true, but Reason (R) is false.
(d) Assertion (A) is false, but Reason (R) is true.

10. **Assertion (A)** A Multi-Tasking Operating System allows multiple programs to run simultaneously by efficiently switching between tasks.

Reason (R) Multi-Tasking Operating Systems execute all processes at the same time using multiple CPUs.

11. **Assertion (A)** A Real-Time Operating System (RTOS) is used in time-critical applications like industrial control systems and medical devices.

Reason (R) A Real-Time Operating System (RTOS) ensures that every task gets executed within a specific time constraint.

Very Short Answer Type Questions

12. What is software? How softwares are classified?

13. Explain the term operating system?

14. What is language processor?

15. Describe proprietary software.

16. Which tool is used to reduce the size of data?

Short Answer Type Questions

17. Explain the need of operating system in computer.

18. Distinguish between single-task and multi-task operating system.

19. Distinguish between freeware and proprietary software.

20. What is booting? How many types of booting are there?

21. What do you mean by inventory management system?

Long Answer Type Questions

22. Explain disk management tools with its example.

23. Explain Word processor.

24. Briefly explain the operating system.

25. Explain language translator and its types.

26. Describe the open source concepts in detail.

Case Study Based Questions

27. Rahul is a computer science student working on a school project. He needs to write and test a program in Python, but he also wants to ensure that his system is secure and optimized for smooth performance. To do this, he installs an Integrated Development Environment (IDE) for coding, an antivirus program for protection, and a disk cleaner to remove unnecessary files. Additionally, he learns about different types of software such as system software, application software, and utility software to understand their roles in a computer system.

Based on the above scenario, answer the following multiple-choice questions:

(i) **Which type of software does Rahul use to write and test his Python program?**
(a) System Software
(b) Utility Software
(c) Programming Software
(d) Application Software

(ii) **The antivirus software Rahul installs is an example of:**
(a) System Software (b) Utility Software
(c) Application Software (d) Firmware

(iii) **Rahul's disk cleaner helps remove unnecessary files to free up space. This software is classified as:**
(a) System Software
(b) Utility Software
(c) Application Software
(d) Real-Time Software

(iv) **Which of the following is an example of system software?**
(a) Microsoft Word
(b) Windows Operating System
(c) Photoshop
(d) VLC Media Player

(v) **Rahul wants to create a presentation for his project. Which type of software should he use?**
(a) System Software
(b) Programming Software
(c) Application Software
(d) Firmware

Answers

1. (d) 2. (b) 3. (d) 4. Machine
5. Compilers 6. human-readable
7. True 8. True 9. False 10. (c) 11. (a)
27. (i) → (c), (ii) → (b), (iii) → (b), (iv) → (b), (v) → (c)

03 CHAPTER

Computer programming is an art, because it applies accumulated knowledge to the world, because it requires skill and ingenuity and especially because it produces objects of beauty.

YOUR STUDY GOALS

3.1 Download and Installation of Python
3.2 Working in Python
3.3 Print "hello world" using command line

YOUR PRACTICE GOAL

- Objective Type Questions (30 Qs ; MCQs, True or False, Fill in the Blanks, Assertion and Reason)
- Subjective Type Questions (31 Qs ; VSA, SA, LA)
- Case Study Based Questions-2

Python Overview

Python is a user-friendly programming language that lets you write code quickly and efficiently. It was created by **Guido Van Rossum** in **1991** and is now maintained by the **Python Software Foundation.**

Python is versatile, which means it can be used for various tasks, from simple scripts to complex software applications. It's easy to learn and understand, which makes it a great choice for both beginners and experienced programmers.

Python is based on two programming languages which are as follows:

- ABC language is an interactive programming and teaching language, originally intended as a good replacement for BASIC.
- Modula-3 supports interfaces, objects and generics.

Python interpreters are available for many operating systems such as Windows, MacOS etc.

Advantages of Python

Python is considered easy to learn and run almost anywhere, it is useful for a number of applications, including education, data analytics and web development. There are various advantages of Python as follows:

- **Easy to Use** Python's simple syntax and readability makes it easier for beginners to pick up and start coding quickly. Unlike many other programming languages, Python doesn't require complex syntax or strict rules, which can often be a barrier for new programmers.

- **Object-Oriented** Python supports both procedural and object-oriented programming paradigms, allowing for flexible and modular code. In object-oriented programming, code is organized into objects. Python's object-oriented features allow you to create classes, objects, and define relationships between them. By using object-oriented concepts like inheritance, polymorphism, and encapsulation, you can write more efficient and well-structured programs.
- **Productivity and Speed** Python's powerful features and integration capabilities enhance development speed and efficiency.
- **Portability** Python code can run on various platforms without significant modifications.
- **Open-Source** Python is freely available and open-source which promotes collaboration and innovation.
- **Extensive Libraries** Python comes with a built-in library that offers a vast collection of modules and functions for various tasks. This means you don't have to write code from scratch for common operations like file handling, network programming, data manipulation, and more. You can simply import the necessary modules and use their functions to perform these tasks efficiently. This significantly reduces development time and effort.
- **Interpreted** Python's interpreted nature makes it easier to debug and test code.
- **Integration** Python can integrate with other programming languages and systems which makes Python a versatile and powerful language.

Disadvantages of Python

There are some disadvantages of Python are as follows:

- **Slower Performance** Python is an interpreted language, which means that the code is executed line by line, one at a time. In contrast, compiled languages like C++ and Java are translated into machine code before execution, which can lead to faster performance. While Python's interpreted nature makes it easier to develop and debug code, it can sometimes result in slower execution times, especially for computationally intensive tasks.
- **Limited Mobile Applications** Python is less commonly used for mobile app development compared to languages like Java and Swift.
- **Runtime Errors** Python's dynamic typing can sometimes lead to unexpected errors if you accidentally assign a value of a different type to a variable. For example, if you try to perform arithmetic operations on a string, Python will raise a `TypeError`. To avoid such errors, it's important to be mindful of the data types you're working with and use appropriate type conversions when necessary.
- **Less Mature Database Access** Python's database access layers are not as mature as those in other languages, making it less suitable for large-scale enterprise applications.
- **Higher Memory Consumption** Python's dynamic typing allows for flexibility, but it can also impact memory usage. When you assign a value to a variable, Python allocates memory to store both the value and its type information. This can lead to higher memory consumption compared to statically typed languages where the type of a variable is determined at compile time.

3.1 Download and Installation of Python

Python is a versatile program that can run on many different computer systems, including those which used by servers that run websites and other online services.

Installing Python on a Windows server is pretty straightforward. All you need to do is download the setup program from the official Python website (Python.org) and run it on your server. It's that easy!

Downloading Python

To download a Python setup, follow the steps given below

(i) Enter Python.org in URL. A window will be appearing. Select Downloads tab, after this a pop-up will appear as shown below:

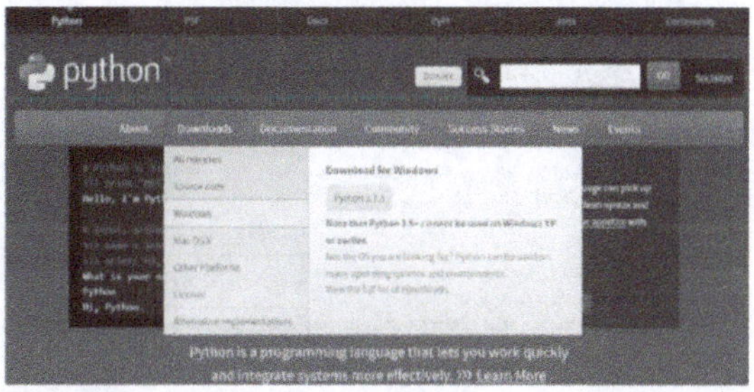

(ii) Click on Python 3.7.3 button to download.

The file named 3.7.3.exe should start downloading into your standard download folder.

(iii) Move this file to more permanent location, so that you can install Python.

Installing Python

To install Python, follow the steps given below:

(i) Open Downloads folder where Python setup was saved.Double click on the file python-3.7.3.exe.

(ii) An Open File-Security Warning dialog box will appear as shown below.

(iii) Click on Run button.

A Python 3.7.3 (32-bit) Setup pop-up window will appear.

(iv) Highlight the install now (or upgrade now) message and then click it. A user account control pop-up window will appear, that asked the question. Do you want to allow the following program to make changes to this computer?

(v) Click on Yes button.

A new Python 3.7.3 (32-bit) Setup pop-up window will appear, with a Setup Progress message and a progress bar.

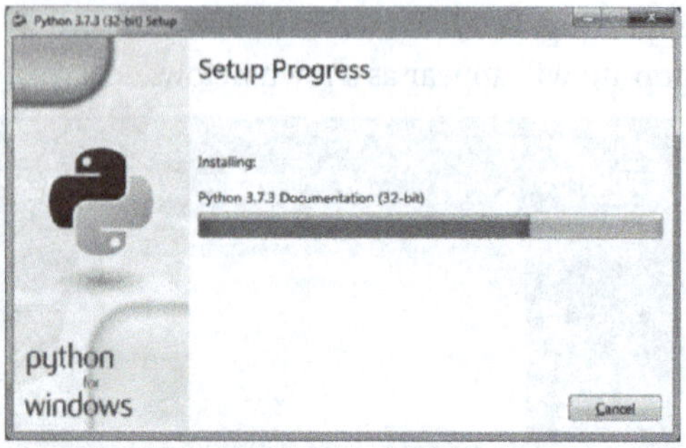

During installation, it will show the various components that are installing and move the progress bar towards completion. Soon, a new Python 3.7.3 (32 bit) Setup pop-up window will appear, with a "Setup was successful" message.

(vi) Click the Close button.

3.2 Working in Python

Programmers typically create individual programs, called scripts, that can work on their own without needing to be connected to something else. These scripts are saved with the ".py" extension, which tells both the computer and the programmer that the file contains Python code.Once you start the interpreter, it reads the script line by line and tells the computer what to do.

User can run a program with three ways in python

(i) Python (Command line)

You can run Python programs directly on your computer. To do this, you'll need to find the Python application on your computer, usually in the Start menu. Once you open it, a window will appear where you can type and run your Python code.

To start Python with command line, follow given step

Start → All Programs → Python 3.7 → Python 3.7 (32-bit).

Python 3.7 (32-bit) window will appear in your computer, where you can write code and execute it.

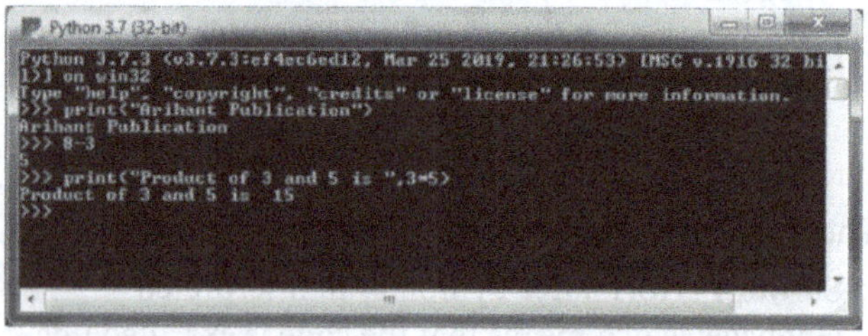

Python gives the output after you entered statement and press enter key. In command line mode, you type

```
>>>print (''Arihant Publication'')
Arihant Publication
>>> 8-3
5
>>> print (''Product of 3 and 5 is'',  3 * 5)
Product of 3 and 5 is 15
```

TEACHER TIP

Indentation plays a very crucial role in Python programming. If you give extra space, it will give syntax error.

(ii) Interactive Mode IDLE (Python GUI)

IDLE is a user-friendly tool that lets you write and run Python code in a window. You can use it to create and test your Python programs.

If you're having trouble setting up IDLE or Python, you can ask your system administrator for help.

Make sure everything is set up correctly so you can start coding.

To start Python with IDLE, follow the given step

Start → All Programs → Python 3.7 → IDLE (Python 3.7 (32-bit)).

Python 3.7.3 Shell window will appear.

In that window, >>> sign will appear, here you can write your code and press Enter.

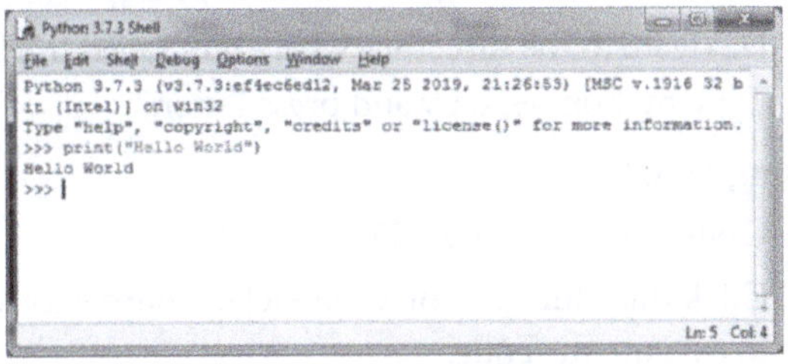

If you want to exit from the IDLE window, there are various options

Press Ctrl+D from keyboard

or Click File → Exit

or Click on cross ☒ button on title bar.

Advantages of Interactive Mode in Python

- **Immediate Execution & Feedback** You can enter a command and get instant results, making it useful for testing small code snippets.
- **Easy Debugging** Errors are identified immediately, allowing quick modifications and corrections.

Disadvantage of Interactive Mode in Python

- **No Permanent Code Storage** Code written in interactive mode is not saved automatically, requiring manual copying to a file for future use.

(iii) Python Script Mode

Python usually shows you the result as soon as you press Enter. However, if you want to see all the results at once after you've finished writing your code, you can use Python's script mode. To work with Python script mode, you will have to follow given steps:

Step 1 Create Script/Program File

To create script/program file, follow the given instructions:

- Start button → All Programs → Python 3.7 → IDLE (Python 3.7 (32-bit)).
- Python 3.7.3 shell window will appear on your screen. From here select File → New File window.

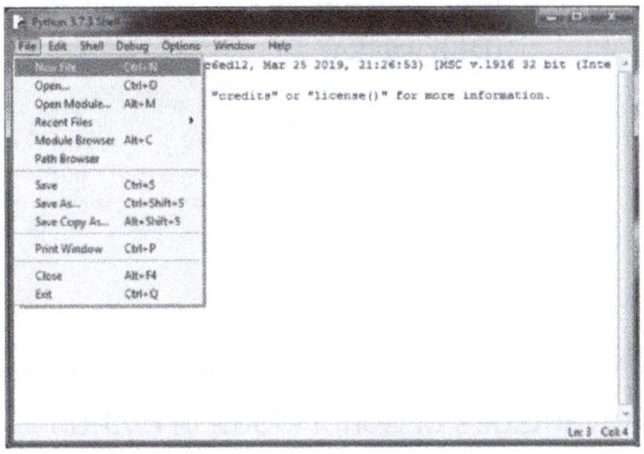

- An Untitled window will appear where you can write your code.

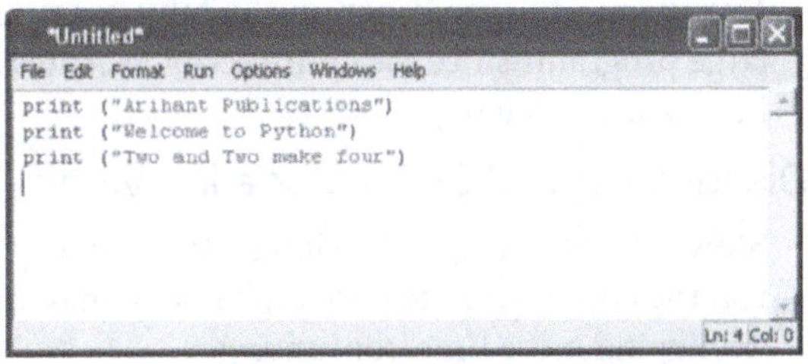

- After finish your code, select File → Save As.
- Save As dialog box will appear. Enter program name in File name: text field with .py extension and click on Save button.

Step 2 Run Script/ Program File

To run script/program file after creation of script, follow the given instructions:

- Now, open the IDLE file, which was opened in step1.
- Select File → Open and type file name in File name: box which file you want to open for executing.
- Click on Open button. Filename.py file will appear on your screen.

- Select Run → Run Module or press F5 key from keyboard.

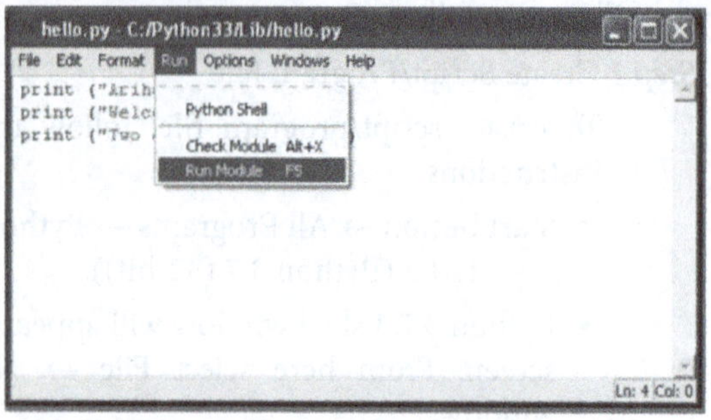

- It will execute and output will print in your IDLE window.

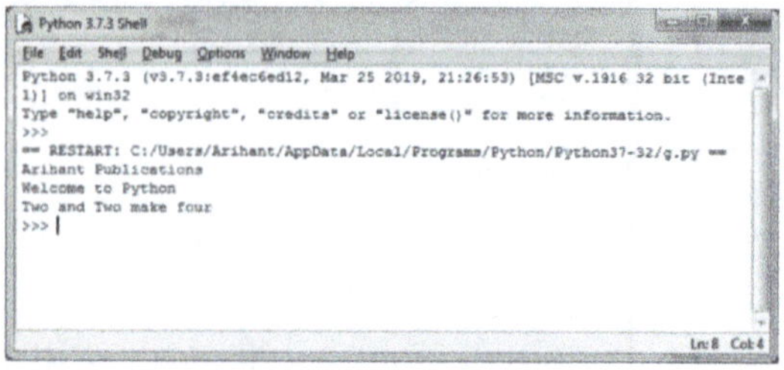

Advantages of Script Mode in Python

- **Code Reusability** You can save the script as a .py file and reuse it multiple times without rewriting the code.
- **Execution of Large Programs** Suitable for running large programs since the entire script executes at once, improving efficiency.

Disadvantage of Script Mode in Python

- **Slower Debugging** Unlike interactive mode, you must run the entire script to check for errors, making debugging more time-consuming.

3.3 Print "hello world" using command line

You can easily write your first program by following these simple steps which are as follow:

1. Install Python

- Download the latest Python version from the official website (python.org).
- Follow the installation instructions for your operating system.

2. Open a Text Editor

- Use a simple text editor like Notepad (Windows), TextEdit (Mac), or a more advanced code editor like Visual Studio Code or PyCharm.

3. Write the Code

- Type the following line of code into the text editor:

```
print("hello world")
```

4. Save the File

- Save the file with a .py extension, like hello.py.

5. Run the Code

- **Using the Command Line**
  1. Open your terminal or command prompt.
  2. Navigate to the directory where you saved the file.
  3. Type python hello.py and press Enter.
- **Using an IDE**
  1. Open the file in your IDE.
  2. Click the "Run" button or use a keyboard shortcut to execute the code.

This will print "hello world" to your console as shown below.

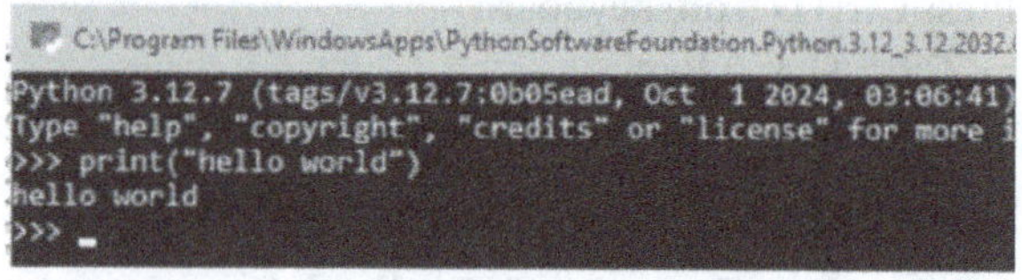

Mistake Alert

Students often make mistakes with indentation, which can lead to syntax errors in their Python code.

Mind Map

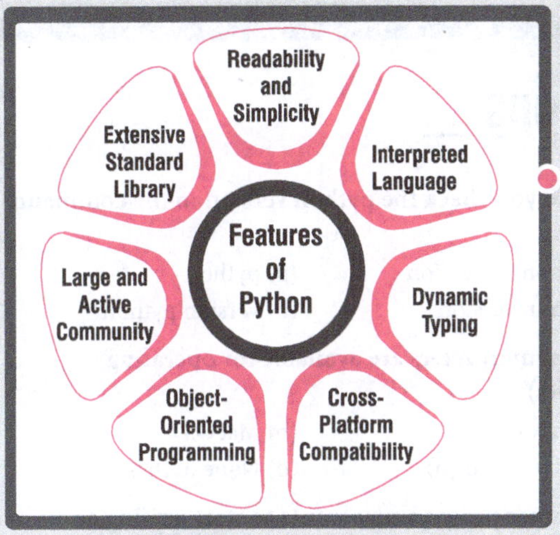

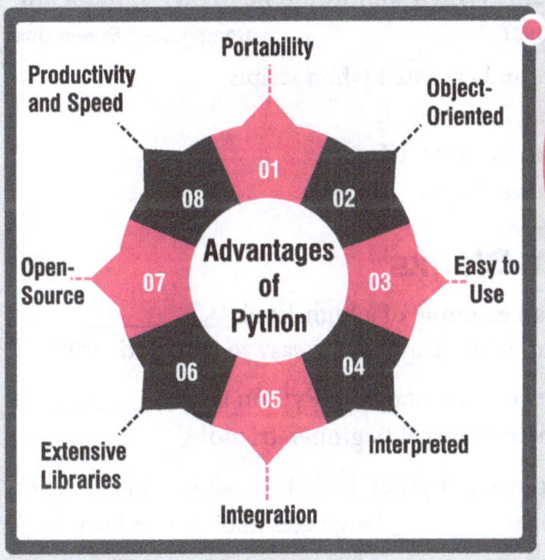

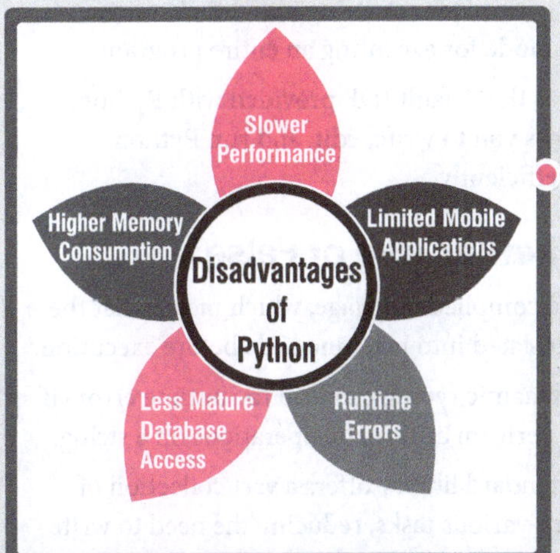

PYTHON OVERVIEW

It was created by **Guido Van Rossum**in **1991** and is now maintained by the **Python Software Foundation.**

Working in Python

User can run a program with three ways in python

Command line

To start Python with command line, follow given step
Start -> All Programs -> Python 3.7 -> Python 3.7 (32-bit).

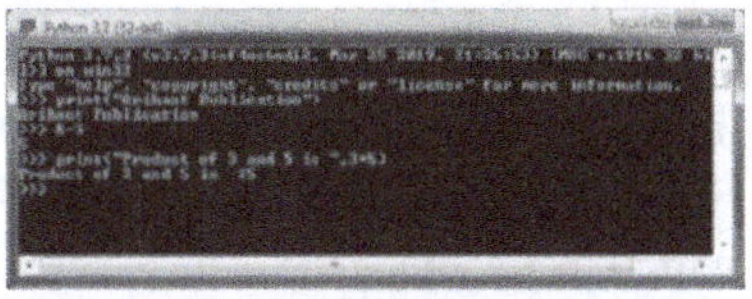

Interactive Mode IDLE (Python GUI)

To start Python with IDLE, follow the given step
Start→All Programs→Python 3.7→IDLE (Python 3.7 (32-bit)).

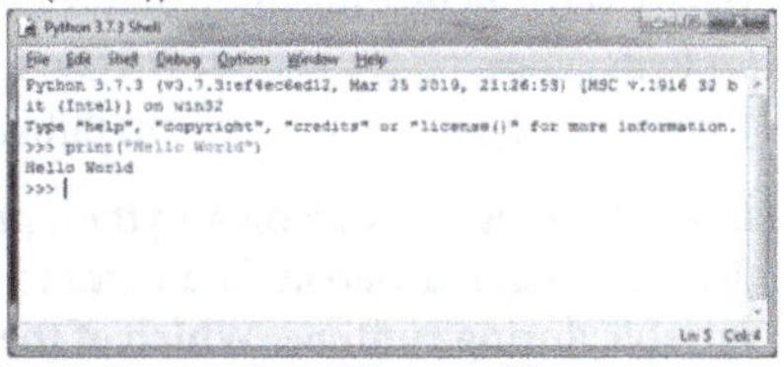

Step 1: Create a Script/Program File

To create a script/program file, follow these instructions:

1. Click on the Start button All Programs Python 3.7 IDLE (Python 3.7 (32-bit)).
2. In IDLE, go to File New File.
3. Type your Python code in the new window.
4. Save the file with a.py extension (e.g., program.py) by selecting File → Save As

Step 2: Run the Script/Program File

To run the script after creating it:

1. Open the saved Python script in IDLE.
2. Click Run Run Module (or press F5).
3. The output will appear in the Python Shell window.

Download and Installation of Python

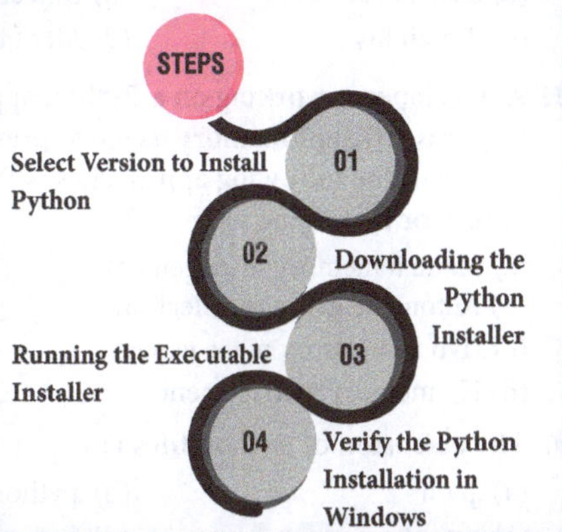

EXAM PATTERN QUESTIONS

Objective Type Questions

Multiple Choice Questions

1. What is Python?

(a) A programming language (b) A software application
(c) A hardware component (d) A network protocol

2. Python is based on

(a) ABC language (b) Modula 3
(c) Both (a) and (b) (d) None of these

3. Where can you download the latest Python installer?

(a) Python.org (b) GitHub
(c) SourceForge (d) Bitbucket

4. A developer is working on a Python project and notices they can assign different data types to the same variable during runtime. Which of the following features of Python enables this behavior? **Competency Based Que.**

(a) Dynamically typed
(b) Interpreted language
(c) Object-oriented programming
(d) Strongly typed

5. In which year was Python 3.0 released?

(a) 2000 (b) 2005
(c) 2008 (d) 2010

6. Python was initially designed by

(a) Guido Van Rossum (b) Charles Babbage
(c) Grace Hopper (d) Dennis Ritchie

7. Which of the following is/are advantage(s) of Python?

(a) Easy to use (b) Object oriented
(c) Portability (d) All of these

8. A developer is working on a Python application that requires efficient memory usage to prevent crashes. Which of the following approaches is Python designed to use for managing memory?

(a) Manual memory management
(b) Automatic garbage collection
(c) Hybrid memory management
(d) No memory management

9. The extension of Python files is

(a) .pyth (b) .python
(c) .py (d) .p

10. How do you check the python version in the command line?

(a) python - - version (b) python –v
(c) python version (d) version python

11. Python interpreters are available for operating system(s)

(a) Windows (b) MacOS
(c) Both (a) and (b) (d) None of these

12. A beginner programmer wants to start writing and running Python code directly within a user-friendly environment. Which tool would be MOST suitable for this purpose? **Competency Based Que.**

(a) To write and execute Python scripts
(b) To debug Python code
(c) To create Python GUIs
(d) To manage Python packages

Fill in the Blanks

13. Python is an example of a high-level, __________ programming language that is easy to read and write.

14. One of the key advantages of Python is its _________ syntax, which makes it beginner-friendly.

15. A disadvantage of Python is that it is slower in execution compared to _________ languages like C++ or Java.

16. Python provides different modes for working, such as __________ mode for running individual commands and script mode for executing an entire program.

17. ________ is the default IDE provided with Python, which allows you to write, edit, and run Python programs efficiently.

State Whether True or False

18. Python is a compiled language, which means that the code is translated into machine code before execution.

19. Python's dynamic typing can lead to runtime errors if you try to perform arithmetic operations on a string.

20. Python's standard library offers a vast collection of modules for various tasks, reducing the need to write code from scratch.

21. Python can only be installed on Windows servers.

22. Python scripts are typically saved with a ".py" extension.

23. Indentation is not important in Python programming.

24. Python scripts can only be run within the IDLE environment.

Assertion and Reason Based Questions

Assertion (A) and Reason (R) Type questions. Choose the correct option as:

(a) Both Assertion (A) and Reason (R) are true, and Reason (R) is the correct explanation of Assertion (A).

(b) Both Assertion (A) and Reason (R) are true, but Reason (R) is not the correct explanation of Assertion (A).

(c) Assertion (A) is true, but Reason (R) is false.

(d) Assertion (A) is false, but Reason (R) is true.

25. Assertion (A) Python is a high-level programming language.

Reason (R) Python syntax is complicated and difficult to learn.

26. Assertion (A) Python is platform-independent.

Reason (R) Python code can be executed on different operating systems without modification.

27. Assertion (A) Python is slower compared to compiled languages like C or Java.

Reason (R) Python uses an interpreter to execute code.

28. Assertion (A) Python installation requires downloading it from python.org.

Reason (R) Python is pre-installed on all operating system.

29. Assertion (A) Python allows both interactive and script-based modes of programming.

Reason (R) Python does not support writing multiple lines of code in a script.

30. Assertion (A) You can print "Hello, world!" in Python using the command.

Reason (R) Python uses the echo command to print messages.

Answers

1. (a) A programming language

2. (c) Both (a) and (b) **3.** (a) Python.org

4. (a) Dynamically typed **5.** (c) 2008

6. (a) Guido Van Rossum **7.** (d) All of these

8. (b) Automatic garbage collection **9.** (c) .py

10. (a) python - - version **11.** (c) Both (a) and (b)

12. (a) To write and execute Python scripts

13. interpreted **14.** simple

15. compiled **16.** interactive

17. IDLE **18.** False **19.** True **20.** True

21. False **22.** True **23.** False

24. False

25. (c) Assertion (A) is true, but Reason (R) is false.

26. (a) Both Assertion (A) and Reason (R) are true, and Reason (R) is the correct explanation of Assertion (A).

27. (a) Both Assertion (A) and Reason (R) are true, and Reason (R) is the correct explanation of Assertion (A).

28. (c) Assertion (A) is true, but Reason (R) is false.

29. (c) Assertion (A) is true, but Reason (R) is false.

30. (c) Assertion (A) is true, but Reason (R) is false.

Subjective Type Questions

Very Short Answer Type Questions

1. Who developed Python?

Ans. Python was initially designed by Guido Van Rossum in 1991 and developed by Python Software Foundation.

2. Python is which type of programming language?

Ans. Python is an object oriented programming language.

3. Is Python free and open source?

Ans. Yes, Python is both free and open-source. This means you can download, use, modify, and distribute it without any cost or licensing restrictions.

4. Python is based on which type of programming language?

Ans. Python is based on two types of programming languages as

- ABC language
- Modula-3

5. Name the core software component that enables Python's cross-platform capability.

Ans. Interpreter

6. List some advantages of Python.

Ans. Some advantages of Python are as follow:

- Easy to learn

- Expressive (can do a lot with few lines)
- Interpreted (no separate compilation step)
- Cross-platform (runs on many systems)
- Free and Open Source

7. Python can run "on any machine or platform." What single word describes this ability?

Ans. Portability

8. Why is Python easy to learn?

Ans. Python's simplicity, clear syntax, and extensive standard library make it easy to learn and use. Its object-oriented nature and cross-platform compatibility further enhance its appeal.

A large and active community provides abundant resources for learning and support.

9. List two disadvantages of Python.

Ans. Two disadvantages of Python are as follow:

- Not as fast as compiled languages
- Not ideal for memory-intensive applications

10. What does IDLE stand for?

Ans. Integrated Development and Learning Environment

11. How to start Python from command prompt?

Ans. Type python on the search box and press enter

12. How can you start Python with a command line?

Ans. Start → All Programs → Python 3.7 → Python 3.7 (32-bit).

13. You need to display the message "Hello" on the screen. What Python command would you use?

Ans. `print("Hello")`

14. What is the extension of Python files?

Ans. Python files have extension .py.

15. What will be the output of the following code at the command line?

```
>>>print ("Sum of 10 and 20 is", 10+20)
```

Ans. Sum of 10 and 20 is 30.

16. Anurag is working on IDLE (Python GUI). He has finished his coding and now wants to exit from IDLE. How can he exit from IDLE? **Competency Based Que.**

Ans. Press Ctrl+D or File → Exit or Click on cross ☒ button on title bar.

Short Answer Type I Questions

17. What is Python? Explain.

Ans. Python is a general purpose interpreted, interactive, object oriented and high level programming language. It was initially designed by Guido Van Rossum in 1991 and developed by Python Software Foundation.

18. Python is free and open source, what does it mean?

Ans. Python language is developed under an OSI-approved open source license, which makes it free to use and distribute, including for commercial purposes.

19. What is the difference between interactive mode and script mode in Python?

Ans. Interactive mode is used when a user wants to run one single line or one block of code. While script mode is used when the user is working with more than one single code or a block of code.

20. You're teaching Python to a group of beginners. Explain how Python's "readability" directly benefits them in learning the language.

Ans. Python code is like reading a simple story. This helps beginners understand how programs work without getting confused by complicated symbols. They can learn faster and focus on the main ideas of coding.

21. What is the role of indentation in python?

Ans. Indentation is used to define code blocks and determines the hierarchical structure of a program. Unlike many other programming languages that use curly braces to delimit code blocks, Python relies only on consistent indentation. This makes Python code more readable and visually appealing.

22. Give any three disadvantages of Python.

Ans. Three disadvantages of Python are as follows:

(i) **Speed Limitation** Python is interpreted language and slow as compared to C/C++ or Java, because interpreted languages are executed line by line.

(ii) **Weak in Mobile Computing** Python has made its presence on many desktop and server platforms, but it is seen as a weak language for mobile computing.

(iii) **Run-time Errors** Python programmers face several issues regarding the design of the language. This language requires more testing and also it has errors that only show up at run-time, this is because the language is dynamically typed.

23. How do you check the Python version in the command line?

Ans. To check the Python version, you can open your terminal or command prompt and type the following command:

Bash

```
python--version or python-V.
```

24. What do you mean by IDLE in Python?

Ans. IDLE (Integrated Development and Learning Environment) is Python's default integrated development environment. It provides a user-friendly interface for writing, running, and debugging Python code. It includes a text editor with syntax highlighting, an interactive shell, and debugging tools, making it a great tool for beginners.

25. **How do you run a Python script named script.py from the command line?**

Ans. To run the script, you can open your terminal or command prompt and type the following command:

Bash, `python script.py`

For Python 3, `python3 script.py`

Short Answer Type II Questions

26. **How do you install Python and set up a development environment?**

Ans.
1. **Download the Installer** Go to the official Python website (https://www.python.org/downloads/) and download the latest Python installer for your operating system.
2. **Run the Installer** Follow the on-screen instructions to install Python.
3. **Verify Installation** Open your terminal or command prompt and type python --version. If it shows, it's version means we successfully installed python in our computer system.
4. **Set Up a Development Environment**
   - **Text Editor/IDE** Choose a suitable text editor or IDE like Visual Studio Code, PyCharm, or Sublime Text.
   - **Virtual Environments** Create virtual environments to isolate project dependencies. Use tools like venv or virtualenv.

27. **How do you execute a Python script in IDLE?**

Ans. To run a Python script in IDLE, follow these steps:

1. Create a New File

- Open IDLE and go to File -> New File.
- This will open a new window where you can write your Python code.

2. Write Your Code

- Type your Python code into the new file.

3. Save the File

- Go to File -> Save As and save the file with a .py extension (e.g., my_script.py).

4. Run the Script

- You can run the script in two ways:
  - **Keyboard Shortcut** Press F5 on your keyboard.
  - **Menu Option** Go to Run -> Run Module.

5. View the Output

- The output of your script will be displayed in the Python shell window.

28. **How do you use Python's interactive mode and command-line interface?**

Ans. **Interactive Mode**

- Open your terminal or command prompt.
- Type python and press Enter.
- You'll be in the Python interactive shell, where you can execute Python code line by line.

Command-Line Interface

- Write Python code in a .py file (e.g., hello.py).
- Open your terminal or command prompt.
- Navigate to the directory containing the script.
- Type python hello.py to execute the script.

29. **Write a Python program to print "hello world" using command line.**

Ans. Refer to text on page no. 46 (Print "hello world" using command line).

Long Answer Type Questions

30. **Explain the concept of a programming language. How does Python work as a high-level programming language, and how does it differ from a compiler-based language?**

Ans. A programming language is a set of instructions used to communicate with a computer to perform specific tasks. Since computers understand only machine language (binary code: 0s and 1s), programming languages provide a way for humans to write instructions in a structured and understandable format.

There are two main types of programming languages:

1. **Low-Level Languages** These include machine language and assembly language, which are closer to hardware but difficult for humans to read and write.
2. **High-Level Languages** These include Python, C++, Java, etc., which are easier to understand and write. They must be translated into machine language using a translator (compiler or interpreter).

Python Works as a High-Level Programming Language

Python is a high-level language that allows developers to write code in a simple, readable, and structured way. Here's how it works:

1. Python code is written in human-readable syntax and saved in a .py file.
2. Since the computer does not understand high-level code, Python uses an interpreter to translate it into machine language.
3. The interpreter executes Python statements line by line, making it easy to debug errors quickly.

Difference Between Python (Interpreter-Based) and Compiler-Based Languages

Python uses an interpreter, while some languages like C++ and Java use a compiler. The key differences are:

Feature	Interpreter (Python)	Compiler (C++, Java)
Execution Process	Translates and executes code line by line	Translates the entire program before execution
Speed	Slower due to step-by-step execution	Faster because the whole code is compiled first
Error Handling	Stops execution at the first error, making debugging easier	Shows all errors after compilation, requiring debugging later

31. What are the advantages of Python programming language?

Ans. Python has several advantages that make it a popular programming language among beginners and professionals. Here are some key advantages:

1. **Easy to Learn and Use** Python has a simple syntax that resembles natural language, making it easier for beginners to learn and use.
2. **High-Level Language** It allows developers to focus on problem-solving rather than low-level details like memory management.
3. **Interpreted Language** Python executes code line by line, making debugging easier compared to compiled languages.
4. **Cross-Platform Compatibility** Python runs on multiple operating systems (Windows, macOS, Linux) without modification.
5. **Large Standard Library** It comes with a vast set of built-in modules and libraries for various applications, such as web development, data science, and automation.
6. **Open-Source and Community Support** Python is free to use and has a large, active community that contributes to its development and provides support.
7. **Strong Support for AI, Machine Learning, and Data Science** Python is widely used in artificial intelligence, machine learning, and data analysis due to libraries like TensorFlow, NumPy, and pandas.
8. **Object-Oriented and Functional Programming** It supports multiple programming paradigms, including object-oriented, procedural, and functional programming.

Case Study Based Questions

Case Study 1

Python, a versatile programming language, was conceived by Guido van Rossum in the late 1980s. It's renowned for its simplicity, readability, and powerful capabilities. Python's syntax is designed to resemble natural language, making it easy to learn and understand.

As an interpreted language, it executes code line by line, which aids in debugging and rapid development. Python's object-oriented nature allows for modular and reusable code, promoting efficient software development. It's widely used in various domains, including web development, data science, machine learning, and automation.

Based on the above paragraph answer the following questions

(i) Who is the creator of the Python programming language?

(a) Dennis Ritchie (b) James Gosling
(c) Guido van Rossum (d) Bjarne Stroustrup

(ii) Python is primarily a:

(a) Compiled language (b) Interpreted language
(c) Assembly language (d) Machine language

(iii) Python's syntax is often compared to:

(a) C++ (b) Java
(c) English (d) Assembly

(iv) One of the key strengths of Python is its:

(a) Complexity (b) Speed
(c) Readability (d) Low-level nature

(v) Python is used in which of the following fields?

(a) Web development
(b) Data science
(c) Artificial intelligence
(d) All of the above

(vi) What is the correct file extension for a Python script?

(a) .txt (b) .py (c) .cpp (d) .java

Ans. (i) (c) Guido van Rossum (ii) (b) Interpreted language
(iii) (c) English (iv) (c) Readability
(v) (d) All of these (vi) (b) .py

Case Study 2

In Python, comments are denoted by a hash symbol (#). They are ignored by the interpreter and are used to explain code or provide documentation. For example, # This is a comment. To print text to the console, we use the print () function. The code print ("Hello, world!") will give the output -> Hello, world!. To declare a variable in Python, we simply assign a value to it. For instance, x = 10 assigns the value 10 to the variable x. The if statement is used to execute a block of code conditionally. It checks a condition and executes the code within the block only if the condition is true. The for loop is used to iterate over a sequence of values. It repeatedly executes a block of code for each item in the sequence.

Based on the above paragraph answer the following questions

(i) Which is a valid Python comment?

(a) // This is a comment
(b) /* This is a comment */
(c) # This is a comment
(d) 'This is a comment'

(ii) What is the output of print ("Hello, world!")?

(a) "Hello, world!" (b) Hello, world!
(c) 'Hello, world!' (d) print ("Hello, world!")

(iii) How to declare a variable in Python?

(a) declare x = 10; (b) int x = 10;
(c) x := 10; (d) x = 10

(iv) What is the purpose of the if statement?

(a) To repeat a block of code
(b) To define a function
(c) To execute a block of code conditionally
(d) To declare a variable

(v) What is the purpose of the for loop?

(a) To define a function
(b) To execute a block of code conditionally
(c) To iterate over a sequence of values
(d) To declare a variable

Ans. (i) (c) # This is a comment
(ii) (b) Hello, world!
(iii) (d) x = 10
(iv) (c) To execute a block of code conditionally
(v) (c) To iterate over a sequence of values

SELF ASSESSMENT TEST

Multiple Choice Questions

1. Which of the following is not an advantage of Python?
(a) Interpreted (b) Integration
(c) Memory consumption (d) Extensive Support Libraries

2. User can run a program with .... ways in Python.
(a) two (b) three (c) four (d) five

3. Python uses .... rather than curly brackets to delimit blocks.
(a) whitespace indentation (b) square brackets
(c) parentheses (d) None of these

Fill in the Blanks

4. ________ is an interactive development environment for Python.

5. Python's ________ allows it to run on different operating systems.

6. The ________ is a disadvantage of Python that affects multithreaded performance.

7. To run a Python script from a file, you can use ________.

State Whether True or False

8. Python is a compiled language.

9. Python is known for its readability and simple syntax.

10. The Global Interpreter Lock (GIL) in Python allows multiple threads to execute simultaneously.

11. IDLE is an integrated development environment for Python.

12. You can run Python code directly from the command line.

13. Python is not platform independent.

Assertion and Reason Based Questions

Assertion (A) and Reason (R) Type questions. Choose the correct option as:
(a) Both Assertion (A) and Reason (R) are true, and Reason (R) is the correct explanation of Assertion (A).
(b) Both Assertion (A) and Reason (R) are true, but Reason (R) is not the correct explanation of Assertion (A).
(c) Assertion (A) is true, but Reason (R) is false.
(d) Assertion (A) is false, but Reason (R) is true.

14. Assertion (A) Python is a dynamically typed language.
Reason (R) Python determines the data type of variables at runtime.

15. Assertion (A) Python is primarily a compiled language.
Reason (R) Python's extensive standard library makes it versatile for many applications.

16. Assertion (A) Python is only suitable for small scripting tasks.
Reason (R) Python is used in data science, web development, and machine learning.

17. Assertion (A) IDLE is a useful tool for learning Python.
Reason (R) IDLE provides an interactive environment for writing and testing Python code.

18. Assertion (A) IDLE is the only way to write python code.
Reason (R) Debugging is a crucial part of software development.

Very Short Answer Type Questions

19. In which year, Python was developed?

20. Python is an interpreted language. Explain.

21. Where can you install Python in your computer?

Short Answer Type Questions

22. How can you start Python with IDLE?

23. What is the output of the following statement?

```
>>> a = 25
>>> print (a)
```

24. Give any two advantages of Python Programming language.

25. Python is weak in mobile computing. Give reason.

26. How many ways can user run a program in Python?

27. Give output of the following code.

```
>>> print (''Hello world !!!'')
>>> print (''Python Program'')
>>> print (''Honesty is the best policy'')
```

Long Answer Type Question

28. What do you mean by script mode in Python?

Case Study Based Questions

29. A software development team needs to build a web application that works seamlessly across different operating systems (Windows, macOS, Linux). They are looking for a language that supports rapid development, has extensive libraries for web frameworks, and is easy to deploy. However, they are concerned about potential performance issues and the Global Interpreter Lock (GIL).

(i) **Which programming language is a strong contender for this project, considering its cross-platform capabilities and extensive libraries?**

(a) C# (b) Java
(c) Python (d) Swift

(ii) **The team's concern about performance issues and the GIL highlights which aspect of Python?**

(a) Advantages of Python
(b) Features of Python
(c) Disadvantages of Python
(d) Installation of Python

(iii) **Using web frameworks like Django or Flask demonstrates which feature of Python?**

(a) Dynamic Typing (b) Extensive Libraries
(c) Interpreted Language (d) Platform Independence

(iv) **The team needs to ensure Python is installed on all target operating systems. This involves:**

(a) Working in Python
(b) Download and Installation of Python
(c) IDLE, Python Script Mode
(d) Printing "hello world" using the command line

(v) **To test a small snippet of code quickly, the team can use:**

(a) Python Script Mode
(b) Command Line
(c) IDLE
(d) All of these

Answers

1. (c) 2. (b) 3. (a) 4. IDLE
5. Platform-independence
6. Global Interpreter Lock (GIL)
7. Python script mode
8. False 9. True 10. False 11. True 12. True
13. False 14. (a) 15. (d) 16. (d) 17. (a)
18. (d)
29. (i) → (c), (ii) → (c), (iii) → (b), (iv) → (b), (v) → (d)

04 CHAPTER

Python is a high-level, interpreted programming language known for its simplicity and readability. It is widely used for web development, data science, artificial intelligence, automation, and more.

Python Fundamental

▼ **YOUR STUDY GOALS**

4.1 Python Character Set
4.2 Python Tokens
4.3 Function
4.4 Variables in Python
4.5 Input and Output in Python
4.6 Basic Structure of Python Program

▼ **YOUR PRACTICE GOAL**

- Objective Type Questions (30 Qs ; MCQs, True or False, Fill in the Blanks, Assertion and Reason)
- Subjective Type Questions (38 Qs ; VSA, SA, LA)
- Case Study Based Questions-2

We face the IPO cycle (Input, Process, Output) in our daily lives and computer activities. This cycle involves taking an input, processing it, and generating an output. To automate this process and transform input into useful output, we use programs.

These programs are written using various programming languages, and to effectively use a language, we need to understand its fundamental elements.

Python, for example, use character sets, tokens, expressions, statements, input/output functions, and more to construct programs.

4.1 Python Character Set

Python's character set is a collection of characters that can be used to create strings and other text-based data. It is a set of valid characters that a language can recognize. A character represents any digit, alphabet and special symbol. It primarily consists of:

ASCII Characters

- **Alphabetic characters** In alphabetic characters we have uppercase (A-Z) and lowercase (a-z) letters which allows us for creating words and identifiers.
- **Numeric characters** Numeric characters containing digits from 0 to 9 which are used to represent numbers and numeric values.

- **Punctuation marks** Punctuation marks such as commas, periods, colons, semicolons, and quotation marks are used to structure and format text.
- **Special Characters** A variety of special characters, including symbols like `@`, `#`, `$`, and `%`, as well as whitespace characters like spaces, tabs, and newlines, are used for various purposes, such as formatting, delimiting code blocks, and representing special characters.

Unicode Characters

Extended Character Set Python supports Unicode, which allows for a much wider range of characters, including characters from different languages and scripts.

Unicode Escape Sequences Unicode escape sequences are a way to represent Unicode characters within text, especially in programming languages. They typically consist of a backslash (\) followed by the letter 'u' and a four-digit hexadecimal code point. For example, the Unicode escape sequence for the character 'A' is '\u0041'.

4.2 Python Tokens

Tokens are the smallest individual units in a program. They are the building blocks of Python code.

There are five main types of tokens in Python, these are as follow:

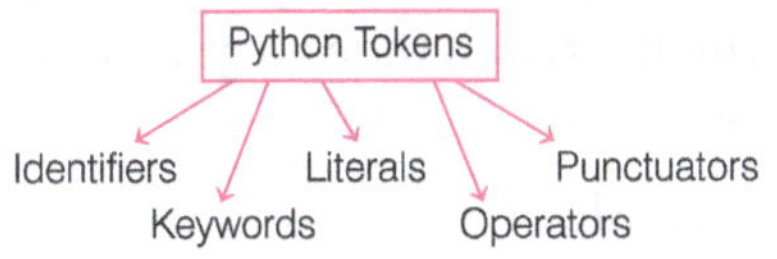

Identifiers

Identifiers are basically the names given to variables, functions, classes, and other entities in a Python program.

The rules in Python for identifiers are

(i) Only alphabets, digits and underscores are allowed.
(ii) Identifier name cannot start with a digit.
(iii) Keywords cannot be used as identifier.
(iv) Uppercase and lowercase letters are distinct because Python is case sensitive language.
(v) Special characters are not allowed.

For example,

Following are the valid identifiers

Identifier	Explanation
Name	Capital letter with small letters are allowed
name	Small letters are allowed
name_1	Digits and underscore are allowed alongwith alphabets
_SUM	Underscore at the first position is allowed
sum_of_the _numbers	We can concatenate multiple words with underscore
PASS	Keywords are allowed but we have to change case of any letter or complete word
FirstName	Best style to concatenate multiple words (changing case of first letter of successive word).

Following are the invalid identifiers

Identifier	Explanation
global	Keywords name cannot be given to identifier
num^2	Special characters are not allowed
num 1	Spaces are not allowed in Python programming language for declaring identifier
2num	Digits are allowed but not as first character

Keywords

These are reserved words in Python that have special meanings. They cannot be used as variable names. Some commonly used keywords in Python, which are listed below

False	assert	del	for	in	or	while
None	break	elif	from	is	pass	with
True	class	else	global	lambda	raise	yield
and	continue	except	if	nonlocal	return	
as	def	finally	import	not	try	

Literals or Constants

Literals are the raw data values assigned to variables in a program. They represent fixed values that do not change during program execution. Python supports various types of literals:

- **Numeric literals** A numeric literal is a fixed number value in code. Numeric literals can belong to three different numerical types as Integer, Float and Complex.

Numeric integers in Python can be of the following types:

Decimal Integers These are regular numbers made of digits from 0 to 9. e.g., 1024, +275, -12.

Octal Integers These start with 0 and use digits from 0 to 7. e.g., 0, 01, 0125, 0555.

Hexadecimal Integers These begin with 0X or 0x and can use digits from 0 to 9 and letters A to F. e.g., 0X0, 0x1, 0XAB125, -0x555.

Floating point These constants are real numbers which hold a fractional part. They express numbers with decimals.

Complex These are in form of a + bj where a is the real number and b is the imaginary number. e.g. 3+2j, 5-4j etc.

- **String literals** A series of characters enclosed in single quotes (' ') or double quotes (" ") is considered a string literal.

  Some valid string constants are

"j"	" ₹ 56,234.50 "	"computer"	'math'
"T"	"The result is: "	"Intel"	'2456'

Some invalid string constants are

No	Not enclosed in double quotes
"h'	Both quotes must be double or single quotes
"She said, "OK"	Number of double quotes must be even

The backslash (\) character is used to escape characters that have a special meaning, such as new line, backslash itself or the quote character.

Escape sequences in Python are as follows

Escape Sequence	Meaning
\\	backslash (\)
\'	single quote (')
\"	double quote (")
\a	ASCII Bell (BEL)
\b	ASCII Backspace (BS)
\f	ASCII Formfeed (FF)
\n	ASCII Linefeed (LF) or new line
\r	ASCII Carriage Return (CR)
\t	ASCII Horizontal tab (TAB)
\v	ASCII Vertical tab (VT)
\000	ASCII character with octal value 000
\xhh	ASCII character with hex value hh

- **Boolean literals** Boolean literals represent logical values, either `True` or `False`.

  For example,

```
>>> a = 7
>>> b = 5
>>> a > 5
True
```

- **Special literal (None)** In Python, you have one special literal None. None is used to define a field that is not created.

  For example,

```
>>> a = None
>>> if a == None:
  Print ("This is none")
This is none
```

- **Literal Collections** In Python, you have literal collections like list, tuple, dictionary and set.

  We will discuss list, and dictionary in forward chapters.

Operators

Operators are the symbols that perform operations on values. It is used in programs to operate on data and variables. Python carries a wide range of operators; these are as follows:

(i) Unary Operators

Those operators that work on single operand to form an expression are known as unary operators.

Following are some unary operators:

+	unary plus
–	unary minus
~	Bitwise complement
not	logical negation

(ii) Binary Operators

The operators that work upon two operands are known as binary operators.

There are various types of binary operators in Python as follows:

- **Arithmetic operator** These operators are used to do arithmetic operations. These operators are

+	Addition
–	Subtraction
*	Multiplication
/	Division
%	Remainder / Modulus
**	Exponent (raise to power)
//	Floor division

- **Logical operators** These operators are used to make a decision on two conditions. Logical operators are typically used with boolean values and what they return is also a boolean value.

  These operators are

and	Logical AND
or	Logical OR

- **Relational operators** Relational operators compare two operands to one another. These operators are

<	less than
>	greater than
<=	less than or equal to
>=	greater than or equal to
==	equal to
!=	Not equal to

- **Assignment operators** Assignments operators are used to assign the value of an expression to a variable. These operators are

=	assignment
/=	assign quotient
+=	assign sum
*=	assign product
%=	assign remainder
–=	assign difference
**=	assign exponent
//=	assign floor division

- **Bitwise operators** Bitwise operators work on bits and perform bit by bit operation. These operators are

<table>
<tr><td>&</td><td>Bitwise AND</td></tr>
<tr><td>^</td><td>Bitwise XOR</td></tr>
<tr><td>|</td><td>Bitwise OR</td></tr>
</table>

- **Shift operators** These operators are used to shift value left or right. These operators are

<<	shift left
>>	shift right

- **Identity operators** These operators are

is	is the identity same ?
is not	is the identity not same?

- **Membership operators** These operators are

in	whether variable in sequence
not in	whether variable not in sequence

We will discuss operators in detail, in next chapter.

Punctuators

Punctuators in Python are symbols that defines code structure and syntax.

The following characters are used as punctuators in Python:

' " # \ ( ) [ ] { } @ , : . ‘ =

Some of them are discussed below:

(i) **Brackets** [ ] indicate list.

(ii) **Parentheses** ( ) indicate tuples, function calls, function parameters for grouping expressions etc.

(iii) **Comma** (,) can be used as a separator in a function argument list or variable declaration.

(iv) **Colon** (:) indicates a labelled statement or conditional operator symbol.

(v) **Equal sign** (=) is used to initialize the value of variable i.e. used as assignment operator in an expression.

Delimiters

A delimiter is a sequence of one or more characters used to specify the boundary between separate, independent regions in plain text or other data streams.

e.g. ( ) { } [ ] , ; :

Quick Test 1

1. Which character set does Python use to represent characters internally?
2. Identify the type of token in the following Python statement: price = 99.99
3. Which category of tokens does the 'not' keyword belong to in Python?
4. What is the difference between a keyword and an identifier in Python?

4.3 Function

A function is a reusable block of code that performs a specific task. It takes inputs (parameters), processes them, and may return a result.

For example,

```
def add():
 a = int(input("Enter the first number: "))
 b = int(input("Enter the second number: "))
 return a + b
```

In above program, we have one function add ( ). All the statements which indented below add ( ) function are the part of add ( ). All statements below Add ( ) are executed by calling this function by following statement: add ( )

Blocks and Indentation

In Python, a block is a group of statements that are executed together, typically under structures like functions or loops.

Indentation is used to define these blocks by indenting the statements, which ensures the correct scope and grouping of code.

For example,

```
if (a == b):
  print ("Value of a is equal to b")
  print ("Finished")
```

This is block with all its statements same indentation. Python uses indentation while other programming languages such as C/C++, Java use curly braces { }.

4.4 Variables in Python

Variables are names used to store data that can be used and changed in the program. The type of the variable is set automatically based on the value it holds. They help in storing and reusing the data.

Key points about variables in Python

No explicit declaration you don't need to declare a variable's data type; it's automatically determined by the assigned value.

Case-sensitive Python distinguishes between uppercase and lowercase letters, so myVariable and MyVariable are different.

Naming Conventions Variable names should be descriptive and follow a consistent naming convention (often snake_case or camelCase).

For example,

```
x = 10              # Integer variable
y = 3.14            # Floating-point variable
name = "Alice"      # String variable
is_student = True   # Boolean variable
print(x, y, name, is_student)
```

l-values and r-values in Python

In Python, the concepts of l-value and r-value are related to understanding how values are assigned and used in expressions. This concept is derived from the typical evaluation process on the left and right sides of an assignment statement.

l-value (Left-value)

An l-value, or left-value, in Python refers to a memory location that can be assigned to a value. It typically appears on the left side of an assignment operator (=). l-values represent variables that can be modified.

For example, in the statement `x = 10`, `x` is an l-value.

r-value (Right-value)

An r-value is simply a value that can be assigned to a variable. It could be a number like 5, a word like "hello", or the result of a calculation. r-values appear on the right side of an assignment operator.

For example, in the statement `x = 10`, `10` is an r-value.

Dynamic Typing

Python is a dynamically typed language, which means that you don't need to declare the type of a variable before using it. The type of a variable is determined at runtime based on the value assigned to it.

This makes Python more flexible and easier to learn, as you can focus on the logic of your code rather than worrying about specific data types.

Syntax `Type (variable_name)`

4.5 Input and Output in Python

When we run a program, it often requires us to input data, such as numbers or text. This data is stored in the computer's memory and processed according to the program's instructions.

The results of these calculations can then be displayed on the screen, saved to a file, or sent to another computer.

Input from User

Python has many built-in functions; one useful built-in function is `input () `.

Python provides two build-in functions to read a line of text from standard input, which by default comes from the keyboard. These functions are as follows.

(i) input ( )

The input() function in Python allows you to get user input as text.

Python can then interpret this input as numbers, strings, or other data types. This makes input() a versatile tool for creating interactive programs.

Syntax

```
variable_name = input (< Message to be
displayed >)
```

e.g.
```
>>> a = input ("Enter a number: ")
Enter a number: 25
>>> print (a)
25
>>> name = input ("Enter your name: ")
Enter your name: Anurag
>>> print (name)
Anurag
```

(ii) raw_input ( )

In older versions of Python, like Python 2.x, the `raw_input()` function was used to get user input. This function takes whatever the user types and converts it directly into a string, regardless of its content.

Syntax

```
variable_name = raw_input ( < Message to be
displayed >)
```

e.g.
```
>>> n = raw_input ("Enter your hobbies: ")
Enter your hobbies: Reading novels
>>> print (n)
Reading novels
```

We can typecast and convert the string input from `raw_input()` to numeric types using `int()` or `float()`.

Syntax

```
variable_name = int (raw_input (Message))
```

e.g.
```
x = int (raw_input ("Enter your marks: "))
Enter your marks: 90
>>> print (x)
90
```

Output by print Statement

The `print()` function is used to display output on the screen. It can print numbers, text, or the results of calculations. To print multiple items on the same line, you can separate them with commas.

Syntax

```
print (expression / constant / variable)
```

e.g.
```
>>> print ("Arihant")
Arihant
>>> print (5.65)
5.65
>>> print (10 * 3)
30
```

Using f-strings in Python

Python's f-strings (formatted string literals), introduced in Python 3.6, simplify string formatting by embedding expressions directly within {}.

They offer a concise and intuitive way to interpolate variables into strings.

Prefix a string with f to create an f-string. It allows embedding expressions directly within {}.

Example:

```
name = "Amit"
age = 25
print(f"My name is {name} and I am {age}
years old.")
```

Note *F-strings are faster than % formatting and str.format().*

4.6 Basic Structure of Python Program

Here, we will discuss the basic structure of Python program and terms which are used in it.

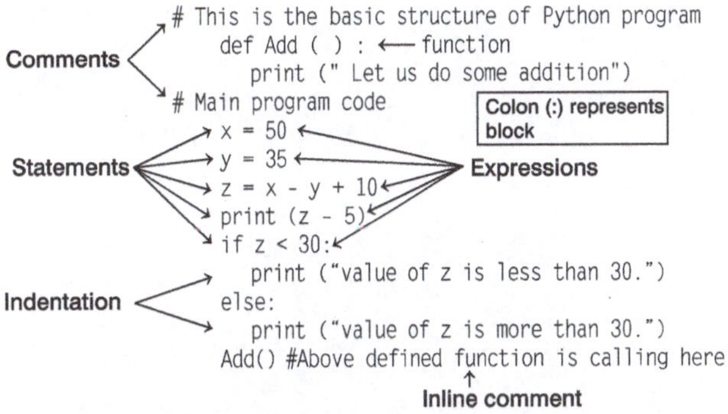

Above structure of Python program contains various components, which are discussed below:

Expressions

An expression is a combination of operators, constants and variables as per rule of the language. Any part in a program which can have a value, is an expression. It will have operands and operators together to produce a value.

e.g. `4 * i, x + y/10, (a < b) etc.`

From the above program, we have 5 expressions

```
50, 35, x-y+10, (z-5), z < 30
```

Statements

A statement in Python is a logical instruction, which Python interpreter can read and execute. In python, it could be an expression or assignment statement. The assignment statement is fundamental to Python.

e.g.
```
if x == y:
    print ("x is equal to y")
```

when expression will be evaluated, statement or group of statements executed.

Comments in Python

Comments are non-executable lines of code that help explain what your code does. They are crucial for readability and understanding, especially in larger projects.

Types of Comments

- **Single-line** Use # to comment out a single line.

  For example, `# This is a comment.`
- **Multi-line** Use triple quotes ("""...""" or '''...''') for comments spanning multiple lines.

  For example
  ```
  """
  This is a
  multi-line comment
  """
  ```

Quick Test 2

1. In Python, what will be the output of the following code?
   ```
   x = 5
   y = x + (x := 10)
   print(y)
   ```
2. Identify the l-value and r-value in the statement below:

   a = b + 10
3. What concept of Python allows a variable to store different types of values at different times during execution?
4. What will be the output of the following code?
   ```
   print("5" + "5")
   ```
5. How does Python differentiate between an expression and a statement, and which of the two can be used inside function's return?

Mind Map

PYTHON FUNDAMENTAL

Python Character Set

Python's character set is a collection of characters that can be used to create strings and other text-based data. It is a set of valid characters that a language can recognize.

ASCII Characters
- Alphabetic characters
- Numeric characters
- Punctuation marks
- Special Characters

Unicode Characters
- Extended Character Set
- Unicode Escape Sequences

Tokens

Tokens are the smallest individual units in a Python program.

Identifiers

Identifiers are basically the names given to variables, functions, classes, and other entities in a Python program.

Valid identifiers	Name, name, name_1, _SUM, sum_of_the_numbers, PASS First Name
Invalid identifiers	global, num^2, num1, 2num

Keywords

These are reserved words in Python that have special meanings. They cannot be used as variable names.

Literals or Constants

Literals are the raw data values assigned to variables in a program. They represent fixed values that do not change during program execution.

Numeric literals	String literals	Boolean literals	Special literal	Literal Collections

Operators

Operators are the symbols that perform operations on values. It is used in programs to operate on data and variables.

- **Unary Operators** +,-,~, not
- **Binary Operators**
  - **Arithmetic operator** +, –, *, /, %, **, //
  - **Assignment operators** =, /=, +=, *=, %=, –=, **=, //=
  - **Logical operators** AND, OR
  - **Bitwise operators** &, ^, |
  - **Shift operators** <<, >>
  - **Relational operators** <, >, <=, >=, ==, !=
  - **Identity operators** is, is not
  - **Membership operators** in, not in

Punctuators

These are symbols used to structure and separate different parts of a Python program.

Function

A function is a self-contained block of statements which are kept together to perform a specific task in related manner.

Blocks and Indentation

In Python, it improves program structure and readability

Variable

In python, variables are used to store data values. They act as containers that hold information.

In Python, the concepts of **l-value** and **r-value** are related to understanding how values are assigned and used in expressions.

Input and Output in Python

- input() function in Python allows you to get user input as text.
- \`print()\` function is used to display output on the screen.

Basic Structure of Python Program

```
# This is the basic structure of Python program
def Add ( ) :  ⟵ function
    print (" Let us do some addition")
# Main program code
x = 50
y = 35
z = x - y + 10
print (z - 5)
if z < 30:
    print ("value of z is less than 30.")
else:
    print ("value of z is more than 30.")
Add() #Above defined function is calling here
```

Comments → the two # lines; Statements → x = 50, y = 35, z = x - y + 10, print (z - 5), if z < 30:; Expressions → 50, 35, x - y + 10, z - 5, z < 30; Indentation → the indented print lines; Colon (:) represents block; Inline comment → #Above defined function is calling here

EXAM PATTERN QUESTIONS

Objective Type Questions

Multiple Choice Questions

1. Which of the following is/are character set?

(a) Alphabets (b) Digits
(c) White spaces (d) All of these

2. Which of the following is a valid identifier in Python?

(a) 123number (b) my_variable
(c) @variable (d) class

3. What is the maximum length of an identifier in Python?

(a) 32 characters (b) 64 characters
(c) 128 characters (d) No fixed limit

4. Which of the following is not a valid identifier in Python?

(a) MyBook (b) @book
(c) _book (d) book23

5. What is the maximum possible length of an identifier in Python?

(a) 16 (b) 32
(c) 64 (d) None of these

6. Which of the following are the most obvious kind of constants?

(a) Keywords (b) Literals
(c) Variables (d) Identifiers

7. Which of the following is not a valid string literal in Python?

(a) "Hello World" (b) 'Python's Power'
(c) '''Multiline String''' (d) "12345"

8. Which of the following is not a valid string in Python?

(a) "Hello" (b) 'Hello'
(c) "Hello' (d) '''Hello'''

9. ………… is a logical instruction which Python interpreter can read and execute.

(a) Expression (b) Statement
(c) Comment (d) Indentation

10. Find the punctuator(s) from the following options.

(a) Brackets (b) Parentheses
(c) Comma (d) All of these

11. Priya is writing a Python program and wants to display the values of a and b on the same line, separated by a space. Which syntax should she use?

Competency Based Que.

(a) print(a, b) (b) print(a, end=" ", b)
(c) print(a, end="$", b) (d) print(a) print(b)

12. How are blocks of code defined in Python?

(a) Using curly braces {}
(b) Using keywords like BEGIN and END
(c) Using indentation
(d) Using parentheses ()

13. Rahul is learning Python and wants to add explanations to his code without affecting execution. He notices that some comments start with the # symbol. Which type of comment should he use?

Competency Based Que.

(a) Double-line (b) Multi-line
(c) Single-line (d) All of these

Fill in the Blanks

14. Python uses the ________ character set to represent text and symbols.

15. The ______ operator in Python is used to calculate the remainder of a division.

16. In Python, a variable is created the moment you assign it a _______.

17. Python is a dynamically typed language, meaning you do not need to declare the _____ of a variable explicitly.

18. The function ______ is used to display output on the screen, while _____ is used to take input from the user.

State Whether True or False

19. The identifier "2name" is considered valid in Python.

20. Special characters like '@', '#', and '$' are allowed within identifiers.

21. Brackets "[ ]" are used to indicate a list in Python.

22. The "<<" operator is used to perform bitwise AND operation.

23. Indentation is used in Python to define blocks of code, similar to how curly braces are used in languages like C or Java.

24. In the Python statement y = x + 5, the variable y is an r-value, and the expression x + 5 is an l-value.

25. In Python, a statement like x = 5 is considered an expression.

26. A multi-line comment in Python can be started with # and ended with ##

Assertion and Reason Based Questions

Assertion (A) and Reason (R) Type questions. Choose the correct option as:

(a) Both Assertion (A) and Reason (R) are true, and Reason (R) is the correct explanation of Assertion (A).
(b) Both Assertion (A) and Reason (R) are true, but Reason (R) is not the correct explanation of Assertion (A).
(c) Assertion (A) is true, but Reason (R) is false.
(d) Assertion (A) is false, but Reason (R) is true.

27. Assertion (A) Python supports both ASCII and Unicode characters.

Reason (R) Unicode allows representing characters from multiple languages.

28. Assertion (A) Keywords, identifiers, literals, and operators are all tokens in Python.

Reason (R) Tokens are the smallest individual units in a Python program.

29. Assertion (A) Python uses indentation to define blocks of code.

Reason (R) Curly braces {} are mandatory to define blocks in Python.

30. Assertion (A) Variables in Python can hold values of any type due to dynamic typing.

Reason (R) Python variables must be declared with a specific data type before use.

Answers

1. (d) All of these
2. (b) my_variable
3. (d) No fixed limit
4. (b) @book
5. (d) None of these
6. (b) Literals
7. (c) '''Multiline String'''
8. (c) "Hello'
9. (b) Statement
10. (d) All of these
11. (a) print(a, b)
12. (c) Using indentation
13. (c) Single line
14. Unicode
15. Modulus (%)
16. Value
17. Data type
18. print, input
19. False
20. False
21. True
22. False
23. True
24. False
25. True
26. False
27. (a) Both Assertion (A) and Reason (R) are true, and Reason (R) is the correct explanation of Assertion (A).
28. (a) Both Assertion (A) and Reason (R) are true, and Reason (R) is the correct explanation of Assertion (A).
29. (c) Assertion (A) is true, but Reason (R) is false.
30. (c) Assertion (A) is true, but Reason (R) is false.

Subjective Type Questions

Very Short Answer Type Questions

1. What is Python character set explaining in short?

Ans. Character set is a set of valid characters that a language can recognize. It represents any letter, digit or other sign.

2. What is token?

Ans. A smallest individual unit in a program is known as token.

3. How do different types of tokens in Python contribute to writing a structured and meaningful program? **Competency Based Que.**

Ans. Python has the following tokens

- Identifiers
- Keywords
- Punctuations
- Literals
- Operators

4. Can keywords be used as identifier?

Ans. No, keywords cannot be used as identifier.

5. While developing a payroll management system, a programmer tries to use the word class as a variable name but encounters an error. Explain why this happens and how reserved words impact programming in Python. **Competency Based Que.**

Ans. Reserved words also known as keywords are predefined by the programming language that have some special or predefined meanings.

6. Explain the concept of constants in Python.

Ans. Constants are the data values that can never change their values during program execution.

7. **Write the name of any four punctuators used in Python program.**

Ans. Brackets [ ], parentheses ( ), comma (,), colon (:)

8. **Explain string literals.**

Ans. The literal which is stored in a variable within double or single quotation mark is called string literal.

9. **What are the different types of integer literals in Python?**

Ans. The main integer constants in Python are decimal, octal and hexadecimal.

10. **What is meant by \' in escape sequence?**

Ans. \' represents single quote.

11. **Define assignment operator?**

Ans. An assignment operator is used to assign values to a variable or a constant.

12. **Which symbol is represented the Bitwise OR?**

Ans. (|) symbol is represented the bitwise OR.

13. **Imagine you are developing a student management system where each student has a unique ID, name, and grade that can change over time. How would you use variables in Python to store and manage this information efficiently?** **Competency Based Que.**

Ans. By using a dictionary to store each student's data (ID, name, grade) as key-value pairs.

14. **Name the two values associated with the symbolic variable.**

Ans. The two values associated with symbolic variables are

(i) r-value (ii) l-value

15. **What is the output of following code?**

```
>>> a = 10
>>> print ("Value of a is:", a + 10 * 2)
```

Ans. Value of a is: 30

Short Answer Type I Questions

16. **Differentiate between identifier and keyword.**

Ans. Differences between identifier and keyword are

Identifier	Keyword
Identifier consists any combination of letters, numbers and underscores.	Keyword must consist only letters.
It allows both uppercase and lowercase.	It allows only lowercase.
e.g. x, sum_5, _mul etc.	e.g. finally, continue, yield etc.

17. **Which of the following are invalid names and why?**

(i) PaidInterest **(ii) S_num**
(iii) Percent **(iv) 123**
(v) abc km **(vi) elif**
(vii) lambda

Ans. (i) Valid (ii) Valid

(iii) Valid

(iv) Invalid, first character must be alphabet.

(v) Invalid, space is not allowed

(vi) Invalid, elif is a keyword.

(vii) Invalid, lambda is a keyword.

18. **(a) Write the one example of following terms.**

(i) Identifier **(ii) Punctuator**
(iii) Keyword **(iv) Constant**

(b) Identify the types of following literals.

False 'True' "False"
45345 00434 435.3

Ans. (a) (i) Identifier → Sum_1

(ii) Punctuator → Bracket ( )

(iii) Keyword → for

(iv) Constant → 'Neha'

(b)

False	Boolean
'True'	String
"False"	String
45345	Integer
00434	Integer (octal)
435.3	Floating point

19. **What do you mean by special literal None ?**

Ans. In Python, you have one special literal None. None is used to define a field that is not created.

e.g.
```
x = None
if x == None:
    print ('This is none')
```

20. **Riya is writing a Python program to automate payroll processing. However, her code throws an indentation error, causing incorrect calculations. Why is indentation important in Python, and how does it impact code execution in real-world applications?** **Competency Based Que.**

Ans. Indentation is used to define code blocks and determines the hierarchical structure of a program.

Unlike many other programming languages that use curly braces to delimit code blocks, Python relies only on consistent indentation. This makes Python code more readable and visually appealing.

21. **Define the term r-value and l-value in Python?**

Ans.
- **r-value** Pulls or fetches the value stored in a variable or constant.
- **l-value** The requirement that operand on the left side of the assignment operator is modifiable, usually a variable.

22. **Find the errors in the following Python code:**

(i) `a + 5 = b` (ii) `1 = 2 b + c * d`

(iii) `name = Aryan` (iv) `a = 20`
`print a;`

Ans. (i) `b = a + 5` (ii) `1 = 2 * b + c *d`

(iii) name = "Aryan" (iv) `a = 20`
`print (a)`

23. **Imagine you are working on a team project where multiple developers contribute to the same Python codebase. How can using comments improve collaboration and code maintainability? Where should comments be placed for better readability?**

Competency Based Que.

Ans. The sequence of character which improves the readability of a program is called comment. It may start anywhere and do not require closing symbol.

24. **What is the difference between statement and expression ?**

Ans. Differences between statement and expression are as follows

Statement	Expression
A statement is a complete line of code that performs some action.	An expression is any section of the code that evaluates to a value.
Statements can only be combined vertically by writing one after another or with block constructs.	Expressions can be combined horizontally into larger expressions using operators.

25. **Anurag is writing a Python program but is encountering an error. Can you identify the issue in the following code?**

```
a = 10
b = 20
c = a + b
print ('The output is:", c)
```

Ans. The above code is having an indentation error and correct code is

```
a = 10
b = 20
c = a + b
  print ("The output is:", c)
```

26. **What will be the output of the following code?**

```
name = "Anurag"
rnk = 1
  print (name, "is a famous singer and his
  rank in India is", rnk)
```

Ans. Output

Anurag is a famous singer and his rank in India is 1.

27. **What will be the output of the following code?**

```
a, b = 10, 5
x, y = a + b, b - 2
z = x - y
print ( "x : " , x, "y:" , y, " z : " , z)
```

Ans. **Output**

x:15 y:3 z:12

28. **Write a program to enter two numbers and print their difference.**

Ans.
```
a = int(input("Enter first number : "))
b = int(input("Enter second number : "))
Difference = a - b
print (" Two numbers are :" , a, b)
print ("Difference is:", Difference)
```

Short Answer Type II Questions

29. **What are identifiers? Also, give the rules in Python for identifiers.**

Ans. Identifiers are the fundamental building blocks of a program which are used to give the name to data items included by the programmer. It is required in all programming languages, where the programmer has to include items like variables, objects, classes, functions, arrays, etc., to specify their names. The identifier is a sequence of characters taken from Python character set.

The rules in Python for identifiers are

(i) Only alphabets, digits and underscores are permitted.
(ii) Identifier name cannot start with a digit.
(iii) Keywords cannot be used as identifier.
(iv) Uppercase and lowercase letters are distinct because Python is case sensitive language.
(v) Special characters are not allowed.

30. **Explain the process of declaring and assigning a variable in Python.**

Ans. Creating of variables means providing an initial value when it is declared. A variable can be created anywhere in Python program.

e.g. x = 20

Subject = 'Mathematics'

Above code is an assignment statements which used to assign values to variables. The equal (=) sign causes the value on the right hand side of the variables to be assigned to the variables on the left.

31. **A software company is developing a payroll system where employee salaries can be stored as integers, but bonuses may be represented as floating-point values. The system should handle both data types without explicit type declarations.** **Competency Based Que.**

How does Python's dynamic typing feature help in this scenario? Provide an example.

Ans. Python's dynamic typing allows variables to change their data type during runtime without explicit declaration. This is beneficial in the payroll system because it can handle both integer salaries and floating-point bonuses without needing to predefine the type.

Example

```
salary = 50000
bonus = 1500.75
total_pay = salary + bonus
print(total_pay) # Output: 51500.75
```

32. Predict the output.

```
a,b=10,15
x=20
y=25
a=x+y-b
x=a+b-y+10
z=y+b*3+a
x=50
a=x+y+z
print("a:",a)
print("b:",b)
print("x:",x)
print("y:",y)
print("z:",z)
```

Ans. Output

a : 175
b : 15
x : 50
y : 25
z : 100

33. Correct the following code

(i)
```
x = 5
  print(x)
y = 10
  print(y)
a = x + y
  print(a)
```

(ii)
```
sub = Math
marks = 80
print("Value of subject and marks
are", sub + marks)
```

(iii)
```
x = 5
b = x + 5
x = "Try"
d = x/20
```

Ans. (i)
```
x = 5
print(x)
y = 10
print(y)
a = x + y
print(a)
```

(ii)
```
sub = "Math"
marks = 80
print("Value of subject and marks
are", sub, marks)
```

(iii)
```
x = 5
b = x + 5
#x = "Try"
d=x/20
```

Long Answer Type Questions

34. Determine which of the following identifiers are valid. If invalid, explain with reason.

(i) name_1
(ii) _SUM
(iii) $sum
(iv) num ^ 2
(v) Name

Ans. The valid identifiers are

Identifier	Reason
name_1	Digits and underscore is allowed along with alphabets
_SUM	Underscore at the first position is allowed
Name	Capital letter with small letters are allowed

The invalid identifiers are

Identifier	Reason
$sum	$ sign can be used in other programming languages for creating identifier, however Python does not support $ sign
num ^ 2	Special character are not allowed

35. What are literals in Python? Explain the different types of literals with examples.

Ans. Refer to text on page no. 57-58 (Literals or constants).

36. Discuss the various types of numeric literals.

Ans. Numeric literals are immutable (unchangeable). Numeric literals can belong to 3 different numerical types as

(i) **Integer Literals** Integers are whole numbers without any fractional part. The following rules are followed for constructing integer constant.

- A decimal point and comma is not allowed in an integer constant.
- It must have atleast one digit.
- Integer constants may have either positive or negative sign.
- In the absence of any sign, it is assumed to be positive.
- Blanks are not permitted in integer constants.

Integers literals can be further divided into three parts as

(a) **Decimal Integer Literals** These constants consist of a sequence of digits, taken from the set 0 to 9. e.g. 1024, +275 etc.

(b) **Octal Integer Literals** These constants are preceded by 0. The first digit must be 0, in order to identify the constant as an octal number. A octal value can contain only digits between 0 and 7. e.g. 01, 055 etc.

(c) **Hexadecimal Integer Literals** These literals must begin with either 0X or 0x. It can then be followed by any combination of digits taken from the set 0 to 9 and A to F. e.g. 0X0, 0x1, –0x523 etc.

(ii) **Floating Point Constants** Floating point literals are real numbers which hold a fractional part.

They express numbers with decimals and / or exponents. Its range is greater than the range of integer constant.

The rules for writing floating point constants in Python as

- It must have atleast one digit before and one digit after the decimal point.
- A floating point constant can be either positive or negative.
- Blanks and commas are not permitted.
- In the absence of any sign, it is assumed to be positive.

37. What do you understand by string literals? Explain.

Ans. The literal which is stored in a variable within single quotation mark or double quotation marks is called string literal.

These represent a sequence of zero or more characters enclosed by double quotes. It can also include blank spaces.

Some valid string constants are

'A'	"Science"	"560.50'	'The output is'
"24567"	"0.34"	'MP'	'Delhi'

Some Invalid string constants are

Neha	Not enclosed in double or single quotes
'Hello"	Number of quotes must be even either double or single.

There are two types of strings supported in Python:

(a) **Single Line String** Strings that are terminated within a single line are known as single line strings.

e.g. >>> value = 'Arihant'

(b) **Multiline String** A piece of text that is spread along multiple lines is known as multiple line string.

There are two ways to create multiline strings:

(I) Adding backslash at the end of each line

e.g.
```
>>> value = 'Arihant\
    Publication'
>>> value
'ArihantPublication'
```

(II) Using triple quotation marks

e.g.
```
>>> value = '''Welcome
    to
    Python '''
    >>> print (value)
    Welcome
    to
    Python
```

38. Write a Python program which calculate the cost of triangle area wise. Also, display its output.

Ans.
```
a = float(input('Enter first side: '))
b = float(input('Enter second side: '))
c = float(input('Enter third side: '))
# calculate the semi-perimeter
s = (a + b + c) / 2
# calculate the area
area = (s*(s-a)*(s-b)*(s-c)) ** 0.5
print('The area of the triangle is
%0.2f', area)
cost=float(input("Enter the cost per
meter square in rupees:`"))
Total_cost=area*cost
print("Total cost of triangle area
wise:`",Total_cost)
```

Output

Enter first side: 12
Enter second side: 13
Enter third side: 5
The area of the triangle is %0.2f 30.0
Enter the cost per meter square in rupees:`15.50
Total cost of triangle area wise:`465.0

Case Study Based Questions

Case Study 1

A variable in Python is a named storage location that holds a value. Unlike many other programming languages, Python is dynamically typed, meaning you don't need to declare a variable's data type explicitly. The interpreter automatically infers the type based on the assigned value. Variable names can be a combination of letters, numbers, and underscores, but they must start with a letter or an underscore.

(i) What is a variable in Python?
   (a) A keyword (b) A data type
   (c) A named storage location (d) A function

(ii) Is Python a statically typed or dynamically typed language?
   (a) Statically typed (b) Dynamically typed
   (c) Both (d) Neither

(iii) Which of the following is a valid variable name in Python?
   (a) 123variable (b) my_variable
   (c) @variable (d) class

(iv) How do you declare and initialize a variable named x with the value 10 in Python?
   (a) int x = 10; (b) var x = 10;
   (c) x = 10 (d) let x = 10;

(v) What happens if you try to use a variable that hasn't been assigned a value?
   (a) The program will continue to run without any errors
   (b) A NameError will be raised
   (c) The program will crash
   (d) The variable will be automatically assigned the value None

(vi) Can you change the data type of a variable after it's been assigned a value?
   (a) Yes, Python is dynamically typed
   (b) No, the data type is fixed once assigned
   (c) It depends on the specific data type
   (d) Only in certain cases

Ans. (i) (c) A named storage location
(ii) (b) Dynamically typed
(iii) (b) my_variable (iv) (c) x = 10
(v) (b) A NameError will be raised
(vi) (a) Yes, Python is dynamically typed

Case Study 2

Variable is a container object that stores a meaningful value that can be used throughout the program.

In a Python program, to store different types of values such as, name of a shop and quantities of items (goods) available in the shop during the run time. We require some sort of storage area called variables. Each variable has a specific type, which determines the size and layout of the variable's memory, the range of values that can be stored within that memory and the set of operations that can be applied to the variable.

A variable is an identifier that is used to represent specific data item. The data item may be a whole number, a fractional number, a sequence of characters, a single character, etc.

Based on the above information, answer the following questions.

(i) What is an identifier that is used to represent a specific data item?
   (a) Function (b) Variable
   (c) Operator (d) Statement

(ii) Which term is used to pull or fetch the value stored in a variable or constant?
   (a) Assigning (b) Accessing
   (c) Storing (d) Declaring

(iii) In Python, a data item may be represented by which type of character(s)?
   (a) Whole number (b) Fractional number
   (c) Sequence of characters (d) All of the above

(iv) Which sign is used to assign a value to a variable?
   (a) == (b) =
   (c) : (d) ->

(v) You can assign a single value to multiple variables using which statement?
   (a) a = b = c = 10 (b) a, b, c = 10
   (c) a == b == c == 10 (d) a -> b -> c = 10

(vi) How do you declare and assign a value to a variable in Python?
   (a) int x = 10; (b) x = 10
   (c) var x = 10 (d) declare x = 10

(vii) How do you swap the values of two variables in Python?
   (a) temp = a; a = b; b = temp (b) a, b = b, a
   (c) swap(a, b) (d) a = b, b = a

Ans. (i) (b) Variable
(ii) (b) Accessing
(iii) (d) All of the above
(iv) (b) =
(v) (a) a = b = c = 10
(vi) (b) x = 10
(vii) (b) a, b = b, a

SELF ASSESSMENT TEST

Multiple Choice Questions

1. The Python recognises these kind(s) of token

(a) identifier (b) keyword
(c) operator (d) All of these

2. Which of the following is invalid identifier?

(a) Name (b) num^2 (c) num 1 (d) _SUM

3. .... is a set of valid characters that a language can recognise.

(a) Variable (b) Datatype (c) Character set (d) Token

Fill in the Blanks

4. In Python, a token is the smallest unit of a program and includes categories like keywords, identifiers, literals, operators, and ________.

5. The input() function in Python always returns data in the ______ type, regardless of the user's input.

6. In Python, the print() function separates multiple arguments by a default separator, which is the _______ character.

7. Python uses ___________ typing, which means that the type of a variable is determined at runtime based on the assigned value.

State Whether True or False

8. Among Python's tokens, 'return' and 'global' are considered identifiers because they define names used in a program.

9. A floating-point literal in Python can contain an underscore (_) to improve readability, such as 1_000.25, without affecting its value.

10. The operators and, or, and not in Python are classified as special literals rather than keywords.

Assertion and Reason Based Questions

Assertion (A) and Reason (R) Type questions. Choose the correct option as:

(a) Both Assertion (A) and Reason (R) are true, and Reason (R) is the correct explanation of Assertion (A).

(b) Both Assertion (A) and Reason (R) are true, but Reason (R) is not the correct explanation of Assertion (A).

(c) Assertion (A) is true, but Reason (R) is false.

(d) Assertion (A) is false, but Reason (R) is true.

11. **Assertion (A)** In Python, an L-value refers to a memory location that can hold a value, whereas an R-value is any valid expression or literal that can be assigned to an L-value.

Reason (R) The expression 5 = x is a valid statement in Python because 5 is an L-value.

12. **Assertion (A)** Python uses dynamic typing, meaning a variable can hold different types of data at different times.

Reason (R) Once a variable is assigned a data type, it cannot change throughout the program.

Very Short Answer Type Questions

13. What is the meaning of ~ in Python?

14. Which escape sequence is represented the ASCII horizontal tab?

15. How many ways are there to write comments in Python program?

16. Write any two keywords which are used in Python.

Short Answer Type Questions

17. Differentiate between ** and //operators.

18. In how many ways can multiple assignments used in Python?

19. State the meaning of the following terms.

(i) ^
(ii) >>
(iii) \n
(iv) \b

20. Write the rules for writing the identifiers.

21. Distinguish between integer literals and floating point literals.

22. Explain the following terms.

(i) Operator
(ii) Indentation
(iii) Expression

23. Define the raw_input() function.

24. What are the comments ? What is the used of these in programming?

Long Answer Type Questions

25. Explain the basic structure of a Python program.

26. Write the short note.

(i) Boolean literal
(ii) Literal collection
(iii) Unary operator
(iv) Binary operator

27. Differentiate between input ( ) and raw_input ( ) with an example.

28. Correct the following code.

(i)
```
x = 10
    print(y)
y = 5
```

(ii)
```
x = 5
y = 10
print("Addition:" x + y)
```

(iii)
```
sub = "Science"
code = 245
print ("Details:", sub + code)
```

(iv)
```
a = 10
b = a + 10
b = "Hello"
c = b/20
```

Case Study Based Questions

29. Rahul is learning Python programming and wrote the following code:

```
name = input("Enter your name: ")
age = input("Enter your age: ")
age = age + 5
print("Hello", name, "You will be", age,
"years old in 5 years.")
```

However, when he runs the code, it throws an error. He is confused about Python's data types, input handling, and tokens. Help Rahul understand the concepts by answering the following questions.

Answer the following questions:

(i) Which type of error will Rahul encounter when he runs this code?

(a) SyntaxError (b) TypeError
(c) NameError (d) ValueError

(ii) What is the correct way to fix Rahul's error?

(a) Change age = input("Enter your age: ") to age = int(input("Enter your age: "))
(b) Change age = age + 5 to age = str(age) + "5"
(c) Use print("Hello" + name + "You will be" + str(age) + "years old in 5 years.")
(d) Remove the input() function and directly assign age = 20

(iii) In the given code, what kind of token will not print?

(a) Identifier (b) Keyword
(c) Operator (d) Function name

(iv) Which concept of Python is demonstrated when age is assigned a string first and later changed to an integer?

(a) Strong Typing (b) Static Typing
(c) Dynamic Typing (d) Explicit Casting

(v) What is the purpose of the input() function in Python?

(a) It takes user input and converts it into an integer automatically.
(b) It is used to display output on the screen.
(c) It takes user input as a string.
(d) It is used to define a variable.

Answers

1. (d)	2. (b)	3. (c)	4. delimiters
5. string	6. space	7. dynamic	
8. False	9. True	10. False	11. (c) 12. (c)

29. (i) → (b), (ii) → (a), (iii) → (b), (iv) → (c), (v) → (c)

05

CHAPTER

Python data types are the classification or categorization of data items. It represents the kind of value that tells what operations can be performed on a particular data.

Data Types and Operators

▼ **YOUR STUDY GOALS**

5.1 Data Types
5.2 Operators
5.3 Type Conversion
5.4 Expressions

▼ **YOUR PRACTICE GOAL**

- Objective Type Questions (34 Qs ; MCQs, True or False, Fill in the Blanks, Assertion and Reason)
- Subjective Type Questions (45 Qs ; VSA, SA, LA)
- Case Study Based Questions-2

Before you start programming in Python, it's important to understand the basic building blocks of the language.

This includes learning about data types, operators and expressions used by Python to perform its various operations on different data types, which are used to perform calculations and manipulate data.

In this chapter, we'll explore these fundamental concepts and how they work in Python. We will learn about the order in which Python evaluates different operations.

This is determined by the type of operation and the number of values involved. Understanding operator precedence is crucial for writing correct and efficient Python code.

5.1 Data Types

Computers can process many different types of data. This data can be numbers (like 1, 2, 3.14), single letters (like 'A', 'b'), or groups of letters and numbers (like "Hello World 01 ").

To handle all these different types of data, programming languages use something called "data types."

A data type tells the computer what kind of data it's dealing with, so it can process and store it correctly.

Python has five standard data types which shown in figure below:

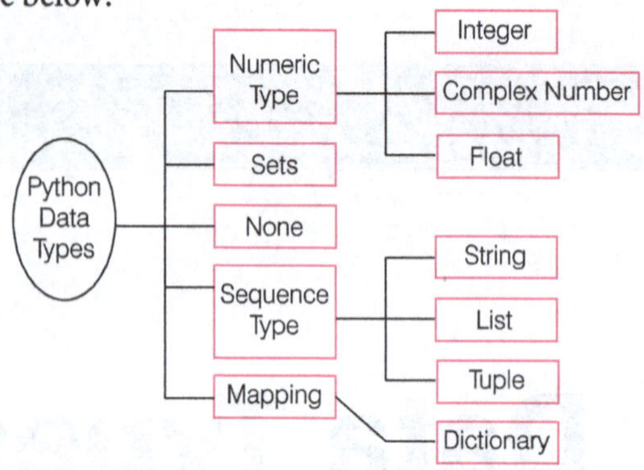

Numbers

Numbers data type contains only numeric values in Python. The types of numbers data type are as follows:

1. Integers

Integers are whole numbers, like 1, 2, 3, -1, -2, and so on having different storage ranges supported by a particular machine. They don't have any decimal parts. Integers can be both positive and negative.

There are two types of integers in Python as follows:

- **Integers (signed)** It is a simple whole number integers. In Python 3.x, integers are represented by any length and its length is limited depending on memory availability. It is a signed representation.
- **Boolean** data type, often termed as "bool," is a subtype of integer. It is a special kind of data that can only be one of two values: True or False. It's like a simple yes or no answer. "True" is represented by a non-zero value, while "False" is represented by zero.

2. Floating Point Numbers

A float is a number with a decimal point. For example, 3.14, 2.718, and 1.0 are all floats. Unlike integers, which are whole numbers, floats can represent fractional values. In Python, you use the float data type to store these kinds of numbers.

Floating point numbers can also be written in exponent notation.

e.g., 786.456 would be written as 7.86456E02.

```
>>> 1.1 + 1.1
2.2
>>> 4.2 % 2.1
0.0
```

Floating-point numbers are used to represent real numbers with decimal points. They're perfect for measuring things like distance, area, temperature, and weight, where precise values are important.

3. Complex Numbers

A complex number is a special kind of number that combines both real and imaginary numbers. It's written in the form a + bi, where 'a' is the real part and 'b' is the imaginary part. The letter 'i' represents the imaginary unit, which is the square root of -1.

So, a complex number is like a combination of two numbers, one real and one imaginary, working together.

e.g., 2 + 3i, 1 + 4i, 2 - 5i etc.

Here, you will learn about how to declare complex numbers in Python and extract their real and imaginary parts.

```
>>> a = complex (2,3)
>>> print (a)
(2 + 3i)
>>> a.real
2.0
>>> a.imag
3.0
```

Where, a.real will give the real part and a.imag will give the imaginary part of a complex number.

Sequence

Python sequences are like ordered lists of items. Each item has a specific position or index, which is a number.

There are three main types of sequences in Python: strings, lists, and tuples. We'll explore each type in more detail later, but here's a quick overview:

1. Strings

Strings are collections of characters, like letters, numbers, or symbols. In Python, they are represented by the str data type. You can define a string by enclosing the characters within either single quotes (' ') or double quotes (" ").

e.g., "Anurag", 'ABC', "??\+", '$ABC' etc all are valid strings.

```
>>> print ("Arihant Publications")
Arihant Publications
>>> type("Arihant Publications")
<class 'str'>
```

A string in Python can contain as many characters as you want. The string limit depends on your machine's memory resources. A string can also be empty.

2. Lists

Lists are like versatile containers in Python. You can store a variety of items within them, such as numbers, text, or even other lists. To create a list, you enclose the items within square brackets [] and separate them with commas. Unlike some other data structures, lists are mutable, meaning you can add, remove, or modify elements after you've created the list.

e.g.,
```
x = [ ]
y = [1,2, 'Neha']
z = [23, 46, 52, 98]
```

Python lists start counting from zero. So, the first item in a list is at index 0, the second at index 1, and so on.

In IDLE Python,
```
value = [20, 25, 'Anurag', 42.6, 'Sharma']
value1 = ['Abhishek', 24, 3.75]
print (value)
print (value [2])
print (value [1: 3])
print (value1[0])
print (value1 * 2)
print (value + value1)
```

Output

[20, 25, 'Anurag', 42.6, 'Sharma']

Anurag

[25, 'Anurag']

Abhishek

['Abhishek', 24, 3.75, 'Abhishek', 24, 3.75]

[20, 25, 'Anurag', 42.6, 'Sharma', 'Abhishek', 24, 3.75]

If you want to change any element in list then follow this,
```
>>> value [3] = 'Harsh'
>>> value
[20, 25, 'Anurag', 'Harsh', 'Sharma']
```

3. Tuples

Tuples are similar to lists in that they are ordered collections of items. However, unlike lists, tuples are immutable, meaning they cannot be changed once they are created.

This makes them useful for protecting data that should not be altered. Tuples are often faster than lists because they are static and don't require dynamic memory allocation. To define a tuple, you enclose the items within parentheses ().

e.g.,
```
sub = ('Maths', 'English', 'Hindi', 'Computer')
add_sub = ('Games', 'Dancing')
print (sub)
print (sub [1])
print (sub [2:])
print (add_sub * 1)
print (sub + add_sub)
```

Output

('Maths', 'English', 'Hindi', 'Computer')

English

('Hindi', 'Computer')

('Games', 'Dancing')

('Maths', 'English', 'Hindi', 'Computer', 'Games', 'Dancing')

Set

A set is a collection of unique items, like a group of friends with no repeats. Unlike lists, sets don't have a specific order, and you can't have the same item appear multiple times. Once you create a set, you can't change its elements. Sets are defined using curly braces {}.

e.g.
```
#create a set
>>>  set1 = {1, 12, 3.14, "New Delhi"}
>>> print(type(set1))
<class 'set'>
>>> print (set1)
{1, 12, 3.14, "New Delhi"}
#duplicate elements are not included in set
>>> set2 = {100,24,1,24}
>>> print (set2)
{100, 24, 1}
```

None

None is a special data type in Python that represents the absence of a value. It's different from zero or False. You can use it to indicate that a variable has no value assigned to it yet, or that a function hasn't returned a specific value. While it doesn't support many operations, it plays a crucial role in various programming scenarios.

e.g.
```
>>> myVar = None
>>> print (type(myVar))
<class 'NoneType'>
>>> print (myVar)
None
```

Mapping

A mapping data type in Python is a collection of items where each item is associated with a unique key. This allows you to efficiently store and retrieve values based on their corresponding keys. Currently, there is only one standard mapping data type in Python called a dictionary.

Dictionary

In Dictionaries, you can store information in key-value pairs. Each key is unique, and it's used to access the corresponding value.

For example, you could store a person's name as a key and their age as the value. Dictionaries are incredibly versatile and can be used to sort, search, and compare data.

You create a dictionary by enclosing key-value pairs within curly braces {}, separating each pair with a comma, and using a colon : to connect the key and value.

e.g.,
```
dict = ['Name' : 'Abhishek', 'Salary' : 80000,]
print (dict.keys())
print (dict.values())
print (dict ['Salary'])
```

Output
```
dict_keys(['Name', 'Salary'])
Dict_values(['Abhishek', 80000])
80000
```

Mutable and Immutable Data Types

Every variable in Python holds an instance of an object. There are two types of objects in Python as follows

1. Mutable Types

The values of mutable types can be changed after it is created. These are list, dictionary and sets.

e.g.
```
Subject = ['Maths', 'Hindi', 'English']
print (subject)
subject [0] = 'History'
subject [-1] = 'Economics'
print ("After change")
print (subject)
```

Output

['Maths', 'Hindi', 'English']

After change

['History', 'Hindi', 'Economics']

2. Immutable Types

The values of immutable cannot be changed after it is created. These are integer, float, boolean, string and tuple.

e.g.
```
tuple1 = ('Maths', 'English', 'Hindi')
tuple1 [1] = 'Computer'
print (tuple1)
```

Output

It will give an error message like tuple object does not support item assignment.

Quick Test 1

1. What are the basic data types in Python?
2. What is the difference between mutable and immutable data types?
3. What is the purpose of the None keyword in Python?
4. Explain the difference between a list and a tuple.
5. What is a dictionary in Python?

5.2 Operators

In Python, **operators** are symbols used to perform operations on values or variables. They can be classified as **unary** or **binary** based on the number of operands they operate on:

Unary Operators

Unary operators operate on a single operand. They are often used to perform operations like negation or to increment/decrement a value.

Common Unary Operators

1. **Unary Plus** (+) Indicates a positive value.
```
num = 5
print(+num)  # Output: 5
```
2. **Unary Minus** (-) Negates the value of the operand.
```
num = 5
print(-num)  # Output: -5
```

Binary Operators

Binary operators operate on two operands. They are used for arithmetic, comparison, logical, and other operations.

Arithmetic Operator

Arithmetic operators are symbols used to perform mathematical operations on numerical values.

Arithmetic operators include addition (+), subtraction (-), multiplication (*), division (/), and modulus (%).

Operator	Description	Example
+	Adds two operands.	5 + 3 = 8
-	Subtracts the second operand from the first.	5 - 3 = 2
*	Multiplies two operands.	5 * 3 = 15
/	Divides the numerator by the denominator.	10 / 2 = 5.0
//	Divides and returns the integer part only.	10 // 3 = 3

Operator	Description	Example
%	Returns the remainder of the division.	10 % 3 = 1
**	Raises the first operand to the power of the second.	2 ** 3 = 8

Relational Operators

Relational operators compare two operands to one another. The relational operators are = =, ! =, <, >, <= and >= . When used in an expression, they all return a boolean value which states the result of comparison.

Relational operators are sometimes called comparison operators and expressions that contain relational operators are called relational expressions.

Following table shows all the relational operators supported by Python language values of A and B are 5 and 9, respectively.

Operator	Name	Description	Example
= =	Equal to	Checks if the values of two operands are equal or not, if yes then condition becomes True.	(A= = B) is not True
! =	Not equal to	Checks if the value of two operands are equal or not, if values are not equal then condition becomes True.	(A ! = B) is True
>	Greater than	Checks if the value of left operand is greater than the value of right operand, if yes then condition becomes True.	(A>B) is not True
<	Less than	Checks if the value of left operand is less than the value of right operand, if yes then condition becomes True.	(A<B) is True
>=	Greater than or equal to	Checks if the value of left operand is greater than or equal to the value of right operand, if yes then condition becomes True.	(A>= B) is not True
<=	Less than or equal to	Checks if the value of left operand is less than or equal to the value of right operand, if yes then condition becomes True.	(A<=B) is True

In relational operators, use of equal to operator (= =) should be avoided with floating point numbers and it also be avoided with signed and unsigned values.

Logical Operators

Logical operators, like AND, OR, and NOT, are used to make decisions based on multiple conditions. They work with true/false values (Boolean values) and produce a true/false result.

These operators are often used to control the flow of a program, determining which parts of the code should be executed. You'll commonly find them in conditional statements like "if" and "while" to make choices based on different conditions.

Following table shows all the logical operators supported by the Python language. Assume variables A holds 5, B holds 7 and C holds 9, then

Operators	Name	Description	Example
and	Logical AND	It returns True, if both the conditions are True, otherwise returns False.	((A<B) and (C<B)) returns False
or	Logical OR	It returns True, if atleast one of the two conditions is True.	((A<B) or (C<B)) returns True
not	Logical NOT	It works on single operand. It is used to reverse the logical state of its operand. If a condition is True then logical NOT operator will make it False.	not ((A<B) or (C<B)) returns True

Bitwise Operators

Bitwise operators work on bits and perform bit-by-bit operation. These operators manipulate the values of data at bit level. These operators are generally used for testing and shifting of bits.

For example, if a = 44 and b = 12.

Now in binary format they will be as follows

a = 00101100

b = 00001100

A table is given to understand bitwise operators more precisely:

Operator	Description	Example
&	Binary AND operator copies 1 to the result if it exists in both operand otherwise copies 0.	(a & b) will give 12 which is 00001100
|	Binary OR operator copies 1 if it exists in either operand, otherwise copies 0.	(a|b) will give 44 which 00101100
^	Binary XOR operator copies 1 if it in one operand. If it is either in both operand or not in any operand the operator copies 0.	(a^b) will give 32 which 00100000
~	Binary one's complement operator is unary and has the effect of flipping bits.	(~a will give 211 which is 11010011)

Operator	Description	Example
<<	Binary left shift operator. The left operand value is moved left by the number of bits specifted by the right operand.	a<<2 will give 176 which is 10110000
>>	Binary right shift operator. The left operands value is moved right by the number of bits specified by the right operand.	a>>2 will give 11 which is 00001011

Assignment Operators

These operators are also known as shorthand operators. These operators are used to assign the value of an expression to a variable.

The following lists are assignment operators:

Operator	Description	Example
+=	Add AND assignment operator, it adds right operand to the left operand and assigns the result to left operand.	c += a is equivalent to c = c + a
−=	Subtract AND assignment operator, it subtracts right operand from left operand and assigns the result to left operand.	c −= a is equivalent to c = c − a
*=	Multiply AND assignment operator, it multiplies right operand with left operand and assigns the result to the left operand.	c *= a is equivalent to c = c * a
/=	Divide AND assignment operator, it divides left operand with the right operand and assigns the result to left operand.	c /=a is equivalent to c = c /a
%=	Modulus AND assignment operator, it divides left operand with right operand and assigns the remainder to the left operand.	c %= a is equivalent to c = c % a
**=	Exponentiation AND assignment operator, it gives left operand raised to the power of right operand and assigns the value to the left operand.	c **= a is equivalent to c = c ** a
//=	Floor division AND assignment operator, it floor divides left operand with the right operand and assigns the result to the left operand.	c //= a is equivalent to c = c//a

Note '=' and '==' are different things. '=' is used for assignment while '==' is used for relational operators.

For example, x = 10 will assign 10 to variable x while if x = = 10 is given, it will test whether the value of x is equal to 10 or not? If it is True, then True else False will be returned.

Membership Operators

Membership operators are used to check if a value is a member of the given sequence or not. Python has two membership operators:

1. **in** **Returns** True if a sequence with the specified value is present in the object.
2. **not in** **Returns** True if a sequence with the specified value is not present in the object.

Example

```
a = [4,6,8,2,5]
print(1 in a)
print(6 in a)
```

Output

False

True

Identity Operators

Identity operators are used to check if two variables point to the same object in memory. They help us determine if two variables are essentially the same or if they represent different objects. Python has two identity operators:

1. **is** Checks if two variables refer to the same object.
2. **is not** Checks if two variables refer to different objects.

Example

```
a = 5
b = a
c = a
d = 2
print(b is a)
print(c is a)
print(d is c)
```

Output

True

True

False

Operator Precedence in Python

Imagine you have a math problem with multiple operations, like addition, subtraction, multiplication, and division.

To solve it correctly, you follow a specific order: multiplication and division come before addition and subtraction. This order is called precedence.

In Python, operators also have a specific order of precedence. This order determines which operation is performed first when there are multiple operators in an expression.

A table of operators is given below according to their precedence from highest to lowest:

Precedence	Operator	Description
1.	( )	Parentheses
	**	Exponentiation
2.	+,–	Unary plus, unary minus
	not	Logical NOT
	~	Bitwise NOT
3.	*	Multiplication
	/	Division
	//	Floor division
	%	Modulus
4.	+	Addition
	–	Subtraction
5.	<<	Bitwise left shift
	>>	Bitwise right shift
6.	<,<=	Less than, less than or equal to
	>,>=	Greater than, greater than or equal to
7.	!=	Not equal to
	==	equal to
8.	&	Bitwise AND
9.	^	Bitwise XOR
10.	|	Bitwise OR
11.	and	Boolean AND
12.	or	Boolean OR
13.	=,+ =,– =,* =,/ =,% =	Assignment

- Logical OR operator and Logical AND operator have a low precedence than relational operators.
  e.g. (10 > 5) or (5 < 4)
  Here, relational operations will be performed first and then logical operations will be executed.
- Logical NOT operator has a higher precedence than relational and arithmetic operators.

Associativity of Python Operators

We can see in the above table that more than one operator exists in the same group. These operators have the same precedence. When two operators have the same precedence, associativity helps to determine the order of operations. Associativity is the order in which an expression is evaluated that has multiple operators of the same precedence. Almost all the operators have left-to-right associativity.

For example, multiplication and floor division have the same precedence. Hence, if both of them are present in an expression, the left one is evaluated first.

e.g. `>>> print (10 * 3 // 6)`

Output 5

```
>>> print (10 * (3//6))
```

Output 0

5.3 Type Conversion

Sometimes we need to change the type of data in Python. For example, we might want to convert a string into a number for calculation purpose.

The below mentioned example will make you more understand:

```
string = input ("Enter a number: ")
number = int(string)
result = number * 3
print ("The result is:", result)
```

Output

Enter a number: 5

The result is: 15

Now, if the user enters "5" as text, the program will treat it as the number 5 and calculate the result, all because of type conversion. There are two ways to do this:

(i) Explicit Conversion

Explicit conversion, or type casting, is when we directly tell Python to change the data type of a value. We use special functions like int(), float(), and str() to do this. However, be careful when converting between data types, as you might lose information.

For example, converting a decimal number like 20.67 to an integer using int(20.67) will result in 20, as the decimal part is discarded.

(ii) Implicit Conversion

Implicit conversion, or coercion, is when Python automatically changes the data type of a value without explicit instruction from the programmer. This happens when Python can safely convert one data type to another, such as converting an integer to a float for calculations.

5.4 Expressions

An expression in Python is a combination of values, variables, and operators that, when evaluated, produces a result.

It's like a mathematical equation where you combine numbers, letters, and symbols to get an answer.

For example, 2 + 3, x * y, and "Hello, " + "world!" are all expressions. The operators in an expression tell Python how to combine the values and variables to produce the final result.

Function	Description
int (x)	Converts x to an integer
float (x)	Converts x to a floating-point number
str (x)	Converts x to a string representation
chr (x)	Converts ASCII value of x to character
ord (x)	Returns the character associated with the ASCII code x

There are various types of expressions as follows.

Arithmetic Expression

These expressions are composed with operators, constants, variables etc. It can be either a pure integer expression, a floating point expression or complex numbers.

e.g.
```
a * b - 5 (integer expression)
x + y/10 (floating expression)
1 + 2i (complex number expression)
```

Logical Expression

Those expressions having logical operators in them are called logical expressions.

e.g. `x and b, a or not b, c or b`

Relational Expression

This type of expression includes relational operators.

e.g. `a == b, a <= b, a != b`

String Expression

This type of expression includes string operators with string operands and integers.

e.g. `>>> "Me" + "Cool"`

Output 'MeCool'

```
>>> "Computer" * 2
```

Output 'ComputerComputer'

TEACHER TIP
Use parentheses to explicitly control the order of operations.

Expression Evaluation

Evaluation means simplifying an expression down to a single numerical value. When a mixed expression evaluates, it is divided into sub-expressions. Expression evaluation is done from left-to-right and based on operator precedence.

e.g.
```
a = b = 10, c = 5
a = b * 3//4 + c//4 + 4-b + 5//6
  = 10*3//4 + 5//4 + 4-10 + 5//6
  = 7 + 5//4 + 4 - 10 + 5//6
  = 7 + 1 + 4 - 10 + 0
  = 12 - 10 + 0
  = 2 + 0
  = 2
```

Some Rules for Expressions

I. Arithmetic expressions may contain just one signed or unsigned variable/constant or it can have two or more variables or/and constants or two/more expressions joined by valid arithmetic operators. Two/more variables or operators should not occur in a continuous manner.

II. Logical expressions may contain just one signed or unsigned variable/constant or it can have two or more variables or/and constants or two/more expressions joined by valid relational and/or logical operators. Two/more variables or operators should not occur in a continuous manner.

Quick Test 2

1. What are the basic arithmetic operators in Python?
2. What is the difference between // and / operators?
3. What are relational operators in Python?
4. What is the purpose of the in and not in operators?
5. What is operator precedence in Python?

Mind Map

DATA TYPES AND OPERATORS

Data Types

Data types in programming defines how data is processed and stored by computer.

Numbers
It contains only numeric values in Python

Integers
These are whole numbers.e.g.,1, 2 , 3, -1, -2,.. and so on.

Floating Point Numbers
Float values are specified with decimal point.

Complex Number
A complex number is expressed in form of (a+ib).

Sequence
Python sequence are ordered list of items including String, List and Tuples.

String
String are collections of characters like letters , numbers or symbols.

List
A list is a mutable variable defined with [].

Tuples
It is an ordered , immutable sequence of items ,defined with ().

Set
A set is an unordered collection of unique items.

None
None in Python represents the absence of a value.

Mapping
It is a collection of items where each item is associated with a unique key.

Dictionary
In dictionary, you can store information in **key-value pairs.** Each key is unique and its used to access the corresponding value.

Note
The values of mutable types can be changed after it is created. These are list , dictionary and sets. The values of immutable types cannot be changed after it is created These are integer, float, boolean, string and tuple.

Type Conversion

It is the process of converting a data type into another data type .

Implicit Conversion
Python ,automatically converts one data type to another .

Explicit Conversion
User convert the data type of an object to require data type .

Expression

Expressions are the combination of operators , constants ,variable ,etc.

01 Arithmetic Expression
02 Relational Expression
03 Logical Expression
04 String Expression

- Concatenation Operator (+)
- Replication Operator (*)

Operators

Operators are the symbols that perform operations on values. It is used in programs to operate on data and variables.

Unary Operators +,–,~, not

Binary Operators

- **Arithmetic operator** +, –, *, /, %, **, //
- **Logical operators** AND, OR
- **Relational operators** <, >, <=, >=, ==, !=
- **Assignment operators** =, /=, +=, *=, %=, –=, **=, //=
- **Bitwise operators** &, ^, |
- **Shift operators** <<, >>
- **Identity operators** is, is not
- **Membership operators** in, not in

Precedence of Python Operators

This is used in an expression with more than one operator with different precedence to determine which operation to perform first.

NCERT Folder

1. Which of the following identifier names are invalid and why?

(i) Serial_no.
(ii) 1st_Room
(iii) Hundred$
(iv) Total Marks
(v) Total_Marks
(vi) total-Marks
(vii) _Percentage
(viii) True

Ans. **Invalid Identifiers**

(i) **Serial_no.** invalid as we cannot use ' . ' in variable names.

(ii) **1st_Room** Starts with a digit (1), which is not allowed. Identifiers must start with a letter or an underscore (_).

(iii) **Hundred$** Contains the special character '$', which is not allowed.

(iv) **Total Marks** As there are two separate words in the variable name.

(vi) **total-Marks** Contains the hyphen '-', which is not allowed.

(viii) **True** As it is a keyword.

2. Write the corresponding Python assignment statements:

(a) Assign 10 to variable length and 20 to variable breadth.

(b) Assign the average of values of variables length and breadth to a variable sum.

(c) Assign a list containing strings 'Paper', 'Gel Pen', and 'Eraser' to a variable stationery.

(d) Assign the strings 'Mohandas', 'Karamchand', and 'Gandhi' to variables first, middle and last.

(e) Assign the concatenated value of string variables first, middle and last to variable fullname. Make sure to incorporate blank spaces appropriately between different parts of names.

Ans. (a) Assigning values to length and breadth

```
length = 10
breadth = 20
```

(b) Calculating and assigning the average to sum

```
sum = (length + breadth) / 2
```

(c) Assigning a list to stationery

```
stationery=['Paper', 'Gel Pen', 'Eraser']
```

(d) Assigning strings to variables

```
first = 'Mohandas'
middle = 'Karamchand'
last = 'Gandhi'
```

(e) Concatenating strings and assigning to fullname

```
fullname=first+' '+middle+' '+last
```

3. Which data type will be used to represent the following data values and why?

(a) Number of months in a year
(b) Resident of Delhi or not
(c) Mobile number
(d) Pocket money
(e) Volume of a sphere
(f) Perimeter of a square
(g) Name of the student
(h) Address of the student

Ans. (a) **Integer** The number of months in a year is a fixed integer value (12).

(b) **Boolean** This represents a true/false value (resident of Delhi or not).

(c) **String** Mobile numbers are sequences of digits, typically represented as strings.

(d) **Float** Pocket money can be a decimal value (e.g., 10.50).

(e) **Float** Volume of a sphere can be a decimal value.

(f) **Integer or Float** The perimeter can be a whole number or a decimal value, depending on the units used.

(g) **String** Names are sequences of characters.

(h) **String** Addresses are typically represented as text.

4. Give the output of the following when num1 = 4, num2 = 3, num3 = 2

(a)
```
num1 += num2 + num3
print (num1)
```
(b)
```
num1 = num1 ** (num2 + num3)
print (num1)
```
(c)
```
num1 **= num2 + c
```
(d)
```
num1 = '5' + '5'
print(num1)
```
(e)
```
print(4.00/(2.0+2.0))
```
(f)
```
num1 = 2+9*((3*12)-8)/10
print(num1)
```
(g)
```
num1 = float(10)
print (num1)
```
(h)
```
num1 = int('3.14')
print (num1)
```
(i)
```
print(10 != 9 and 20 >= 20)
```
(j)
```
print(5 % 10 + 10 < 50 and 29 <= 29)
```

Ans. (a) 9 (b) 1024

(c) NameError (d) 55

(e) 1.0 (f) 27.2
(g) 10.0 (h) ValueError
(i) True (j) True

5. Write a Python program to calculate the amount payable if money has been lent on simple interest. Principal or money lent = P, Rate of interest = R% per annum and Time = T years. Then Simple Interest (SI) = (P × R × T)/ 100.

Amount payable = Principal + SI.

P, R and T are given as input to the program.

Ans.
```
# Input the principal amount, rate of
                     interest, and time period
P = float(input("Enter the principal
                              amount (P): "))
R = float(input("Enter the rate of
                      interest (R) in %: "))
T = float(input("Enter the time period
                            (T) in years: "))
# Calculate simple interest (SI)
SI = (P * R * T) / 100
# Calculate total amount payable
Amount = P + SI
print(f"Simple Interest (SI) = {SI}")
print(f"The total amount payable =
                                 {Amount}")
```

Output

Enter the principal amount (P): 20000
Enter the rate of interest (R) in %: 5
Enter the time period (T) in years: 1
Simple Interest (SI) = 1000.0
The total amount payable = 21000.0

6. Write a program to find the average of three numbers.

Ans.
```
# Input three numbers
num1 = float(input("Enter the first
                              number: "))
num2 = float(input("Enter the second
                              number: "))
num3 = float(input("Enter the third
                              number: "))
# Calculate the average
average = (num1 + num2 + num3) / 3
print(f"The average of the three
                    numbers is: {average}")
```

Output

Enter the first number: 0
Enter the second number: 60
Enter the third number: 45
The average of the three numbers is: 35.0

7. Write a program that asks the user to enter their name and age. Print a message addressed to the user that tells the user the year in which they will turn 100 years old.

Ans.
```
# Input user's name and age
name = input("Enter your name: ")
age = int(input("Enter your age: "))
# Get the current year
current_year = 2025
# Calculate the year when the user will
                                  turn 100
year_100 = current_year + (100 - age)
print(f"Hello, {name}! You will turn 100
        years old in the year {year_100}.")
```

Output

Enter your name: Shivam
Enter your age: 30
Hello, Shivam! You will turn 100 years old in the year 2095.

EXAM PATTERN QUESTIONS

Objective Type Questions

Multiple Choice Questions

1. Which data type contains only numeric values in Python?

(a) Numbers (b) Strings (c) Lists (d) Tuples

2. In complex number, a + ib, where b represents as

(a) real part (b) imaginary part
(c) special part (d) None of these

3. A software company is developing a large-scale financial application where accuracy in calculations is crucial. The developers initially used the float data type for monetary values but noticed small precision errors. Which of the following data types is the most appropriate choice to handle financial transactions accurately in Python? **Competency Based Que.**

(a) float (b) int
(c) decimal.Decimal (d) complex

4. Which of the following are sequences of character data?

(a) Lists (b) Tuples
(c) Strings (d) Dictionaries

5. A data scientist is working with large datasets and wants to optimize memory usage. He needs a data type that is immutable and takes less memory compared to a list while still allowing indexing. Which of the following should he choose? **Competency Based Que.**

(a) list (b) tuple (c) set (d) dict

6. Which operator is used to find the remainder of a division operation?

(a) / (b) // (c) % (d) *

7. How do you calculate the power of a number in Python, for example, 2 raised to the power of 3?

(a) 2^3 (b) pow (2, 3)
(c) 2**3 (d) 3^2

8. If x = 15 and y = 10, what will be the value of x after the operation x += y?

(a) 10 (b) 15 (c) 25 (d) 5

9. Consider the following Python expressions:

```
x = 5
y = 10
result = x < y == True
```

What will be the output of result and why? **Competency Based Que.**

(a) True, because < and == are evaluated from left to right.
(b) False, because comparison operators have different precedence levels.
(c) SyntaxError, because the comparison is invalid.
(d) True, because Python allows chaining of comparison operators.

10. Which data type can only store the values True or False?

(a) int (b) float (c) str (d) bool

11. Given the following Python expression:

a = True + 5 * False

What will be the value of a and why? **Competency Based Que.**

(a) True, because Boolean operations take precedence.
(b) 6, because True is treated as 1 and False as 0.
(c) 5, because multiplication is evaluated first.
(d) SyntaxError, because Booleans cannot be used in arithmetic operations.

12. These operators are used to make a decision on two conditions.

(a) Logical (b) Arithmetic
(c) Relational (d) Assignment

13. Which of the following is/are expressions?

(a) Arithmetic (b) Logical
(c) Relational (d) All of these

14. What will be the output of the following Python expression?

```
"hello" + " " + "world"
```

Use code with caution.

(a) hello world (b) "hello world"
(c) hello+world (d) Error

Fill in the Blanks

15. ______ data types can change their values in place.

16. Plain integers use ________ bytes to store a value.

17. ________ is an unordered set of key: value pairs where the keys are unique.

18. _________ are special symbols which perform some computations.

State Whether True or False

19. In Python, a string can only be defined using single quotes (') and cannot use double quotes (").

20. A complex number in Python is represented as a combination of two integers, where the first integer represents the real part and the second integer represents the imaginary part.

21. The unary minus operator changes the sign of a negative decimal value to positive.

22. The modulus operator can only be used with integer operands.

23. The logical OR operator returns True if both expressions are True, and False otherwise.

24. Relational operators have higher precedence than logical AND and logical OR operators.

25. The augmented assignment operator %= is equivalent to c = c % a, where c is the left operand and a is the right operand.

26. The **= operator (Exponentiation AND assignment) can only be used with integer operands.

Assertion and Reason Based Questions

Assertion (A) and Reason (R) based questions. Mark the correct choice as

(a) Both (A) and (R) are true and (R) is the correct explanation for (A).

(b) Both (A) and (R) are true but (R) is not the correct explanation for (A).

(c) Assertion (A) is true, but Reason (R) is false.

(d) Reason (R) is true, but Assertion (A) is false.

27. Assertion (A) Python is a strongly-typed language.

Reason (R) Variables in Python must be declared with a specific data type.

28. Assertion (A) Lists are mutable data structures.

Reason (R) Elements in a list can be changed, added, or removed after creation.

29. Assertion (A) Tuples are immutable data structures.

Reason (R) Once a tuple is created, its elements cannot be changed.

30. Assertion (A) The + operator can be used to concatenate strings.

Reason (R) String concatenation is the process of joining two or more strings together.

31. Assertion (A) Dictionaries are unordered collections of key-value pairs.

Reason (R) The order of elements in a dictionary is preserved.

32. Assertion (A) The % operator is used to calculate the remainder of a division operation.

Reason (R) It's known as the modulo operator.

33. Assertion (A) Operator precedence determines the order in which operations are performed in an expression.

Reason (R) Parentheses can be used to override the default precedence.

34. Assertion (A) Sets are unordered collections of unique elements.

Reason (R) Sets do not allow duplicate elements.

Answers

1. (a) Numbers
2. (b) imaginary part
3. (c) decimal.Decimal
4. (c) Strings
5. (b) tuple
6. (c) %
7. (c) 2**3
8. (c) 25
9. (d) True, because Python allows chaining of comparison operators.
10. (d) bool
11. (b) 6, because True is treated as 1 and False as 0.
12. (a) Logical
13. (d) All of these
14. (a) hello world
15. Mutable
16. 4
17. Dictionary
18. Operators
19. False
20. False
21. True
22. False
23. False
24. True
25. True
26. False
27. (c) Assertion (A) is true, but Reason (R) is false.
28. (a) Both Assertion (A) and Reason (R) are true, and Reason (R) is the correct explanation of Assertion (A).
29. (a) Both Assertion (A) and Reason (R) are true, and Reason (R) is the correct explanation of Assertion (A).
30. (a) Both Assertion (A) and Reason (R) are true, and Reason (R) is the correct explanation of Assertion (A).
31. (c) Assertion (A) is true, but Reason (R) is false.
32. (a) Both Assertion (A) and Reason (R) are true, and Reason (R) is the correct explanation of Assertion (A).
33. (a) Both Assertion (A) and Reason (R) are true, and Reason (R) is the correct explanation of Assertion (A).
34. (a) Both Assertion (A) and Reason (R) are true, and Reason (R) is the correct explanation of Assertion (A).

Subjective Type Questions

Very Short Answer Type Questions

1. (a) **What is the data type?**

(b) **What are some examples of mutable data types in Python?**

Ans. (a) Data type is a term that is used to show the kind of data values or the type of data that is expected to be handled.

(b) Python offers only two data types that are mutable:

(1) Lists (e.g., [1, "hello", True])

(2) Dictionaries (e.g., {"name": "Alice", "age": 30})

2. Define the term operator.

Ans. Operators are symbols which take one or more operands to perform arithmetic or logical computations.

3. Explain unary operator.

Ans. A unary operator is an operator that performs its operation on only one operand.

4. Differentiate between / and % operators.

Ans. / operator is used to find the quotient while % operator is used to find the remainder.

5. The proper Python syntax for testing that value of A is between 2 and 9 inclusively is

(i) 2 < =A < = 9

(ii) 2> =A and A < = 9

(iii) A > = 2 and A < = 9

(iv) 2 < =A and A > = 9

Ans. (iii) A > = 2 and A < = 9

6. What is the use of a relational operator?

Ans. The relational operators are used for comparison between two or more operands.

7. Differentiate between = and = = operators.

Ans. = is an assignment operator whereas = = is a relational operator.

8. Write the augmented assignment operators used in Python.

Ans. + =,- =,* =,/ =,% =,// =,** =

9. What will be the output of the following code?

```
X= 2
Y= 6
X= X+Y/2 + Y//4
print(X)
```

Ans. 6.0

10. Name three logical operators.

Ans. (i) AND operator (and)

(ii) OR operator (or)

(iii) NOT operator (not)

11. What will be the result of the following expression?

```
-a <= 5
```

(i) if a = 5

(ii) if a = - 5

Ans. (i) True (ii) True

12. Write the value stored in the variable Num by each of the following statements.

(i) Num = 2 * 3 – 4

(ii) Num = 2+3-1*3

(iii) Num = (2+3)*2

Ans. (i) Num = 2

(ii) Num = 2

(iii) Num = 10

13. Convert the equation into corresponding Python statement $y = a^3 + b^2 + c + 2bc$

Ans. y = (a * *3 + b * *2 + c + 2 * b * c)

14. What are the two common string representations in Python?

Ans. Python supports str (Unicode) and bytes (Byte String) as its two common string representations.

15. A bank maintains customer balances using Python. Consider the following code snippet:

Competency Based Que.

```
balance = 5000
withdrawal = "2000"
new_balance = balance - int(withdrawal)
print(type(new_balance))
```

What will be the output of type(new_balance)?

Ans. <class 'int'>

16. A scientist is performing calculations using Python and writes the following code:

```
x = 3 + 4.0 * 2 / 2 + 5 // 2
print(x)
```

What will be the output of x? **Competency Based Que.**

Ans. 9.0

17. An e-commerce platform records the number of items in a cart as a string:

```
items = "7"
price_per_item = 199.50
```

```
total_cost = float(items) * price_per_item
print(type(total_cost))
```

What will be the output of type(total_cost)? **Competency Based Que.**

Ans. <class 'float'>

Short Answer Type I Questions

18. Imagine you are developing a banking application where account numbers, once assigned, should never be altered. Similarly, customer names should remain unchanged unless explicitly updated through a secure process.

Based on this scenario, explain why Python's immutable data types, such as strings and numbers, are useful in ensuring data integrity and security in applications. **Competency Based Que.**

Ans. Immutable data types in Python, like strings and numbers, prevent unintended changes, ensuring data integrity in applications like banking. Since modifying an immutable object creates a new one instead of altering the original, critical data (e.g., account numbers) remains secure and consistent, reducing risks in financial transactions.

19. Determine the Output.

```
x = -4
y = -x
print ("value of x =", x)
print ("value of y =", y)
x = 2
y = 3
z = x ** y + 3
x = y + 5
print ("value of z =", z)
print ("value of x =", x)
```

Ans. value of x = -4

value of y = 4

value of z = 11

value of x = 8

20. How does the logical OR operator work when the operands are not relational expressions?

Ans. When using the logical OR operator (or) with non-relational operands in Python, it follows a specific evaluation process:

(a) **Evaluate the first operand** Python first evaluates the truth value of the first operand.

(b) **If the first operand is True** If the first operand is True, the entire expression is considered True, and the second operand is not evaluated.

(c) **If the first operand is False** If the first operand is False, Python evaluates the second operand. If the second operand is True, the entire expression is True. Otherwise, if the second operand is also False, the entire expression is False.

21. What is the difference between unary and binary operators?

Ans. **Unary** This operator works on a single operand. It negates the value of the operand. For example, -5 negates the number 5.

Binary This operator works on two operands. It subtracts the second operand from the first. For example, 10 - 5 subtracts 5 from 10.

22. Predict the output of the following code fragment.

```
b = 20
a = 90/b
print ("value of a is :", a)
```

Ans. value of a is : 4.5

23. Using the given values of x, y and z, evaluate the following.

```
(x >= y) and (not(z ==y)) or (z < x)
```

(i) x =5, y = 6, z = 20

(ii) x = 10, y = 4, z = 11

Ans. (i) False (ii) True

24. Predict the output of the following program.

```
a = 5
b = a = 15
c = (a < 15)
print ("a =", a)
print ("b =", b)
print ("c =", c)
```

Ans.

```
a = 15
b = 15
c = False
```

25. Write the corresponding Python expression for the following mathematical expression.

(i) $z = a / a + b - d^2$

(ii) $z = x^2 + y^3$

Ans. (i) z = a / (a + b) - (d * d)

(ii) z = (x * *2) + (y * *3)

26. Determine the hierarchy of operations and evaluate the following expression.

```
A = 3*4//5 + 5//7 + 8 - 2 + 4//2
```

Ans. The * operator will be performed before //. Though both have same priority but in this expression * is prior to //.

```
A = 12 //5 + 5//7 +8 - 2 + 4//2
  = 2 + 5//7 + 8 - 2 + 4//2
  = 2 + 0 + 8 - 2 + 4//2
  = 2 + 0 + 8 - 2 + 2
  = 2 + 0 + 6 + 2 = 10
```

27. **What will be the value of following if a = 2?**

(i) (12 / + a)%3

(ii) (21* + a)%9

(iii) (21//+a)%3

Ans. (i) 0.0 (ii) 6 (iii) 1

28. **Determine the hierarchy of operations and evaluate the following expression.**

```
a = 2 *3//4 + 4//4 + 8 - 2 + 5//8
```

Ans.

```
a = 2*3//4 + 4//4 + 8 - 2 + 5//8
  = 6//4 + 4 //4 + 8 - 2 + 5//8   operation : *
  = 1 + 4//4 + 8 - 2 + 5//8       operation : //
  = 1 + 1 + 8 - 2 + 5//8          operation : //
  = 1 + 1 + 8 - 2 + 0             operation : //
  = 2 + 8 - 2 + 0                 operation : +
  = 10 - 2 + 0                    operation : + , -
  = 8 + 0 = 8                     operation : +
```

29. **What value will be stored in different variables when the following Python statements are executed?**

```
i = 10
j = i + 5
k = i + j/5
l = k + 1 + 4
m = l + 1 - i
n = k + m*l
print ("i: ", i)
print ("j: ", j)
print ("k: ", k)
print ("l: ", l)
print ("m: ", m)
print ("n: ", n)
```

Ans. i: 10

j: 15

k: 13.0

l: 18

m: 9

n: 175

Short Answer Type II Questions

30. **How are strings stored and manipulated in Python?**

Ans. A string in Python is an immutable sequence of characters enclosed in single (') or double (") quotes.

Example: text = "Hello, World!" assigns a string to the variable text.

Common operations include concatenation (+), repetition (*), and slicing ([:]).

Example: "Hello" + " World" results in "Hello World", and "Python"[0:3] gives "Pyt".

Since strings are immutable, modifying a string creates a new one instead of changing the original.

31. **What is the difference between a list and a tuple in Python?**

Ans.

List	Tuple
A list is a collection that is mutable, meaning its elements can be changed.	A tuple, on the other hand, is immutable, meaning once defined, it cannot be altered.
Lists are created using square brackets [], e.g., my_list = [1, 2, 3].	Tuples are created using parentheses (), e.g., my_tuple = (1, 2, 3).
Tuples are immutable, they are faster and preferred when data should not be changed.	Lists are commonly used for dynamic data, while tuples are for fixed collections.

32. **What is the difference between set and dictionary in Python?**

Ans. The difference between set and dictionary in Python are as follows

Parameter	Set	Dictionary
Definition	An unordered collection of unique elements.	An ordered collection of key-value pairs.
Representation	Curly braces {}.	Curly braces {}, but with key-value pairs.
Order	Unordered.	Ordered (from Python 3.7 onwards).
Duplicates	Does not allow duplicate elements.	Does not allow duplicate keys.
Mutability	Mutable (can add or remove elements).	Mutable (can add, modify, or remove key-value pairs).
Access Method	Elements are accessed directly.	Values are accessed using keys.
Use Case	To store unique elements.	To store related pieces of information.
Example	my_set = {1, 2, 3}	my_dict = {"name": "Alice", "age": 30}

33. **Determine which of the arithmetic expressions are valid. If invalid, explain the reason. [(a, b, c) are integers, (p, q, r) are float and (x, y, z) are float].**

(i) p/q + a – c

(ii) q (a + b – z/4)

(iii) p/q + a – c

(iv) x/y + p * a/b

(v) a * + b

(vi) a//+b*c*2

Ans. (i) p/q + a – c valid

(ii) q (a + b – z/4) invalid because operator missing between q and a

(iii) p/q + a – c valid

(iv) x/y + p * a/b valid

(v) a * + b invalid because use of two operators together

(vi) a//+b*c*2 invalid because use of two operators together.

34. Write a program to calculate the GST.

Ans.
```
prod = int(input("Enter the original
                        amount of product:"))
gst = int(input("Enter the percentage of
                        GST on that product:"))
GST_Amount = (prod*gst)/100
Net_price = prod + GST_Amount
print ("Net Price:", Net_price)
```

Output

Enter the original amount of product: 800

Enter the percentage of GST on that product: 2

Net Price: 816.0

35. The distance between two cities (in km) is input through the keyboard, write a Python program to convert this distance in meters.

Ans.
```
km = float (input ("Enter the distance
                        in km:"))
print ("Distance in km:", km)
meters = km * 1000
print ("Distance in meters :", meters)
```

Output

Enter the distance in km : 2.5

Distance in km : 2.5

Distance in meters : 2500.0

36. Write a Python program to find the perimeter of a rectangle.

Ans.
```
l = int (input ("Enter the length:"))
b = int (input ("Enter the breath:"))
print ("Length:", l)
print ("Breath:", b)
p = 2 * (l+b)
print ("Perimeter of the rectangle:", p)
```

Output

Enter the length : 6

Enter the breath: 4

Length : 6

Breath : 4

Perimeter of the rectangle : 20

Long Answer Type Questions

37. Write a Python program which input the time in seconds and convert it into days. Also, display its output.

Ans.
```
time = float (input("Enter the time in
                        seconds:"))
day = time // (24*3600)
time = time % (24* 3600)
hour = time // 3600
time %= 60
seconds = time
print ("Days:", day)
print ("Hours:", hour)
print ("Minutes:", minutes)
print ("Seconds:", seconds)
```

Output

Input time in seconds: 360425060

Days: 4171.0

Hours: 14.0

Minutes: 4.0

Seconds: 20.0

38. Write a program which input three sides of triangle and calculate its perimeter, semi perimeter and area.

Ans.
```
a = float (input("Enter the First side of
                        a Triangle:"))
b = float (input("Enter the Second side of
                        a Triangle:"))
c = float(input("Enter the Third side of
                        a Triangle:"))
  #calculate the Perimeter
Perimeter = a + b + c
  #calculate the semi-perimeter
s = (a+b+c)/2
  #calculate the area
Area = (s*(s-a)*(s-b)*(s-c)) ** 0.5
print ("\n The perimeter of Triangle =
                        %.2f" %perimeter)
print ("The Semi Perimeter of Triangle
                        = %.2f" %s)
print ("The Area of a Triangle is %0.2f" %Area)
```

Output

Enter the First side of a Triangle: 13

Enter the Second side of a Triangle: 12

Enter the Third side of a Triangle: 5

The perimeter of Triangle = 30.00

The Semi Perimeter of Triangle = 15.00

The Area of a Triangle is 30.00

39. Evaluate the following expressions.

(a) A = 10*4//2 + 4 - 2//2 + 4 - 3 + 5//8

(b) A = 5 + 6//3 + 10*3//4 + 2 + 3//4

(c) A = 5*5 + 4 //5 + 15 - 9//2 + 10

Ans. (a) A =10*4//2 + 4 - 2//2 + 4 - 3 + 5//8

= 40//2 + 4 - 2//2 + 4 - 3 + 5//8

= 20 + 4 - 2//2 + 4 - 3 + 5//8

= 20 + 4 - 1 + 4 - 3 + 5//8

= 20 + 4 - 1 + 4 - 3 + 0

= 20 + 4 - 1 + 4 - 3 + 5//8
= 20 + 4 - 1 + 4 - 3 + 0
= 24 - 1 + 4 - 3 + 0
= 23 + 4 - 3
= 27 - 3
= 24

(b) A = 5 + 6//3 + 10*3//4 + 2 + 3//4
= 5 + 2 + 10*3//4 + 2 + 3//4
= 5 + 2 + 30//4 + 2 + 3//4
= 5 + 2 + 7 + 2 + 0
= 7 + 7 + 2
= 16

(c) A = 5*5 + 4//5 + 15 - 9//2 + 10
= 25 + 4//5 + 15 - 9//2 + 10
= 25 + 0 + 15 - 4 + 10
= 40 - 4 + 10
= 36 + 10
= 46

40. **A software company stores employee details in a dictionary format, where each key represents an employee ID, and the values are stored as a list containing their name, age, and salary.**

```
employees = {
    101: ["Ali", "28", "55000.50"],
    102: ["Bunny", "30", "62000.75"],
    103: ["Charu", "26", "48000.25"]
}
```

I. **Identify the data types of age and salary values for each employee.**

II. **Convert the age to an integer type and the salary to a float type for all employees.**

III. **Calculate and display the average salary of all employees after conversion.** **Competency Based Que.**

Ans. **Step I** Identifying Data Types Before Conversion

- The age values are stored as strings ("28", "30", "26").
- The salary values are also stored as strings ("55000.50", "62000.75", "48000.25").

Step II Converting age to int and salary to float:

```
for emp_id in employees:
  employees[emp_id][1] =
                int(employees[emp_id][1])
# Convert age to int
   employees[emp_id][2] =
         float(employees[emp_id][2])
# Convert salary to float
```

Step III Calculating Average Salary

```
total_salary = sum([employees[emp_id][2]
                for emp_id in employees])
average_salary = total_salary
                         / len(employees)
print(f"Average Salary: {average_salary}")
```

Output:

Average Salary: 55000.5

41. **A company assigns bonus points to employees based on their performance scores. The formula for calculating bonus points is:**

Bonus Points=(Performance Score×2+Experience in years)%7

The employee details are stored in a list of tuples, where each tuple contains:

```
employees = [
   ("Dev", 85, 5),
     # (Name, Performance Score, Experience)
   ("Mohit", 92, 3),
   ("Priya", 78, 7)
]
```

(i) **Write Python code to calculate the Bonus Points for each employee using the given formula.**

(ii) **Identify the operator types used in the formula (*, +, %).**

(iii) **Determine which employee receives the highest Bonus Points and display their name.**

Competency Based Que.

Ans. **Step (i)** Calculate Bonus Points

```
bonus_points = {}
for emp in employees:
  name, score, experience = emp
  bonus = (score * 2 + experience) % 7
  bonus_points[name] = bonus
```

Step (ii) Identifying Operators in the Formula

- * (Multiplication): Arithmetic Operator
- + (Addition): Arithmetic Operator
- % (Modulus): Arithmetic Operator

Step (iii) Find the Employee with the Highest Bonus Points

```
max_bonus_employee = max(bonus_points,
key=bonus_points.get)
print(f"Employee with highest bonus points:
{max_bonus_employee}")
```

Output:

Employee with highest bonus points: Mohit

42. **Write a program to calculate the volume of the sphere and hemisphere using math modules. Also, display the appropriate output.**

Volume of sphere = $4/3\pi r^3$

Volume of hemisphere = $2/3\pi r^3$

Ans.

```
print ("Calculate the Volume of Sphere")
radius = int(input("Enter the radius of
                                  a sphere:"))
print ("Radius of Sphere:", radius)
```

```
print ("volume of sphere:", volume)
print ("\nCalculate the volume of
                              Hemisphere")
radius1 = int (input("Enter the radius of
                           a hemisphere:"))
print ("Radius of Hemisphere:", radius1)
#volume of hemisphere
volume1 = (2/3)*3.14*(radius1**3)
print ("Volume of Hemisphere:", volume1)
```

Output

Calculate the Volume of Sphere
Enter the radius of a sphere: 5
Radius of Sphere: 5
Volume of Sphere: 523.3333333333334
Calculate the Volume of Hemisphere
Enter the radius of a hemisphere: 4
Radius of Hemisphere: 4
Volume of Hemisphere: 133.97333333333333

43. Predict the output:

(i)
```
a = 3
b = a *2
print(a*3+6+b)
```

(ii)
```
a, b = 12, 10
c = a//b + 4 * 2
d = c – 10
print(d)
```

(iii)
```
a = 5
b = 6
print((a and b)
or (a > b))
```

(iv)
```
a = 4
b = 6
c = 10
print((a >= b)
or ((c = = b)
and (not(c < a))))
```

(v)
```
a = 4
b = 6
c = 10
print((a <= b) and
((c == a)and
(not(c < b))))
```

(vi)
```
a = 60
b = 10
c = 85/b + a
print(c)
```

(vii)
```
a = 3
b = 4
c = a ** b + 5
print(c)
```

(viii)
```
b = 89
a = 78
c = (a <= b)
print(c)
```

Ans. (i) 21 (ii) –1
(iii) 6 (iv) False
(v) False (vi) 68.5
(vii) 86 (viii) True

44. Find the output

(i)
```
x = 20
y = 24
print('x > y  is',x>y)
print('x < y  is',x<y)
print('x == y is',x == y)
print('x != y is',x!=y)
print('x >= y is',x>=y)
print('x <= y is',x<=y)
```

(ii)
```
x = 19
y = 4
print('x + y =',x+y)
print('x - y =',x-y)
print('x * y =',x*y)
print('x / y =',x/y)
print('x // y =',x//y)
print('x ** y =',x**y)
```

Ans. (i) **Output**

x > y is False
x < y is True
x == y is False
x != y is True
x >= y is False
x <= y is True

(ii) **Output**

x + y = 23
x - y = 15
x * y = 76
x / y = 4.75
x // y = 4
x ** y = 130321

45. Describe the expressions in Python.

Ans. Refer to text on page no. 80 (Expressions).

Case Study Based Questions

Case Study 1

Operators are special symbols that perform specific operations on values or variables. They are the building blocks of expressions and form the core of programming logic. Python offers a wide range of operators, including arithmetic, comparison, assignment, logical, bitwise, membership, and identity operators.

Based on the above information, answer the following questions.

(i) Which operator is used to perform integer division in Python?

(a) / (b) // (c) % (d) **

(ii) What is the result of the expression 5 ** 2?

(a) 7 (b) 10 (c) 25 (d) 3

(iii) Which operator is used to check if two values are equal?

(a) == (b) != (c) > (d) <

(iv) What is the output of 10 % 3?

(a) 3 (b) 2 (c) 1 (d) 0

(v) Which operator is used to assign a value to a variable?

(a) = (b) == (c) := (d) ->

(vi) What is the result of the expression True and False?

(a) True (b) False (c) None (d) Error

Ans. (i) (b) // (ii) (c) 25
(iii) (a) == (iv) (c) 1
(v) (a) = (vi) (b) False

Case Study 2

Data Type The data that needs to be processed by a computer can be in various form. It can be numbers with or without decimal places or it can be just a single character or a sequence of characters.

The data to be handled by the computer can also be in group. All computer programming languages support wide variety of data that can be stored, processed and manipulated in a computer system.

Data type is a term that is used to show the kind of data values or the type of data that is expected to be handled. Python has five standard data types: Numbers, Strings, Lists, Tuples and Dictionaries.

Based on the above information, answer the following questions.

(i) Which data type contains only numeric values in Python?

(a) String (b) List
(c) Number (d) Dictionary

(ii) Which term is used to show the kind of data values?

(a) Variable (b) Data Type
(c) Operator (d) Function

(iii) Tuples are defined by which type of bracket?

(a) Square brackets [ ] (b) Curly braces { }
(c) Parentheses ( ) (d) Angle brackets < >

(iv) In Python, what are the uses of data types?

(a) To store data in different formats
(b) To define variables and their usage
(c) To perform specific operations on data
(d) All of the above

(v) Integer data type can be represented by which term(s)?

(a) int (b) float
(c) str (d) list

Ans. (i) (c) Number
(ii) (b) Data Type
(iii) (c) Parentheses ( )
(iv) (d) All of the above
(v) (a) int

SELF ASSESSMENT TEST

Multiple Choice Questions

1. These operators work on single operand

(a) Binary (b) Unary
(c) Ternary (d) None of these

2. Which of the following symbol is used for exponentiation?

(a) // (b) **
(c) * (d) ^^

3. Dictionary data types are created by using

(a) { } (b) [ ]
(c) ( ) (d) < >

Fill in the Blanks

4. In Python, the function _______ is used to check the data type of a variable.

5. The expression 5 + 3 * 2 ** 2 - 4 // 2 evaluates to _______, following Python's operator precedence rules.

State Whether True or False

6. In Python, the is operator checks whether two variables have the same value, similar to the == operator.

7. In Python, a set can contain both mutable and immutable data types as its elements.

Assertion and Reason Based Questions

Assertion (A) and Reason (R) Type questions. Choose the correct option as:

(a) Both Assertion (A) and Reason (R) are true, and Reason (R) is the correct explanation of Assertion (A).
(b) Both Assertion (A) and Reason (R) are true, but Reason (R) is not the correct explanation of Assertion (A).
(c) Assertion (A) is true, but Reason (R) is false.
(d) Assertion (A) is false, but Reason (R) is true.

8. **Assertion (A)** In Python, the int and float data types are both immutable.

Reason (R) Immutable data types in Python cannot be changed after they are created.

9. **Assertion (A)** The // operator in Python performs floor division and always returns an integer.

Reason (R) The // operator rounds the result towards zero.

10. **Assertion (A)** The + operator in Python can be used for both arithmetic addition and string concatenation.

Reason (R) Python allows operator overloading, enabling operators to perform different operations based on operand types.

Very Short Answer Type Questions

11. Which operator is used to connect relational expression?

12. What will be the value of z?
z = 2 * 3 + 4 – 3/2 * 4

13. Convert the equation into corresponding Python statement $a^3 + b^2 + 5c$.

Short Answer Type Questions

14. Define conditional operator with the help of an example.

15. Construct logical expression to represent the following condition

(i) a is odd.
(ii) age is less than 35 and greater than 18.

16. What will be the output of following program?

```
i = 4
j = -1
k = 0
w = i or j or k
x = i and j and k
print("w = ", w)
print("x = ", x)
```

17. Write the output of the following program:

```
x = 5
y = 3
z = ++ x + -- y
print ("z = ", - - z)
```

18. Evaluate the following expression and show their hierarchy

```
a = b * c/2 + 3/2 * c + 2 + d
(if b = 4, c = 1, d = 3.2)
```

Long Answer Type Questions

19. Any year is input through the keyboard. Write a program to determine whether the year is a leap year or not.

20. If a three digit number is input through the keyboard, write a program to reverse the number.

21. Write a Python program to input a number, if number is even print its cube otherwise print its square.

22. If the marks obtained by a student in five different subjects are input through the keyboard, find out the aggregate marks and percentage marks obtained by the student. Assume the maximum marks that can be obtained by a student in each subject is 100.

23. Ravish's basic salary is input through the keyboard. His dearness allowance is 40% of basic salary and house rent allowance is 20% of basic salary. Write a program to calculate his gross salary.

Case Study Based Questions

24. A software development company is designing an application that helps users analyze their monthly expenses. The application takes inputs for different expense categories, processes the data, and provides useful insights. The developer has implemented the following Python code to handle the data:

```
salary = 50000
rent = 12000
groceries = 8500
transport = 3200
utilities = 4100
savings = salary - (rent + groceries
                      + transport + utilities)
print("Remaining Balance:", savings)
print("Is rent greater than groceries?",
                            rent > groceries)
print("Total expenditure:", rent
      + groceries + transport + utilities)
print("Average expense per category:",
      (rent + groceries + transport + utilities)
                                          / 4)
```

Based on the above information, answer the following questions.

(i) What is the data type of the variable salary in the given Python code?

(a) int (b) float
(c) str (d) bool

(ii) What type of operator is used in the expression rent > groceries?

(a) Arithmetic Operator
(b) Logical Operator
(c) Comparison Operator
(d) Assignment Operator

(iii) What will be the output of the following expression: type(savings)

(a) <class 'int'> (b) <class 'float'>
(c) <class 'bool'> (d) <class 'str'>

(iv) Which of the following operators is used to calculate the average expense in the given code?

(a) + (Addition) (b) / (Division)
(c) - (Subtraction) (d) * (Multiplication)

(v) If the salary is changed to 50000.50, what will be the data type of savings?

(a) int (b) float
(c) str (d) bool

Answers

1. (b)	2. (b)	3. (a)	4. type()	5. 15
6. False	7. False	8. (a)	9. (a)	10. (a)

24. (i) → (a), (ii) → (c), (iii) → (a), (iv) → (b), (v) → (b)

06

CHAPTER

Programming is all about making decisions and automating repetitive tasks. Python provides powerful constructs for decision-making (conditional statements) and iteration (looping statements) that allow programmers to control the flow of execution efficiently.

YOUR STUDY GOALS

6.1 Control Structure
- Sequence
- Selection
- Iteration

6.2 Programs

YOUR PRACTICE GOAL

- Objective Type Questions (30 Qs ; MCQs, True or False, Fill in the Blanks, Assertion and Reason)
- Subjective Type Questions (39 Qs ; VSA, SA, LA)
- Case Study Based Questions-2

Conditional and Looping Statements

A computer program is a collection of instructions that tell a computer what to do. These instructions, or statements, are the building blocks of programs. The simplest statement is a null statement, which does nothing.

Compound statements are groups of statements that work together to perform a specific task. Control statements, like if, else, for, and while, determine the order in which these statements are executed.

This flow of control allows programmers to create complex programs with different execution paths.

6.1 Control Structure

A control structure is a programming language construct which affects the flow of the execution of a program.

Various types of control structure are described below.

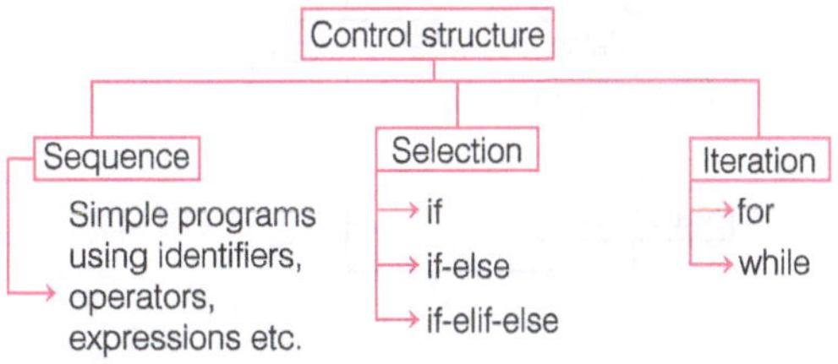

Sequence

Sequence control means the statements are being executed sequentially.

Sequence structure is also known as straight line path.

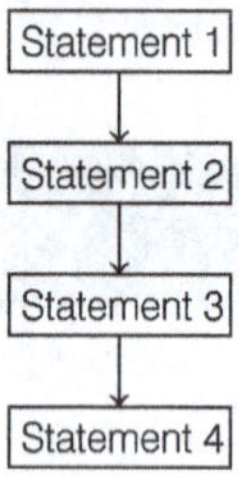

Sequence Statements

Sequence statements are instructions that are executed one after the other, in the order they appear in the program.

When a program runs, it follows a specific path, executing each **statement sequentially**.

For example,

```
print ("A program which adds two integers\n")
x = int(input("Enter first integer:"))
y = int(input("Enter second integer:"))
sum = x + y
print ("Sum is :", sum)
```

Output

A program which adds two integers

Enter first integer: 5

Enter second integer: 5

Sum is: 10

Selection or Branching

Selection or Branching statements allow us to control the flow of the program and execute different parts of the code depending on whether a certain condition is true or false.

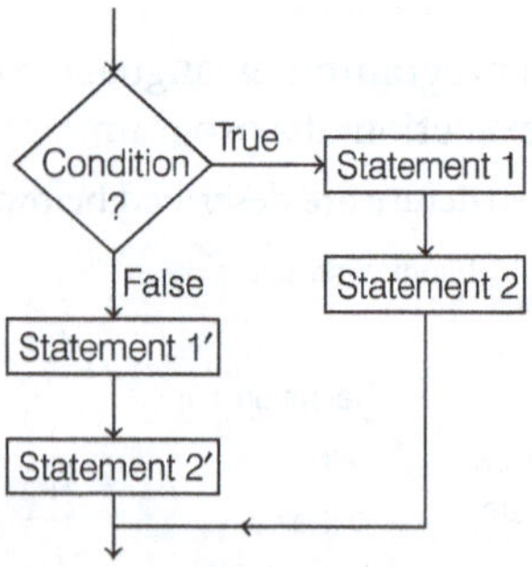

Selection Statements

Selection statements, also known as conditional statements or decision statements, allow a program to make choices.

This decision-making process is often based on the result of a boolean expression. Relational operators like ==, !=, <, >, <=, and >= are used to create these boolean expressions.

Python language provides the following selection statements

(i) if statement

(ii) if-else statement

(iii) if-elif-else statement

if Statement

The simplest and most common selection structure is the if statement.

If the condition evaluates true, an action is followed; otherwise, the action is ignored.

Syntax

```
if (conditional expression):
  statement(s)
```

Points to be remember

1. Logical statements in Python can only evaluate to either True or False.
2. In Python, any non-zero value (positive or negative) is considered True, while zero is considered False.
3. It's generally not recommended to use floating-point numbers to control conditional statements, as it can lead to unexpected behavior due to floating-point precision issues.

For example,

```
x = 1
y = 3
x = x + y
if (x > y):
  print ("x is greater")
```

In the above example, the conditional statement under if() will be always evaluated as True, i.e the output of the above code would be "x is greater".

Following flowchart illustrates if statement:

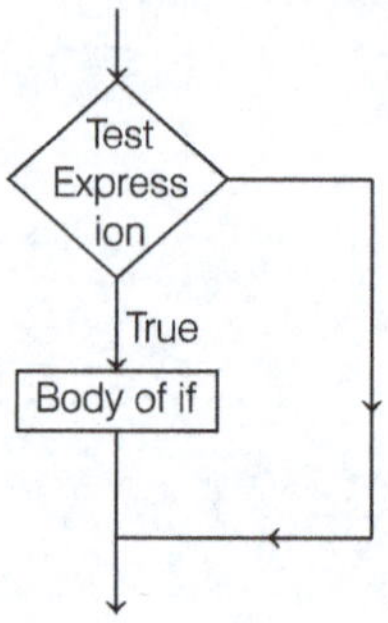

if-else Statement

This statement also tests a conditional expression. If the condition is True, the entire block of statements following the if will be executed.

Otherwise, the entire block of statements following the else will be executed.

Syntax
```
if (conditional statement):
        statement(s)
else:
        statement(s)
```

Following flowchart illustrates if-else statement:

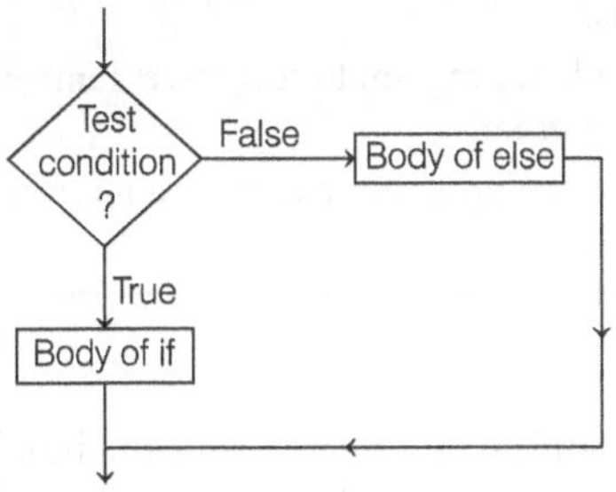

e.g.,
```
x = 0
y = 3
x = x + y
if (x > y):
    print ("x is greater")
else:
    print ("we are in else part because x is
not greater")
```

The above code produces an output as "we are in the else part because x is not greater". Because the conditional statement under if ( ) evaluates as False x is not greater than y, it is the same as that of y.

Some of valid if-else statements are

(i)
```
if((ch>='a') and (ch<='z')):
     print(ch, "is a lowercase letter")
else:
     print(ch, "is not a lowercase letter")
```

(ii)
```
if((age==50) or (age==20)):
     print("You are old")
else:
     print("You are young")
```

if-elif-else statement

Sometimes, we need to make decisions based on multiple conditions. We can use a series of if-else statements to check each condition one by one.

If a condition is true, the corresponding code block is executed. If not, the next condition is checked, and so on. This allows us to create more complex decision-making processes.

Syntax
```
if (condition 1):
       statement 1
elif(condition 2):
       statement 2
else:
       statement 3
```

or
```
if(condition 1):
       statement 1
elif(condition 2):
       statement 2
```

Expression is tested from the top towards the downside. As soon as the true condition is found, the associated set of statement is executed.

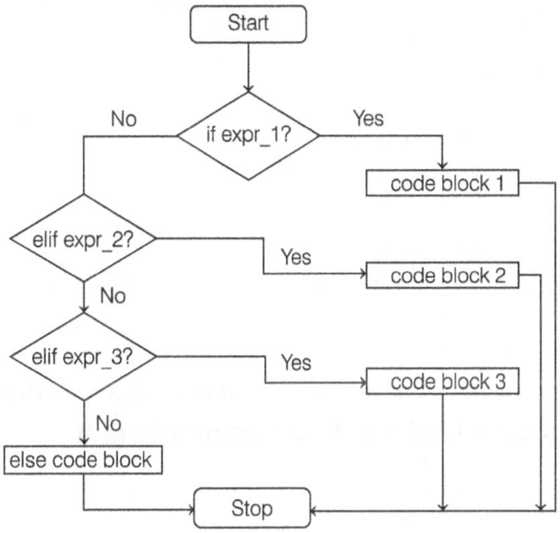

e.g.
```
if((x % 5 = = 0) and (x % 8 = = 0)):
       print("Divisible by both 5 and 8")
elif(x % 8 = = 0):
       print("Divisible by 8")
elif (x % 5 = = 0):
       print("Divisible by 5")
else:
       print("Divisible by none")
```

Output

The code checks if a number is divisible by 5, 8, or both. It prints a message accordingly:

Divisible by both 5 and 8 (e.g., 40)

Divisible by 8 (e.g., 16)

Divisible by 5 (e.g., 25)

Divisible by none (e.g., 17)

For an if-elif-else

(i) Other than 0(zero), all other values are considered as True.

(ii) (==) must be used for comparision in the expression of if condition, if you use (=) the expression will always return True, because it performs assignment not comparison.

Nested if statement

A nested if statement is an if statement that is placed inside another if statement. It allows you to make more complex decisions by testing additional conditions after the first if condition is evaluated.

Syntax

```
if(condition 1):
    if(condition 2):
        statement 1
    else:
          statement 2
else:
        statement 3
```

e.g.
```
if(a > b):
    if(a > c):
        result = a
    else:
        result = c
else:
        if(b>c):
            result = b
        else:
            result = c
```

The nested if can have one of the following four forms:

(i) **if nested inside both, if part and else part**

```
if(condition 1):
    if(condition 2):
        statement 1
    else:
        statement 2
else:
        if(condition 3):
            statement 3
        else:
            statement 4
```

(ii) **if nested inside if part**

```
if(condition 1):
    if(condition 2):
        statement 1
    else:
        statement 2
else :
        statement 3
```

(iii) **if nested inside else part**

```
if(condition 1):
        statement 1
else:
        if(condition 2):
            statement 2
        else:
            statement 3
```

(iv) **One if inside another if statements**

```
if(condition 1):
    statement 1
    if (condition 2):
        statement 2
```

Quick Test 1

1. What is sequential flow in programming?
2. What is the purpose of conditional statements in programming?
3. Explain the difference between if, if-else and if-elif-else statements.
4. Write a Python program to sort three numbers in descending order.
5. Write a Python program to check if a number is divisible by 3 and 5.

Iteration

Iteration, or looping, is a way to repeat a block of code multiple times. We use it when we need to perform the same task over and over again until a certain condition is met. For example, if we want to print the numbers from 1 to 10, we can use a loop to repeat the printing process 10 times.

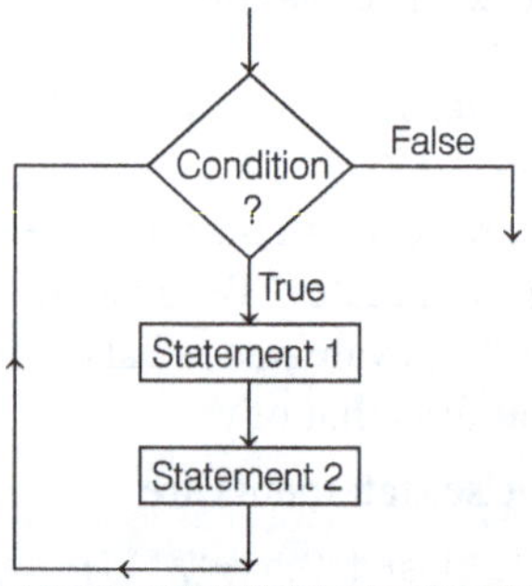

range( ) Function

The range( ) function is used to generate a sequence of numbers overtime. At its simplest, it accepts an integer and returns a range object (a type of iterable).

Syntax `range(start, stop, step)`

where,

- **start** This is where you want to begin your count. If you don't specify a number, it defaults to 0.
- **stop** This is where you want to end your count. You need to provide a number here (Required).
- **step** This tells you how much to increase the count each time. If you don't specify a number, it defaults to 1, meaning you'll count by ones.

e.g., if you set start to 2, stop to 10, and step to 2, you'll count: 2,4,6,8.

Iterative Statements

Loops in Python are used to repeatedly execute a block of code. This repetition is controlled by a condition, which is evaluated before each iteration. If the condition is true, the code block is executed. Once the condition becomes false, the loop terminates.

Python offers two main types of loops:

(i) for loop (ii) while loop

for loop

The for loop is a tool that lets you repeat a set of instructions a specific number of times. It iterates through a sequence (like a range, string, list, or tuple), processing each value. Once all items are processed, the loop ends, and control moves to the next statement.

Syntax
```
for variable in <sequence>:
    statement (s)
```

In general
```
for i in range(start, stop, step):
    statement (s)
```

Flowchart

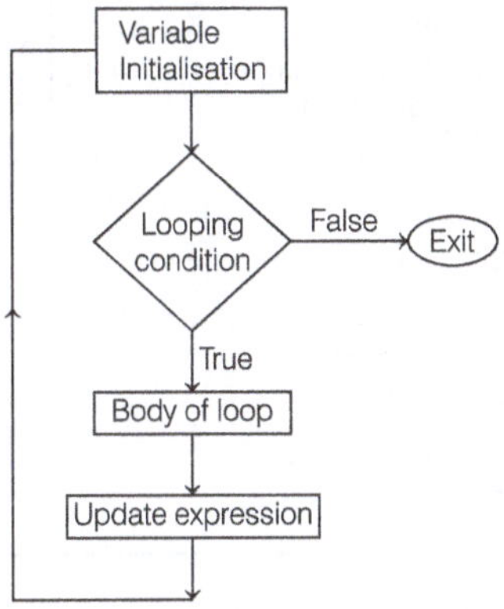

Example

(i)
```
for i in range (1,5):
    print("A")
    print("B")
```

Output

A
B
A
B
A
B
A
B

(ii)
```
a = "Arihant"
for i in a:
    print(i)
```

Output

A
r
i
h
a
n
t

while loop

A while loop is like a set of instructions that keeps repeating as long as a certain condition is true. Before it starts, it checks if the condition is true. If it is, it runs the instructions inside the loop.

Once the condition becomes false, the loop stops.

Note *If the condition is false right at the beginning, the loop won't run even once. This is why it's called an "entry control loop."*

Syntax
```
while (loop-condition):
    statement (s)
```

Example
```
x = 5
sum = 0
while (x>0):
    sum = sum + x
    x = x - 1
print ("Sum is:", sum)
```

Output

Sum is: 15

In the above example, The loop keeps running as long as the value of x is more than 0. Once x reaches 0, the loop stops. Inside the loop, we keep subtracting 1 from x with each repetition. At the same time, we add the current value of x to a total sum. This process continues until x becomes 0.

Let's understand the iterations of the above example with the help of a table.

Initial	Condition	Sum	x
Initial	_	0	5
1st Iteration	5 > 0 (True)	0 + 5 = 5	5 - 1 = 4
2nd Iteration	4 > 0 (True)	5 + 4 = 9	4 - 1 = 3
3rd Iteration	3 > 0 (True)	9 + 3 = 12	3 - 1 = 2
4th Iteration	2 > 0 (True)	12 + 2 = 14	2 - 1 = 1
5th Iteration	1 > 0 (True)	14 + 1 = 15	1 - 1 = 0
6th Iteration	0 > 0 (False)	*Loop ends*	

> **TEACHER TIP**
> Always ensure that the loop condition will eventually become false.

Break and Continue

Loops are a great way to repeat tasks, but sometimes we need more control over when and how the loop runs. Python provides two special statements, break and continue, to help us with this.

break statement

The break statement is like a shortcut to exit a loop. When the program reaches a break statement, it immediately stops the loop and continues with the code that comes after the loop.

It's like saying, "I'm done with this loop, let's move on."

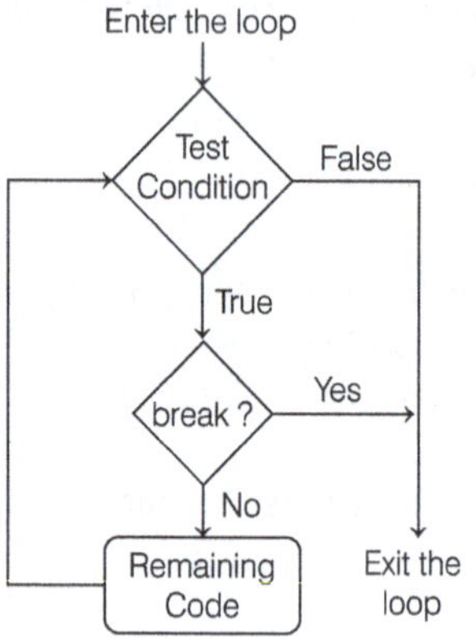

continue statement

The continue statement in Python is used to skip the current iteration of a loop and move to the next iteration.

It only affects the current loop cycle, and the remaining code in the loop for that iteration is not executed.

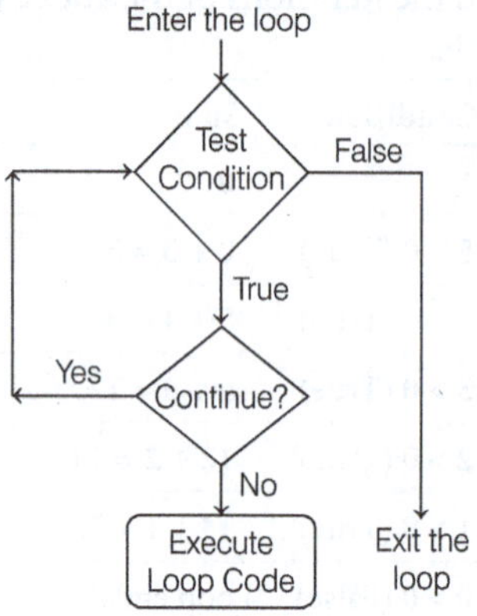

Nested Loops

A nested loop is a loop within a loop. Python has two main types of loops: for loops and while loops. We can combine these loops to create nested loops. It's a way to create more complex patterns of repetition.

Imagine a loop as a box. A nested loop is a smaller box inside the bigger one.

The inner loop runs completely for each iteration of the outer loop.

Syntax of Nested for loop

```
for outer_var in outer_sequence:
  for inner_var in inner_sequence:
    statement_innerLoop
  statement_outerLoop
```

Syntax of Nested while loop

```
while outer_condition:
  while inner_condition:
    statement_innerLoop
  statement_outerLoop
```

e.g.

```
for i in range(2):
  print(i)
  for j in range (10, 13):
    print(j)
```

Inner loop ← (for j in range (10, 13): print(j))
→ Outer loop (whole block)

Output

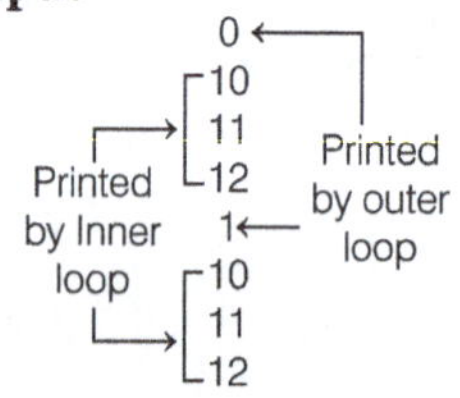

> ## Quick Test 2
> 1. What is a loop in programming? What are the two main types of loops in Python?
> 2. What is the purpose of the range () function in Python?
> 3. When would you use a while loop instead of a for loop?
> 4. What is the output of the following code?
> ```
> for i in range (1, 5):
>   print(i)
> ```
> (a) 1 2 3 4 (b) 0 1 2 3 4
> (c) 1 2 3 4 5 (d) 0 1 2 3
> 5. What is the role of the break and continue statements in loops?
> 6. What are nested loops?

6.2 Programs

1. For accepting an integer from user and checking if this integer is greater than 10.

Ans.
```
a = int(input ("Enter a number:"))
print ("Number is", a)
if (a>10):
    print (a, "is greater than 10")
```

Output

Enter a number: 56
Number is 56
56 is greater than 10

2. For adding a number to non-zero real number x.

Ans.
```
sum = 100.00
x = float (input("Please enter a real
number:"))
print("Real number is",x)
if(x ! = 0.0):
    sum=sum + x
    print("The sum is:", sum)
```

Output

Please enter a real number: 45.9
Real number is 45.9
The sum is: 145.9

3. For asking a user to answer Yes or No to a question such as "Are you ready to provide your credit card number"?

Ans.
```
ans = input ("Are you ready to provide your
credit card number (1=Yes/0 = No):")
print ("Your choice:", ans)
if(ans = = '1'):
    print ("Now we will continue the
    processing of transaction")
elif(ans = = '0'):
    print ("Now we will not continue the
    processing of transaction")
```

Output

Are you ready to provide your credit card number (1=Yes/0 = No):0
Your choice: 0
Now we will not continue the processing of transaction

4. To find the number is even or odd with compound statement.

Ans.
```
n = int(input("Enter a number:"))
print("The number is",n)
d = n%2
if(d= = 0):
    print ("Remainder on division by 2 is:" , d)
    print ("The number is an even number.")
else:
    print("Remainder on division by 2 is:", d)
    print("The number is an odd number.")
```

Output

Enter a number:45
The number is 45
Remainder on division by 2 is: 1
The number is an odd number.

5. To accept a positive value from a user and prints the square of the number.

Ans.
```
n=int(input(" Enter a number:"))
if (n<0):
    print ("Number is negative")
else:
    print (" The square of " ,n, "is" ,n ** 2)
```

Output

Enter a number:6
The square of 6 is 36

6. To enter a character and print whether a given character is an alphabet, digit or any character.

Ans.
```
ch = input ("Enter a character:")
if (((ch>='A') and (ch<='Z')) or ((ch>='a')
and (ch<='z'))):
    print ("You entered an alphabet")
elif(ch>='0' and ch<='9'):
    print ("You entered a digit")
else:
    print ("You entered a character other than
    alphabets and digits")
```

Output

Enter a character:a
You entered an alphabet
>>>
Enter a character:2
You entered a digit

7. To print the largest number out of 3 numbers.

Ans.
```
i = int(input("Enter first number: "))
j = int(input("Enter second number: "))
k = int(input("Enter third number: "))
print("i =", i)
print("j =", j)
print("k =", k)
largest = i
if j > largest:
    largest = j
if k > largest:
    largest = k
print("The largest number is", largest)
```

Output

Enter first number: 78
Enter second number: 54
Enter third number : 23
i = 78
j = 54

k = 23
The largest number is 78

8. For fibonacci series using while loop.

Ans.
```
n=int(input("Enter the limit:"))
i = 1
a = 0
b = 1
while(i<=n):
    print(a)
    c = a+b
    a = b
    b = c
    i = i+1
```
Output
Enter the limit: 10
0
1
1
2
3
5
8
13
21

9. To find the factorial of a given number.

Ans.
```
num = int(input("Enter any number:"))
n = num
f = 1
while(n>0):
    f = f*n
    n = n - 1
print("The factorial of", num," is ", f)
```
Output
Enter any number:5
The factorial of 5 is 120

10. To display quotient and remainder.

Ans.
```
num = int(input("Enter Numerator:"))
den = int(input("Enter Denominator:"))
print("The Quotient is:", num//den)
print("The Remainder is:", num% den)
```
Output
Enter Numerator: 77
Enter Denominator: 2
The Quotient is: 38
The Remainder is: 1

11. Program to print all numbers in a range divisible by a given number.

Ans.
```
l = int(input("Enter lower range:"))
u = int(input("Enter upper range:"))
n = int(input("Enter the number to be divided by:"))
for i in range (l, u+1):
    if (i% n= = 0):
        print (i)
```
Output
Enter lower range : 50
Enter upper range : 100
Enter the number to be divided by : 7
56
63
70
77
84
91
98

Mind Map

CONDITIONAL AND LOOPING STATEMENTS

Control Structure

Sequence

These statements refers to the instructions that are executed in the sequence.

Selection

Conditional statements executes specific action based on a given condition .

01 • **if Statement**

Syntax if(conditional expression):
statement(s)

02 • **if-else Statement**

Syntax if(conditional expression):
statement(s)
else:
statement(s)

03 • **if-elif-else Statement**

Syntax if(condition 1):
statement 1
elif(condition 2):
statement 2
else:
statement 3

04 • **Nested if Statement**

Syntax if(condition 1):
if(condition 2):
statement 1
else:
statement 2
else:
statement 3

Jump Statements

It is used to break the normal flow of the program and jump onto a specific line of code in the program if the specific condition is true.

break Statement

```
for val in sequence
  # code
  if condition:
    break
  # code
```

```
while condition:
  #   code
  if condition:
    break
  # code
```

Continue Statement

```
for val in sequence
  # code
  if condition:
    continue

  # code
```

```
while condition:
  #   code
  if condition:
    continue
  # code
```

Iteration

It commonly known as loops, are statements in programming used to execute part of code repeatedly based on condition or set of conditions.

01 • **for Loop**

Syntax for variable in sequence:
statements(s)

02 • **while Loop**

Syntax while expression:
statement(s)

03 • **Nested Loop**

For nested for loop,

Syntax for iterator_var in sequence:
for iterator_var in sequence:
statements(s)
statements(s)

For nested while loop,

Syntax while expression:
while expression:
statement(s)
statement(s)

Note

range() function returns a sequence of numbers, starting from 0 by default, and increments by 1 (by default), and stops before a specified number.

Syntax range(*start, stop, step*)

NCERT Folder

1. Write a program to repeat the string "GOOD MORNING" n times. Here n is an integer entered by the user.

Ans.
```
n = int(input("Enter the number of times to
repeat: "))
for i in range(n):
print("GOOD MORNING")
```

2. What is the difference between else and elif construct of if statement?

Ans. (a) **else**

- Executes only when the condition of all preceding if and elif statements is False.
- It's a default block that runs if none of the previous conditions are met.
- There can be only one else block in an if statement.

(b) **elif**

- Short for "else if."
- It's used to check additional conditions after the initial if statement.
- Multiple elif blocks can be used to check different conditions sequentially.
- An elif block only executes if the preceding if and elif conditions are False, and its own condition is True.

3. Find the output of the following program segments:

(i)
```
for i in range(20,30,2):
    print(i)
```

(ii)
```
country = 'INDIA'
for i in country:
    print (i)
```

(iii)
```
i = 0; sum = 0
while i < 9:
    if i % 4 == 0:
        sum = sum + i
    i = i + 2
print (sum)
```

Ans. (i) **Output**

20
22
24
26
28

(ii) **Output**

I
N
D
I
A

(iii) **Output**

4

EXAM PATTERN QUESTIONS

Objective Type Questions

Multiple Choice Questions

1. Which Python construct allows you to repeat a block of code multiple times?

(a) Looping (b) Decision (c) Condition (d) Sequence

2. When you use a for loop in Python, where does the counting usually start from?

(a) -1 (b) 0 (c) 1 (d) 10

3. Which statement is a sequence of more than one statements?

(a) Control statement (b) Compound statement
(c) Single statement (d) Sequence statement

4. Which function is used to generate a sequence of numbers overtime?

(a) range ( ) (b) len ( ) (c) limit ( ) (d) lim ( )

5. You are designing a program to simulate a game where players take turns making moves. The game continues until a player wins or a draw occurs. Which programming paradigm is most suitable for implementing the turn-based logic that repeats until a game-ending condition is met? **Competency Based Que.**

(a) Sequence programming
(b) Compound programming
(c) Single-statement programming
(d) Iterative programming

6. **while loops are called as**
(a) entry control loops (b) exit control loops
(c) Both (a) and (b) (d) None of these

7. **A computer program is a set of instructions and are also known as**
(a) compounds (b) statements
(c) blocks (d) comments

8. **Which Python keyword is often used as a placeholder, meaning "do nothing"?**
(a) break (b) continue
(c) pass (d) jump

9. **You are writing a program to determine if a student has passed an exam. The passing score is 60. You have a variable student_score that holds the student's score. Which if statement condition would correctly determine if the student has passed?**
Competency Based Que.
(a) if student_score < 60:
(b) if student_score == 60:
(c) if student_score >= 60:
(d) if student_score != 60:

10. **Which Python statement allows you to choose between two options?**
(a) if (b) for
(c) while (d) print

Fill in the Blanks

11. ________ is the simplest form of decision statement.

12. ______ is used to chain multiple conditions.

13. A set of statements is usually indented ______ spaces inside the if statement.

14. In a for loop, the ______ function is commonly used to generate a sequence of numbers.

15. A _______ statement skips the rest of the loop and jumps over to the statement following the loop.

16. ________ is the only way to figure out the level of nesting.

17. A loop that continues indefinitely without a condition to terminate it is called an ______ loop.

State Whether True or False

18. In Python, you can use the elif statement multiple times within an if-elif-else block. It allows you to check for multiple conditions sequentially.

19. The if statement can only be used to check for equality conditions.

20. You can use logical operators (and, or, not) within the conditions of if and elif statements.

21. A break statement can only be used within a for loop.

22. A continue statement in a loop will immediately terminate the loop and move to the next statement after the loop.

23. In nested loops, the inner loop completes all its iterations for each iteration of the outer loop.

Assertion and Reason Based Questions

Assertion (A) and Reason (R) Type questions. Choose the correct option as:

(a) Both Assertion (A) and Reason (R) are true, and Reason (R) is the correct explanation of Assertion (A).
(b) Both Assertion (A) and Reason (R) are true, but Reason (R) is not the correct explanation of Assertion (A).
(c) Assertion (A) is true, but Reason (R) is false.
(d) Assertion (A) is false, but Reason (R) is true.

24. **Assertion (A)** Indentation is crucial in Python to define code blocks.
Reason (R) Indentation helps the interpreter to understand the structure of the code.

25. **Assertion (A)** An if statement can exist without an accompanying else statement.
Reason (R) The else clause is mandatory when using an if statement to handle all possible conditions.

26. **Assertion (A)** The break statement can be used to exit a loop prematurely.
Reason (R) The break statement immediately terminates the innermost loop.

27. **Assertion (A)** A while loop is an entry-controlled loop.
Reason (R) The loop condition is checked at the end of each iteration.

28. **Assertion (A)** Nested loops can be used to create complex patterns and structures.
Reason (R) Nested loops involve one loop inside another, allowing for multiple levels of iteration.

29. **Assertion (A)** A for loop in Python is used when the number of iterations is known beforehand.
Reason (R) A for loop always executes at least once, even if the condition is false.

30. **Assertion (A)** The range() function in Python generates a sequence of numbers.
Reasong (R) range(5) generates the numbers 0,1,2,3, and 4.

Answers

1. (a) Looping
2. (b) 0
3. (b) Compound statement
4. (a) range ( )
5. (d) Iterative programming
6. (a) entry control loops
7. (b) statements
8. (c) pass
9. (c) if student_score >= 60:
10. (a) if
11. if
12. if-elif
13. 4
14. range
15. break
16. indentations
17. infinite
18. True
19. False
20. True
21. False
22. False
23. True
24. (a) Both Assertion (A) and Reason (R) are true, and Reason (R) is the correct explanation of Assertion (A).
25. (c) Assertion (A) is true, but Reason (R) is false.
26. (a) Both Assertion (A) and Reason (R) are true, and Reason (R) is the correct explanation of Assertion (A).
27. (c) Assertion (A) is true, but Reason (R) is false.
28. (a) Both Assertion (A) and Reason (R) are true, and Reason (R) is the correct explanation of Assertion (A).
29. (c) Assertion (A) is true, but Reason (R) is false.
30. (a) Both Assertion (A) and Reason (R) are true, and Reason (R) is the correct explanation of Assertion (A).

Subjective Type Questions

Very Short Answer Type Questions

1. Define sequence statement.

Ans. Sequence statements refer to the instructions that are executed in the sequence in which they are written in the program.

2. What type of programming logic uses 'if' to decide what to do next? **Competency Based Que.**

Ans. Selection.

3. (a) Define iteration.

(b) What determines how a program runs?

Ans. (a) Iteration is a process of executing a statement or a set of statements repeatedly, until some specific condition is specified.

(b) Flow of control

4. (a) What is the minimum number of iterations that a while loop could make?

(b) What is looping?

Ans. (a) while loop could make minimum 0 iteration.

(b) Looping is also an iteration. It is the ability to perform the same set of operations repeatedly till a specific condition is met.

5. Explain entry controlled loop.

Ans. In an entry controlled loop, the loop control condition is evaluated at the entry point of the loop.

6. What must be defined for a loop to function correctly? **Competency Based Que.**

Ans. Body and exit condition.

7. For iterating over a list with a known length, which loop is most efficient? **Competency Based Que.**

Ans. for loop.

8. Give the output for the following program segment given below.

```
for i in range(-5, -7, -1):
  print (i + 1)
```

Ans. –4

–5

9. Find the output of the following code.

```
i = 1
while (i < 5):
  print (i)
  i = i * 2
```

Ans. Output

1

2

4

10. Write an appropriate loop for the condition-A loop is to be repeated 100 times.

Ans. for i in range (0, 100, +1):

11. List the two looping structures.

Ans. (i) for loop

(ii) while loop

12. What do flowcharts visualize?

Ans. Program flow

13. **How does a flowchart typically read?**

Ans. Top to bottom

14. **How can you create an infinite loop using a while loop? Give an example.**

Ans. To create an infinite while loop, use a condition that's always true.

For example,

```
while True:
  # Code to be repeated infinitely
```

15. **What is the purpose of an else block in a try-except block?**

Ans. The else block in a try-except runs only if no exceptions occur in the try block.

16. **What are the three basic control flow structures in programming?**

Ans. Sequence, Selection, Iteration

Short Answer Type I Questions

17. **Write two different forms of if statement.**

Ans. (i)
```
if (condition):
       statement (s)
```
(ii)
```
if (condition):
       statement 1
else:
       statement 2
```

18. **What is the purpose of the `else` clause in a loop?**

Ans. The `else` clause is executed only if the loop completes normally, without encountering a `break` statement.

19. **What are loops and when do they end?**

Ans. Loops are used to repeatedly execute a block of code. They continue as long as a certain condition remains true. Once the condition becomes false, the loop terminates.

20. **(a) What is the difference between `for` and `while` loops?**

(b) How does a `while` loop work?

Ans. (a) A `for` loop is used to iterate over a sequence of values, while a `while` loop continues as long as a given condition is true.

(b) A `while` loop repeatedly executes a block of code as long as the specified condition is true. Once the condition becomes false, the loop terminates.

21. **Find the syntax error in the following program and underline after correct them.**

```
w = 90:
while (w > 60)
  print(w)
  w = w - 50
```

Ans. Correct code is

```
w = 90
while (w > 60):
  print (w)
  w = w - 50
```

22. **Construct logical expressions to represent the following conditions.**

(i) Weight is greater than or equal to 115 but less than 125.

(ii) Donation is in the range of 4000-5000 or Guest is 1.

Ans. (i) (weight >=115 and weight < 125)

(ii) ((Donation > = 4000 and Donation <= 5000) or Guest = =1)

23. **Write a python program to calculate simple interest and display it.**

Ans.
```
p = int(input("Enter the principle:"))
r = int(input("Enter rate of interest:"))
t = int(input("Enter time:"))
si = (p*r*t)/100
print ("The simple interest is:", si)
```

Output

Enter the principle: 5000

Enter rate of interest: 10

Enter time: 2

The simple interest is 1000.0

24. **Write a program to input three angles and determine if they make a triangle or not.**

Ans.
```
a = float (input("Enter first angle:"))
b = float(input("Enter second  angle:"))
c = float(input("Enter third angle:"))
sum = a+b+c
if (sum == 180):
  print ("These angles will make a triangle")
else:
  print ("These angles will not make a
                                  triangle"
```

Output

Enter first angle: 45.6

Enter second angle: 44.4

Enter third angle: 90.0

These angles will make a triangle

25. **What happens when a `break` statement is encountered in a loop?**

Ans. A `break` statement immediately terminates the loop, and the program continues with the next statement outside the loop.

Short Answer Type II Questions

26. Write a Python program that takes a number n as input and prints the first n Fibonacci numbers. However, for numbers in the Fibonacci sequence that are divisible by 3, print "Fizz", and for numbers divisible by 5, print "Buzz". If a number is divisible by both 3 and 5, print "FizzBuzz". **Competency Based Que.**

Ans.
```
n = int(input("Enter a number: "))
a, b = 0, 1
for i in range(n):
    if a % 3 == 0 and a % 5 == 0:
        print("FizzBuzz", end=" ")
    elif a % 3 == 0:
        print("Fizz", end=" ")
    elif a % 5 == 0:
        print("Buzz", end=" ")
    else:
        print(a, end=" ")
    a, b = b, a + b
```

27. Write a Python program that prints a right-angled triangle pattern of numbers. The number of rows should be taken as input, and the pattern should look like this for n=5: **Competency Based Que.**

```
1
2  3
4  5  6
7  8  9  10
11 12 13 14 15
```

Ans.
```
n = int(input("Enter the number of rows: "))
num = 1  # Start from number 1
for i in range(1, n+1):
    for j in range(i):
        print(num, end=" ")
        num += 1
    print()
```

28. Write a Python program that accepts a series of integers from the user and returns the second smallest odd number. If no odd number is found or if there is only one unique odd number, print "No second smallest odd number". The program should also ignore any negative numbers while processing the input. **Competency Based Que.**

Ans.
```
smallest_odd = float('inf')
second_smallest_odd = float('inf')
n = int(input("Enter the number of
                        integers: "))
for _ in range(n):
    num = int(input("Enter an integer: "))
    if num < 0:
        continue
    if num % 2 != 0:
        if num < smallest_odd:
            second_smallest_odd = smallest_odd
            smallest_odd = num
        elif num < second_smallest_odd and
                        num != smallest_odd:
            second_smallest_odd = num
if second_smallest_odd == float('inf'):
    print("No second smallest odd number")
else:
    print(f"The second smallest odd number
                is: {second_smallest_odd}")
```

Long Answer Type Questions

29. Write a Python program that takes a list of integers and calculates the sum of all prime numbers in the list. The program should also find and print the largest prime number in the list. If no prime number is found, print "No primes found". **Competency Based Que.**

Ans.
```
numbers = [10, 15, 7, 23, 19, 11, 4]
prime_sum = 0
largest_prime = -1
for num in numbers:
    if num <= 1:
        continue
    is_prime = True
    for i in range(2, int(num ** 0.5) + 1):
        if num % i == 0:
            is_prime = False
            break
    if is_prime:
        prime_sum += num
        if num > largest_prime:
            largest_prime = num
if largest_prime == -1:
    print("No primes found")
else:
    print(f"Sum of primes: {prime_sum}")
    print(f"Largest prime: {largest_prime}")
```

Output

Sum of primes : 60

Largest prime : 23

30. An electricity board charges according to the following rules:

- For the first 100 units - 40 P per unit
- For the next 200 units - 50 P per unit
- Beyond 300 units - 60 P per unit
- All users have to pay a meter charge also, which is 50.

Write a program to read the number of units consumed and print out the charges.

Ans.
```
units = int(input("Enter the number of
units consumed: "))
charges = 0.0
if units <= 100:
  charges = units * 0.4 + 50
elif units <= 300:
  charges = (units - 100) * 0.5 + 40 + 50
else:
  charges = (units - 300) * 0.6 + 140 + 50
print("The charges is:", charges)
```

Output

Enter the number of units consumed: 125

The charges is: 102.5

31. **Write a program in Python to find and display income tax with the help of following rules:**

Monthly Salary	Income Tax
9000 or more	40% of monthly salary
7500-8999	30% of monthly salary
7499 or less	20% of monthly salary

Ans.
```
salary = int(input("Enter monthly salary: "))
if (salary >= 9000):
  itax = salary * 0.40
elif (salary >= 7500 and salary < 9000):
  itax = salary * 0.30
elif (salary <= 7499):
  itax = salary * 0.20
print("Income tax is:", itax)
```

Output

Enter monthly salary: 15000

Income tax is: 6000.0

32. **A small retail store is developing an inventory management system. They need a module that calculates the profit or loss for each item sold. Write a Python program that takes the cost price and selling price of an item as input and determines whether there is a profit, a loss, or no gain/loss. Ensure the program handles invalid inputs appropriately.**

Competency Based Que.

Ans.
```
cost_price = float(input("Enter Cost
                              Price: "))
selling_price = float(input("Enter
                         Selling Price: "))
if cost_price < 0 or selling_price < 0:
    print("Invalid input! Prices cannot be
                              negative.")
elif selling_price > cost_price:
    profit = selling_price - cost_price
    print(f"Profit: {profit}")
elif selling_price < cost_price:
    loss = cost_price - selling_price
    print(f"Loss: {loss}")
else:
    print("No Profit, No Loss")
```

Output

Enter Cost Price : 500

Enter Selling Price : 300

Loss : 200.0

33. **A science education website wants to provide a simple temperature conversion tool for its users. Write a Python program that takes a temperature value and its unit (Celsius or Fahrenheit) as input and converts it to the other unit. Ensure the program handles invalid inputs appropriately.**

Ans.
```
temperature = float(input("Enter
                       temperature value: "))
unit = input("Enter unit (C for Celsius,
      F for Fahrenheit): ").strip().upper()
if unit == "C":
    fahrenheit = (temperature * 9/5) + 32
    print(f"{temperature}°C is equal to
                        {fahrenheit:.2f}°F")
elif unit == "F":
    celsius = (temperature - 32) * 5/9
    print(f"{temperature}°F is equal to
                           {celsius:.2f}°C")
else:
    print("Invalid unit! Please enter 'C'
        for Celsius or 'F' for Fahrenheit.")
```

Output

Enter temperature value : 52

Enter unit (C for Celsius, F for Fahrenheit) : C

52.0°C is equal to 125.60°F

34. **Write a Python program to input the marks of 5 subjects and print their sum and average. Also, find the grade according to given conditions:**

Average	Grade
>=90 and <=100	A+
>=81 and <=90	A
>=71 and <=80	B+

Average	Grade
>=61 and <=70	B
>=51 and <=60	C+
>=41 and <=50	C
>=0 and <=40	F

Ans.
```
print("Enter marks obtained in 5 subjects: ")
mark1 = int(input())
mark2 = int(input())
mark3 = int(input())
mark4 = int(input())
mark5 = int(input())
sum = mark1 + mark2 + mark3 + mark4 + mark5
average = sum  / 5
print("Total of marks:", sum)
print("Average:", average)
if (average > 91 and average <= 100):
  print("Your Grade is A+")
elif (average > 81 and average <= 90):
  print("Your Grade is A")
elif (average > 71 and average <= 80):
  print("Your Grade is B+")
elif (average > 61 and average <= 70):
  print("Your Grade is B")
elif (average > 51 and average <= 60):
  print("Your Grade is C+")
elif (average >= 41 and average <= 50):
  print("Your Grade is  C")
elif (average >= 0 and average <= 40):
  print("Your Grade is F")
else:
  print ("Strange Grade..!!")
```

Output

Enter marks obtained in 5 subjects:

95

88

92

89

90

Total of marks: 454

Average: 90.8

Your Grade is A+

35. Write a Python program to input some amount and calculate discount based on the amount and give rate. Also, display its output.

Average	Grade
0-5000	5%
5000-15000	12%
15000-25000	20%
above-25000	30%

Ans.
```
amount = int(input('Enter Sale Amount: '))
if amount <= 0:
    print('Invalid Amount')
    # No discount for invalid amounts
elif amount <= 5000:
    discount = amount * 0.05
    # 5%
elif 5000 < amount <= 15000:
    discount = amount * 0.12
    # 12%
elif 15000 < amount <= 25000:
    discount = amount * 0.2
    # 20%
else:
    discount = amount * 0.3
    # 30%
print('Discount:', discount)
print('Net Pay:', amount - discount)
```

Output

Enter Sale Amount: 10000

Discount: 1200.0

Net Pay: 8800.0

36. Explain the concept of loop control elements in the context of a `while` loop in Python. How do these elements work together to control the flow of a loop?

Ans. Loop control elements are essential components that govern the execution of a `while` loop in Python. They work together to determine when the loop starts, continues, and ultimately terminates.

Key Loop Control Elements

- **Initialization Expression** This expression initializes the loop variable before the loop begins. - It sets an initial value for the variable that will be used in the test expression.
- **Test Expression** This expression is evaluated at the beginning of each iteration. - If the expression evaluates to `True`, the loop body is executed. - If the expression evaluates to `False`, the loop terminates.
- **Loop Body** The loop body contains the statements that are executed repeatedly. - The statements within the loop body are indented to indicate their belonging to the loop.
- **Update Expression** This expression modifies the loop variable during each iteration. It ensures that the loop eventually terminates by changing the value of the test expression.

Example

```
count = 0                   # Initialization
while count < 5:            # Test expression
  print("Hello, world!")
  count += 1                # Update expression
```

37. Write a Python program to generate and print:

(i) All prime numbers between 1 and 50.

(ii) Numbers in the sequence 5, 10, 15, ..., 50, but replace multiples of 10 with "X".

Ans. (i)
```
print("Prime numbers between 1 and 50:")
for num in range(2, 51):
    is_prime = True
    for i in range(2, int(num ** 0.5) + 1):
        if num % i == 0:
            is_prime = False
            break
    if is_prime:
        print(num, end=" ")
print("\n")
```

Output

Prime numbers between 1 and 50:

2 3 5 7 11 13 17 19 23 29 31 37 41 43 47

(ii)
```
print("Sequence with multiples of 10 replaced by 'X':")
for num in range(5, 51, 5):
    if num % 10 == 0:
        print("X", end=" ")
    else:
        print(num, end=" ")
```

Output

Sequence with multiples of 10 replaced by 'X':

5 X 15 X 25 X 35 X 45 X

38. Write a program to display a triangle of numbers using a for loop within a while loop.

Ans.
```
x = 1
while x <= 6:
    for y in range(1, x + 1):
        print(x, end="")
            print()
x = x + 1
```

Output

1

22

333

4444

55555

666666

39. Write a Python program to input the price of items and calculate the sales tax on 6%. Also, display its output.

Ans.
```
n = int(input("Enter the number of items
                      which you want to buy: "))
sub_total = 0
i = 1
while i <= n:
    item = int(input("Enter the price of an
                                  item: "))
    i = i + 1
    sub_total = sub_total + item
    sales_tax = sub_total * 0.06
    total = sub_total + sales_tax
print ("Sub total:", sub_total)
print ("Sales tax:", sales_tax)
print ("Amount including sales tax:", total)
```

Output

Enter the number of items which you want to buy:5

Enter the price of an item:120

Enter the price of an item:100

Enter the price of an item:350

Enter the price of an item:450

Enter the price of an item:840

Sub total: 1860

Sales tax: 1116.0

Amount including sales tax: 2976.0

Case Study Based Questions

Case Study 1

Looping is a powerful programming construct that allows us to repeatedly execute a block of code. Python provides two primary loop structures: `for` loops and `while` loops.

- **A `for` loop is used to iterate over a sequence of items, such as a list, tuple, or string. It's often used when we know the number of iterations in advance.**
- **A `while` loop repeatedly executes a block of code as long as a given condition is true. It's useful when we don't know the exact number of iterations beforehand.**

Based on the above information, answer the following questions.

(i) What is the purpose of a loop in Python?
(a) To execute a block of code repeatedly.
(b) To make decisions based on conditions.
(c) To define functions.
(d) To handle input and output.

(ii) Which loop is used to iterate over a sequence of items?
(a) while loop (b) for loop
(c) do-while loop (d) repeat-until loop

(iii) What is the condition for a while loop to continue execution?
(a) The loop variable must be less than a certain value.
(b) The loop variable must be greater than a certain value.
(c) The loop condition must evaluate to True.
(d) The loop condition must evaluate to False.

(iv) What is the difference between a for loop and a while loop?
(a) A for loop is used for definite iteration, while a while loop is used for indefinite iteration.
(b) A for loop is used for indefinite iteration, while a while loop is used for definite iteration.
(c) Both loops are used for the same purpose.
(d) None of the above.

(v) Which loop is more suitable for iterating over a list of items?
(a) while loop (b) for loop
(c) Both are equally suitable (d) Neither is suitable

(vi) Can a while loop execute indefinitely?
(a) Yes, if the loop condition is always true.
(b) No, a while loop always terminates after a fixed number of iterations.
(c) It depends on the specific implementation of the loop.
(d) None of the above.

Ans. (i) (a) To execute a block of code repeatedly
(ii) (b) for loop
(iii) (c) The loop condition must evaluate to True.
(iv) (a) A for loop is used for definite iteration, while a while loop is used for indefinite iteration.
(v) (b) for loop
(vi) (a) Yes, if the loop condition is always true.

Case Study 2

Consider the following program to find the number is even or odd with compound statement.

```
n = int(input("Enter a number: "))          #Line 1
print("The number is", __)                  #Line 2
d = _____                                   #Line 3
if d == _:                                  #Line 4
  print("Remainder on division by 2 is:", d)
                                            #Line 5
  print("The number is an even number.")
                                            #Line 6
_____                                       #Line 7
  print("Remainder on division by 2 is:",
  ________)                                 #Line 8
  print("The number is an odd number.")
                                            #Line 9
```

Based on the above program, answer the following questions.

(i) Name the variable which will print by Line 2.
(a) d (b) n
(c) input (d) "Enter a number: "

(ii) Fill in the blank in Line 3.
(a) n / 2 (b) n * 2 (c) n % 2 (d) n - 2

(iii) Which value will be equal to d to satisfy the condition in Line 4?
(a) 1 (b) 2
(c) 0 (d) Any number

(iv) Fill in the blank in Line 7.
(a) if d == 1: (b) else:
(c) elif d == 1: (d) if d != 0:

(v) Which value will come to print to the odd number?
(a) 0 (b) 1 (c) n (d) d

Ans. (i) (b) n (ii) (c) n % 2
(iii) (c) 0 (iv) (b) else: (v) (d) d

SELF ASSESSMENT TEST

Multiple Choice Questions

1. for loop is also known as

(a) entry control loop (b) exit control loop
(c) Both (a) and (b) (d) None of these

2. Iterative statements evaluate the loop condition either.

(a) True (b) False
(c) Both (a) and (b) (d) None of these

3. Find the appropriate loop for the condition when a for loop is to be repeated 50 times.

(a) for i in range (0, 50, 1) : (b) for i in in range (1, 50, 1) :
(c) for i in range (0, 51, 1) : (d) for i in range (0, 1, 50) :

Fill in the Blanks

4. ________ is used to define code blocks in Python.
5. The ________ statement is used to exit a loop prematurely.
6. The ________ statement is used to skip the current iteration of a loop.
7. A loop within a loop is called a ________ loop.
8. ________ statements are used for decision-making in Python.

State Whether True or False

9. Indentation is optional in Python.
10. The break statement exits the current loop.
11. The continue statement skips the remaining code in the current iteration.
12. Nested loops cannot be used in Python.
13. The if-elif-else statement allows multiple conditions to be checked.

Assertion and Reason Based Questions

Assertion (A) and Reason (R) Type questions. Choose the correct option as:

(a) Both Assertion (A) and Reason (R) are true, and Reason (R) is the correct explanation of Assertion (A).
(b) Both Assertion (A) and Reason (R) are true, but Reason (R) is not the correct explanation of Assertion (A).
(c) Assertion (A) is true, but Reason (R) is false.
(d) Assertion (A) is false, but Reason (R) is true.

14. **Assertion (A)** Indentation is crucial in Python.
Reason (R) Indentation defines code blocks and ensures proper flow control.

15. **Assertion (A)** The break statement can be used to terminate a loop.
Reason (R) The break statement immediately exits the innermost loop.

16. **Assertion (A)** The continue statement exits the entire loop.
Reason (R) Python supports nested loops for complex iterations.

17. **Assertion (A)** Nested loops allow for complex iterations.
Reason (R) Nested loops are used when an inner loop needs to be executed multiple times for each iteration of an outer loop.

18. **Assertion (A)** Python loops always require a break statement to terminate.
Reason (R) Python's indentation rules enhance code readability.

Very Short Answer Type Question

19. Write one difference between for loop and while loop.

Short Answer Type Questions

20. Find the syntax errors, if any, in the following program.

```
max = 0
a = int (input("Enter the value of a"))
b = int (input ("Enter the value of b"))
if (a>>b):
max = a
print (max):
```

21. What are the logical constructs used in for loop?
22. Write a program to find the sum of 3 numbers.
23. Is it necessary to write else with every if statement while writing nested if statements?
24. What will be the output?

(a)
```
if (44):
    print ("Forty four")
else:
    print ("None")
```

(b)
```
if (0):
    print ("Zero")
```

(c)
```
if(10 == 5):
    print ("Equal")
else:
    print("Not equal")
```

Long Answer Type Questions

25. Differentiate between if and if-else statements.

26. Give the purpose of iteration statement. What are the other names by which a iteration statement is referred to?

27. Describe a nested if statement.

28. Write a program that will allow an integer from 1 to 7 to be input and the name of the day of week corresponding to the integer to be output.

29. Write a program to input marks in five subjects. Find average and awards grades as per the following guidelines.

Percentage	Grade
90% and above	A
89% and 80%	B
79% and 70%	C
69% and 60%	D
59% and 50%	E
Less than 50%	Fail

30. Write Python program to sum the following series.

(i) $S = 1 + \frac{1}{2} + \frac{1}{3} + \frac{1}{4} + \frac{1}{5} + \frac{1}{6} + ... + n \text{ terms}$

(ii) $S = 1 + \frac{1}{1^2} + \frac{1}{2^3} + \frac{1}{3^4} + ... + n \text{ terms}$

Case Study Based Questions

31. A ticket vending machine needs to determine the ticket price based on the customer's age. If the customer is under 12, the ticket price is half. If the customer is 65 or older, the ticket price is also half. Otherwise, the ticket price is full. The machine also needs to handle invalid inputs gracefully.

(i) Which flow control structure is most suitable for determining the ticket price based on age?

(a) for loop (b) while loop
(c) if-elif-else statement (d) break statement

(ii) To ensure the machine handles invalid age inputs, what type of flow control would be useful?

(a) continue statement (b) nested loops
(c) selection (d) repetition

(iii) If the machine needs to repeat the process until a valid age is entered, which flow control structure would be used?

(a) for loop
(b) while loop
(c) break statement
(d) continue statement

(iv) If the machine needs to stop the current transaction and start a new one if an error occurs, the machine will use:

(a) nested loops
(b) continue statement
(c) break statement
(d) if statements.

(v) The code blocks within the if-elif-else statements are defined by:

(a) Semicolons (b) Curly braces
(c) Indentation (d) Parentheses

Answers

1. (a)	2. (a)	3. (a)	4. Indentation
5. break	6. continue	7. nested	8. if-elif-else
9. False	10. True	11. True	12. False	13. True
14. (a)	15. (a)	16. (d)	17. (a)	18. (d)

31. (i) → (c), (ii) → (c), (iii) → (b), (iv) → (b), (v) → (c)

07
CHAPTER

In this chapter, we will explore different types of errors in Python, debugging techniques, and tools that help troubleshoot and resolve issues efficiently.

YOUR STUDY GOALS

YOUR PRACTICE GOAL

- Objective Type Questions
  (21 Qs ; MCQs, True or False, Fill in the Blanks, Assertion and Reason)
- Subjective Type Questions
  (27 Qs ; VSA, SA, LA)
- Case Study Based Question-1

Debugging Programs

When a computer program doesn't work as expected, there's likely a mistake in the code, called a bug. Developers use debugging to carefully examine the code, piece by piece, to find and fix these bugs.

This helps to ensure the program works correctly and reliably. While debugging helps to identify and fix problems, testing is still necessary to make sure the program meets all its requirements.

7.1 Error Messages

An error message is a notification displayed by a computer or software program when something goes wrong. It's like a warning sign that alerts you to a problem.

A computer program error, caused by human mistakes in code or design, can lead to incorrect results or unexpected behavior.

Some common form of program errors are as given below

Compile-time Errors

All the errors that are detected and displayed by the compiler or interpreter are known as compile-time errors. Whenever the compiler displays an error, it will not be able to run.

It is therefore necessary that we fix all the errors so that we can successfully compile and run the program.

There are two categories of compile-time errors as follows

(i) Syntax errors
(ii) Semantic errors

Syntax Error

When a formal set of rules defined for writing a program in a particular language is not followed then error raised is known as syntax error.

Syntax errors occur when syntax rules of any programming language are violated.

Common Python syntax errors include

- Leaving out a keyword
- Putting a keyword in the wrong place
- Leaving out a symbol, such as a colon, comma or brackets
- Misspelling a keyword
- Incorrect indentation
- Empty block

For example,

```
def add_function( )
  msg = "How are you ?"
  print(msg)
  add_function( )
```

Here, Python is telling us that there's a mistake in the way we've written the code on the first line. The problem is that we forgot to put a colon (:) at the end of line 1 where we define the function.

If we fix that, we'll find another mistake. The lines inside the function aren't lined up correctly. They should all start at the same place to show that they belong together.

The correct code is

```
def add_function ():
  msg = "How are you ?"
  print (msg)
add_function ()
```

Semantic Error

This type of compile time error indicates an improper use of Python statements.

These errors occur when statements are not meaningful. The word "semantics" relates to the meaning of words, **sentences or programs.**

For example,

```
a = 10
b = 15
a + b = c
print (c)
```

Output

```
SyntaxError: can't assign to operator.
```

In the above code, the statement a + b = c will result in a semantic error as an expression cannot come on the left side of an assignment operator.

So, it will show an error message.

> **Mistake Alert**
>
> Some students might not pay attention to error messages, which can make it harder for them to find and fix problems in their code.

Run-time Errors

A run-time error occurs during a program's execution, after it has started running. It happens when the program encounters a situation it cannot handle, like dividing by zero or accessing invalid memory. These errors cause the program to abruptly stop or produce incorrect results.

Debugging tools are often needed to identify and fix run-time errors.

Common Python run-time errors include

- Division by zero
- Performing an operation on incompatible types
- Using an identifier which has not been defined
- Accessing a list element, dictionary value or object attribute which does not exist
- Trying to access a file which does not exist

For example,

```
b = 0
a = 5
c = a / b
print ("The value of c is : ", c)
```

Output

```
ZeroDivisionError: integer division or module by zero
```

Here, this program will crash when it runs because you can't divide a number by zero.

Logical Errors

A logical error in programming occurs when a program runs without crashing but produces incorrect or unintended results. It happens due to flaws in the program's logic, such as incorrect conditions or calculations. These errors are difficult to detect because there are no syntax or runtime errors, and debugging requires careful testing.

Note *When a wrong formula is used to calculate any mathematical expression it gives logical error.*

Common Python logical errors include

- Using the wrong variable name
- Indenting a block to the wrong level
- Getting operator precedence wrong
- Making a mistake in a boolean expression

For example,

```
a = 7
b = 6
c = 5
avg = a * b * c/3
print(" The average is: ", avg)
```

Output

The average is 70.

The code should give us the answer 6, but it's actually giving 70. Even though the code looks right to the computer, there's a mistake in how we told it to calculate the average. We used the wrong formula.

The correct formula should be:

```
avg = (a + b + c) / 3
```

TEACHER TIP

Error messages are like hints that can help you find and fix problems in your code. Always pay attention to them and use them to figure out what's wrong.

Quick Test 1

1. Describe the process of "debugging" and why it's important for programmers.
2. Which of the following is NOT a type of runtime error in Python?
   (a) Division by zero (b) Index out of range
   (c) Syntax error (d) File not found
3. What is the difference between a syntax error and a semantic error?
4. Discuss the common types of runtime errors that can occur in Python programs and how to handle them.

7.2 Python Exception

An exception is like a roadblock in a program's journey. When this happens, the program stops and can't continue. To handle these roadblocks, we use exception handling. This helps us to deal with errors and unexpected situations in the program, which makes it more robust.

Exception Handling

Exception handling is a way to automatically deal with errors in a program. Many programming languages, including Python, have built-in tools for this. There are certain situations where errors are more likely to happen while the program is running.

When we try to read a file or get input from a user, things can sometimes go wrong.

For example, the file might be missing or the user might enter the wrong type of data. To handle these situations, we use a try-except block. We put the code that might cause an error in the try block. If an error occurs, the code in the except block will run, allowing us to handle the problem gracefully.

Syntax

```
try :
   {Run this code}
except:
   {Run this code if an exception occurs}
```

For example,

```
try:
   age = int (input ("Please enter your
                                    age: "))
   print (" I see that you are % d years
                          old . " % age)
except:
   print (" Hey, that was not a number !!")
```

Python will try to run the code inside the try block. If it encounters an error, it will stop running the try block and immediately jump to the except block. Any code that comes after the error in the try block will be skipped.

7.3 Python Built-in Exceptions

Python provides some basic exception classes which are already defined and can be used in generic cases.

Exception Class	Event
Exception	Base class for all exceptions.
ArithmeticError	Raised when numeric calculations fails.
AssertionError	Raised when Assert statement fails.
FloatingPointError	Raised when a floating point calculation fails.
ImportError	Raised when the imported module is not found.
IndexError	Raised when index of a sequence is out of range.
IndentationError	Raised when there is incorrect indentation.

Exception Class	Event
IOError	Raised when an input / output operation fails.
KeyboardInterrupt	Raised when the user interrupts program execution, generally by pressing Ctrl + C.
KeyError	Raised when the specified key is not found in the dictionary.
OverflowError	Raised when result of an arithmetic operation is too large to be represented.
NameError	Raised when an identifier is not found in the local or global namespace.
RuntimeError	Raised when a generated error does not fall into any category.
SyntaxError	Raised by parser when syntax error is encountered.
TypeError	Raised when a function or operation is applied to an object of incorrect type.
ValueError	Raised when a function gets argument of correct type but improper value.
ZeroDivisionError	Raised when division or module by zero takes place for all numeric types.
StopIteration	Raised when the next ( ) method of an iterator does not point to any object.
AttributeError	Raised in case of failure of attribute reference or assignment.
EOFError	Raised when there is no input from either raw_input ( ) or input ( ) function and the end of file is reached.

The finally block

The finally block in Python is used in exception handling and always executes, regardless of whether an exception occurs or not. It is typically used for cleanup actions like closing files or releasing resources.

Syntax

```
try:
   # block of code
   # this may throw an exception
finally:
   # block of code
   # this will always be executed
```

For example,

```
try:
   file1 = open ("Dairy.txt", "r")
   try:
      file1 . write ("Python Programming")
   finally:
      file1.  close ( )
      print (" Diary file closed")
except:
   print (" Error")
```

Output

Diary file closed

Error

Raising Exceptions

Raising an exception in Python is done using the raise keyword, which lets you manually trigger a specific exception to indicate an error or unwanted condition in the program.

Syntax

```
raise Exception_class, <value>
```

For example,

```
try:
   marks = int (input ("Enter the marks: "))
   if marks <30:
      raise ValueError
   else:
      print ("The marks are valid")
except ValueError:
   print ("The marks are not valid")
```

Output

Enter the marks: 25

The marks are not valid

Quick Test 2

1. What is the base class for all exceptions in Python?
2. Explain the concept of exception handling in Python. What are the key components involved?
3. How can you use the try-except block to handle exceptions in Python? Provide an example.
4. What is the purpose of the finally block in Python exception handling?

Mind Map

DEBUGGING PROGRAMS

Error Messages

An error message is a notification displayed by a computer or software program when something goes wrong.

Compile-time Errors

All the errors that are detected and displayed by the compiler or interpreter are known as compile-time errors. Whenever the compiler displays an error, it will not be able to run.

Syntax Error

When a formal set of rules defined for writing a program in a particular language is not followed then error raised is known as syntax error.

Semantic Error

These errors occur when statements are not meaningful. The word "semantics" relates to the meaning of words, sentences or programs.

Run-time Errors

Even if a program compiles and links without errors, it doesn't guarantee that it will run correctly. Sometimes, errors can occur while the program is running, leading to unexpected results or the program crashing. These are known as runtime errors.

Logical Errors

Sometimes, a program can run without crashing, but it still gives the wrong answer. This is because of logical errors, which are mistakes in the way the programmer has designed the program. These errors are the hardest to find and fix.

Exception Handling

Exception handling is a way to automatically deal with errors in a program

try-except Block

Syntax

```
try :
   {Run this code}
except:
   {Run this code if an
    exception occurs}
```

finally Block

Syntax

```
try:
   # block of code
   # this may throw an
     exception
finally:
   # block of code
   # this will always be
     executed
```

Raising Exceptions

Syntax

```
raise Exception_class,<value>
```

Python Built-in Exceptions

Exception	Class Event
Exception	Cause of Error
Arithmetic Error	Raised when numeric calculations fails.
Assertion Error	Raised when an assert statement fails.
Attribute Error	Raised when attribute assignment or reference fails.
EOF Error	Raised when the input() function hits end-of-file condition.
Floating Point Error	Raised when a floating point operation fails.
Import Error	Raised when the imported module is not found.
Index Error	Raised when the index of a sequence is out of range.
IO Error	Raised when an input/output operation fails.
Key Error	Raised when a key is not found in a dictionary.
Keyboard Interrupt	Raised when the user hits the interrupt key (Ctrl+C or Delete).
Name Error	Raised when a variable is not found in local or global scope.
Overflow Error	Raised when the result of an arithmetic operation is too large to be represented.
Runtime Error	Raised when an error does not fall under any other category.
Stop Iteration	Raised by next() function to indicate that there is no further item to be returned by iterator.
Syntax Error	Raised by parser when syntax error is encountered.
Indentation Error	Raised when there is incorrect indentation.
Type Error	Raised when a function or operation is applied to an object of incorrect type.
Value Error	Raised when a function gets an argument of correct type but improper value.
Zero Division Error	Raised when the second operand of division or modulo operation is zero.

EXAM PATTERN QUESTIONS

Objective Type Questions

Multiple Choice Questions

1. Errors are called as

(a) bugs (b) defects
(c) Both (a) and (b) (d) None of these

2. The process of identifying and fixing errors in a program is called:

(a) Compiling (b) Debugging (c) Testing (d) Executing

3. All the errors that are detected and displaced by the compiler or interpreter are known as

(a) Run time errors (b) Compile time errors
(c) Logical errors (d) None of these

4. Which of the following code snippets would prevent a Python program from being executed due to a syntax error? **Competency Based Que.**

(a) if x > 5 (b) print("Hello")
(c) for i in range(10): print(i) (d) All of the above

5. A program is running and encounters a problem that causes it to halt execution abruptly. Which of the following error types is most likely the cause? **Competency Based Que.**

(a) Run time (b) Compile time (c) Semantic (d) Syntax

6. _______ is a computer program used by programmers to test and debug a target program.

(a) Logical error (b) Runtime error
(c) Debugger (d) Break point

7. Which two activities are closely related and often go hand-in-hand in software development?

(a) Coding and Debugging
(b) Testing and Debugging
(c) Compiling and Linking
(d) Designing and Implementing

Fill in the Blanks

8. __________ is an error in the code.

9. Compile time errors can _____ or _____.

10. Debugging is the process of finding error in a _____.

11. Logical error is due to some mistake in the ____.

12. A set of rules which give the meaning of a statement are _________.

State Whether True or False

13. A syntax error in Python will always prevent a program from running, even if the logic is correct.

14. A program that compiles without errors is guaranteed to run correctly and produce the desired output.

15. Indentation is crucial in Python and incorrect indentation can lead to syntax errors.

16. Logical errors are the easiest type of programming errors to find and fix because they always produce obvious incorrect output.

17. The finally block in Python is only executed if no exceptions occur within the corresponding try block.

Assertion and Reason Based Questions

Assertion (A) and Reason (R) Type questions. Choose the correct option as:

(a) Both Assertion (A) and Reason (R) are true, and Reason (R) is the correct explanation of Assertion (A).
(b) Both Assertion (A) and Reason (R) are true, but Reason (R) is not the correct explanation of Assertion (A).
(c) Assertion (A) is true, but Reason (R) is false.
(d) Assertion (A) is false, but Reason (R) is true.

18. **Assertion (A)** Debugging is a crucial step in software development.

Reason (R) Debugging helps to identify and fix errors in code, leading to more reliable and efficient software.

19. **Assertion (A)** Syntax errors are detected during the compilation process.

Reason (R) Syntax errors are caused by violations of the programming language's grammar rules.

20. **Assertion (A)** Runtime errors occur during the execution of a program.

Reason (R) Runtime errors are caused by logical errors in the code.

21. **Assertion (A)** A debugger is a tool used to identify and fix errors in code.

Reason (R) A debugger allows programmers to step through code execution line by line and inspect variables.

Answers

1. (c) Both (a) and (b)
2. (b) Debugging
3. (b) Compile time errors
4. (a) if x > 5
5. (a) Run time
6. (c) Debugger
7. (b) Testing and Debugging
8. Bug
9. syntax error, semantic errors
10. program
11. program logic
12. semantics
13. True
14. False
15. True
16. False
17. False
18. (a) Both Assertion (A) and Reason (R) are true, and Reason (R) is the correct explanation of Assertion (A).
19. (a) Both Assertion (A) and Reason (R) are true, and Reason (R) is the correct explanation of Assertion (A).
20. (c) Assertion (A) is true, but Reason (R) is false.
21. (a) Both Assertion (A) and Reason (R) are true, and Reason (R) is the correct explanation of Assertion (A).

Subjective Type Questions

Very Short Answer Type Questions

1. What do you mean by a bug?

Ans. An error, sometimes called 'a bug' is anything in the code that prevents a program from compiling and running correctly.

2. Define debugging in the context of software development. **Competency Based Que.**

Ans. Debugging is the process of identifying and removing errors (bugs) from a computer program.

3. How many types of compile-time errors?

Ans. There are two types of compile-time errors as follows.

(i) Syntax error (ii) Semantic error

4. Name the different types of errors.

Ans. (i) Syntax error (ii) Run-time error (iii) Logical error

5. What do you mean by syntax of a program?

Ans. Syntax are the set of rules and regulations governing to the construction of a valid statement in a programming language.

6. What do you mean by syntax error ?

Ans. Errors which occur when the programming rules are violated called syntax errors.

7. What type of errors can be detected by a compiler?

Ans. Syntax error

8. Identify the type of error that occurs during program execution. **Competency Based Que.**

Ans. Run-time errors

9. When is the IndexError exception class used in a program ?

Ans. IndexError is raised when the index of a sequence is out of range.

10. Which exception class is used when the imported module is not found ?

Ans. ImportError

11. Write the syntax of raising exceptions.

Ans. raise Exception_class, <value>

12. Name the block in exception handling that guarantees execution regardless of whether an exception occurs.

Ans. Finally block **Competency Based Que.**

Short Answer Type I Questions

13. What is debugging?

Ans. Debugging is the process of finding and fixing errors in a program that cause it to malfunction or behave unexpectedly.

14. Differentiate between testing and debugging.

Ans. Differences between testing and debugging errors are as follows:

Feature	Testing	Debugging
Goal	To uncover errors within a software program.	To find the cause of errors and correct them within a software program.
Process	Running the software and observing its behavior.	Examining the code to understand its execution and identify the source of errors.
Outcome	A list of issues found (or confirmation that none were found).	Improved code where the identified errors have been removed or resolved.

15. What do you mean by compile-time error?

Ans. All the errors that are detected and displayed by the compiler or interpreter are known as compile-time errors.

Whenever the compiler displays an error, it will not be able to run. It is therefore necessary that we fix all the errors so that we can successfully compile and run the program.

16. Identify and describe two distinct categories of errors that can prevent a program from compiling successfully.

Ans. Two major categories of compile-time errors are

(i) **Syntax errors** These are violations of the programming language's rules, like missing semicolons or incorrect keywords. The compiler can't understand the code's structure.

(ii) **Semantic errors** These happen when the code is grammatically correct but doesn't make logical sense, like using an undeclared variable or mismatched data types. The compiler understands the structure but can't execute it due to logical flaws.

17. Underline the syntax errors in the following program.

```
a = int(input(" Enter first number : ")
b = int(input(" Enter second number : "))
print(" a = ", a, end = "", "b = ", c)
c = a + b:
print d
```

Ans. The syntax errors are

```
a = int (input (" Enter first number : "))
b = int (input (" Enter second number : "))
print(" a = ", a, end = " ", "b = ", b)
c = a + b
print c
```

18. What are differences between compile-time and run-time errors?

Ans. Differences between compile-time and run-time errors are as follows:

Compile-time error	Run-time error
Compile-time errors are caught by the compiler, when we compile the program for error.	Run-time errors arise, when a program is in execution state.
For example, an incorrect syntax like missing paranthesis or semicolon.	*For example,* division by zero.

19. Differentiate between a logical error and syntax error. Also, give suitable examples of each in Python.

Ans. Differences between a logical error and syntax error are as follows:

Logical Error	Syntax Error
It occurs because of wrong implementation of logic.	It occurs when statements are wrongly written violating rules of the programming language.
With logical errors, the code is syntactically correct and compiler will not show any error message.	With syntax errors, the code is not syntactically correct and compiler will show the error messages.
It produces the output, but undesired.	It does not produce any output.
For example, if in place of (c = a * b); if by mistake (c = a + b); is written, it will be a logical error.	*For example,* if in place of if (a == b): if by mistake if (a == b), is written, it will be a syntax error.

20. The code given below will give an error on execution. Identify the type of the error and modify the code to handle such type of an error.

```
a = int(input(" Enter the value of a : "))
b = int(input(" Enter the value of b : "))
c = a/b
```

Ans. The error is run-time error

```
a = int(input("Enter the value of a:"))
b = int(input("Enter the value of b:"))
   if(b! = 0):
   c = a/b
```

21. Analyze the provided code snippet. Identify the line that will cause a run-time error and explain why that error occurs **Competency Based Que.**

```
a = int (input (" Enter a : "))
b = 0
c = a/b
```

Ans. The line c = a/b will cause a run-time error. This is because it attempts to divide the value of a by b, which is initialized to 0. Division by zero is an undefined mathematical operation and results in a ZeroDivisionError during program execution.

22. Define any two exception classes which are used in Python.

Ans. **KeyboardInterrupt** Raised when the user interrupts program execution, generally by pressing Ctrl + C.

OverflowError Raised when result of an arithmetic operation is too large to be represented.

Short Answer Type II Questions

23. Explain the difference between a syntax error and a semantic error in programming, providing an example of each.

Ans. Differences between syntax error and semantic error are as follows:

Feature	Syntax Error	Semantic Error
Nature of Error	Violation of the grammatical rules of the programming language	Code is grammatically correct, but doesn't make logical sense
Detection	Detected by the compiler or interpreter during the compilation or interpretation phase.	Not detected by the compiler; occurs during program execution (runtime)
Error Messages	Usually points to the exact location of the syntax error in the code.	Often harder to pinpoint; might lead to unexpected behavior or crashes
Examples	• Missing a semicolon or parenthesis • Misspelling a keyword • Incorrect indentation	• Using a variable before it's declared • Type mismatch (e.g., assigning a string to an integer variable) • Dividing by zero
Impact	Prevents the program from being executed.	Program runs but produces incorrect results or crashes

Example of Syntax Error

`print "Hello" (missing parentheses in Python 3) or a + b = c (attempting to assign a value to an expression).`

Example of Semantic Error

Using a variable before it has been declared or trying to assign a value of the wrong data type to a variable.

24. Describe what a runtime error is and give two common examples of runtime errors in Python.

Ans. A runtime error occurs during the execution of a program. These errors are not detected by the compiler or interpreter but arise when the program is running. They often cause the program to terminate abruptly.

Example 1: Division by zero (e.g., c = a / b where b is 0).

Example 2: Accessing a list element that doesn't exist (e.g., trying to access my_list[10] when my_list only has 5 elements).

25. Explain the purpose of exception handling in Python using a try-except block and provide a simple code example to illustrate its usage.

Ans. The purpose of exception handling in Python is to gracefully manage errors or unexpected situations that may occur during the execution of a program, preventing it from crashing. It allows the program to continue running even when errors arise, making it more robust. This is achieved using a try-except block.

try block: The code that might raise an exception is placed within the try block.

except block: If an exception occurs within the try block, the program immediately jumps to the except block, where the error is handled.

Code Example:

```
try:
age = int(input("Please enter your age: "))
print("I see that you are",age,"years
old.")
except ValueError:
    print("Hey, that was not a number!")
```

Long Answer Type Questions

26. What do you mean by logical errors?

Ans. In this case, the program does not give any error but still gives an incorrect output, it is due to logical errors. These errors occur due to mistakes of the programmer. This is the most difficult task to find and debug a logical error.

For example, when a wrong formula is used to calculate any mathematical expression it gives logical error.

Some Python logical errors include

- Using the wrong variable name
- Indenting a block to the wrong level
- Getting operator precedence wrong
- Making a mistake in a boolean expression

e.g.

```
a = 17
b = 11
c = 12
avg = (a * b)/(c +3)
print (" The average is : " , avg)
```

The above program, gives the result 12.4666667, but the expected output is 13.3333333.

Here is logical error that formula to find the average of numbers should be $avg = \frac{(a+b+c)}{3}$

27. Define the following exception classes.

(a) NameError **(b) RuntimeError**
(c) OverflowError **(d) IOError**

Ans. (a) **NameError** This error raised when a variable or function name is used that has not been defined or is out of scope. This often occurs when you try to access a variable that doesn't exist, or when you misspell a variable or function name.

e.g. `print(undefined_variable)`

(b) **RuntimeError** A broad class of exceptions that occur during runtime but don't fall into more specific categories like TypeError or ValueError. It's often raised when the interpreter encounters an unexpected condition or behavior.

e.g.
```
import math
math.sqrt(-1)
# Raises a ValueError, which is
        a subclass of RuntimeError
```

(c) **OverFlowError** This error raised when a calculation results in a value that is too large to be represented by the available data type. This often occurs when working with very large or very small numbers.

e.g.
```
import math
math.exp(1000)
# May raise an OverflowError
        depending on the system
```

(d) **IOError** Raised when an input/output operation fails. This can include errors related to reading from or writing to files, network sockets, or other input/output devices.

e.g.
```
f = open("nonexistent_file.txt", "r")
# Raises an IOError if the file
        doesn't exist
```

Case Study Based Question

Case Study

Debugging is the systematic process of identifying, locating, and rectifying errors or bugs in computer programs or software. It involves analyzing code, testing inputs and outputs, and using debugging tools to pinpoint the exact cause of the issue.

Effective debugging is crucial for ensuring software quality, reliability, and performance. Common debugging techniques include using print statements, setting breakpoints, and utilizing a debugger to step through code execution.

By understanding the types of errors (syntax, runtime, and logical) and employing appropriate debugging strategies, developers can efficiently resolve issues and deliver high-quality software.

(i) **What is a syntax error?**
(a) An error in the logic of the code
(b) An error in the grammar or structure of the code
(c) An error that occurs during program execution
(d) An error caused by hardware malfunction

(ii) **What is a runtime error?**
(a) An error that occurs while the program is running
(b) An error in the design of the program
(c) An error in the input data
(d) An error in the compiler

(iii) **What is a logical error?**
(a) An error in the syntax of the code
(b) An error in the logic or algorithm of the code
(c) An error in the hardware of the computer
(d) An error in the operating system

(iv) **Which of the following is a common debugging technique?**
(a) Using comments
(b) Using print statements
(c) Using a text editor
(d) Using a web browser

(v) **What is a debugger?**
(a) A tool for writing code
(b) A tool for compiling code
(c) A tool for debugging code
(d) A tool for running code

(vi) **What is the importance of debugging?**
(a) To make code more efficient
(b) To make code more readable
(c) To ensure code quality and reliability
(d) To create more complex programs

(vii) **Which of the following is a common debugging strategy?**
(a) Divide and conquer
(b) Trial and error
(c) Guessing
(d) Ignoring the error

Ans. (i) (b) An error in the grammar or structure of the code
(ii) (a) An error that occurs while the program is running
(iii) (b) An error in the logic or algorithm of the code.
(iv) (b) Using print statements
(v) (c) A tool for debugging code
(vi) (c) To ensure code quality and reliability
(vii) (a) Divide and conquer

SELF ASSESSMENT TEST

Multiple Choice Questions

1. Which exception classes raised when a generated error does not fall into any category?
(a) RuntimeError
(b) TypeError
(c) KeyError
(d) AttributeError

2. Identify the syntax error from the following options
(a) Leaving out a keyword
(b) Division by zero
(c) Using the wrong variable name
(d) Trying to access a file which does not exist

3. Which type of compile time error indicates an improper use of Python statements?
(a) Syntax error
(b) Semantic error
(c) Logical error
(d) Express error

Fill in the Blanks

4. A ________ occurs when the program violates the rules of the programming language.

5. An error that occurs during the execution of a program is a ________ error.

6. ________ errors produce incorrect results without crashing the program.

7. The ________ block is used to ensure that code is always executed, regardless of whether an exception occurs.

8. The ________ statement is used to force an exception to occur.

9. ________ are used to handle errors in a structured way.

State Whether True or False

10. A SyntaxError occurs during runtime.

11. Logical errors cause a program to crash.

12. Exception handling allows a program to continue running after an error.

13. The finally block is executed only if an exception occurs.

14. Raising exceptions allows you to create custom error messages.

15. Compile time errors are found when the program is executing.

Assertion and Reason Based Questions

Assertion (A) and Reason (R) Type questions. Choose the correct option as:

(a) Both Assertion (A) and Reason (R) are true, and Reason (R) is the correct explanation of Assertion (A).
(b) Both Assertion (A) and Reason (R) are true, but Reason (R) is not the correct explanation of Assertion (A).
(c) Assertion (A) is true, but Reason (R) is false.
(d) Assertion (A) is false, but Reason (R) is true.

16. Assertion (A) Syntax errors are detected by the interpreter before execution.
Reason (R) Syntax errors violate the grammatical rules of the programming language.

17. Assertion (A) Logical errors are difficult to detect.
Reason (R) Logical errors do not cause the program to crash, but result in incorrect output.

18. Assertion (A) Exception handling improves program robustness.
Reason (R) Exception handling allows a program to gracefully handle runtime errors.

19. Assertion (A) The finally block is executed only when an exception is raised.
Reason (R) Debugging tools help identify and fix errors in code.

20. Assertion (A) Raising exceptions allows for custom error control.
Reason (R) Raising exceptions enables developers to create specific error messages and handle them appropriately.

Very Short Answer Type Questions

21. What do you mean by error in program?

22. Which type of error occurs in program when a number will be divided by zero?

23. Write the syntax of try_except block in Python.

24. What is meant by AttributeError exception class ?

Short Answer Type Questions

25. How can you stop debugging?

26. Distinguish between syntax error and semantic error.

27. The code is given below will give an error on execution. Identify the type of error and modify the code to handle such type of an error.

```
x = int (input (" Enter the value of x : "))
y = int (input (" Enter the value of y : "))
x = y + 10
d = x/y
```

28. Write some conditions which occur logical errors in Python.

29. What are the use of exception handling in Python?

30. Define two forms of program errors.

31. Explain run-time error with an example in Python.

Long Answer Type Questions

32. Explain the following terms.

(i) Exception (ii) EOFError
(iii) StopIteration (iv) ValueError

33. Write the output of the following code.

```
try:
    file2 = open ("File.txt" ,"r")
    try:
        file2.write ("Programming Langauge")
    finally:
        file2.close( )
        print("File closed")
except :
    print(" Error occurred ")
```

Case Study Based Questions

34. A data analysis script is designed to read a CSV file, perform statistical calculations, and output results. However, when processing large files, the script occasionally crashes with "ZeroDivisionError" and "FileNotFoundError." The script lacks proper exception handling.

(i) The "ZeroDivisionError" and "FileNotFoundError" are examples of which type of error?

(a) Syntax errors
(b) Compile-time errors
(c) Runtime errors
(d) Logical errors

(ii) To prevent the script from crashing, the developer should implement:

(a) Syntax correction
(b) Exception handling
(c) Logical correction
(d) Compile-time checks

(iii) Using a try-except block to catch and handle these errors is a form of:

(a) Raising exceptions
(b) Python build-in exceptions
(c) Exception handling
(d) The finally block

(iv) If the developer wants to ensure that the file is always closed, regardless of whether an exception occurs, they should use:

(a) try-except block (b) raise statement
(c) finally block (d) pass statement

(v) If the developer wants to force a specific error to occur during testing, they can use:

(a) try block (b) raise statement
(c) except block (d) finally block

Answers

1.	(a)	2.	(a)	3.	(a)	4.	Syntax error
5.	Runtime	6.	Logical	7.	Finally	8.	raise
9.	Exceptions			10.	False	11.	False	12. True
13.	False	14.	True	15.	False	16.	(a)	17. (a)
18.	(a)	19.	(d)	20.	(a)		

34. (i) → (c), (ii) → (b), (iii) → (c), (iv) → (c), (v) → (b)

08

CHAPTER

In Python, lists allow us to store multiple items in a single variable. For example, if you need to store the ages of all the students in a class, you can do this task using a list.

YOUR STUDY GOALS

- 8.1 Creating and Initializing a List
- 8.2 Accessing Lists
- 8.3 Traversing a List
- 8.4 List Operators
- 8.5 List Operations
- 8.6 Built-in Functions
- 8.7 Programs

YOUR PRACTICE GOAL

- Objective Type Questions (27 Qs ; MCQs, True or False, Fill in the Blanks, Assertion and Reason)
- Subjective Type Questions (33 Qs ; VSA, SA, LA)
- Case Study Based Question-1

Lists

A list in Python is an ordered, mutable collection used to store multiple items. It can hold elements of different data types, including numbers, strings, or even other lists.

Lists are defined using square brackets [], and elements are accessed via their index. Because of their mutability, lists allow dynamic modifications like adding, removing, or updating elements.

8.1 Creating and Initializing a List

Creating a list in Python refers to defining a variable and assigning it an empty or filled collection of items, which are enclosed in square brackets [].

Example `my_list = []  # Creating an empty list`

Initializing a list refers to the process of adding values to it when you create it. This is done by directly placing the elements within square brackets [].

Example
```
my_list = [1, 2, 3, 4, 5]
        # Initializing a list with values
```

We can create different types of list in Python as follows:

(i) Empty List

Empty list can be created in Python using [ ] . It takes the truth value as false. Here is the two ways to create empty list as

```
>>>a = [ ]
>>>print (a)
```

Output [ ]

Or
```
>>>a = list ( )
>>>print (a)
```

Output [ ]

(ii) Mixed Data Types List

It can be created to place different data types such as integers, strings, double etc., into one list.

For example,

```
>>>a = ['Neha', 'Sharma', 25, 75, 6, 47]
>>>print(a)
```

Output

```
['Neha', 'Sharma', 25, 75, 6, 47]
```

(iii) Nested List

Nested lists are list objects where the elements in the lists can be lists themselves.

For example,

```
>>> A = ['Neha', 4, 1, [5, 23, 4], 98]
>> print (A)
```

Output

```
['Neha', 4, 1, [5, 23, 4], 98]
```

List A contains 5 elements while inner list contains 3 elements ([5, 23, 4]). List A is considered [5, 23, 4] as one element.

Lists are Mutable

In Python, lists are mutable. It means that the contents of the list can be changed after it has been created. #List list1 of colors

```
>>> list1 =
['Red','Green','Blue','Orange']
#change/override the fourth element of
list1
 >>> list1[3] = 'Black'
>>> list1 #print the modified list list1
['Red', 'Green', 'Blue', 'Black']
```

Creating List from an Existing Sequence

(a) **Using the list () Function** You can convert sequences like tuples or strings into lists.

Syntax

```
new_list_name = list (sequence / string)
  #Here, the sequence includes tuples,
lists etc.
```

For example,

```
my_tuple = (1, 2, 3)
my_list = list(my_tuple)
```

Output

[1, 2, 3]

(b) **Directly from input** You can create lists by taking input from the user.

For example,

```
# Creating an empty list
new_list = [ ]
# Numbers of elements as input
n = int (input ("Enter no. of elements ="))
#iterating till the range
for i in range (0, n):
   element = int (input ())
   #adding the element
   new_list.append (element)
print (new_list)
```

Output

Enter no. of elements = 4

12

10

'Arihant'

'Publications'

[1, 10, 'Arihant', 'Publications']

8.2 Accessing Lists

To access the list's elements, index number is used. Use the index operator [ ] to access the elements of a list. The index should be an integer. Index of 0 refers to first element, 1 refers to second element and so on. While the index of –1 refers to the last element, –2 refers to the second last element and so on.

For example,

```
l1 = [5, 7, 3, 4, 5, 6, 9, 0, 8]
```

It is called positive index ↑

0	1	2	3	4	5	6	7	8
5	7	3	4	5	6	9	0	8
-9	-8	-7	-6	-5	-4	-3	-2	-1

↓ It is called negative index

```
>>>l1 = [34, 87, 'Computer', 12, 'Python',
11, 76, 'Option']
>>>l1 [0]
34
>>>l1 [6]
76
>>>l1 [-4]
'Python'
>>>l1 [3]
12
```

```
>>>l1 [-3]
11
>>>l1 [8]
```

It will give an error as `IndexError: list index out of range`. Because it has 8 elements for which indexing are 0 to 7.

8.3 Traversing a List

Traversing a list is a technique to access an individual element of that list. It is also called iterate over a list.

There are multiple ways to iterate over a list in Python. These are as follows

Using for loop

The most common and easy way to traverse a list is with a for loop. For loop is used when you want to traverse each element of a list.

For example,

```
a = ['P', 'R', 'O', 'G', 'R', 'A', 'M']
for i in a:
  print (i, end = " ")
```

Output

P R O G R A M

Or

```
a = ['P', 'R', 'O', 'G', 'R', 'A', 'M']
for i in range (len(a)):
  print ((a [i]), end = "-")
```

Output

P-R-O-G-R-A-M

Program to display the elements of list

['P', 'Y', 'T', 'H', 'O', 'N']

in a separate line with their index number.

For example,

```
list1 = ['P', 'Y', 'T', 'H', 'O' 'N']
L1 = len (list1)
for i in range (L1):
  print ("Element :", list1 [i], "at index number", i)
```

Output

Element : P at index number 0

Element : Y at index number 1

Element : T at index number 2

Element : H at index number 3

Element : O at index number 4

Element : N at index number 5

Using while loop

A while loop can also be used to iterate over the elements of a list, but it requires more explicit index management.

For example,

```
list = ['A', 'r', 'i', 'h', 'a', 'n', 't']
index = 0
while index < len(list):
  print((list[index]), end = " ")
  index += 1
```

Output

A r i h a n t

8.4 List Operators

We can manipulate lists in different ways using operators. These are as follows:

Membership Operators

These operators are used to find out whether a value is a member of a sequence such as string, list, tuple, dictionary etc. There are two types of membership operator as follows

(i) in operator

It evaluates True, if the value in the left operand appears in the sequence found in the right operand.

For example,

```
l1 = [45, 76, [3, 98], 6]
l2 = [60, [23, 43], 65]
for item in l1:
  if item in l2:
    print ("Exist")
else :
  print ("Not Exist")
```

Output

Not Exist

(ii) not in operator

It evaluates True, if the value in the left operand does not appear in the sequence found in the right operand.

For example,

```
a = 54
b = 87
list1 = [45, 65, 30, 78, 512, 87]
if (a not in list1):
  print ("a is NOT present in given
  list")
```

```
    else :
        print ("a is present in given list")
    if (b in list1):
        print ("b is present in given list")
    else :
        print ("b is NOT present in given list")
```

Output

a is NOT present in given list
b is present in given list

8.5 List Operations

We can perform various operations on list in Python, some of them are describe below.

Concatenate Lists

The most conventional method to perform on the list is concatenation, the use of (+) operator can easily add the whole of one list to other list and hence perform the concatenation.

Syntax `list = list1 + list2`

For example,

```
>>>l1 = [43, 56, 34]
>>>l2 = [22, 34, 98]
>>>l = l1 + l2
>>>l
[43, 56, 34, 22, 34, 98]
```

The (+) operator cannot add list with other type as number or string because this operator is used only with list types.

For example,

```
>>>l1 = [2, 5, 7]
>>>l = l1 + 5
Trackback (most recent call last) :
File "<pyshell#5>", line 1, in <module>
  l = l1 + 5
TypeError : can only concatenate list
                        (not "int") to list.
```

For example,

```
>>>l1 = [3, 2, 6]
>>>l = l1 + "Try"
Trackback (most recent call last):
File "<pyshell#1>", line 1, in <module>
l = l1 + "Try"
TypeError : can only concatenate list
                        (not "str") to list.
```

Replicating List

You can repeat the elements of the list using (*) operator. This operator is used to replicate the list.

Syntax `list = list1 * digit`

For example,

```
>>>l1 = [3, 2, 6]
>>>l = l1 * 2
>>>l
[3, 2, 6, 3, 2, 6]
```

Slicing of a List

If we want to display only a specific portion of the list, we use a technique called slicing. Slicing involves using the colon (:) symbol to indicate the range of elements we want to extract.

Below are the operators used for slicing:

Operators	Syntax	Example
Basic Slicing	`list[start : end]`	`list1 = [4, 3, 7, 6, 4, 9, 5, 0, 3, 2]` `print(list1 [2 : 5])` **Output** [7, 6, 4]
Omitting Indices	`string[: end]` `string[start :]`	`print(list1[:5])` **Output** [4, 3, 7, 6, 4] `print(list1[3:])` **Output** [6, 4, 9, 5, 0, 3, 2]
Step Sizing	`string[start:end: step]`	`print(list1[1:10:3])` **Output** [3, 4, 0]
Negative Indexing	`string[-start : -end]`	`print(list1[-6:-1])` **Output** [4, 9, 5, 0, 3]

List Modification using Slicing

List can be modified after creating using slicing.

For example,

```
>>> l1 = [2, 4, "Try", 54, "Again"]
>>> l1[0:1] = [34, "Hello"]
>>> l1
[34, 'Hello', 4, 'Try', 54, 'Again']
>>> l1[4] = ["World"]
>>> l1
[34, 'Hello', 4, 'Try', ['World'], 'Again']
>>> l1[2] = "Hiiii"
>>> l1
[34, 'Hello', 'Hiiii', 'Try', ['World'], 'Again']
```

TEACHER TIP

Negative indices can be used to access elements from the end of the list.

8.6 Built-in Functions

Python has large number of build-in functions and methods that make programming easier. Some of them are follows:

Function	Description	Example

list()	Converts an iterable into a list.
	Syntax `list(sequence)`
		`>>l=list("hello")`
		`>>l`
		`['h', 'e', 'l', 'l', 'o']`

append()	Adds an element to the end of a list.
	Syntax `list.append(item)`
		`>>lst = [1, 2, 3]`
		`>>lst.append(4)`
		`>>lst`
		`[1, 2, 3, 4]`

extend()	Adds all elements from another sequence to the end of the list.
	Syntax `list.extend(list_2)`
		`>>lst = [1, 2]`
		`>>lst.extend([3, 4])`
		`>>lst`
		`[1, 2, 3, 4]`

insert()	Inserts an element at a specified position.
	Syntax `list.insert(index, item)`
		`>>lst = [1, 3]`
		`>>lst.insert(1,2)`
		`>>lst`
		`[1, 2, 3]`

sum()	Returns the sum of elements in a list.
	Syntax `sum(sequence)`
		`>>lst = [1, 2, 3]`
		`>>sum(lst)`
		`6`

max()	Returns the largest element in a list.
	Syntax `max(sequence)`
		`>>lst = [1, 3, 2]`
		`>>max(lst)`
		`3`

min()	Returns the smallest element in a list.
	Syntax `min(sequence)`
		`>>lst = [1, 3, 2]`
		`>>min(lst)`
		`1`

len()	Returns the length (number of elements) in a list.
	Syntax `len(sequence)`
		`>>lst = [1, 2, 3, 'hi']`
		`>>len(lst)`
		`4`

index()	Returns the index of the first occurrence of an element.
	Syntax `list.index(item)`
		`>>lst = [1, 2, 3, 'Hello']`
		`>>lst.index('Hello')`
		`3`

count()	Returns the number of occurrences of an element in the list.
	Syntax `list.count(item)`
		`>>lst = [1, 'New',2, 2, 3]`
		`>>lst.count(2)`
		`2`

reverse()	Reverses the elements of the list in place.
	Syntax `list.reverse()`
		`>>lst = [1, 2, 3]`
		`>>lst.reverse()`
		`[3, 2, 1]`

pop()	Removes and returns an element at a specified index (default is the last element).
	Syntax `list.pop(index)`
		`>>lst = [1, 2, 3, 78, 99]`
		`>>lst.pop(4)`
		`99`
		`Updated List: [1,2,3,78]`

remove()	Removes the first occurrence of a specified element.
	Syntax `list.remove(item)`
	If the item(argument)
		`>>lst = [1, 3, 6]`
		`>>lst.remove(3)`
		`[1, 6]`

sort()	Sorts the elements of a list in place (ascending by default).
	Syntax `list.sort()` or `list.sort(reverse=True)`
		`>>lst = [3, 1, 2]`
		`>>lst.sort()`
		`[1, 2, 3]`

sorted()	It takes a list as parameter and creates a new list consisting of the same elements arranged in sorted order.
	Syntax `list1.sorted(list2)`
		`>> list1 = [23,45, 11,67,85,56]`
		`>> list2 = sorted(list1)`
		`>> list1`
		`[23,45,11,67,85,56]`
		`>> list2`
		`[11,23,45,56,67,85]`

clear()	Removes all elements from the list.
	Syntax `list.clear()`
		`>>lst = [1, 2, 3]`
		`>>lst.clear()`
		`[]`

8.7 Programs

1. Find the Maximum, Minimum, and Mean of Numeric Values in a List.

Ans.
```
def find_stats(num_list):
  max_num = max(num_list)
  min_num = min(num_list)
  mean_num = sum(num_list) / len(num_list)
  return max_num, min_num, mean_num
numbers = [10, 25, 5, 30, 15]
max_val, min_val, mean_val
                    = find_stats(numbers)
print("Maximum value is = :", max_val)
print("Minimum value is = :", min_val)
print("Mean is = :", mean_val)
```

2. Linear Search on a List of Numbers.

Ans.
```
def linear_search(num_list, target):
  for i in range(len(num_list)):
    if num_list[i] == target:
      return i
  return -1
```

```
numbers = [10, 25, 5, 30, 15]
target_value = 30
index = linear_search(numbers, target_value)
if index != -1:
  print(f"Target value {target_value}
                    found at index {index}")
else:
  print("Target value not found")
```

3. Counting the Frequency of Elements in a List.

Ans.
```
def count_frequencies(num_list):
  freq_dict = {}
  for num in num_list:
    if num in freq_dict:
      freq_dict[num] += 1
    else:
      freq_dict[num] = 1
  return freq_dict
numbers = [10, 25, 5, 30, 15, 10, 25, 5]
freq_dict = count_frequencies(numbers)
print(freq_dict)
Programs
```

4. Write a menu driven program to perform various list operations, such as:

- **Append an element**
- **Insert an element**
- **Append a list to the given list**
- **Modify an existing element**
- **Delete an existing element from its position**
- **Delete an existing element with a given value**
- **Sort the list in ascending order**
- **Sort the list in descending order**
- **Display the list.**

Ans.
```
# Menu driven program to do various list operations
myList = [22, 4, 16, 38, 13] # myList already has
                                        5 elements
while True:
  print("The list 'myList' has the following
                              elements:", myList)
  print("\nL I S T O P E R A T I O N S")
  print(" 1. Append an element")
  print(" 2. Insert an element at the desired
                                        position")
  print(" 3. Append a list to the given list")
  print(" 4. Modify an existing element")
  print(" 5. Delete an existing element by its
                                        position")
  print(" 6. Delete an existing element by its value")
  print(" 7. Sort the list in ascending order")
  print(" 8. Sort the list in descending order")
  print(" 9. Display the list")
  print(" 10. Exit")
  choice = int(input("ENTER YOUR CHOICE (1-10): "))
  # Append element
  if choice == 1:
    element = int(input("Enter the element to be
                                        appended: "))
    myList.append(element)
    print("The element has been appended.\n")
  # Insert an element at desired position
  elif choice == 2:
    element = int(input("Enter the element to be
                                        inserted: "))
    pos = int(input("Enter the position: "))
    if 0 <= pos <= len(myList):
      myList.insert(pos, element)
      print("The element has been inserted.\n")
    else:
      print("Invalid position.\n")
  # Append a list to the given list
  elif choice == 3:
    newList = input("Enter the elements separated
                by commas (e.g. 1,2,3): ").split(',')
    newList = [int(x) for x in newList]
    myList.extend(newList)
    print("The list has been appended.\n")
  # Modify an existing element
  elif choice == 4:
    i = int(input("Enter the position of the
                            element to be modified: "))
    if 0 <= i < len(myList):
      newElement = int(input("Enter the new
                                        element: "))
      oldElement = myList[i]
      myList[i] = newElement
      print(f"The element {oldElement} has been
                                        modified.\n")
    else:
      print("Position of the element is more than
                            the length of the list.\n")
  # Delete an existing element by position
  elif choice == 5:
    i = int(input("Enter the position of the
                            element to be deleted: "))
    if 0 <= i < len(myList):
      element = myList.pop(i)
      print(f"The element {element} has been
                                        deleted.\n")
    else:
      print("Position of the element is more than
                            the length of the list.\n")
```

```
    # Delete an existing element by value
    elif choice == 6:
        element = int(input("Enter the element to be
                                              deleted: "))
        if element in myList:
            myList.remove(element)
            print(f"The element {element} has been
                                              deleted.\n")
        else:
            print(f"Element {element} is not present in
                                              the list.\n")
    # Sort the list in ascending order
    elif choice == 7:
        myList.sort()
        print("The list has been sorted in ascending
                                              order.\n")
    # Sort the list in descending order
    elif choice == 8:
        myList.sort(reverse=True)
        print("The list has been sorted in descending
                                              order.\n")
    # Display the list
    elif choice == 9:
        print("The list is:", myList)
    # Exit from the menu
    elif choice == 10:
        print("Exiting the program.")
        break
    else:
        print("Choice is not valid. Please enter a
                                    valid option (1-10).\n")
    # Pause to let the user read output
    input("Press any key to continue...")
```

5. Write a Python program to display all the common elements of two lists.

Ans.

```
list1 = []
num = int(input("Enter number of elements
                                    in List1: "))
for i in range(1, num+1):
    x = int(input("Enter element: "))
    list1.append(x)
list2 = []
num1 = int(input("Enter number of elements
                                    in List2: "))
for i in range(1, num1+1):
    y = int(input("Enter element: "))
    list2.append(y)
a_set = set(list1)
b_set = set(list2)
if (a_set & b_set):
  print("Common elements are:", a_set &
                                        b_set)
else:
  print("No common elements found")
```

6. Write a Python program to reverse a list in-place without creating a new list.

Ans.

```
def reverse_list(lst):
  lst.reverse()
  return lst
n = int(input("How many elements you want
                           to enter in a list? "))
my_list = []
for i in range(n):
  element = int(input("Enter the element: "))
  my_list.append(element)

print("Original List is:", my_list)
reversed_list = reverse_list(my_list)
print("List after reversing in place is:",
                                 reversed_list)
```

Mind Map

LISTS

Creating a List

We can create different types of list in Python as follows:

Empty List

```
>>>a = [ ]
>>>print (a)
Or
>>>a = list ( )
>>>print (a)
```

Mixed data Type List

```
>>>a = ['Neha', 'Sharma', 25, 75, 6, 47]
>>>print(a)
```

Nested List

```
>>> A = ['Neha', 4, 1, [5, 23, 4], 98]
>> print (A)
```

Note

In Python, lists are mutable. It means that the contents of the list can be changed after it has been created. #List list1 of colors

Accessing Lists

To access the list's elements, index number is used. Use the index operator [ ] to access the elements of a list. The index should be an integer. Index of 0 refers to first element, 1 refers to second element and so on.While the index of −1 refers to the last element, −2 refers to the second last element and so on.

```
>>>l1 = [34, 87, 'Computer', 12, 'Python', 11 ]
>>>l1 [0]
```

Output 34

Traversing a Lists

Traversing a list is a technique to access an individual element of that list. It is also called iterate over a list.

There are multiple ways to iterate over a list in Python.

Using for loop

```
a = ['P', 'R', 'O', 'G', 'R', 'A', 'M']
for i in a:
print (i, end = " ")
```

Using While loop

```
list = ['A', 'r', 'i', 'h', 'a', 'n', 't']
index = 0
while index < len(list):
print((list[index]), end = " ")
index += 1
```

List Operators

Comparison Operators

Comparison operators in Python are like scales that weigh two values and tell us if one is bigger, smaller, or equal to the other.

They use symbols like <, >, ==, != , >= , and <=

When we use these operators, they give us a True or False answer.

Membership Operators

These operators are used to find out whether a value is a member of a sequence such as string, list, tuple, dictionary etc. There are two types of membership operator as follows-

in operator, not in operator

List Operations

Concatenate Lists

Syntax list = list1 + list2

Replicating List

Syntax list = list1 * digit

Slicing of a List

If we want to display only a specific portion of the list, we use a technique called slicing. Slicing involves using the colon (:) symbol to indicate the range of elements we want to extract.

Built-in Functions

Methods	Syntax
list( )	list(sequence)
append( )	list.append(item)
extend ( )	list.extend(list_2)
insert()	list.insert (index, item)
sum()	sum(sequence)
max()	max(sequence)
min()	min(sequence)
len()	len(sequence)
index()	list.index(item)
count()	list.count(item)
reverse()	list. reverse(item)
pop()	list. pop(item)
remove()	list. remove(item)
sort()	list.sort() or list.sort(reverse=True)
sorted()	list1.sorted(list2)
clear()	list.clear()

NCERT Folder

Exercise Questions

1. **What will be the output of the following statements?**

(i)
```
list1 = [12,32,65,26,80,10]
list1.sort()
print(list1)
```
(ii)
```
list1 = [12,32,65,26,80,10]
sorted(list1)
print(list1)
```
(iii)
```
list1 = [1,2,3,4,5,6,7,8,9,10]
print (list1[::-2])
print (list1[:3] + list1[3:])
```
(iv)
```
list1 = [1,2,3,4,5]
print (list1[len(list1)-1])
```

Ans. **Output**

(i) [10, 12, 26, 32, 65, 80]

(ii) [12, 32, 65, 26, 80, 10]

(iii) [10, 8, 6, 4, 2]
[1, 2, 3, 4, 5, 6, 7, 8, 9, 10]

(iv) 5

2. **Consider the following list myList. What will be the elements of myList after the following two operations?**

```
myList = [10,20,30,40]
```

(i) `myList.append([50,60])`

(ii) `myList.extend([80,90])`

Ans. (i) [10, 20, 30, 40, [50, 60]]

(ii) [10, 20, 30, 40, [50, 60], 80, 90]

3. **What will be the output of the following code segment?**

```
myList = [1,2,3,4,5,6,7,8,9,10]
for i in range(0,len(myList)):
  if i%2 == 0:
    print(myList[i])
```

Ans. **Output**

1
3
5
7
9

4. **What will be the output of the following code segments?**

(a)
```
myList = [1,2,3,4,5,6,7,8,9,10]
del myList[3:]
print(myList)
```
(b)
```
myList = [1,2,3,4,5,6,7,8,9,10]
del myList[:5]
print(myList)
```
(c)
```
myList = [1,2,3,4,5,6,7,8,9,10]
del myList[::2]
print(myList)
```

Ans. **Output**

(a) [1, 2, 3]

(b) [6, 7, 8, 9, 10]

(c) [2, 4, 6, 8, 10]

5. **Differentiate between append() and extend()**

Ans.

Feature	append()	extend()
Purpose	Adds a single element to the end of a list.	Adds all elements of an iterable (like another list, tuple, etc.) to the end of a list.
Argument Type	Any object (single element).	Any iterable object (list, tuple, set, string, etc.).
Effect on List	Increases the list's length by 1.	Increases the list's length by the number of elements in the iterable.
How Elements are Added	Adds the argument as a single element, even if it's a list itself.	Adds each element of the iterable individually.
Example	my_list = [1, 2, 3] my_list.append(4) print(my_list) # Output: [1, 2, 3, 4]	my_list = [1, 2, 3] my_list.extend([4, 5, 6]) print(my_list) # Output: [1, 2, 3, 4, 5, 6]

6. **Consider a list:**

```
list1 = [6,7,8,9]
```

What is the difference between the following operations on list1?

(a) `list1 * 2`

(b) `list1 *= 2`

(c) `list1 = list1 * 2`

Ans. (a) `list1 * 2`

Creates a new list This operation multiplies the list by 2, creating a new list that contains the original list repeated twice.

Does not modify the original list The original list1 remains unchanged.

e.g.
```
list1 = [6, 7, 8, 9]
new_list = list1 * 2
print(new_list)
[6, 7, 8, 9, 6, 7, 8, 9]
print(list1)
[6, 7, 8, 9]
```

(b) `list1 *= 2`

Modifies the original list This operation multiplies the list by 2 in-place, doubling the elements of the original list1.

Changes the original list The original list1 is now modified to contain the repeated elements.

e.g.
```
list1 = [6, 7, 8, 9]
list1 *= 2
print(list1)
[6, 7, 8, 9, 6, 7, 8, 9]
```

(c) `list1 = list1 * 2`

Assigns a new list to the variable This operation multiplies the list by 2, creating a new list, and then assigns this new list back to the variable list1.

Modifies the original list The original list1 is now replaced with the new, doubled list.

e.g.
```
list1 = [6, 7, 8, 9]
list1 = list1 * 2
print(list1)
[6, 7, 8, 9, 6, 7, 8, 9]
```

7. The record of a student (Name, Roll No., Marks in five subjects and percentage of marks) is stored in the following list:

```
stRecord =
['Raman','A-36',[56,98,99,72,69], 78.8]
```

Write Python statements to retrieve the following information from the list stRecord:

(a) Percentage of the student

(b) Marks in the fifth subject

(c) Maximum marks of the student

(d) Roll no. of the student

(e) Change the name of the student from 'Raman' to 'Raghav'

Ans. (a) `print(stRecord[3])`

(b) `print(stRecord[2][4])`

(c) `print(max(stRecord[2]))`

(d) `print(stRecord[1])`

(e) `stRecord[0] = 'Raghav'`

Programming Based Questions

1. Write a program to find the number of times an element occurs in the list.

Ans.
```
def count_occurrences(lst, element):
  count = lst.count(element)
  print(f"The element {element} occurs
                                  {count} times.")
my_list = [1, 2, 3, 2, 1, 4, 2]
element_to_count = 2
count_occurrences(my_list,
                              element_to_count)
```

2. Write a program to read a list of n integers (positive as well as negative). Create two new lists, one having all positive numbers and the other having all negative numbers from the given list. Print all three lists.

Ans.
```
def separate_positive_negative(num_list):
  positive_list = []
  negative_list = []
  for num in num_list:
    if num > 0:
      positive_list.append(num)
    else:
      negative_list.append(num)
  return positive_list, negative_list
numbers = [1, -2, 3, -4, 5, -6]
positive, negative =
separate_positive_negative(numbers)
print("Original list:", numbers)
print("Positive numbers:", positive)
print("Negative numbers:", negative)
```

3. Write a program to find the largest and the second largest elements in a given list of elements.

Ans.
```
nums = eval(input("Enter the list: "))
first = nums[0]
second = nums[0]
for num in nums[2:]:
    if num > first:
        second = first
        first = num
    elif num > second and num != first:
        second = num
print("Largest element:", first)
print("Second largest element:", second)
```

4. Write a program to read a list of n integers and find their median.

Note The median value of a list of values is the middle one when they are arranged in order. If there are two middle values then take their average.

Hint You can use an built-in function to sort the list

Ans.
```
def find_median(num_list):
  num_list.sort()
  n = len(num_list)
  if n % 2 == 0:
    median = (num_list[n//2 - 1] +
                             num_list[n//2]) / 2
  else:
    median = num_list[n//2]
  return median
numbers = [10, 25, 5, 30, 15]
median = find_median(numbers)
print("Median:", median)
```

5. Write a program to read a list of elements. Modify this list so that it does not contain any duplicate elements, i.e., all elements occurring multiple times in the list should appear only once.

Ans.
```
def remove_duplicates(lst):
  unique_list = []
  for num in lst:
    if num not in unique_list:
      unique_list.append(num)
  return unique_list
numbers = [1, 2, 3, 2, 1, 4, 2]
unique_numbers =
                 remove_duplicates(numbers)
print("Unique numbers:", unique_numbers)
```

6. Write a program to create a list of elements. Input an element from the user that has to be inserted in the list. Also input the position at which it is to be inserted.

Ans.
```
list1 = eval(input("Enter list: "))
new_element = int(input("Enter the element
to be inserted: "))
position = int(input("Enter the position at
which the element should be inserted: "))
list1.insert(position, new_element)
print("Updated list:", list1)
```

7. Write a program to read elements of a list and do the following.

(a) The program should ask for the position of the element to be deleted from the list and delete the element at the desired position in the list.

(b) The program should ask for the value of the element to be deleted from the list and delete this value from the list.

Ans.
```
nums = eval(input("Enter list: "))
```

(a) Delete element by position
```
position = int(input("Enter the position
                of the element to delete: "))
if 0 <= position < len(nums):
    del nums[position]
    print("List after deletion
                         by position:", nums)
else:
   print("Error: Position out of bounds.
          Please enter a valid position.")
```

(b) Delete element by value
```
value = int(input("Enter the value of the
                     element to delete: "))
if value in nums:
    nums.remove(value)
   print("List after deletion by value:",
                                      nums)
else:
   print("Element", value, "not found in
                                the list.")
```

EXAM PATTERN QUESTIONS

Objective Type Questions

Multiple Choice Questions

1. **Which value is used to represent the first index of the list?**

(a) 1 (b) 0 (c) -1 (d) a

2. **You have a list my_list = [10, 20, 30, 40, 50] and you need to retrieve the last element (50) without knowing the exact length of the list. Which of the following methods is the most efficient and direct way to achieve this?** **Competency Based Que.**

(a) my_list[len(my_list) - 1]
(b) my_list.pop()
(c) my_list[-1]
(d) my_list[4:5]

3. **Choose the output of the following Python code.**

```
l1 = list ()
print (l1)
```

(a) [] (b) () (c) [,] (d) Empty

4. **How do you create a true copy (a new, independent copy) of a Python list L1?**

(a) L2 = L1 (b) L2 = list(L1)
(c) L2.copy(L1) (d) It's not possible

5. **Suppose list**

```
l1 = [10, 20, 30, 40, 50, 60, 70]
print (l1[-3])
```

(a) 30 (b) 50 (c) 40 (d) Error

6. **Choose the output from the following code.**

```
list1 = ['A', 'R', 'I', 'H', 'A', 'N', 'T']
print (list1[7])
```

(a) T (b) N (c) A (d) Error

7. **You have a list data = [1, 2, 4, 5] and you need to insert the number 3 between 2 and 4. Which method would you use to achieve this?** **Competency Based Que.**

(a) data.extend(3) (b) data.append(3)
(c) data.insert(2, 3) (d) data.add(3)

8. **What is the output of the following Python code?**

```
L = ['A', 'r', 'i', 'h', 'a', 'n', 't']
print(len(L))
```

(a) 7 (b) 8
(c) 9 (d) None of these

Fill in the Blanks

9. Creating lists using L = [expression for variable in sequence] is called ________.

10. ______ method is used to add multiple elements to a given list.

11. [] indicates an _____ list.

12. The sort() function sorts the items of the list by default in ascending order and in _______.

13. ______ method is used to delete an element when its index is not known.

State Whether True or False

14. Lists in Python cannot be nested inside each other.

15. List comprehensions can be used to create a new list by filtering and transforming an existing list.

16. The clear() method removes all elements from the list and deletes the list itself.

17. Lists in Python can be directly compared for equality using ==.

18. Using the * operator on a list duplicates its elements.

19. Slicing a list with list[1:3] includes the elements at indexes 1 and 3.

20. The pop() method removes the first element from the list by default.

21. The insert() method in Python lists can add an element at a specific index.

Assertion and Reason Based Questions

Assertion (A) and Reason (R) Type questions. Choose the correct option as:

(a) Both Assertion (A) and Reason (R) are true, and Reason (R) is the correct explanation of Assertion (A).
(b) Both Assertion (A) and Reason (R) are true, but Reason (R) is not the correct explanation of Assertion (A).
(c) Assertion (A) is true, but Reason (R) is false.
(d) Assertion (A) is false, but Reason (R) is true.

22. **Assertion (A)** Lists in Python are homogeneous.

Reason (R) They can only store elements of the same data type.

23. **Assertion (A)** Lists in Python are mutable.

Reason (R) Elements of a list can be changed after the list is created.

24. **Assertion (A)** Negative indexing can be used to access elements from the end of a list.

Reason (R) The index -1 refers to the last element, -2 to the second last, and so on.

25. **Assertion (A)** Slicing can be used to extract a portion of a list.

Reason (R) It involves using the colon (:) operator to specify the start and end indices.

26. **Assertion (A)** The append() method adds an element to the beginning of a list.

Reason (R) It modifies the original list.

27. **Assertion (A)** The len() function returns the number of elements in a list.

Reason (R) It counts the number of items in the list.

Answers

1. (b) 0
2. (c) my_list[-1]
3. (a) []
4. (b) L2 = list(L1)
5. (b) 50
6. (d) Error
7. (c) data.insert(2, 3)
8. (a) 7
9. list comprehensions
10. extend()
11. empty
12. place
13. remove()
14. False
15. True
16. False
17. True
18. True
19. False
20. False
21. True
22. (d) Assertion (A) is false, but Reason (R) is true.
23. (a) Both Assertion (A) and Reason (R) are true, and Reason (R) is the correct explanation of Assertion (A).
24. (a) Both Assertion (A) and Reason (R) are true, and Reason (R) is the correct explanation of Assertion (A).
25. (a) Both Assertion (A) and Reason (R) are true, and Reason (R) is the correct explanation of Assertion (A).
26. (d) Assertion (A) is false, but Reason (R) is true.
27. (a) Both Assertion (A) and Reason (R) are true, and Reason (R) is the correct explanation of Assertion (A).

Subjective Type Questions

Very Short Answer Type Questions

1. What do you mean by list in Python ?

Ans. List is a type of container in data structures which is used to store multiple data at the same time.

2. Are lists mutable or immutable ?

Ans. Lists are mutable which means they can be changed after creation.

3. If my_list = ['a', 'b', 'c'], what is the index of 'a'?

Ans. 0

4. Write the syntax to create a list from an existing sequence.

Ans. new_list_name = list(sequence/string)

5. Write the output of the below code.

```
>>> l1 = list()
>>> print(l1)
```

Ans. []

6. If you need to look at every item in a list, what technique do you use?

Ans. Traversing

7. What is the use of the list() method?

Ans. The list() method takes sequence types and converts them to lists. This is used to convert a given tuple into a list.

8. Give the syntax for slicing a list's elements which are not consecutive.

Ans. sliced_list = list_name[start:stop:step]

9. What do you mean by the insert() method?

Ans. The insert() method is used to insert an element at a specified position in the list.

10. Define the min() function used in a list.

Ans. The min() function is used to return the minimum element out of the elements of a list.

```
min(list_name)
```

11. How to count the elements of a list?

Ans. list_name.count(element)

12. What sort() option arranges items from highest to lowest?

Ans. reverse=True

Short Answer Type I Questions

13. What is a nested list ? Explain with an example.

***Or* Distinguish between string and list.**

Ans. Nested lists are list objects where the elements in the lists can be lists themselves.

For example,

```
list1 = [45, 43, 12, 'Math', 'Eng', [75,
                                   34, 'A'], 5]
```

list1 contains 7 elements while inner list contains 3 elements. list1 is considered [75, 34, 'A'] as one element.

Or

Feature	String	List
Data Type	Immutable sequence of characters	Mutable sequence of items of any data type
Mutability	Cannot be changed after creation	Can be modified after creation (add, remove, change items)
Syntax	Enclosed in single (' ') or double (" ") quotes	Enclosed in square brackets []
Iteration	Can iterate through individual characters	Can iterate through individual items
Operations	Concatenation (+), repetition (*), slicing, etc.	Append, insert, remove, sort, etc.
Example	"Hello"	[1, 2, 'a', 3.14]

14. Observe the given list and find the answer of questions that follows.

```
list1 = [45, 77, 87, "Next", "Try", 33, 43]
```

(i) list1[-2] **(ii) list1[2]**

Ans. (i) 33 (ii) 87

15. What is the output of the below program?

```
l2 = [75, 43, 40, 36, 28, 82]
l2.sort(reverse=True)
print(l2)
```

Ans. [82, 75, 43, 40, 36, 28]

16. Find the errors.

```
L1 = [2, 4, 5, 9]
L2 = L1 * 3
L4 = L1.pop(5)
L3 = L1 + 3
```

Ans. **Error 1** L3 = L1 + 3 cannot add a list and an integer.

Error 2 L1.pop(5) tries to access an index out of range.

17. Predict the output.

```
L2 = [5, 4, 3, 1, 11]
print(L2.count(1))
print(L2.index(3))
print(L2.remove(11))
print(L2)
```

Ans. **Output**

1
2
None
[5, 4, 3, 1]

18. Find the output.

```
L = [3, 4, 53, 4, 0, 2, 4, 7, 29]
print(L[2:5])
print(L[::-1])
```

Ans. [53, 4, 0]

[29, 7, 4, 2, 0, 4, 53, 4, 3]

19. Find the output of the given code.

```
list1 = ["A", "R", "T", "H", "U", "R"]
for i in range(len(list1)):
  print(list1[i], end = " ")
```

Ans. A R T H U R

20. Describe the outcome when you multiply a Python list by an integer. What does this operation achieve?

Ans. Multiplying a Python list by an integer repeats its elements the specified number of times. It does not perform element-wise multiplication but creates a new list with repeated values.

e.g.
```
nums = [1, 2, 3] * 3
print(nums)
  # Output: [1, 2, 3, 1, 2, 3, 1, 2, 3]
```

21. Consider the following list and answer the below questions:

```
list1 = [89, 45, "Taj", "Qutub", 93, 42,
"Delhi", "Agra"]
```

(i) list1[5] **(ii) "Qutab" not in list1**
(iii) list1[-3] **(iv) list1[9]**
(v) list1[2:5] **(vi) list1[-2:]**

Ans. (i) 42 (ii) False
(iii) 42 (iv) IndexError (out of range)
(v) ["Taj", "Qutub", 93] (vi) ["Delhi", "Agra"]

22. Predict the output.

```
L1 = [3, 4, 5, 9, 11, 2, 27]
print(max(L1))
print(len(L1))
```

Ans. Output

27
7

23. You have a list of numbers and need to find the index of the first occurrence of the number 5. Write a short Python code snippet that demonstrates how to do this using the appropriate list method.

Ans.
```
my_list = [1, 2, 5, 3, 5]
index_of_5 = my_list.index(5)
print(index_of_5)
```
Output 2

Short Answer Type II Questions

24. **If L1 = [1, 2, 3, 2, 1, 2, 4, 2, ...] and L2 = [10, 20, 30, ...], then (Answer using built-in functions only)**

(I) (A) Write a statement to count the occurrences of 2 in L1.

***Or* (B) Write a statement to remove the first occurrence of 1 from L1.**

(II) (A) Write a statement to insert the number 5 at the third position in L2.

***Or* (B) Write a statement to return the index of the first occurrence of 20 in L2.**

Ans. (I) (A) count_of_2 = L1.count(2)
```
print(count_of_2)
```
Or (B) L1.remove(1)
```
print(L1)
```
(II) (A) L2.insert(2, 5)
```
print(L2)
```
Or (B) index_of_20 = L2.index(20)
```
print(index_of_20)
```

25. **If L1 = ['apple', 'banana', 'cherry', 'date', 'elderberry'] is a Python list, then:**

(I) (A) Explain how you would traverse the entire list L1 using a for loop and print each element.

***Or* (B) Explain how you would access and print the element at index 2 of list L1.**

(II) (A) Explain how you would traverse the list L1 using a while loop and print each element.

***Or* (B) Explain how you would access and print the last element of list L1 without knowing its length beforehand.**

Ans. (I) (A) Use a for loop to iterate over the list and print each element:
```
for item in L1: print(item)
```
(B) Access and print the element at index 2 using L1[2]:
```
print(L1[2])  # Prints 'cherry'
```
(II) (A) Use a while loop with an index counter to print each element:
```
index = 0; while index < len(L1):
         print(L1[index]); index += 1
```
(B) Access the last element using negative indexing L1[-1]:
```
print(L1[-1]) # Prints 'elderberry'
```

26. **(A) What is the result of the following Python code:**
```
my_list = [1, 2, 3]
my_list.append(4)
print(my_list)
```
Explain why you get this result.

***Or* (B) Explain how you would create a list of squares of numbers from 1 to 5 using a list comprehension in Python.**

Ans.(A) The result of the code is [1, 2, 3, 4].

The append() method adds the value 4 to the end of the existing list my_list. Therefore, after my_list.append(4), the list becomes [1, 2, 3, 4].

(B) To create a list of squares of numbers from 1 to 5 using a list comprehension:
```
squares = [x**2 for x in range(1, 6)]
print(squares)
```
Output [1, 4, 9, 16, 25]

Long Answer Type Questions

27. **You are developing a program that manages a dynamic list of tasks. This list needs to be flexible enough to allow for various types of modifications, including inserting new tasks at specific positions and integrating tasks from other lists.** Competency Based Que.

(i) Which Python list method is best for inserting a new task at a specific position? Explain its syntax and how it handles different insertion points. Provide a short code example.

(ii) Which Python list method is best for adding the contents of one task list to another? Explain its behavior and provide a short code example.

(iii) Briefly discuss the time complexity of these methods and suggest a scenario where an alternative data structure might be more efficient.

Ans. (i) Inserting an element at a specified position:

The insert() method is best.

Syntax `list.insert(index, element)`

Explanation Inserts element before the given index.

Example `tasks.insert(1, "New Task")`

(ii) Adding contents from one list to another:

The extend() method is best.

Explanation Appends all elements from one list to the end of another.

Example tasks.extend(additional_tasks)

(iii) Time Complexity and Alternatives:

insert() O(n) time complexity (n = elements after insertion).

extend() O(k) time complexity (k = length of added list).

Alternative If frequent insertions/deletions at both ends are needed, use a deque for O(1) time complexity.

28. Write a program to move all zeroes to the end of the list.

Ans.
```
list1 = [4, 7, 0, 9, 8, 0, 2, 0, 4, 9, 0]
count = 0
for i in range(len(list1)):
    if list1[i] != 0:
        list1[count] = list1[i]
        count += 1
while count < len(list1):
    list1[count] = 0
    count += 1
print("List after pushing all zeros to end
                                of list:")
print(list1)
```

Output

List after pushing all zeros to end of list:

[4, 7, 9, 8, 2, 4, 9, 0, 0, 0, 0]

29. You are analyzing a Python list list1 that contains mixed data types, including a nested list.

```
list1 = [45, 65, "The", [65, "She", "He"],
90, 12, "This", 21]
```

(i) **Explain how list1[3:4] works and what it returns. Why?**

(ii) **What value is returned by list1[4]? Explain.**

(iii) **What elements are included in list1[:7]? Why?**

(iv) **What is the result of list1[1:2] + list1[3:4]? Explain the steps.**

Ans. (i) This slice extracts elements from index 3 up to (but not including) index 4. This includes only the element at index 3, which is the nested list [65, "She", "He"]. Therefore, it returns [[65, "She", "He"]].

(ii) This accesses the element at index 4, which is the fifth element in the list. This element is 90.

(iii) This slice extracts elements from the beginning of the list up to (but not including) index 7. It includes elements at indices 0 through 6. The result is [45, 65, "The", [65, "She", "He"], 90, 12, "This"].

(iv) **list1[1:2]** extracts the element at index 1, which is 65. Result: [65].

list1[3:4] extracts the nested list at index 3: [[65, "She", "He"]].

The + operator concatenates these two lists.

Result [65, [65, "She", "He"]].

30. You are tasked with developing a robust and efficient solution for analyzing numerical data entered by a user. This data represents a series of measurements, and your goal is to identify and report the third largest value. Competency Based Que.

Ans.
```
numbers = input("Enter numbers separated
                    by spaces: ").split()
  # Take input as a list of strings
numbers = [int(num) for num in numbers]
if len(numbers) < 3:
    print("Not enough values to determine
                    the third largest.")
else:
    numbers = list(set(numbers))
    numbers.sort(reverse=True)
    print("Third largest value:", numbers[2])
```

Output

Enter numbers separated by spaces: 3 54 22 44 11 1

Third largest value: 22

31. Write a Python program to find the odd and even numbers from entered list and display them in two different list.

Ans.
```
num = int(input("Enter number of
                        elements: "))
a = []
even = []
odd = []
for i in range(1, num+1):
    x = int(input("Enter element: "))
    a.append(x)
for y in a:
    if (y%2 == 0):
        even.append(y)
    else:
        odd.append(y)
print("The even list", even)
print("The odd list", odd)
```

Output

Enter number of elements: 5

Enter element: 56

Enter element: 67

Enter element: 88

Enter element: 33

Enter element: 65

The even list [56, 88]

The odd list [67, 33, 65]

32. Write a Python program to count positive and negative numbers in a list.

Ans.
```
num = int(input("Enter number of
                        elements: "))
x = []
for i in range(1, num+1):
    element = int(input("Enter element: "))
    x.append(element)
```

```
pos_count = 0
neg_count = 0
for i in x:
    if i > 0:
        pos_count += 1
    elif i < 0:
        neg_count += 1
print("Positive numbers in the list:",
                                    pos_count)
print("Negative numbers in the list:",
                                    neg_count)
```

Output

Enter number of elements: 4
Enter element: 23
Enter element: 53
Enter element: 77
Enter element: 33
Positive numbers in the list: 4
Negative numbers in the list: 0

33. Write a program to search a number entered by a user in a list of 5 numbers and then print the index position of that number. Now swap it with the number 1 places previous to it.

Ans.

```
numbers = [10, 20, 30, 40, 50]
search_number = int(input("Enter a number
                          to search: "))
if search_number in numbers:
    index = numbers.index(search_number)
    print(f"Index: {index}")
    if index > 0:
        numbers[index], numbers[index - 1]
        = numbers[index - 1], numbers[index]
        print("Updated list:", numbers)
    else:
        print("Cannot swap, number is at
                        the first position.")
else:
    print("Number not found.")
```

Output

Enter a number to search: 30
Index: 2
Updated list: [10, 30, 20, 40, 50]

Case Study Based Question

Case Study

A Python list is a versatile data structure that allows you to store a collection of items. It's like a dynamic array, capable of holding elements of various data types, including integers, strings, and even other lists. Lists are mutable, meaning you can modify their contents after creation.

Based on the above information, answer the following questions.

(i) Which of the following is a correct way to create a list in Python?

(a) list1 = list() (b) list1 = [1, 2, 3, 4]
(c) Both (a) and (b) (d) None of these

(ii) Which of the following is true about Python lists?

(a) Lists are immutable.
(b) List size must be declared beforehand.
(c) List elements are stored contiguously in memory.
(d) The size(list1) function is used to find the size of a list.

(iii) Which of the following Python code snippets will result in an error?

(a) list1 = [] (b) list1 = [] * 3
(c) list1 = [2, 8, 7] (d) None of these

(iv) What is the output of the following code?

```
L = [1, 2, 3, 4, 5, [6, 7, 8]]
print(L[5])
```

(a) [6, 7, 8] (b) 6
(c) Error (d) None of these

(v) Consider the following list:

```
L1 = [10, 56, 23, 45, 55, 23, 11, 65, 47,
                                [15, 13], 75]
```

What will be the output of the following statement?

```
print(L1[::-3])
```

(a) [75, 65, 55, 56] (b) [75, 65, 55, 10]
(c) [75, 65, 55, 56, 10] (d) Error

(vi) Which of the following operations will sort a list in descending order?

(a) list_name.sort() (b) max(list_name)
(c) list_name.reverse() (d) list_name[-1]

Ans. (i) (c) Both (a) and (b)
(ii) (c) List elements are stored contiguously in memory.
(iii) (d) None of the above
(iv) (a) [6, 7, 8]
(v) (a) [75, 65, 55, 56]
(vi) (c) list_name.reverse ()

SELF ASSESSMENT TEST

Multiple Choice Questions

1. **What is the output of following code?**

```
list1=[4, 3, 7, 6, 4, 9, 5, 0, 3, 2]
l1=list1[1:10:3]
print(l1)
```

(a) [3, 7, 6]   (b) [3, 4, 0]
(c) [3, 6, 9]   (d) [7, 9,2]

2. **Identify the output of following Python statement.**

```
a = [[0, 1, 2], [3, 4, 5, 6]]
b=a [1] [2]
print (b)
```

(a) 2   (b) 1
(c) 4   (d) 5

3. **Identify the output of following code.**

```
list1 = [2, 3, 9, 12, 4]
list1.insert(4, 17)
list1.insert(2, 23)
print(list1 [-4])
```

(a) 4   (b) 9
(c) 12   (d) 23

Fill in the Blanks

4. An ordered, mutable sequence of elements is a ______.

5. The ________ method is used to insert an element at a specific index.

6. The ________ method is used to remove an element from a list by its index.

7. ________ is accessing each element of a list sequentially.

8. The ________ method reverses the order of elements in a list.

9. ________ lists enable creating data structures with multiple dimensions.

State Whether True or False

10. Lists are immutable in Python.

11. List slicing modifies the original list.

12. The insert() method adds an element to the end of a list.

13. Nested lists can contain lists of the same length only.

14. Passing a list as an argument to a function creates a copy of the list.

15. The reverse() method modifies the original list.

Assertion and Reason Based Questions

Assertion (A) and Reason (R) Type questions. Choose the correct option as:

(a) Both Assertion (A) and Reason (R) are true, and Reason (R) is the correct explanation of Assertion (A).
(b) Both Assertion (A) and Reason (R) are true, but Reason (R) is not the correct explanation of Assertion (A).
(c) Assertion (A) is true, but Reason (R) is false.
(d) Assertion (A) is false, but Reason (R) is true.

16. **Assertion (A)** Lists in Python are mutable.

Reason (R) Elements in a list can be modified after the list is created.

17. **Assertion (A)** List slicing creates a new list object.

Reason (R) List slicing extracts a portion of the original list without modifying it.

18. **Assertion (A)** The insert() method adds elements at a specified index.

Reason (R) The insert() method modifies the original list by adding elements at the given index.

19. **Assertion (A)** The sort() method returns a new sorted list without modifying the original.

Reason (R) List methods are built-in functions for list operations.

20. **Assertion (A)** Lists in Python can only store elements of the same data type.

Reason (R) List copying methods create independent copies of lists.

Very Short Answer Type Questions

21. Which type of data can be store in list?

22. Write an example of mixed data type list.

23. How to compare a list in Python ?

24. Write the syntax for finding the min element in list.

Short Answer Type Questions

25. What is the use of (*) operator in list?

26. Define the max ( ) function with an example.

27. Explain the parameters of given syntax.

```
l = list_name [Start : Stop : Step]
```

28. Find the errors.

```
L = [43, 47, 40, 72]
L1 = "L + Math"
L2 = L . extend (L1)
```

29. What is the output of below questions?

```
L = [45, 89, 74, 12, 9, 83]
```

(i) L. remove ( ) (ii) L. remove (12)

30. Predict the output.

```
L1 = [3, 2, 1]
L2 = [5, 9, 8]
print (L1 * L2)
print (L2.sort ( ))
print (L1.reverse( ))
```

31. Write a Python program to move all zeroes to the starting of the list.

32. Write a program to count the even numbers in a list.

Long Answer Type Questions

33. Write the best suited method's name for the following conditions.

(i) Remove the value from the list.
(ii) Sort the elements in descending order.
(iii) Calculate the sum of all the elements of list.
(iv) Return the minimum element out of elements.

34. Write the program to print second largest number from the list.

35. Write a program to find maximum and minimum sum of elements of list in a list. Also, display its output.

Case Study Based Questions

36. A library wants to create a system to track books that are currently checked out. The system should allow librarians to store book titles and the member IDs of those who borrowed them, identify overdue books, and calculate the total number of books checked out.

(i) Which Python data type would be most suitable for storing book titles and member IDs?
(a) Dictionary (b) Tuple
(c) String (d) List

(ii) To calculate the total number of books checked out, the system needs to perform:
(a) List sorting
(b) List traversal and counting
(c) List slicing
(d) List concatenation

(iii) To identify overdue books, the system should use:
(a) List sorting
(b) List concatenation
(c) List traversal and conditional checks
(d) List slicing

(iv) If the librarian wants to add a new book to the system, which list method would be used?
(a) sort() (b) pop()
(c) append() (d) remove()

(v) To store details for multiple copies of the same book, the system would use:
(a) Tuples (b) Single list
(c) Dictionaries (d) Nested lists

Answers

1. (b)	2. (d)	3. (b)	4. list	5. insert()
6. pop()	7. Traversing		8. reverse()	
9. Nested	10. False	11. False	12. False	13. False
14. False	15. True	16. (a)	17. (a)	18. (a)
19. (d)	20. (d)			

36. (i) → (d), (ii) → (b), (iii) → (c), (iv) → (c), (v) → (d)

09 CHAPTER

A dictionary serves as a bridge between words and their meanings, helping us understand, learn and use language effectively.

Dictionary

▼ **YOUR STUDY GOALS**

▼ **YOUR PRACTICE GOAL**

- Objective Type Questions (23 Qs ; MCQs, True or False, Fill in the Blanks, Assertion and Reason)
- Subjective Type Questions (44 Qs ; VSA, SA, LA)
- Case Study Based Questions-2

A dictionary in Python is like a real-world dictionary. It's a collection of words (keys) and their meanings (values). Each word is unique, and you can use it to find its meaning.

In Python, a dictionary also has unique keys, which are usually **strings or numbers**. Each key is paired with a value, which can be anything: **a number, a word, a list,** or **even another dictionary**. You can use the key to access its corresponding value.

9.1 Creating and Initializing a Dictionary

To creating an empty dictionary in Python, you can either use the curly braces {} or the dict() constructor. Both methods will create an empty dictionary ready to store key-value pairs.

1. **Using curly braces** `empty_dict = {}`
2. **Using dict() constructor** `empty_dict = dict()`

For initializing a dictionary, inside the braces each key-value pair is separated by colon (:), and different pairs are separated by commas (,).

Syntax `dictionary_name = [key1 : value1, key2 : value2, …]`

For example,

```
>>> Employees = {"Abhi" : "Manager", "Manish" :
"Project Manager", "Aasha" : "Analyst", "Deepak" :
"Programmer", "Ishika" : "Tester"}
```

Here is the example of dictionary name Employees in which Employees names are stored as keys and their designation stored as values of respected keys.

Output

```
{'Abhi': 'Manager', 'Manish' : 'Project Manager', 'Aasha' :
'Analyst', 'Deepak' : 'Programmer', 'Ishika' : 'Tester'}
```

We can separate these dictionaries as follows

Key : Value Pair	Key	Value
"Abhi" : "Manager"	"Abhi"	"Manager"
"Manish" : "Project Manager"	"Manish"	"Project Manager"
"Aasha" : "Analyst"	"Aasha"	"Analyst"
"Deepak" : "Programmer"	"Deepak"	"Programmer"
"Ishika" : "Tester"	"Ishika"	"Tester"

We can also create empty dictionary.

For example, `dic1 = { }`

Dictionaries are also called **mappings** or **hashes** or **associative arrays.**

If you give list as key, then it will give Error

```
>>> dic = {[1, 2], "math"}
Trackback (most recent call last):
  File "<pyshell#7>", line 1, in <module>
    dic = {[1, 2], "math"}
TypeError : unhashable type : 'list'
```

Properties of Dictionary Keys

There are following points while using dictionary keys as follows.

(i) More than one entry per key is not allowed (no duplicate key is allowed).

(ii) Dictionaries' keys are case sensitive, same key name but with the different case are treated as different in Python.

(iii) The values in the dictionary can be of any type while the keys must be immutable like numbers, tuples or strings.

> **Mistake Alert**
>
> Students often forget to use quotation marks around string keys when creating dictionaries.

9.2 Accessing Elements from a Dictionary

In Python, to access the elements from a dictionary, keys are used. While in tuple and list, index is used to access the elements.

Syntax `dictionary_name[key]`

To access the respective value of key, that key has to given in square bracket with dictionary name.

For example,

```
>>>Employees ["Deepak"]
'Programmer'
>>>Employees ["Ishika"]
'Tester'
```

You can also give this as

```
>>>print ("Manish works as a", Employees
                                ['Manish'])
Manish works as a Project Manager
```

If you give a key that does not exist in dictionary, then it will give error. So, before to access the value first ensure that key is available in dictionary or not.

```
>>>Employees ["Tushar"]
Trackback (most recent call last):
  File "<pyshell#11>", line1, in <module>
  Employees ["Tushar"]
KeyError : 'Tushar'
```

If you do not give any key with dictionary name, then it will give whole dictionary with different order.

For example,

```
>>>dic = {'1' : "Math", '2' : "Science",
                          '3' : "English"}
>>>dic
{'1' : 'Math', '3' : 'English', '2' :
                              'Science'}
```

9.3 Traversing a Dictionary

Traversing a dictionary means access each and every element of it. We can traverse a dictionary using **for loop**.

For example,

```
dic = {1 : "Math", 2 : "Science", 3 :
"English" 4 : "Music"}
```

There are multiple ways to iterate over (traversing) a dictionary in Python as follows.

(i) Iterate through All Keys

In above example, the order of subject number will change every time because the dictionary does not store keys in a particular order.

```
>>>print ("keys are")
>>>for i in dic :
       print(i)
```

Output

Keys are
1
2
3
4

(ii) Iterate through All Values

Again, in above example, the order of subjects are printed will change every time.

For example,

```
>>>print (“Values are”)
>>>for i in dic:
        print(dic [i])
```

Output

Values are

Math

Science

English

Music

(iii) Iterate through All Keys Value Pairs

For example,

```
>>>print (“Keys :Values”)
>>>for i in dic :
        print(i, “:”, dic [i])
```

Output

Keys : Values

1 : Math	2 : Science
3 : English	4 : Music

Accessing Keys or Values Separately

You can access the keys or values of a dictionary separately.

- To access the keys in a dictionary named dict, you can use **dict.keys()**.
- To access the values, you can use **dict.values()**.

For example,

```
>>> dict = {1 : “Math”, 2 : “Science”, 3 : “English”, 4 :
                                              “Music”}
>>> dict.keys()
dict_keys([1, 2, 3, 4])
>>>dict.values()
dict_values(['Anurag', 'Sharma', 'Khushi', 'Deepika'])
```

You can also access the key-value pairs in a dictionary by using **dict.items()** method.

```
>>> dict = {1 : “Math”, 2 : “Science”, 3 : “English”, 4 :
                                              “Music”}
>>> dict.items()
dict_items([(1, 'Anurag'), (2, 'Sharma'), (3, 'Khushi'),
                                     (4, 'Deepika')])
```

9.4 Adding Elements to Dictionary

In Python dictionary, adding elements in dictionary extend it with a single pair of values. One value at a time can be added to a dictionary by defining value along with the key.

Syntax `dictionary_name[key] = value`

For example,

```
>>> Teacher = {'Neha': 'Hindi', 'Akshay':
                'Math', 'Parul': 'English'}
>>> Teacher['Nisha']= 'Computer'
>>> Teacher
{'Akshay': 'Math', 'Nisha': 'Computer',
       'Neha': 'Hindi', 'Parul': 'English'}
```

You can also add elements into an empty dictionary by: dictionary_name[key] = value.

For example,

```
>>> dic = {}
>>> dic[1] = "Delhi"
>>> dic[2] = "Meerut"
>>> dic[3] = "Agra"
>>> dic[4] = "Chandigarh"
>>> dic
{1: 'Delhi', 2: 'Meerut', 3: 'Agra', 4:
                             'Chandigarh'}
```

9.5 Updating Elements in a Dictionary

You can update elements that are already exist in a dictionary.

Syntax `dictionary_name [key] = value`

For example,

```
>>> Student = {11: 'Ashi', 12: 'Shivam',
13: 'Shrey', 14: 'Vicky'}
>>> Student[12] = 'Nishant'
>>> Student
{11: 'Ashi', 12: 'Nishant', 13: 'Shrey',
14: 'Vicky'}
```

If you enter a key that doesn't exist in the dictionary, it will add that key with the specified value.

```
>>> Student[15] = 'Kansal'
>>> Student
{11: 'Ashi', 12: 'Nishant', 13: 'Shrey',
14: 'Vicky', 15: 'Kansal'}
```

9.6 Deleting Elements from a Dictionary

These are following ways to delete elements from a dictionary as follows

(i) Using del Keyword

This keyword is used to delete a specific key-value pair from a dictionary.

Syntax `del dictionary_name[key]`

For example,

```
>>> Teacher = {"Name": "Ashi", "Subject":
                "Math", "Id": 2546, "Salary": 25000}
>>> del Teacher["Id"]
>>> Teacher
{'Name': 'Ashi', 'Subject': 'Math', 'Salary': 25000}
```

Note *If you try to delete a key that doesn't exist, it will raise a KeyError.*

```
>>> del Teacher["Age"]
Traceback (most recent call last):
  File "<pyshell#4>", line 1, in <module>
    del Teacher["Age"]
KeyError: 'Age'
```

(ii) Using pop() Method

This method removes a key-value pair and returns the removed value.

Syntax `dictionary_name.pop(key)`

For example,

```
>>> Teacher = {"Name": "Ashi", "Subject":
                "Math", "Id": 2546, "Salary": 25000}
>>> Teacher.pop("Id")
2546
>>> Teacher
{'Name': 'Ashi', 'Subject': 'Math', 'Salary': 25000}
```

An advantage of pop() over del is that you can provide a default value to be returned if the key is not found:

```
>>> Teacher.pop("Age", "Key not found in dictionary")
'Key not found in dictionary'
```

9.7 in and not in Membership Operators

in and not in membership operators are used with dictionary. These operators check whether a specific key is present in dictionary or not. If it is present, then it will give True otherwise False.

Syntax

```
key in dictionary_name
key not in dictionary_name
```

For example,

```
>>> Employee = {'Id': 4598, 'Name':
        'Shubham', 'Dept': 'Programmer',
                    'Salary': 35000}
>>> 'Age' in Employee
False
>>> 'Id' in Employee
True
>>> 'Designation' not in Employee
True
```

Note These operators only work with keys, not values.

```
>>> 'Shubham' in Employee
False
```

To check if a value exists in a dictionary, you need to use the values() method:

```
>>> 'Shubham' in Employee.values()
True
```

9.8 Built-in Methods

Python has some built-in methods that dictionary objects can call. Some of them are described below.

Method	Description
len()	This method is used to return the total length of the dictionary. **Syntax** `len(dictionary_name)`
clear()	This method is used to remove the elements of the dictionary. It produces an empty dictionary. It will only delete elements, not a dictionary. It does not take any parameter and does not return any value. **Syntax** `dictionary_name.clear()`
get()	This method returns the value associated with a given key. If the key is not found, it returns a default value (None by default). **Syntax** `dictionary_name.get(key, value)`
keys()	This method returns a view object containing all the keys in the dictionary. **Syntax** `dictionary_name.keys()`
values()	This method returns a view object containing all the values in the dictionary. **Syntax** `dictionary_name.values()`
items()	This method returns a view object containing key-value pairs as tuples. **Syntax** `dictionary_name.items()`

Method	Description

dict()	This function is used to create a new dictionary. It can create an empty dictionary, a dictionary from another dictionary, or a dictionary from a sequence of key-value pairs.
	Syntax `dict()`
	`dict(mapping)`
	`dict(iterable)`

update()	This method updates a dictionary with key-value pairs from another dictionary or an iterable. **Syntax** `dictionary_name.update(other_dictionary)`
sorted()	This function returns a sorted sequence of the keys in the dictionary. **Syntax** `sorted(dictionary_name)` **Note** *If a dictionary contains both string and integer keys, it will raise a TypeError as they are not comparable.*

9.9 Programs

1. Write a Program which counts the number of times a character appears in a given string using a dictionary.

Ans.
```
string = "Mississippi"
char_count = {}
for char in string:
    if char in char_count:
        char_count[char] += 1
    else:
        char_count[char] = 1
print(char_count)
```

Output

{'M': 1, 'i': 4, 's': 4, 'p': 2}

2. Write a Program to create a dictionary with names of employees, their salary and access them.

Ans.
```
employees = {
    "Arjun": 50000,
    "Bheem": 60000,
    "chaaru": 45000
}
# Accessing salary of an employee
print(employees["Bheem"])
# Printing all employee names and salaries
for name, salary in employees.items():
    print(f"{name}: {salary}")
```

Output

60000
Arjun: 50000
Bheem: 60000
chaaru: 45000

Mind Map

DICTIONARY

Creating a Dictionary

To create a dictionary, you use curly braces {}. Inside the braces, each key-value pair is separated by a colon (:), and different pairs are separated by commas (,).

Syntax dictionary_name = [key1 : value1, key2 : value2, …]

Accessing Elements from a Dictionary

In Python, to access the elements from a dictionary, keys are used.While in tuple and list, index is used to access the elements.

Syntax dictionary_name[key]

Modifying a Dictionary

Adding Elements to Dictionary

In Python dictionary, adding elements extend it with a single pair of values. One value at a time can be added to a dictionary by defining value along with the key.

Syntax dictionary_name[key]=value

Updating Elements to Dictionary

You can update elements that are already exist in a dictionary.

Syntax dictionary_name[key]=value

Deleting Elements from a Dictionary

Using del Keyword

Syntax del dictionary_name[key]

Using pop() Method

Syntax dictionary_name.pop(key)

Traversing a Dictionary

Iterate Through All Keys

```
>>>print ("keys are")
>>>for i in dic :
print(i)
```

Iterate Through All Values

```
>>>print ("Values are")
>>>for i in dic:
print(dic [i])
```

Iterate Through All Keys Values Pairs

```
>>>print ("Keys :Values")
>>>for i in dic :
print(i, ":", dic [i])
```

'in' and 'Not in' Membership Operators

in and not in membership operators are used with dictionary. These operators check whether a specific key is present in dictionary or not. If it is present, then it will give True otherwise False.

Syntax

key in dictionary_name

key not in dictionary_name

Built-in Methods

Methods	Syntax
len()	len(dictionary_name)
clear()	dictionary_name.clear()
get()	dictionary_name.get(key, value)
keys()	dictionary_name.keys()
values()	dictionary_name.values()
items()	dictionary_name.items()
update()	dictionary_name.update(other_dictionary)
sorted()	sorted(dictionary_name)
fromkeys()	dict.fromkeys(seq, value)
copy()	dict.copy()
popitem()	dict.popitem()
setdefault()	dict.setdefault(key[, default_value])
max()	max(dict)
min()	min(dict)

NCERT Folder

1. Consider the following dictionary stateCapital:

```
stateCapital =
{"AndhraPradesh":"Hyderabad",
"Bihar":"Patna","Maharashtra":"Mumbai",
"Rajasthan":"Jaipur"}
```

Find the output of the following statements:

(i) `print(stateCapital.get("Bihar"))`

(ii) `print(stateCapital.keys())`

(iii) `print(stateCapital.values())`

(iv) `print(stateCapital.items())`

(v) `print(len(stateCapital))`

(vi) `print("Maharashtra" in stateCapital)`

(vii) `print(stateCapital.get("Assam"))`

(viii)
```
del stateCapital["Rajasthan"]
print(stateCapital)
```

Ans. **Output**

(i) Patna

(ii) dict_keys(['AndhraPradesh', 'Bihar', 'Maharashtra', 'Rajasthan'])

(iii) dict_values(['Hyderabad', 'Patna', 'Mumbai', 'Jaipur'])

(iv) dict_items([('AndhraPradesh', 'Hyderabad'), ('Bihar', 'Patna'), ('Maharashtra', 'Mumbai'), ('Rajasthan', 'Jaipur')])

(v) 4

(vi) True

(vii) None

(viii) {'AndhraPradesh': 'Hyderabad', 'Bihar': 'Patna', 'Maharashtra': 'Mumbai'}

2. Write a Python program to find the highest 2 values in a dictionary.

Ans.
```
my_dict = {'a': 10, 'b': 25, 'c': 5, 'd':
                                  30, 'e': 25}
   # Get a list of values
               values = list(my_dict.values())
   # Sort the values in descending order
                      values.sort(reverse=True)
print("Highest 2 values:", values[:2])
```

3. Write a Python program to create a dictionary from a string.

Note Track the count of the letters from the string.

Sample string : 'w3resource'

Expected output : {'3': 1, 's': 1, 'r': 2, 'u': 1, 'w': 1, 'c': 1, 'e': 2, 'o': 1}

Ans.
```
string = 'w3resource'
char_count = {}
for char in string:
    if char in char_count:
        char_count[char] += 1
    else:
        char_count[char] = 1
print(char_count)
```

4. Write a program to input your friends' names and their Phone Numbers and store them in the dictionary as the key-value pair. Perform the following operations on the dictionary:

(a) Display the name and phone number of all your friends

(b) Add a new key-value pair in this dictionary and display the modified dictionary

(c) Delete a particular friend from the dictionary

(d) Modify the phone number of an existing friend

(e) Check if a friend is present in the dictionary or not

(f) Display the dictionary in sorted order of names

Ans.
```
friends = {}
while True:
    name = input("Enter friend's name
                (or type 'quit' to exit): ")
    if name.lower() == 'quit':
        break
    phone_number = input("Enter phone
                                  number: ")
    friends[name] = phone_number
```

(a) Display all friends and their phone numbers
```
    print("\nAll friends and their phone
    numbers:")
    for name, number in friends.items():
        print(f"{name}: {number}")
```

(b) Add a new friend
```
    new_name = input("\nEnter a new friend's
                                    name: ")
    new_number = input("Enter the new
                   friend's phone number: ")
    friends[new_name] = new_number
    print("\nDictionary after adding a new
                                   friend:")
    for name, number in friends.items():
        print(f"{name}: {number}")
```

(c) Delete a friend
```
    delete_name = input("\nEnter a friend's
                          name to delete: ")
    if delete_name in friends:
        del friends[delete_name]
        print(f"\n{delete_name} has been
```

```
                                deleted.")
    else:
        print(f"{delete_name} is not in your
                                friend list.")
```

(d) Modify a phone number

```
    modify_name = input("\nEnter a friend's
        name to modify their phone number: ")
    if modify_name in friends:
        new_number = input("Enter the new phone
                                number: ")
        friends[modify_name] = new_number
        print(f"\n{modify_name}'s phone
                    number has been updated.")
    else:
        print(f"{modify_name} is not in your
                                friend list.")
```

(e) Check if a friend is present

```
    check_name = input("\nEnter a friend's
                            name to check: ")
    if check_name in friends:
        print(f"{check_name} is in your friend
                                    list.")
    else:
        print(f"{check_name} is not in your
                                friend list.")
```

(f) Display the dictionary in sorted order of names

```
    sorted_friends =
    sorted(friends.items())
    print("\nSorted dictionary:")
    for name, number in sorted_friends:
        print(f"{name}: {number}")
```

EXAM PATTERN QUESTIONS

Objective Type Questions

Multiple Choice Questions

1. What will be the output of the following Python code snippet?

```
d1 = {"Neha" : 86, "Yash" : 92}
d2 = {"Neha" : 86, "Yash" : 88}
d1 > d2
```

(a) True (b) False
(c) Error (d) None

2. What will be the output of the following Python code?

```
Dic1 = {}
Dic1 [2] = 85
Dic1 [1] = [22, 23, 24]
print(Dic1[1][1])
```

(a) [22,23,24] (b) 23
(c) 22 (d) Error

3. What will be the output of the following Python code?

```
dic1 = {0 : 'One', 1 : 'Two', 2 : 'Three'}
for x, y in dic1:
    print (x, y)
```

(a) 0 1 2
(b) One Two Three
(c) 0 One 1 Two 2 Three
(d) Error

4. What will be the output of the following Python code snippet?

```
d = {"Neha" : 140, "Paras" : 145}
print (list(d.keys()))
```

(a) ["Neha", "Paras"]
(b) ["Neha" : 140, "Paras" : 145]
(c) ("Neha", "Paras")
(d) ("Neha" : 140, "Paras" : 145)

5. What will be the output of the following Python code snippet?

```
dic1 = {1 : 'One', 2 : 'Two', 3 : 'Three'}
dic1 = {}
print (len(dic1))
```

(a) 1 (b) 0 (c) 3 (d) 2

6. You have a dictionary student_grades = {'Alice': 85, 'Bob': 92}. You need to change Alice's grade to 90 and add a new student, Charlie, with a grade of 78.

Which sequence of operations would correctly update the student_grades dictionary?

(a) student_grades['Alice'] = 90; student_grades.update({'Charlie': 78})
(b) student_grades.update({'Alice': 90, 'Charlie': 78})
(c) student_grades['Alice'] = 90; student_grades['Charlie'] = 78
(d) All of the above

7. You want to count the occurrences of each letter in the word "banana".

Which of the following dictionaries would be the correct output after counting the character frequencies?

(a) {'b': 1, 'a': 3, 'n': 2}
(b) {'a': 3, 'n': 2, 'b': 1}
(c) {'b': 1, 'a': 3, 'n': 2, 'c': 0}
(d) Either a or b

8. You have a dictionary employee_salaries = {'John': 50000, 'Jane': 60000, 'Peter': 55000}.

Which method would you use to get a list of all employee names (keys) in the dictionary?

(a) employee_salaries.values()
(b) employee_salaries.items()
(c) employee_salaries.keys()
(d) employee_salaries.get('John')

Fill in the Blanks

9. To add a new key-value pair to a dictionary or modify an existing one, you can use the syntax dictionary[key] = ______.

10. The ______ method removes all items from a dictionary.

11. The ______ method returns a copy of the dictionary.

12. The ______ method returns the value for the specified key if the key is in the dictionary. If not, it inserts the key with a specified value.

13. The ______ method returns a list of tuples, where each tuple is a key-value pair in the dictionary.

State Whether True or False

14. Dictionaries in Python are mutable, meaning you can change their contents after creation.

15. The keys() method returns a list of all keys in a dictionary.

16. The get() method will raise an error if the specified key is not found in the dictionary.

17. The popitem() method removes and returns an arbitrary key-value pair from the dictionary.

18. The len() function returns the number of key-value pairs in a dictionary.

Assertion and Reason Based Questions

Assertion (A) and Reason (R) based questions. Mark the correct choice as

(a) Both (A) and (R) are true and (R) is the correct explanation for (A).
(b) Both (A) and (R) are true and (R) is not the correct explanation for (A).
(c) (A) is true and (R) is false.
(d) (A) is false but (R) is true.

19. Assertion (A) Dictionaries are mutable data structures.

Reason (R) You can add, remove, or modify elements in a dictionary after it's created.

20. Assertion (A) Dictionaries are unordered.

Reason (R) The order of elements in a dictionary is not guaranteed.

21. Assertion (A) You can use the in operator to check if a key exists in a dictionary.

Reason (R) The in operator is used to check membership in dictionaries.

22. Assertion (A) Dictionaries can be nested.

Reason (R) A dictionary can contain other dictionaries as values.

23. Assertion You can iterate over the keys of a dictionary using a for loop.

Reason (R) The keys() method returns a view of the dictionary's keys.

Answers

1. (c) Error
2. (b) 23
3. (d) Error
4. (a) ["Neha", "Paras"]
5. (b) 0
6. (d) All of the above
7. (d) Either (a) or (b)
8. (c) employee_salaries.keys()
9. value
10. clear()
11. copy()
12. setdefault()
13. items()
14. True
15. True
16. False
17. True
18. True
19. (a) Both (A) and (R) are true and (R) is the correct explanation for (A).
20. (a) Both (A) and (R) are true and (R) is the correct explanation for (A).
21. (a) Both (A) and (R) are true and (R) is the correct explanation for (A).
22. (a) Both (A) and (R) are true and (R) is the correct explanation for (A).
23. (a) Both (A) and (R) are true and (R) is the correct explanation for (A).

Subjective Type Questions

Very Short Answer Type Questions

1. What is a dictionary?

Ans. Dictionary is an unordered collection of data values that stored the key : value pair instead of a single value as an element.

2. If you have a dictionary my_dict and you need to add a new key-value pair to it, can you directly modify my_dict or do you need to create a new dictionary? **Competency Based Que.**

Ans. You can directly modify my_dict.

3. Write the syntax to create a dictionary.

Ans. dictionary_name = {key1 : value1, key2 : value2, ...}

4. Can we create an empty dictionary?

Ans. Yes, we can create an empty dictionary.
For example, dic1 = {}

5. If you try to assign two different values to the same key in a dictionary, what will happen?

Ans. The second value will overwrite the first.

6. Which feature is used to access the elements from a dictionary?

Ans. Keys are used to access the elements from a dictionary.

7. What do you mean by traversing a dictionary?

Ans. Traversing a dictionary means accessing each and every element of it.

8. How many ways are there to iterate over a dictionary?

Ans. There are three ways to iterate over a dictionary as
(i) Iterate through all keys
(ii) Iterate through all values
(iii) Iterate through all keys value pairs

9. Write the output.

```
>>> dic = {'A' : 'One', 'B' : 'Two', 'C' :
                                    'Three'}
>>> dic.keys()
```

Ans. dict_keys (['B', 'C', 'A'])

10. How to convert keys of a dictionary into a list?

Ans. list(dictionary_name.keys())

11. Riya made a dictionary. She wants to convert the values of the dictionary into lists. How can she do this? **Competency Based Que.**

Ans. list(dictionary_name.values())

12. Find the error and write correct code.

```
>>> dic = {}
>>> dic[Rahul] = (Computer)
```

Ans.

```
>>> dic = {}
>>> dic ['Rahul'] = 'Computer'
```

13. Write the syntax to update elements in a dictionary.

Ans. dictionary_name[key] = value

14. What is the use of del keyword?

Ans. del keyword is used to delete the key that is present in the dictionary.

15. Find out the error and underline the error after correct it. `dictionary_name(key).pop`

Ans. `dictionary_name.pop(key)`

16. Give the output.

```
>>> dic = {'A' : 'One', 'B' : 'Two', 'C' :
'Three'}
>>> 'E' in dic
```

Ans. Output
False

17. What will be the output?

```
d = {"Ansh" : 18, "Varsha" : 20}
"Ansh" in d
```

Ans. True

18. What will be the output?

```
dic1 = {"Sahil" : 25, "Muskan" : 22}
dic2 = {"Sahil" : 26, "Muskan" : 23}
dic1 = dic2
```

Ans. False

19. What will be the output?

```
dic = ["Ansh" : 25, "Ritu" : 26]
dic['Ritu']
```

Ans. 26

Short Answer Type I Questions

20. Write any two properties of dictionary keys.

Ans. (i) Dictionaries keys are case sensitive, same key name but with the different case are treated as different keys in Python dictionaries.
(ii) The values in the dictionary can be of any type while the keys must be immutable like numbers, tuples or strings.

21. How can you add the following data in an empty dictionary?

Keys	Values
A	Agra
B	Bengaluru
C	Chennai
D	Delhi

Ans.

```
dic = {}
dic['A'] = 'Agra'
```

```
dic['B'] = 'Bengaluru'
dic['C'] = 'Chennai'
dic['D'] = 'Delhi'
```

22. Find the output:

```
Student = {1: 'Aman', 2: 'Bablu', 3: 'Chandan'}
Student[2] = 'Sahil'
print(Student)
Student[4] = 'Aasha'
print(Student)
```

Ans. {1: 'Aman', 2: 'Sahil', 3: 'Chandan'}

```
{1: 'Aman', 2: 'Sahil', 3: 'Chandan', 4: 'Aasha'}
```

23. What is the advantage of the pop() method over the del keyword?

Ans. The advantage of the pop() method over the del keyword is that it provides a mechanism to print the desired value if tried to remove a non-existing dictionary pair.

Syntax `dictionary_name.pop(key, "Text")`

24. You are given a dictionary containing product names as keys and their prices as values. You need to write code to check if a specific product exists in the dictionary and, if it does, print its price.

Write Python code to implement the above scenario.

Ans.

```
products = {"apple": 1.0, "banana": 0.5,
                              "orange": 1.2}
product_to_check = "banana"
if product_to_check in products:
    print(f"The price of {product_to_check}
        is: {products[product_to_check]}")
else:
    print(f"{product_to_check} not found
                         in the dictionary.")
```

25. You have a dictionary my_dict = {'b': 2, 'a': 1, 'c': 3}. How would you obtain a sorted list of its keys without modifying the original dictionary? Explain the type of data returned. **Competency Based Que.**

Ans. To obtain a sorted list of the keys in the dictionary my_dict = {'b': 2, 'a': 1, 'c': 3}, you can use the sorted() function. This function returns a sorted list of the dictionary keys without modifying the original dictionary.

```
my_dict = {'b': 2, 'a': 1, 'c': 3}
sorted_keys = sorted(my_dict.keys())
print(sorted_keys)
```

Type of Data Returned The sorted() function returns a list of keys sorted in ascending order. In this case, it will return ['a', 'b', 'c'].

26. Find the output of the following code:

```
my_dict = {'data1': 200, 'data2': 154,
                              'data3': 277}
print(sum(my_dict.values()))
```

Ans. 631

27. Find the output:

```
dic = {'data1': 200, 'data2': 56, 'data3': 47}
result = 1
for key in dic:
    result = result * dic[key]
print(result)
```

Ans. 526400

28. Predict the output:

```
dic = {1: [45, 89, 65], 'A': (23, 45, 6)}
print(dic.keys())
print(dic.values())
```

Ans.

```
dict_keys([1, 'A'])
dict_values([[45, 89, 65], (23, 45, 6)])
```

29. Predict the output:

```
dic = {'a': 1, 'b': 2, 'c': 3, 'd': 4}
if 'a' in dic:
    del dic['a']
print(dic)
```

Ans. {'b': 2, 'c': 3, 'd': 4}

30. You have a dictionary student_grades with 7 key-value pairs. What will len(student_grades) return? Briefly explain why. **Competency Based Que.**

Ans. len(student_grades) will return 7.

The len() function, when used with a dictionary, counts the number of key-value pairs (items) present in the dictionary. Since student_grades has 7 key-value pairs, len() will return 7.

Short Answer Type II Questions

31. Given the dictionary d = {"Ansh": 18, "Varsha": 20}, explain the concept of dictionary keys in Python. Discuss the properties of dictionary keys, including their uniqueness and immutability. **Competency Based Que.**

Ans. In Python, a dictionary is a collection of key-value pairs. The keys in a dictionary are used to uniquely identify and access the associated values.

Properties of Dictionary Keys

1. **Uniqueness** Keys must be unique. If a key is repeated, the last value overwrites the previous one (e.g., d = {"Ansh": 18, "Varsha": 20}).
2. **Immutability** Keys must be immutable (e.g., strings, numbers, tuples) and cannot be changed after creation.
3. **Hashable** Keys must be hashable, meaning they can be used efficiently in hashing algorithms. Mutable types like lists cannot be keys.

32. What will be the output of this code

```
dic = {"Ansh": 25, "Ritu": 26}
keys_view = dic.keys()
keys_list = list(keys_view)
dic["Neha"] = 30
del dic["Ansh"]
print(keys_list)
print(list(keys_view))
```

Ans. ['Ansh', 'Ritu']
['Ritu', 'Neha']

33. Given a dictionary data with product IDs as keys and product details as values, write a Python function print_product_report(data) that iterates and prints a report including ID, name, price, quantity, and total value (price * quantity). Handle missing details with KeyError. **Competency Based Que.**

Ans.
```
def print_product_report(data):
    print("Product Report")
    for pid, details in data.items():
        try:
            name = details['name']
            price = details['price']
            qty = details['quantity']
            total_value = price * qty
            print(f"ID: {pid}, Name: {name},
             Price: ${price:.2f}, Qty: {qty},
                  Total: ${total_value:.2f}")
        except KeyError as e:
            print(f"Error: Missing
                 '{e.args[0]}' for ID {pid}")
Example Usage:
inventory =
{
    'A1': {'name': 'Laptop', 'price': 1200,
                               'quantity': 5},
    'B2': {'name': 'Mouse', 'price': 25,
                              'quantity': 20},
    'C3': {'name': 'Keyboard', 'price':
                 80}, # Missing 'quantity'
    'D4': {'name': 'Monitor', 'price': 300,
                               'quantity': 2}
}
print_product_report(inventory)
```

Output

Product Report
ID: A1, Name: Laptop, Price: $1200.00, Qty: 5, Total: $6000.00
ID: B2, Name: Mouse, Price: $25.00, Qty: 20, Total: $500.00
Error: Missing 'quantity' for ID C3
ID: D4, Name: Monitor, Price: $300.00, Qty: 2, Total: $600.00

34. Define the clear() method in the context of Python dictionaries. Explain its functionality, syntax, and provide a detailed example.

Ans. The clear() method in Python dictionaries is a built-in function that serves to remove all key-value pairs from a dictionary, effectively emptying it.

Functionality

When invoked, clear() modifies the dictionary object in place. It doesn't create a new dictionary; instead, it removes all existing elements from the original dictionary. The result is an empty dictionary {}.

Syntax

The syntax for using the clear() method is:

dictionary_name.clear()

Example

```
>>> dic = {1: "One", 2: "Two"}
>>> dic.clear()
>>> dic
{}
```

35. You have a dictionary student_grades = {'Alice': 85, 'Bob': 92, 'Charlie': 78}. Write a Python code snippet that iterates through this dictionary and prints each student's name along with their grade.

Ans.
```
student_grades = {'Alice': 85, 'Bob': 92,
'Charlie': 78}
for student, grade in
student_grades.items():
    print(f"{student}: {grade}")
```

Output Alice: 85
Bob: 92
Charlie: 78

36. You have three dictionaries representing product inventory from different stores: store1 = {'apple': 10, 'banana': 20}, store2 = {'orange': 15, 'grape': 25}, and store3 = {'kiwi': 30, 'mango': 35}. Write a Python function that takes these dictionaries as input and returns a single dictionary combining all the inventory items.

Ans.
```
def combine_inventories(store1, store2,
                                   store3):
    # Combine all dictionaries into one
    combined_inventory = {**store1,
                          **store2, **store3}
    return combined_inventory
```

Example dictionaries

```
store1 = {'apple': 10, 'banana': 20}
store2 = {'orange': 15, 'grape': 25}
store3 = {'kiwi': 30, 'mango': 35}
```

```
result = combine_inventories(store1,
                             store2, store3)
print(result)
```

Output {'apple': 10, 'banana': 20, 'orange': 15, 'grape': 25, 'kiwi': 30, 'mango': 35}

37. Write a Python function multiply_numeric_values(data) that takes a dictionary data as input. The dictionary may contain a mix of different data types as values. The function should calculate and return the product of only the numeric values (integers, floats) present in the dictionary. If no numeric values are found, the function should return 1. Implement error handling to ignore non-numeric values.

Ans.

```
def multiply_numeric_values(data):
    result = 1
    has_numeric = False
    for value in data.values():
        if isinstance(value, (int, float)):
            result *= value
            has_numeric = True
    return result if has_numeric else 1
```

Example Usage:

```
dic = {'A': 50, 'B': 30, 'C': 20, 'D': 53,
'E': 'string'}
print(multiply_numeric_values(dic))
```

Output 1590000

Long Answer Type Questions

38. Write a Python program to split dictionary keys and values into separate lists.

Ans.

```
dic = {'A': 'Apple', 'B': 'Ball', 'C': 'Cat', 'D':
                             'Dog', 'E': 'Elephant'}
print("Original Dictionary:", str(dic))
# Split dictionary into keys and values
keys = dic.keys()
values = dic.values()
# Printing keys and values separately
print("keys:", str(keys))
print("values:", str(values))
```

Output

Original Dictionary: {'A': 'Apple', 'B': 'Ball', 'C': 'Cat', 'D': 'Dog', 'E': 'Elephant'}

keys: dict_keys(['A', 'B', 'C', 'D', 'E'])

values: dict_values(['Apple', 'Ball', 'Cat', 'Dog', 'Elephant'])

39. Write a short note on the following with an example:

(i) update() (ii) len()

Ans. (i) **update()** This method is used to update the dictionary with the elements from another dictionary object or from an iterable of key/value pairs.

Syntax

```
dictionary_name1.update(dictionary _name2)
```

For Example,

```
student = {"name": "Alice", "age":
                             20, "grade": "B"}
student.update({"age": 21, "grade":
                    "A", "city": "New York"})
print(student)
```

Output

{'name': 'Alice', 'age': 21, 'grade': 'A', 'city': 'New York'}

(ii) **len()** This method is used to return the total length of the dictionary.

Syntax `len(dictionary_name)`

e.g.,

```
dic = {'A' : 'One', 'B' : 'Two', 'C' :
                    'Four', 'D' : 'Four'}
dic1 = {'A' : 'One', 'B' : 'Two', 'C' :
        'Four', 'D' : 'Four', 'E' : 'Five'}
dic.update(dic1)
print (dic)
a = len(dic)
print ('The length is' , a)
```

Output

{'A' : 'One', 'B' : 'Two', 'C' : 'Four', 'D' : 'Four', 'E' : 'Five'}

The length is 5

40. Write a Python program to remove a dictionary from a list of dictionaries:

Ans.

```
list1 = [{"id": 101, "data": "Happy"}, {"id": 102,
"data": "Birthday"}, {"id": 103, "data": "Vyom"}]
print("The original list is:")
for a in list1:
    print(a)
for i in range(len(list1)):
    if list1[i]['id'] == 103:
        del list1[i]
        break
print("List after deletion of
dictionary:")
for b in list1:
    print(b)
```

Output

The original list is:

{'id': 101, 'data': 'Happy'}

{'id': 102, 'data': 'Birthday'}

{'id': 103, 'data': 'Vyom'}

List after deletion of dictionary:

{'id': 101, 'data': 'Happy'}

{'id': 102, 'data': 'Birthday'}

41. Analyze the code snippet x = {(1, 2): 1, (2, 3): 2} and print(x[(1, 2)]). Explain what data type is being used as keys in the dictionary x. Describe how Python accesses values in a dictionary using these keys. Predict the output of the print statement and justify your answer based on the properties of dictionaries and the provided code.

Ans. In the given code snippet x = {(1, 2): 1, (2, 3): 2} and print(x[(1, 2)]), a dictionary is created where the keys are tuples and the values are integers.

Data Type of Keys

The keys in the dictionary x are tuples. In this case, the keys are (1, 2) and (2, 3). Tuples are immutable data types in Python, which allows them to be used as dictionary keys.

Accessing Values in a Dictionary

Python accesses dictionary values using keys. When you access x[(1, 2)], Python looks for the key (1, 2) in the dictionary. Since the key (1, 2) exists, it retrieves the associated value, which is 1.

Predicted Output

The print statement print(x[(1, 2)]) will output: 1

42. Predict the output

(i)
```
dic = {}
dic[1] = 1
dic['1.0'] = 2
dic[1.0] = 4
sum = 0
for i in dic:
    sum += dic[i]
print(sum)
```

(ii)
```
dic = {}
dic[(1, 2, 4)] = 8
dic[(1, 2)] = 24
sum = 0
for i in dic:
    sum += dic[i]
print(sum)
print(dic)
```

Ans. (i) 6

(ii) 32

{(1, 2, 4) : 8, (1, 2) : 24}

43. Write Python program to test if dictionary contains unique keys and values.

Ans.
```
dict1 = {'Nikunj': 1, 'Akshat': 2, 'Akansha': 3,
                                  'Manish': 1}
print("The original dictionary: "
                                  + str(dict1))
flag = False
val = {}
for keys in dict1:
    if dict1[keys] in val:
        flag = True
        break
    else:
        val[dict1[keys]] = 1
print("Does dictionary contain repetition:
                                  " + str(flag))
```

Output

The original dictionary: {'Nikunj': 1, 'Akshat': 2, 'Akansha': 3, 'Manish': 1}

Does dictionary contain repetition : True

44. Find the output of the given Python program to swap keys and values in dictionary.

```
old_dict = {'One' : 742, 'Two' : 145,
'Three' : 654, 'Four' : 321, 'Five' : 120,
'Six' : 365, 'Seven' : 459, 'Eight' : 449}
new_dict = dict([(value, key) for key,
value in old_dict.items()])
print("Original dictionary is:")
print(old_dict)
print()
print("Dictionary after swapping is:")
print("Keys:Values")
for i in new_dict:
    print(i, ":", new_dict[i])
```

Ans. Output

Original dictionary is:

{'One': 742, 'Two': 145, 'Three': 654, 'Four': 321, 'Five': 120, 'Six': 365, 'Seven': 459, 'Eight': 449}

Dictionary after swapping is:

Keys: Values

742 : One

145 : Two

654 : Three

321 : Four

120 : Five

365 : Six

459 : Seven

449 : Eight

Case Study Based Questions

Case Study 1

A Python dictionary is a versatile data structure that stores data in key-value pairs. It's mutable, meaning you can add, remove, or modify elements after creation. Unlike lists and tuples, dictionaries are unordered, so the order of elements is not guaranteed. Dictionaries are defined using curly braces {} and are accessed using their keys. You can add new key-value pairs to a dictionary using the assignment operator =.

To access a value, you use the key within square brackets []. The keys(), values(), and items() methods allow you to iterate over the keys, values, or key-value pairs of a dictionary, respectively. Dictionaries offer efficient key-based access with a time complexity of O(1), making them a powerful tool for various data manipulation tasks.

(i) **What is the primary characteristic of a Python dictionary?**
(a) Ordered and immutable
(b) Unordered and mutable
(c) Ordered and mutable
(d) Unordered and immutable

(ii) **Which of the following is used to define a dictionary in Python?**
(a) Square brackets []
(b) Parentheses ()
(c) Curly braces {}
(d) Angle brackets <>

(iii) **How can you access a value in a dictionary?**
(a) By its index (b) By its key
(c) By its position (d) By its order

(iv) **What is the correct way to add a new key-value pair to a dictionary?**
(a) dictionary[key] = value
(b) dictionary.add(key, value)
(c) dictionary.insert(key, value)
(d) dictionary.append(key, value)

(v) **How can you iterate over the keys and values of a dictionary?**
(a) Using a for loop with the items() method
(b) Using a for loop with the keys() method
(c) Using a for loop with the values() method
(d) All of the above

(vi) **What is the time complexity of accessing a value in a dictionary by its key?**
(a) O(n) (b) O(log n)
(c) O(1) (d) O(n^2)

Ans. (i) (b) Unordered and mutable
(ii) (c) Curly braces { }
(iii) (b) By its key
(iv) (a) dictionary[key] = value
(v) (d) All of the above
(vi) (c) O(1)

Case Study 2

Consider the following dictionary :

```
dic = {1 : [45, 89, 65], 'A' : (23, 45, 6)}
```

Based on the above dictionary, answer the following questions.

(i) Find the output of print (dic. keys ()).
(a) dict_keys(['A', 1]) (b) dict_keys ['A', 1]
(c) dict_keys ('A', 1) (d) dict_keys [('A', 1)]

(ii) Which of the following is the correct output of given statement?

```
print(dic.values())
```

(a) dict_values (45, 89, 65, 23, 45, 6)
(b) dict_values ([45, 89, 65], (23, 45, 6))
(c) dict_values ([[45, 89, 65], (23, 45, 6)])
(d) None of the above

(iii) Find the output of len(dic).
(a) 3 (b) 6
(c) 8 (d) 2

(iv) Which output is best suited for given statement?

```
dic.get('A')
```

(a) (23, 45, 6) (b) [23, 45, 6]
(c) 45, 89, 65 (d) [45, 89, 65]

(v) Each key is separated by a
(a) , (b) ;
(c) : (d) Space

Ans. (i) (a) dict_keys(['A', 1])
(ii) (c) dict_values ([[45, 89, 65], (23, 45, 6)])
(iii) (d) 2
(iv) (a) (23, 45, 6)
(v) (a) ,

SELF ASSESSMENT TEST

Multiple Choice Questions

1. Suppose d = {"Rahul":40, "Riya":45}.
To obtain the number of entries in dictionary which command do we use? **Competency Based Que.**
(a) d.size() (b) len(d)
(c) size(d) (d) d.len()

2. Which of the following is not true about dictionary keys?
(a) More than one key is not allowed.
(b) Keys must be immutable.
(c) Keys must be integers.
(d) When duplicate keys encountered, the last assignment wins.

3. What will be the output of the following Python code?
```
a={1:5,2:3,3:4}
a.pop(3)
print(a)
```
(a) {1: 5}
(b) {1: 5, 2: 3}
(c) Error, syntax error for pop() method
(d) {1: 5, 3: 4}

Fill in the Blanks

4. A collection of key-value pairs is called a ______.

5. The ______ method returns a list of keys in a dictionary.

6. The ______ method returns a list of key-value pairs in a dictionary.

7. The ______ method adds or updates key-value pairs in a dictionary.

8. The ______ method removes a key-value pair from a dictionary.

9. The ______ function returns the number of key-value pairs in a dictionary.

State Whether True or False

10. Dictionaries are mutable.

11. Dictionary keys can be of any data type.

12. The values() method returns a list of keys in a dictionary.

13. The get() method returns the value for a given key, or a default value if the key is not found.

14. The clear() method removes a specific key-value pair from a dictionary.

15. sorted() method returns a new sorted dictionary.

Assertion and Reason Based Questions

Assertion (A) and Reason (R) Type questions. Choose the correct option as:
(a) Both Assertion (A) and Reason (R) are true, and Reason (R) is the correct explanation of Assertion (A).
(b) Both Assertion (A) and Reason (R) are true, but Reason (R) is not the correct explanation of Assertion (A).
(c) Assertion (A) is true, but Reason (R) is false.
(d) Assertion (A) is false, but Reason (R) is true.

16. **Assertion (A)** Dictionaries are mutable.
Reason (R) You can add, modify, or remove key-value pairs in a dictionary.

17. **Assertion (A)** The keys() method returns a list of values.
Reason (R) Dictionaries are mutable data structures.

18. **Assertion (A)** Dictionary keys must be immutable.
Reason (R) Dictionary keys are used for hashing, and mutable objects cannot be hashed.

19. **Assertion (A)** The update() method creates a new dictionary instead of modifying the existing one.
Reason (R) Dictionaries can store key-value pairs of different data types.

Very Short Answer Type Questions

20. Read the code shown below and pick out the keys.
```
d = {"Sahil" : 25, "Muskan" : 22}
```

21. What will be the output?
```
d = {"Ansh" : 18, "Varsha" : 20}
"Varsha" in d
```

22. Write the syntax to traverse a dictionary.

Short Answer Type Questions

23. What will be the output?
```
dic = {'Ansh' : 25, 'Varsha' : 26}
print(list(dic.values()))
```

24. Which function is used to remove the first element of a set and the last element of a list?

25. Predict the output.

```
dic1 = {2 : (4, 5, 6), 'B' : [45, 3, 2]}
print (dic1.values())
print (dic1.keys())
```

26. Find the output.

```
dic = {'A' : 400, 'B' : 43, 'C' : 33}
print (sum (dic.values()))
```

27. Write the short note on pop() method.

28. Find out the error and correct it.

```
dic = {'One' : 1, 1 : 'One', 2 : 'Two', [1,
'One'] : 'Three'}
```

29. Find the errors.

```
s = "abbcdccba"
counter = {}
for i in s :
    counter [i] = counter [i] + 1
```

Long Answer Type Questions

30. Write a python program that checks if two same values in dictionary have different keys.

31. Write a Python program to create two dictionary and swap their values.

32. Write a Python program to create a dictionary and make two lists for dictionary keys and values.

33. Write a Python program to create dictionary of an Employee detail in which user add two keys after creation and delete one key after that.

34. Define any two functions which are used in dictionary.

Case Study Based Questions

35. A teacher wants to create a system to store and manage student information. The system should store student names, roll numbers, and grades. The teacher needs to access, modify, and traverse this information efficiently.

(i) Which Python data structure is most suitable for storing student information?

(a) List (b) Tuple
(c) Dictionary (d) Set

(ii) To access a student's grade using their roll number, the teacher should use:

(a) List indexing (b) Dictionary keys
(c) Tuple slicing (d) Set iteration

(iii) To add a new student's information to the system, the teacher would use:

(a) append()
(b) insert()
(c) Dictionary key assignment
(d) extend()

(iv) To get a list of all student roll numbers, the teacher should use:

(a) values() (b) items()
(c) keys() (d) get()

(v) To remove a student's information from the system, the teacher can use:

(a) del() (b) remove()
(c) discard() (d) clear()

Answers

1.	(b)	2.	(c)	3.	(b)	4.	Dictionary		
5.	keys()	6.	items()	7.	update()			8.	pop()
9.	len()	10.	True	11.	False	12.	False	13.	True
14.	False	15.	False	16.	(a)	17.	(d)	18.	(a)
19.	(d)								

35. (i) → (c), (ii) → (b), (iii) → (c), (iv) → (c), (v) → (a)

10 CHAPTER

Introduction to NumPy

NumPy is widely used in various domains such as:
- Efficiently handling large datasets and performing statistical computations.
- Accelerating matrix operations and numerical computations.
- Manipulating pixel data and performing transformations.
- Solving mathematical problems with speed and accuracy.

YOUR STUDY GOALS

10.1 Array
10.2 NumPy Array
10.3 Indexing and Slicing in NumPy

YOUR PRACTICE GOAL

- Objective Type Questions (21 Qs ; MCQs, True or False, Fill in the Blanks, Assertion and Reason)
- Subjective Type Questions (14 Qs ; VSA, SA, LA)
- Case Study Based Question-1

NumPy, short for "Numerical Python," is a powerful package for data analysis and scientific computing in Python. It provides an efficient multi-dimensional array object along with a comprehensive set of functions and tools for array manipulation.

The n-dimensional array in NumPy significantly enhances data processing speed.

Additionally, NumPy seamlessly integrates with other Python libraries and supports interoperability with programming languages like C and C++.

Installing NumPy

To install NumPy, use the following command:

```
pip install numpy
```

10.1 Array

We have learned about various data types like lists, tuples, and dictionaries. In this chapter, we will explore another important data type which is **array**.

An array is a data type used to store multiple values under a single identifier (variable name). It consists of an **ordered collection** of elements, where each element is of the same type and can be accessed using its **index** (position).

Key Characteristics of an Array

- All elements in an array are of the same data type, though their values may differ.

- The entire array is stored contiguously in memory, making operations on it faster.
- Each element is accessed using the array's name and index, where the index uniquely identifies each element.

  For example, consider an array containing five numbers:

  [10, 9, 99, 71, 90]

  Here, indexing starts from 0:

  - The first value 10 has an index [0].
  - The second value 9 has an index [1], and so on.
  - The last value 90 (5th element) has an index [4].

  This is known as **zero-based indexing**, similar to how lists are indexed in Python.

Arrays are a fundamental concept in programming and are supported by most programming languages in various forms.

> ***Contiguous Memory Allocation***
>
> The memory space must be divided into fixed-sized partitions, with each partition allocated to a single data unit only.
>
> ***Non-Contiguous Memory Allocation***
>
> Data is divided into multiple blocks and placed in different parts of memory based on available space.

10.2 NumPy Array

NumPy arrays are used to store numerical data, including lists, vectors, and matrices. The NumPy library provides a comprehensive set of built-in functions for creating, manipulating, and transforming arrays.

While Python has a native array data structure, it is less versatile, efficient, and useful compared to NumPy arrays. The official name for a NumPy array is **ndarray**, but it is commonly referred to as an **array**.

Differences Between List and Array

Feature	List	Array
Data Type	Can contain elements of different data types, e.g., [1, 3.4, 'hello', 'a@'].	All elements must be of the same data type, e.g., an array of floats: [1.2, 5.4, 2.7].
Memory Storage	Elements are not stored contiguously in memory.	Elements are stored in contiguous memory locations, making operations faster.
Element-wise Operations	Does not support element-wise operations like addition or multiplication because elements may be of different types.	Supports element-wise operations. For example, if A1 is an array, A1/3 divides each element by 3.
Memory Efficiency	Requires more memory as Python stores both the value and type information for each element.	More memory-efficient since it does not store type information separately for each element.
Availability	Built into core Python.	Part of the NumPy library (ndarray).

Creating NumPy Arrays from a List

NumPy provides multiple ways to create arrays. To use NumPy arrays and their methods, we first need to import the NumPy library.

```
import numpy as np
```

The array() function in NumPy converts a given list into an array.

Example 1 Creating an array called array1 from the given list.

```
# Creating an array from a list
array1 = np.array([10, 20, 30])
# Displaying the array
print(array1)
```

Output

[10 20 30]

Creating a 1-D Array

A one-dimensional (1-D) array has a single row of elements.

Example 2 Create a 1-D array from a list which contains numbers as well as string.

```
array2 = np.array([5, -7.4, 'a', 7.2])
# Displaying the array
print(array2)
```

Output

['5', '-7.4', 'a', '7.2'], dtype='<U32'

Since the list contains mixed data types, NumPy converts all elements to strings (dtype='<U32').

Creating a 2D Array

A **two-dimensional (2D) array** can be created by passing a **nested list** to np.array().

Example 3

```
array3 = np.array([[2.4, 3], [4.91, 7], [0, -1]])
print(array3)
```

Output

([[2.4 , 3.],
[4.91, 7.],
[0. , -1.]]

The integers 3, 7, 0, and -1 have been **promoted to floats** to maintain a uniform data type.

Mistake Alter!

A common mistake occurs when passing arguments to array() if square brackets are omitted. Ensure that a single argument containing a list of values is passed.

Incorrect way `>>> a = np.array(1, 2, 3, 4)`

Correct way `>>> a = np.array([1, 2, 3, 4])`

Attributes of NumPy Array

Some important attributes of a NumPy ndarray object are

Attribute	Description	Example	Output
ndarray .ndim	• Returns the number of dimensions (axes) of the array. • Arrays can be 1-D, 2-D, or n-D. Here, we focus on 1-D and 2-D arrays only.	print(array 1.ndim)	1
ndarray .shape	• Returns a tuple indicating the size of the array along each dimension. • For a 2-D array, (rows, columns) format is used.	print(array 1.shape)	(3,)
ndarray .size	• Returns the total number of elements in the array. • Equal to the product of shape dimensions.	print(array 1 .size)	3
ndarray .dtype	• Returns the data type of array elements. • All elements in an array must have the same data type. • **Common types** int32, int64, float32, float64, U32, etc.	print(array 1.dtype)	dtype ('int32')
ndarray .itemsize	• Returns the size (in bytes) of each array element. • **Example** int32 and float32 take 4 bytes, int64 and float64 take 8 bytes. • **Calculation** itemsize = bits/8 (e.g., int32 = 32/8 = 4 bytes).	print(array 1.itemsize)	4 (Integer: int32)

Quick Test 1

1. What is the full form of NumPy?
2. How is a NumPy array different from a Python list in terms of memory storage?
3. What will be the output of the following code?

```
import numpy as np
arr = np.array([10, 20, 30])
print(arr.ndim)
```

4. What function is used to convert a list into a NumPy array?

10.3 Indexing and Slicing in NumPy

NumPy arrays allow indexing, slicing, and iteration over elements efficiently.

1. Indexing

For **1-D arrays**, elements are indexed starting from **0**. For **2-D arrays**, each element is accessed using two indices:

- i → Represents the **row number**
- j → Represents the **column number**

Consider the following table representing the weekly sales (in units) of three products in four stores:

Store	Product A	Product B	Product C
Store 1	120	85	90
Store 2	150	95	100
Store 3	130	80	75
Store 4	140	90	85

We can store these values in a 2-D NumPy array named sales:

```
import numpy as np
sales = np.array([[120, 85, 90],
            [150, 95, 100],
            [130, 80, 75],
            [140, 90, 85]])
```

This array has **4 rows** (stores) and **3 columns** (products), making it a sales[4][3] array with 4 × 3 = 12 elements.

Each element in the array is accessed using sales[i, j], where:

- i refers to the **row index** (store).
- j refers to the **column index** (product).

Accessing Elements

- **Find sales of Product C in Store 3** (row index 2, column index 2):

```
sales[2, 2]
75
```

- **Find sales of Product B in Store 4** (row index 3, column index 1):

```
sales[3, 1]
90
```

- **Accessing an out-of-range index results in an error**

```
sales[1, 3]
```

IndexError index 3 is out of bounds for axis 1 with size 3

2. Slicing

Slicing is used to extract a portion of an array using the [start:end] notation. The end index is excluded.

Slicing in a 1-D Array

Example 4 Take a 1-D array of daily temperature readings (in °C).

```
temp = np.array([22, 24, 26, 28, 30, 32, 34])
```

- **Extract temperatures from index 2 to 4 (excluding 5)**

```
temp[2:5]
array([26, 28, 30])
```

- **Reverse the array**

```
temp[::-1]
array([34, 32, 30, 28, 26, 24, 22])
```

Slicing in a 2-D Array

Example 5 Consider the weekly production of three factories (in metric tons) for four weeks.

```
production = np.array([[500, 550, 600, 650],
                       [480, 510, 530, 590],
                       [520, 560, 610, 640]])
```

Week	Factory 1	Factory 2	Factory 3
Week 1	500	550	600
Week 2	480	510	530
Week 3	520	560	610
Week 4	650	590	640

Extracting Specific Data

- **Get production data for Factory 2 (column index 1) for Weeks 1 to 3**

```
production[0:3, 1]
array([550, 510, 560])
```

- **Extract production data for Weeks 2 & 3 (row index 1:3) and Factories 1 & 2 (column index 0:2)**

```
production[1:3, 0:2]
array([[480, 510],
       [520, 560]])
```

- **Extract all production values of Factory 3 (column index 2)**

```
production[:, 2]
array([600, 530, 610])
```

Quick Test 2

1. How do you access the sales value of Product B in Store 4 from the given NumPy array?
2. What will be the output of temp[2:5] if temp = np.array([22, 24, 26, 28, 30, 32, 34])?
3. Write a NumPy slicing expression to extract all production values of Factory 3.
4. What happens if you try to access an index out of range in a NumPy array?

NCERT Folder

1. What is NumPy? How to install it?

Ans. Refer to text on page no. 163 (Introduction to NumPy).

2. What is an array, and how is it different from a list? What is the name of the built-in array class in NumPy?

Ans. An array is a collection of elements of the same data type stored in contiguous memory locations.

A list in Python is a general-purpose data structure that can store elements of different data types and is more flexible but slower than NumPy arrays for numerical operations.

The built-in array class in NumPy is called ndarray (N-dimensional array).

3. What do you understand by the rank of an ndarray?

Ans. The rank of an ndarray refers to the number of dimensions (axes) it has :

- A 1D array has a rank of 1, a 2D array has a rank of 2, and so on.
- We can find the rank of an array using the .ndim attribute

```
import numpy as np
```

```
array1 = np.array([1, 2, 3])
print(array1.ndim)
```
Output 1
```
array2 = np.array([[1, 2, 3], [4, 5, 6]])
print(array2.ndim)
```
Output 2

4. **Create the following NumPy arrays:**

(a) **A 1-D array called zeros having 10 elements and all the elements are set to zero.**

(b) **A 1-D array called vowels having the elements 'a', 'e', 'i', 'o' and 'u'.**

(c) **A 2-D array called ones having 2 rows and 5 columns and all the elements are set to 1 and dtype as int.**

(d) **Use nested Python lists to create a 2-D array called myarray1 having 3 rows and 3 columns and store the following data:**

2.7, -2, -19
0, 3.4, 99.9
10.6, 0, 13

(e) **A 2-D array called myarray2 using arange() having 3 rows and 5 columns with start value = 4, step size 4 and dtype as float.**

Ans.
```
import numpy as np
```
(a)
```
zeros = np.zeros(10, dtype=int)
```
(b)
```
vowels = np.array(['a', 'e', 'i', 'o', 'u'])
```
(c)
```
ones = np.ones((2, 5), dtype=int)
```
(d)
```
myarray1 = np.array([[2.7, -2, -19],
           [0, 3.4, 99.9],
           [10.6, 0, 13]])
```
(e)
```
myarray2 = np.arange(4, 4 + 3 * 5 * 4, 4,
    dtype=float).reshape(3, 5)
```

5. **Using the arrays created in Question 4 above, write NumPy commands for the following:**

(a) **Find the dimensions, shape, size, data type of the items and itemsize of arrays zeros, vowels, ones, myarray1 and myarray2.**

(b) **Reshape the array ones to have all the 10 elements in a single row.**

(c) **Display the 2nd and 3rd element of the array vowels.**

(d) **Display all elements in the 2nd and 3rd row of the array myarray1.**

(e) **Display the elements in the 1st and 2nd column of the array myarray1.**

(f) **Display the elements in the 1st column of the 2nd and 3rd row of the array myarray1.**

(g) **Reverse the array of vowels.**

Ans. (a)
```
arrays = [zeros, vowels, ones, myarray1,
          myarray2]
array_names = ['zeros', 'vowels', 'ones',
               'myarray1', 'myarray2']
for name, arr in zip(array_names,
                     arrays):
    print(f"\nArray: {name}")
    print(f"Dimensions: {arr.ndim}")
    print(f"Shape: {arr.shape}")
    print(f"Size: {arr.size}")
    print(f"Data Type: {arr.dtype}")
    print(f"Item Size: {arr.itemsize}
        bytes")
```
(b)
```
ones_reshaped = ones.reshape(1, 10)
print("\nReshaped 'ones' array:\n",
      ones_reshaped)
```
(c)
```
print("\n2nd and 3rd elements of
      'vowels':", vowels[1:3])
```
(d)
```
print("\n2nd and 3rd row of
      'myarray1':\n", myarray1[1:3])
```
(e)
```
print("\nElements in 1st and 2nd column of
      'myarray1':\n", myarray1[:, :2])
```
(f)
```
print("\nElements in 1st column of 2nd and
      3rd row of 'myarray1':\n",
      myarray1[1:3, 0])
```
(g)
```
vowels_reversed = vowels[::-1]
print("\nReversed 'vowels' array:",
      vowels_reversed)
```

Mind Map

INTRODUCTION TO NUMPY

NumPy, short for "Numerical Python"

NumPy Array

NumPy arrays are used to store numerical data, including lists, vectors, and matrices.

Indexing and Slicing in NumPy

Indexing

For 1-D arrays, elements are indexed starting from 0.
For 2-D arrays, each element is accessed using two indices:

- i Represents the row number
- j Represents the column number

Slicing

Slicing is used to extract a portion of an array using the [start:end] notation. The end index is excluded.

Slicing in a 1-D Array

e.g.
```
temp = np.array([22, 24, 26,
                 28, 30, 32, 34])
```

Slicing in a 2-D Array

e.g.
```
production = np.array([[500,
    550, 600, 650],
    [480, 510, 530, 590],
    [520, 560, 610, 640]])
```

Creating NumPy Arrays from a List

The array() function in NumPy converts a given list into an array.

Example Creating an array called array1 from the given list.

```
array1=np.array([10, 20, 30])
print(array1)
```

Creating a 1-D Array

A one-dimensional (1-D) array has a single row of elements.

Example Create a 1-D array from a list which contains numbers as well as string.

```
array2 = np.array([5, -7.4, 'a', 7.2])
print(array2)
```

Creating a 2D Array

A two-dimensional (2D) array can be created by passing a nested list to np.array().

Example

```
array3 = np.array([[2.4, 3],
[4.91, 7], [0, -1]])
print(array 3)
```

EXAM PATTERN QUESTIONS

Objective Type Questions

Multiple Choice Questions

1. What will be the output of the following code?

```
import numpy as np
arr = np.array([10, 20, 30, 40, 50])
print(arr[-3:-1])
```

(a) [10, 20] (b) [30, 40]
(c) [30, 40, 50] (d) [20, 30, 40]

2. What is the default data type of a NumPy array created using np.array([1, 2, 3])?

(a) int (b) float
(c) complex (d) object

3. What will be the shape of arr after executing the following code?

```
import numpy as np
arr = np.zeros((3, 4, 2))
```

(a) (3, 4, 2) (b) (4, 3, 2) (c) (3, 2, 4) (d) (3, 4, 1)

4. What will be the output of the following slicing operation?

```
import numpy as np
arr = np.array([[1, 2, 3], [4, 5, 6],
                                 [7, 8, 9]])
print(arr[1:, 1:])
```

(a) [[5, 6], [8, 9]] (b) [[2, 3], [5, 6]]
(c) [[4, 5], [7, 8]] (d) [[1, 2], [4, 5]]

5. What will be the shape of the array created by this command?

```
arr = np.zeros((4, 2, 3))
```

(a) (4, 2, 3) (b) (2, 3, 4)
(c) (4, 3, 2) (d) (3, 4, 2)

6. What will be the output of this NumPy command?

```
import numpy as np
arr = np.array([[1, 2], [3, 4], [5, 6]])
print(arr[:, 1])
```

(a) [2, 3, 5] (b) [2, 4, 6]
(c) [1, 3, 5] (d) [1, 2, 3]

7. What does the following code do?

```
import numpy as np
arr = np.array([10, 20, 30, 40, 50])
print(arr[::-2])
```

(a) [50, 30, 10]
(b) [10, 30, 50]
(c) [50, 40, 30, 20, 10]
(d) [50, 30]

State Whether True or False

8. NumPy stands for Numerical Python.

9. NumPy arrays can store elements of different data types in the same array.

10. The arange() function in NumPy creates an array with evenly spaced values within a given range.

11. In NumPy, slicing an array creates a new independent copy of the original array.

12. The reshape() function in NumPy can change the dimensions of an array without changing its data.

Fill in the Blanks

13. NumPy is an _______ module of Python.

14. An array consists of ________ and _______.

15. NumPy array supports ______________ operations which is not supported in Python List.

16. Slicing is specified by using __________ operator.

Assertion and Reason Based Questions

Assertion (A) and Reason (R) Type questions. Choose the correct option as:

(a) Both Assertion (A) and Reason (R) are true, and Reason (R) is the correct explanation of Assertion (A).
(b) Both Assertion (A) and Reason (R) are true, but Reason (R) is not the correct explanation of Assertion (A).
(c) Assertion (A) is true, but Reason (R) is false.
(d) Assertion (A) is false, but Reason (R) is true.

17. **Assertion (A)** NumPy arrays are more efficient than Python lists for numerical computations.

Reason (R) NumPy arrays allow vectorized operations, which reduces the need for explicit loops.

18. **Assertion (A)** NumPy arrays are mutable, meaning their elements can be changed after creation.

Reason (R) NumPy arrays store elements in contiguous memory locations, improving performance.

19. **Assertion (A)** The np.zeros(5) function creates an array with five elements, all set to zero.

Reason (R) The np.zeros() function creates an array filled with ones by default.

20. **Assertion (A)** NumPy supports multi-dimensional arrays, unlike Python lists.

Reason (R) Python lists can only store elements in a single dimension.

21. **Assertion (A)** The shape of a NumPy array can be changed using the reshape() function.

Reason (R) The reshape() function modifies the original array directly.

Answers

1. (b) [30, 40]
2. (a) int
3. (a) (3, 4, 2)
4. (a) [[5, 6], [8, 9]]
5. (a) (4, 2, 3)
6. (b) [2, 4, 6]
7. (a) [50, 30, 10]
8. True
9. False
10. True
11. False
12. True
13. open-source
14. Element and index
15. vectorized
16. colon
17. (a) Both Assertion (A) and Reason (R) are true, and Reason (R) is the correct explanation of Assertion (A).
18. (b) Both Assertion (A) and Reason (R) are true, but Reason (R) is not the correct explanation of Assertion (A).
19. (c) Assertion (A) is true, but Reason (R) is false.
20. (c) Assertion (A) is true, but Reason (R) is false.
21. (c) Assertion (A) is true, but Reason (R) is false.

Subjective Type Questions

Very Short Type Questions

1. What is NumPy in Python?

Ans. NumPy is a Python library used for numerical computing and handling arrays efficiently.

2. How do you create a NumPy array from a Python list?

Ans. Using np.array(list_name).

3. What function is used to create an array of zeros in NumPy?

Ans. np.zeros(shape)

4. How do you find the shape of a NumPy array?

Ans. Using .shape attribute.

5. What does np.arange(5, 15, 2) do?

Ans. Creates an array with values [5, 7, 9, 11, 13].

6. What will be the output of the following code?

```
import numpy as np
A = np.array([24, 46, 57, 14, 68, 34, 89, 92])
print(A[7:3:-1])
print(A[2:6])
```

Ans. [92 89 34 68]

[57 14 68 34]

7. What will be the output of the following code?

```
import numpy as np
A = np.array([1, 2, 3, 4, 5, 6, 7, 8, 9, 10,
                                          11, 12])
print(A[10:5:-2])
```

Ans. [11 9 7]

Short Answer Type I Questions

8. Write a NumPy program to convert a list of numeric values into a one-dimensional NumPy array.

Ans.

```
# Importing the NumPy library with an alias 'np'
import numpy as np
# Creating a Python list 'l' containing
                        floating-point numbers
l = [12.23, 13.32, 100, 36.32]
# Printing the original Python list
print("Original List:", l)
# Creating a NumPy array 'a' from the
                              Python list 'l'
a = np.array(l)
# Printing the one-dimensional NumPy array 'a'
print("One-dimensional NumPy array: ", a)
```

Output

Original List: [12.23, 13.32, 100, 36.32]

One-dimensional NumPy array: [12.23 13.32 100. 36.32]

9. Write a NumPy program to reverse an array (the first element becomes the last).

Ans.

```
# Importing the NumPy library with an
                                   alias 'np'
import numpy as np
# Creating an array 'x' using arange()
         function with values from 12 to 37
                                 (inclusive)
x = np.arange(12, 38)
# Printing the original array 'x'
           containing values from 12 to 37
print("Original array:")
print(x)
# Reversing the elements in the array 'x'
           and printing the reversed array
print("Reverse array:")
x = x[::-1]
print(x)
```

Output

Original array:

[12 13 14 15 16 17 18 19 20 21 22 23 24 25 26 27 28 29 30 31 32 33 34 35 36 37]

Reverse array:

[37 36 35 34 33 32 31 30 29 28 27 26 25 24 23 22 21 20 19 18 17 16 15 14 13 12]

Short Answer Type II Questions

10. Write a NumPy program to create an array of 10 zeros, 10 ones, and 10 fives.

Ans.

```
# Importing the NumPy library with an alias 'np'
import numpy as np
# Creating an array of 10 zeros using
                                  np.zeros()
array = np.zeros(10)
# Printing a message indicating an array
                                 of 10 zeros
print("An array of 10 zeros:")
# Printing the array of 10 zeros
print(array)
# Creating an array of 10 ones using
                                   np.ones()
array = np.ones(10)
```

```
# Printing a message indicating an array
                                   of 10 ones
print("An array of 10 ones:")
# Printing the array of 10 ones
print(array)
# Creating an array of 10 fives by
        multiplying an array of 10 ones by 5
array = np.ones(10) * 5
# Printing a message indicating an array
                                  of 10 fives
print("An array of 10 fives:")
# Printing the array of 10 fives
print(array)
```

Output

An array of 10 zeros:

[0. 0. 0. 0. 0. 0. 0. 0. 0. 0.]

An array of 10 ones:

[1. 1. 1. 1. 1. 1. 1. 1. 1. 1.]

An array of 10 fives:

[5. 5. 5. 5. 5. 5. 5. 5. 5. 5.]

11. Write a code to create an ndarray having six zeros in it. Write statements to change 3rd and 5th elements of this array to 15 and 25 respectively.

Ans.

```
import numpy as n
p=n.zeros(6,dtype=int)
print(p)
p[2]=15
p[4]=25
print(p)
```

12. Consider the following ndarrays:

```
A=[10,20,30,40,50,60,70,80,90]
B=[[0,1,2,3],
  [4,5,6,7],
  [8,9,10,11],
  [12,13,14,15]]
```

What will be the array slices as per the following?

(i) B[0:2,1:3] **(ii) A[2:6:3]**

(iii) A[-1:-3] **(iv) B[::-1]**

(v) B[:3,2:]

Ans. (i) [[1 2]
[5 6]]

(ii) [30 60]

(iii) Empty Array

(iv) [[12 13 14 15]
[8 9 10 11]
[4 5 6 7]
[0 1 2 3]]

(v) [[2 3]
[6 7]
[10 11]]

Long Answer Type Questions

13. Explain the difference between NumPy arrays and Python lists. Why are NumPy arrays preferred for numerical computations?

Ans. Refer to text on page no. 164. (Differences between list and Array).

Python provides a built-in data structure called list, which is flexible and can store different data types. However, for numerical computations, NumPy arrays are preferred over lists due to several reasons:

1. **Memory Efficiency** NumPy arrays require less memory compared to Python lists. A NumPy array stores elements of the same data type in a contiguous memory block, reducing overhead.
2. **Speed** NumPy arrays are significantly faster than lists for numerical operations. This is because NumPy is implemented in C and supports vectorized operations, eliminating the need for explicit loops in Python.
3. **Functionality** NumPy provides powerful mathematical functions like sum, mean, standard deviation, trigonometric functions, and linear algebra operations, which are not available in Python lists.
4. **Broadcasting** NumPy allows operations on arrays of different shapes and sizes using broadcasting, whereas lists require explicit looping.

Example

```
import numpy as np
   # Creating a NumPy array
arr = np.array([1, 2, 3, 4, 5])
   # Performing arithmetic operation
print(arr * 2)
   # Multiplies each element by 2
   # Creating a Python list
lst = [1, 2, 3, 4, 5]
   # Performing the same operation using
                                   a list
print([x * 2 for x in lst])
```

Output

[2 4 6 8 10] # NumPy array operation

[2, 4, 6, 8, 10] # List operation

14. What is slicing in NumPy? Explain with examples.

Ans. Slicing is used to extract a portion of an array using the [start:end] notation. The end index is excluded.

Slicing in a 1-D Array

Example Take a 1-D array of daily temperature readings (in °C).

```
temp = np.array([22, 24, 26, 28, 30, 32,
34])
```

- **Extract temperatures from index 2 to 4 (excluding 5)**

```
temp[2:5]
array([26, 28, 30])
```

- **Reverse the array**

```
temp[::-1]
array([34, 32, 30, 28, 26, 24, 22])
```

Slicing in a 2-D Array

Example Consider the weekly production of three factories (in metric tons) for four weeks.

```
production = np.array([[500, 550, 600, 650],
              [480, 510, 530, 590],
              [520, 560, 610, 640]])
```

Week	Factory 1	Factory 2	Factory 3
Week 1	500	550	600
Week 2	480	510	530
Week 3	520	560	610
Week 4	650	590	640

Extracting Specific Data

- **Get production data for Factory 2 (column index 1) for Weeks 1 to 3**

```
production[0:3, 1]
array([550, 510, 560])
```

- **Extract production data for Weeks 2 & 3 (row index 1:3) and Factories 1 & 2 (column index 0:2)**

```
production[1:3, 0:2]
array([[480, 510],
  [520, 560]])
```

- **Extract all production values of Factory 3 (column index 2)**

```
production[:, 2]
array([600, 530, 610])
```

Case Study Based Question

Case Study

Aryan is learning NumPy in his Python programming class. His teacher gave him a task to create and manipulate a NumPy array. He created the following 2D array:

```
import numpy as np
A = np.array([[5, 10, 15],
            [20, 25, 30],
            [35, 40, 45]])
```

He performed different operations on this array and recorded the outputs.

Answer the following questions based on the above data:

(i) **What will be the output of print(A[1, 2])?**
 (a) 10 (b) 15
 (c) 30 (d) 25

(ii) **What will be the shape of the array A?**
 (a) (3,) (b) (3,3)
 (c) (3,2) (d) (1,9)

(iii) **What will be the output of print(A[:, 1])?**
 (a) [10 25 40]
 (b) [5 10 15]
 (c) [20 25 30]
 (d) [35 40 45]

(iv) **Which command will reverse the rows of array A?**
 (a) A[::-1, :]
 (b) A[:, ::-1]
 (c) A.T
 (d) np.flip(A, axis=1)

(v) **What will be the output of print(A.flatten())?**
 (a) [5 10 15 20 25 30 35 40 45]
 (b) [[5 10 15] [20 25 30] [35 40 45]]
 (c) (3,3)
 (d) (9,)

Ans. (i) (c) 30
 (ii) (b) (3,3)
 (iii) (a) [10 25 40]
 (iv) (a) A[::-1, :]
 (v) (a) [5 10 15 20 25 30 35 40 45]

SELF ASSESSMENT TEST

Multiple Choice Questions

1. What will be the output of the following code?

```
import numpy as np
arr = np.array([1, 2, 3, 4, 5])
print(arr[1:4])
```

(a) [1, 2, 3] (b) [2, 3, 4]
(c) [3, 4, 5] (d) [1, 2, 3, 4]

2. Which of the following functions is used to create an array of ones in NumPy?

(a) np.ones() (b) np.one_array()
(c) np.fill_ones() (d) np.unit_array()

3. What will be the shape of the following NumPy array?

```
import numpy as np
arr = np.zeros((3, 4))
print(arr.shape)
```

(a) (4, 3) (b) (3, 4)
(c) (3, 3) (d) (4, 4)

4. Which of the following statements is TRUE about NumPy arrays?

(a) NumPy arrays can store only integer values
(b) NumPy arrays are slower than Python lists
(c) NumPy arrays support vectorized operations
(d) NumPy arrays cannot be multi-dimensional

5. What will be the output of the following code?

```
import numpy as np
arr = np.array([10, 20, 30, 40, 50])
print(arr[::-1])
```

(a) [10, 20, 30, 40, 50] (b) [50, 40, 30, 20, 10]
(c) [30, 40, 50, 10, 20] (d) [20, 10, 50, 40, 30]

State Whether True or False

6. NumPy arrays are slower than Python lists when performing mathematical operations.
7. The zeros() function creates an array filled with ones.
8. NumPy supports broadcasting, which allows operations between arrays of different shapes.

Fill in the Blanks

9. NumPy stands for __________ and is used for numerical computing in Python.
10. The function used to create an array in NumPy is __________.
11. NumPy, the __________ function is used to generate an array of evenly spaced values within a given range.
12. The shape of a NumPy array can be found using the __________ attribute.

Assertion and Reason Based Questions

Assertion (A) and Reason (R) Type questions. Choose the correct option as:

(a) Both Assertion (A) and Reason (R) are true, and Reason (R) is the correct explanation of Assertion (A).
(b) Both Assertion (A) and Reason (R) are true, but Reason (R) is not the correct explanation of Assertion (A).
(c) Assertion (A) is true, but Reason (R) is false.
(d) Assertion (A) is false, but Reason (R) is true.

13. **Assertion (A)** NumPy allows arithmetic operations on arrays of different shapes through broadcasting.

Reason (R) Broadcasting works by automatically expanding arrays to match compatible shapes.

14. **Assertion (A)** The np.linspace(1,10,5) function creates an array with elements [1, 3, 5, 7, 9].

Reason (R) The linspace() function generates equally spaced values between the given start and end values.

15. **Assertion (A)** NumPy arrays are more memory-efficient than Python lists.

Reason (R) NumPy arrays store data of different types in a single array, reducing memory usage.

Very Short Answer Type Questions

16. Which function is used to create an array in NumPy?
17. What is the default data type of elements in a NumPy array if not specified?
18. How do you find the shape of a NumPy array?

Short Answer Type Questions

19. What is the difference between a Python list and a NumPy array?
20. What is broadcasting in NumPy, and how does it help in array operations?

Long Answer Type Questions

21. Explain the different ways to create a NumPy array. Provide examples for each method.
22. Discuss the different types of indexing in NumPy. Explain integer indexing, slicing, and Boolean indexing with examples.

Case Study Based Questions

23. Rohit is a data science student who recently started learning NumPy. He created a 2D NumPy array to store the marks of five students in three subjects: Mathematics, Physics, and Computer Science. The data is stored as follows:

```
import numpy as np
marks = np.array([[78, 85, 90],
                  [92, 88, 76],
                  [84, 91, 89],
                  [75, 81, 95],
                  [89, 79, 84]])
```

Here, each row represents a student, and each column represents a subject.

Now, answer the following questions:

(i) What will be the output of print(marks.shape)?

(a) (5, 3) (b) (3, 5)
(c) (5,) (d) (3,)

(ii) What will be the output of print(marks[2, :])?

(a) [84, 91, 89] (b) [92, 88, 76]
(c) [75, 81, 95] (d) [89, 79, 84]

(iii) How can Rohit access the marks of the 4th student in Physics (2nd column)?

(a) marks[4,2] (b) marks[3,1]
(c) marks[3,2] (d) marks[4,1]

(iv) What will be the result of print(marks[:, 1])?

(a) [85, 88, 91, 81, 79]
(b) [78, 92, 84, 75, 89]
(c) [90, 76, 89, 95, 84]
(d) [88, 92, 75, 79, 84]

(v) What will be the output of print(marks[marks > 90])?

(a) [92, 91, 95]
(b) [92, 91, 95, 90]
(c) [85, 88, 91, 81, 79]
(d) [78, 92, 84, 75, 89]

Answers

1. (b) 2. (a) 3. (b) 4. (c) 5. (b)
6. False 7. False 8. True
9. Numerical Python 10. numpy.array() 11. arange
12. shape 13. (a) 14. (d) 15. (c)
23. (i) → (a), (ii) → (a), (iii) → (b), (iv) → (a), (v) → (a)

11

CHAPTER

This chapter introduces fundamental database concepts, exploring why databases are essential for modern applications and how they organize and manage data, focusing on the relational model and its key components.

YOUR STUDY GOALS

YOUR PRACTICE GOAL

- Objective Type Questions (40 Qs ; MCQs, True or False, Fill in the Blanks, Assertion and Reason)
- Subjective Type Questions (28 Qs ; VSA, SA, LA)
- Case Study Based Questions-2

Database Concepts

A database can be defined as a collection of information organized in such a way that a computer program is used to quickly retrieve data. You can think of a database as an electronic filing system.

The contents of a database are obtained by combining the data from all the different sources in an organization. This data then forms the base for all further activities such as performing logical, mathematical and other operations and maintains any information that may be necessary to the decision-making processes involved in the management of that organization.

A database has the following properties

- It is a collection of data elements representing real-world information.
- It is logical, coherent and internally consistent.

For example, consider the names, telephone numbers and addresses of the relatives. You may have recorded this data in an indexed address book or you may have stored it on a hard drive, using application software such as Microsoft Access or Excel. This collection of related data with an implicit meaning is known as a **DATABASE**.

11.1 Database Management System (DBMS)

A Database Management System is a software system that enables users to define, create, and maintain the database and provides controlled access to this database.

The primary goal of a DBMS is to provide a way to store and retrieve database information that is both convenient and efficient. Data in a database can be added, deleted, changed, sorted or searched, all using a DBMS.

Application program accesses the data stored in the database by sending request to the DBMS. *For example*, MySQL, INGRES, MS-ACCESS etc.

The purpose of a Database Management System is to bridge the gap between information and data. The data stored in memory or on disk must be converted to usable information.

The basic processes that are supported by a DBMS are

(i) Specification of data types, structures and constraints to be considered in an application.
(ii) Storing the data itself into persistent storage.
(iii) Manipulation of the database.
(iv) Querying the database to retrieve desired information.
(v) Updating the content of the database.

Advantages of DBMS

(i) Reduced data redundancy
(ii) Elimination of inconsistency
(iii) Data sharing
(iv) Data integrity
(v) Data security
(vi) Backup and recovery

Limitations of DBMS

(i) High cost
(ii) Database failure
(iii) Data quality
(iv) Confidentiality, privacy and security

DBMS vs File Processing System

Database Management System	File Processing System
A database management system co-ordinates both the physical and the logical access to the data.	File processing system co-ordinates only the physical access.
A database management system is a bundle of applications i.e. dedicated for managing data stored in a database.	A file processing system is a collection of raw data files stored in the hard drive of a system.
A database management system is designed to allow flexible access to data (i.e. queries).	File processing system is designed to allow predetermined access to data (i.e. compiled programs).
A database management system is designed to co-ordinate multiple users accessing the same data at the same time.	A file processing system is usually designed to allow one or more programs to access different data files at the same time.

11.2 Need of Database System

The need of database systems arose in the early 1960s in response to the **traditional file processing system**. In the file processing system, the data is stored in the form of files, and a number of application programs are written by programmers to add, modify, delete, and retrieve data to and from appropriate files.

New application programs are added to the system as the need arises. *For example*, suppose that a saving bank decides to offer checking accounts.

As a result, the bank creates new permanent files that contain information about all the checking accounts maintained in the bank, and it may have to write new application programs to deal with situations that do not arise in saving accounts, such as overdrafts.

Thus, as time goes by, the system acquires more files and more application programs.

However, the file processing system has a number of disadvantages, which are given below

- Some information may be duplicated in several files.
- The file processing system lacks the insulation between program and data.
- Handling new queries is difficult, since it requires change in the existing application programs or requires a new application program.
- In this system, all the integrity rules need to be explicitly programmed in all application programs, which are using that particular data item.
- This system lacks security features. To overcome these problems, database system was designed.

11.3 Components of Database System

A database system is composed of four components- User, Hardware, Software and Data, which coordinate with one another to form an effective database system.

The major components of a database system are described below

(i) **User** The users are the people who manage the database and perform different operations on it.

Basically, users are those persons who need the information from the database to carry out their primary business responsibilities i.e. personnel, staff, clerical etc.

There are mainly three kinds of people who plays different roles in database system. They are **application programmers**, who develop the application programs, the **end-users** access the database from a terminal using a query language provided by database system and **database administrator**, who is responsible for the design, construction and maintenance of a database system.

Database Administrator (DBA)

The person having the central control over the system is called Database Administrator. The DBA may be department or group rather than one person. It should have an accurate knowledge of computers and organization structures.

The DBA has many different responsibilities but the overall goal of a DBA is to maintain the database system and to provide users with access to the required information when they need it. The DBA makes sure that the database is protected.

Some responsibilities of DBA are as follows

(i) Ensuring regular and accurate update of the database.

(ii) Identifying and resolving user's problem.

(iii) Schema and physical organization modification.

(iv) Storage structure and access method definition.

(v) Processing and maintaining database.

(ii) **Hardware** The hardware consists of various secondary storage devices, such as magnetic tapes, hard disks, floppy disks, CD-ROM's etc, on which data is stored and the input/output devices, such as mouse, keyboard, lightpen, printers, scanners etc., which are used for storing (by providing commands) and retrieving the required data in an efficient manner.

Since database can range from those of a single user with a desktop computer to those on mainframe computers with thousands of users, therefore proper care should be taken for choosing appropriate hardware devices for a required database.

(iii) **Software** This is the most important component of database. It acts as an interface between the user and the database.

In other words, software interacts with the users, application programs, and database of a particular storage media to insert, update, delete and retrieve data.

For performing these operations such as insertion, deletion and updation we can either use the query languages like SQL, QUEL or application softwares such as Visual Basic, etc.

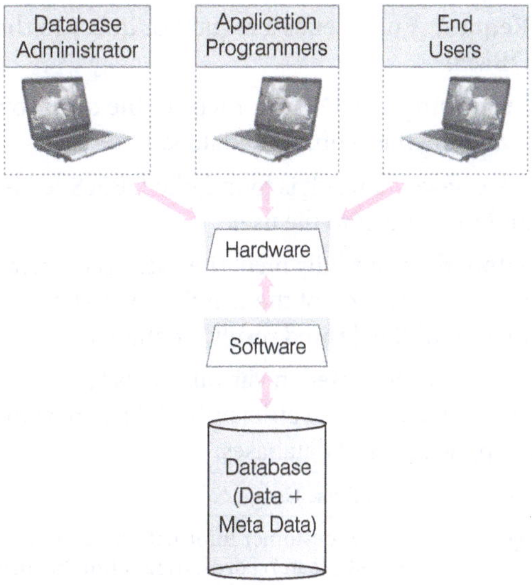

(iv) **Data** It is an important component of database. Most of the organizations generate, store and process large amount of data. The data act as a bridge between the hardware, software and the users. A database contains various types of data

(a) **User Data** It contains a table of data in the form of rows (records) and columns (fields).

(b) **Meta Data** It means 'data about data' *i.e.*, a logical description of the structure of a data.

(c) **Application Data** It contains the structure and format queries, reports and other application components.

11.4 Working of Database

Databases are designed to handle large amounts of information by allowing users to input, store, retrieve, and manage data efficiently.

A database serves as a centralized location that enables multiple users to access the same data simultaneously without creating separate copies of a particular data file. This ensures data consistency and prevents redundancy.

As shown in the diagram below, a Database Management System (DBMS) facilitates all database operations.

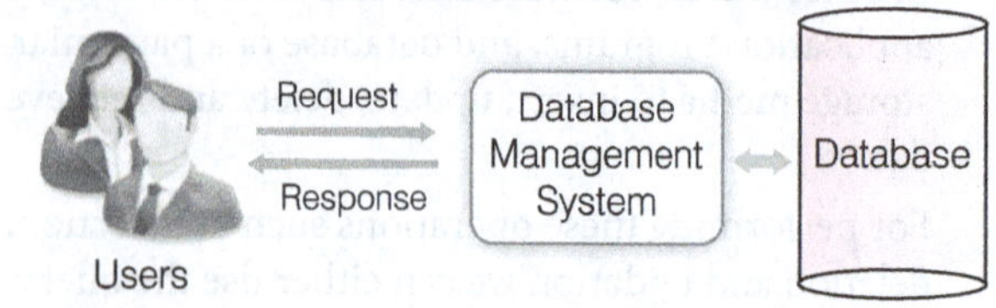

Database Working Process

1. **Request** A user sends a request or query to the DBMS.
2. **Processing** The DBMS processes the query by searching the centralized database.
3. **Response** If a result is found, the DBMS retrieves and forwards it to the user.

If the output does not fully meet the user's requirements, a rollback (re-execution of the search process) is performed until the desired result is obtained.

Databases are widely used in various fields to store, manage, and retrieve data efficiently. Below are some real-life applications of databases:

Application	Database Usage
Banking	Stores customer information, account details, loan records, transaction history, etc.
Crop Loan	Manages Kisan Credit Card data, farmer's personal details, land and cultivation records, loan history, and repayment data.
Inventory Management	Keeps track of product details, customer orders, delivery records, and stock levels.
Organizational Resource Management	Maintains employee records, salary details, department information, and branch locations.
Online Shopping	Stores product descriptions, user login details, purchase history, and customer preferences.

11.5 View of Data (Data Abstraction)

A database system provides users with an abstract view of data by hiding storage details. To ensure efficiency, complex data structures are used. Since many users lack technical knowledge, multiple levels of abstraction simplify interactions.

Levels of Abstraction

1. **Internal Level (Physical Level)** Describes how data is physically stored and organized using complex structures and access methods.
2. **Conceptual Level (Logical Level)** Provides a logical view of the database, showing data relationships without concern for physical storage. It is used by database administrators.
3. **External Level (View Level)** Defines customized views for different user groups, ensuring security by restricting access to certain data.

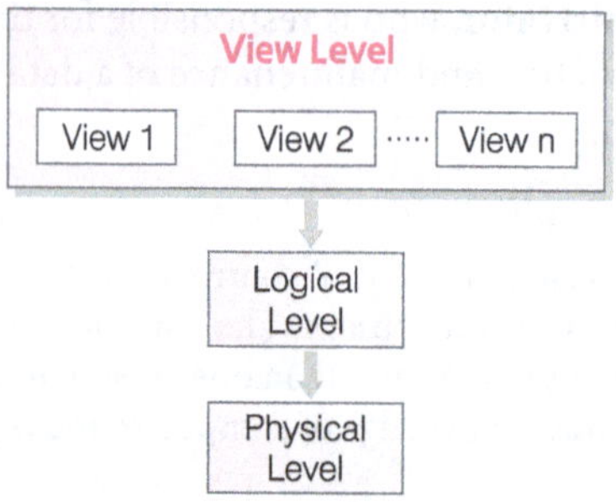

Three Levels of Data Abstraction

To understand the concept of data abstraction, consider the example of the database of a banking organization.

Example Banking Database

- **Internal Level** Stores raw data like client records, employee details, and account information along with storage locations.
- **Conceptual Level** Defines data structures, such as client details (code, name, address, account info).
- **External Level** Provides restricted views, e.g., payroll staff access only employee details, not client accounts.

11.6 Data Models

Data model can be defined as an integrated collection of concepts for describing and manipulating data, relationship between data and constraints on the data in an organisation.

A data model provides a way to describe the design of a database at the internal, conceptual and external level.

A data model comprises of three components, which are given below:

- A **structural part,** consisting of a set of rules according to which databases can be constructed.
- A **manipulative part**, defining the types of operations that are allowed on the data (this includes the operations that are used for updating or retrieving data from the database and for changing the structure of the database).
- Possibly a set of **integrity rules**, which ensures that the data is accurate.

The purpose of a data model is to represent data and to make the data understandable. The different data models that are used for database management system are:

Hierarchical Data Model

In hierarchical data model, data is organised in a tree-like structure. There is a hierarchy of parent and child data segments.

It comprises a set of records connected to one another through links.

The link is an association between two or more records. To create links between these records, the hierarchical model uses parent child relationship.

In a hierarchical database, the parent child relationship is One to Many. This restricts a child segment to having only one parent segment but a parent segment can have one or more child segments. Top of the structure consists of a single segment and known as **root segment**. The operations that can be performed on hierarchical model are retrieval, insertion, deletion and modification of records.

Network Data Model

In network data model, data is represented by collection of records and relationships among data are represented by links like hierarchical data model.

The only difference is that in the network model, records are organized as arbitrary graphs rather than trees. In this model, the parent child relationship is Many to Many, i.e. one child segment can have multiple parent segments.

Relational Data Model

In a relational data model, data is stored in different tables with relationship to each other. These tables are called **relations.** These tables communicate and show information which facilitates data search ability, organisation and reporting.

11.7 Relational Database

A tabular database in which data is defined so that it can be reorganized and accessed in a number of different ways.

In a relational database, data is stored in different tables with relationships to each other. These tables communicate and share information, which facilitates data search ability, organization and reporting.

Various terms related to relational database are as follows

(i) **Relation** A relation is a table with columns and rows which represent the data items and relationships among them. Relations have three important properties a name, cardinality and a degree.

These properties help us to further define and describe relations

(a) **Name** The first property of a relation is its name, which is represented by the title or the entity identifier.

(b) **Cardinality** The second property of a relation is its cardinality, which refers to the number of tuples (rows) in a relation.

(c) **Degree** The third property of a relation is its degree, which refers to the number of attributes (columns) in each tuple.

Mistake Alert!

Students gets confused to differentiate between degree and cardinality.

(ii) **Domain** A domain is a collection of all possible values from which the values for a given column or an attribute is drawn. A domain is said to be atomic if elements are considered to be indivisible units.

(iii) **Attributes** The heading columns of a table are known as attributes. Each attribute of a table has a distinct name.

(iv) **Tuples** The rows in a relation are also known as tuples. Each row or tuple has a set of permitted values for each attribute.

Attributes	Emp_Id	Emp_Name	Emp_Salary	Years
Tuples	100	Jim	20000	2
	101	James	21000	1
	102	Anne	21001	3

Relational Database Management System (RDBMS)

A Relational Database Management System (RDBMS) is a database management system. It is developed by Dr. E.F. Codd, of IBM's San Jose Research Laboratory.

RDBMS stores data in the form of related tables. RDBMS are powerful because they require few assumptions about how data is related or how it will be extracted from the database.

An important feature of relational database is that a single database can be spread across several tables. Today, popular commercial for large databases include Oracle, Microsoft SQL server, Sybase, MySQL.

11.8 Keys

The key is defined as the column or attribute or a combination of attributes that is used to identify records of the database table. Sometimes we might have to retrieve data from more than one table, in those cases we require to join tables with the help of keys.

A key is also used to arrange the records either in ascending or descending order. It also controls and maintains the integrity of information store in the database.

There are various types of keys, which are as follows.

Primary Key

The primary key of a relational table uniquely identifies each record in the table. In some tables, combination of more than one attributes is declared as primary key. In that case, primary key is known as composite key.

Every relation does have a primary key.

For example, in the given table StudentId works as a primary key because it contains Id's, which are unique for each student.

Candidate Keys | Alternate Keys | Relationship | Primary Key

StudentId	FirstName	LastName	CourseId
L0002345	Jim	Black	C002
L0001254	James	Harradine	A004
L0002349	Amanda	Holland	C002
L0001198	Simon	McCloud	S042
L0023487	Peter	Murray	P301
L0018453	Anne	Norris	S042

Primary Key

Student table

CourseId	CourseName
A004	Accounts
C002	Computing
P301	History
S042	Short Course

Course table

Candidate Key

The set of all attributes which can uniquely identify each tuple of a relation are known as candidate keys. Each table may have one or more candidate keys and one of them will become the primary key. *For example*, column StudentId and the combination of FirstName and LastName work as the candidate keys for the given table.

A candidate key must possess the following properties

(i) For each row the value of the key must uniquely identify that row.

(ii) No attribute in the key can be discarded without destroying the property of unique identification.

Alternate Key

From the set of candidate keys after selecting one of the key as primary key, all other remaining keys are known as alternate keys. These keys are also unique but they allow nulls. *For example*, from the candidate keys (StudentId, FirstName and LastName), StudentId chosen as a primary key then the FirstName and LastName column work as a alternate keys.

Foreign Key

A foreign key is a non-key attribute whose value is derived from the primary key of another table. The relationship between two tables is established with the help of foreign key. A table may have multiple foreign keys, and each foreign key can have different referenced table. Foreign keys play an essential role in database design, when tables are broken apart then foreign keys make it possible for them to be reconstructed.

For example, CourseId column of Student table work as a foreign key for student table, as well as a primary key for Course table (referenced table).

Referential Integrity

Referential integrity ensures consistency in a database by enforcing rules on foreign keys. It states that a foreign key must either:

Reference a valid primary key in another table.

Be NULL, indicating no relationship or an unknown relationship. This prevents orphan records and maintains data accuracy. It concerns the concept of a foreign key. The referential integrity rules states that any foreign key value can only be in one of two states. The usual state of affairs is that the foreign key value refers to a primary key value of some table in the database.

Occasionally and this well depend on the rules of the data owner, a foreign key value can be null. In this case, we are explicitly saying that either there is no relationship between the objects represented in the database or that this relationship is unknown.

Mind Map

DATABASE CONCEPTS

Data Models

It is a conceptual framework used to define and organize the structure, relationships and rules of data in a database.

Relational Data Model

The relational data model uses a collection of tables to represent both data and the relationship among data. A table is a collection of records and each record in a table contains the same fields.

Network Data Model

In network data model, the data is represented by collection of records and relationships among data by links like hierarchical data model. In this model, the parent child relationship is Many-to-Many.

Hierarchical Data Model

In this data model, data is organised in a tree-like structure. There is a hierarchy of parent and child data segments. In a hierarchical database, the parent child relationship is One-to-Many.

Relational Database

Relation
A relation is a table with columns and rows, which represent the data items and relationships among them.

- Name
- Cardinality
- Degree

Domain
A domain is a collection of all possible values from which the values for a given column or an attribute is drawn.

Tuples
The rows in a relation are also known as tuples. Each row or tuple has a set of permitted values for each attribute.

Attributes
The heading columns of a table are known as attributes. Each attribute of a table has a distinct name.

Keys
Used to uniquely identify and record or row of data from the table.

- Primary Key
- Candidate key
- Alternate key
- Foreign key

DBMS

A Database Management System is a software system that enables users to define, create, and maintain the database and provides controlled access to this database.

Components of Database System

A database system is composed of four components- User, Hardware, Software and Data, which coordinate with one another to form an effective database system.

User

The users are the people who manage the database and perform different operations on it.

Hardware

The hardware consists of various secondary storage devices, such as magnetic tapes, hard disks, floppy disks, CD-ROM's etc, on which data is stored and the input/output devices, such as mouse, keyboard, lightpen, printers, scanners etc., which are used for storing (by providing commands) and retrieving the required data in an efficient manner.

Software

It acts as an interface between the user and the database. In other words, software interacts with the users, application programs, and database of a particular storage media to insert, update, delete and retrieve data.

Data

The data act as a bridge between the hardware, software and the users. A database contains various types of data: User Data, Meta Data, Application Data

View of Data (Data Abstraction)

The views of data are the different ways to present the data to users. These views are created to hide the complexity of the data structure from the end user.

Levels of Abstraction

- **Internal/Physical Level** Deals with the physical storage of the data.
- **Conceptual Level** Describes the logical structure and relationships of the data.
- **External Level** Also known as the view level, this level provides customized data access for individual users or groups.

Working of Database

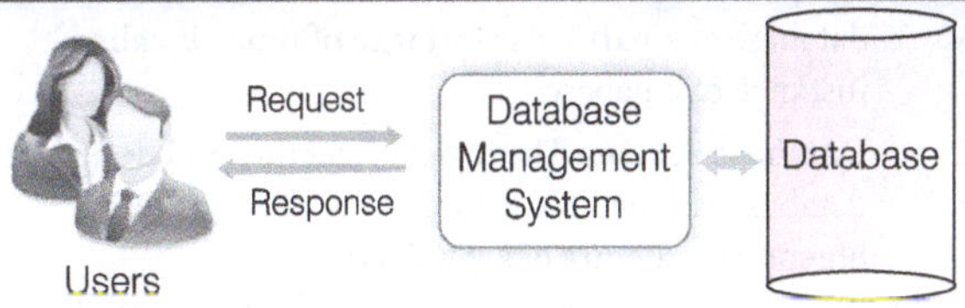

Database Working Process

Request A user sends a request or query to the DBMS.

Processing The DBMS processes the query by searching the centralized database.

Response If a result is found, the DBMS retrieves and forwards it to the user.

NCERT Folder

1. Give the terms for each of the following:

(a) Collection of logically related records.

(b) DBMS creates a file that contains description about the data stored in the database.

(c) Attribute that can uniquely identify the tuples in a relation.

(d) Special value that is stored when actual data value is unknown for an attribute.

(e) An attribute which can uniquely identify tuples of the table but is not defined as primary key of the table.

(f) Software that is used to create, manipulate and maintain a relational database.

Ans. (a) Table/Relation

(b) Data Dictionary

(c) Primary key

(d) NULL

(e) Alternate key

(f) Database Management System. MySQL, Oracle

2. Why foreign keys are allowed to have NULL values? Explain with an example.

Ans. The values of foreign key is derived from primary key of primary table. Sometimes we want to enter a record which is not related. To handle this situation it is allowed to enter NULL value in foreign key.

3. Differentiate between:

(a) Database state and database schema

(b) Primary key and foreign key

(c) Degree and cardinality of a relation

Ans. (a) **Database State/Instance** The data stored in a database at a particular moment of time i.e the state of the database at a particular instance of time , is called instance of database.

Database schema The logical structure and design of a database is called the database schema. It is the blueprint structure of a database.

(b) **Primary key** A column or group of columns that uniquely identify the records in a table.

Foreign key A non key attribute that is key field in another table and links the two tables is called Foreign key.

(c) **Degree** The total number of columns in a table.

Cardinality The total number of rows in a table

4. Compared to a file system, how does a database management system avoid redundancy in data through a database?

Ans. A database stores the data at a central location from where all applications can access data. This avoids to save data in multiple files, thus reducing data redundancy.

5. What are the limitations of file system that can be overcome by a relational DBMS?

Ans. (a) Difficulty in data access

(b) Data redundancy

(c) Data inconsistency

(d) Data isolation

(e) Data dependence.

6. A school has a rule that each student must participate in a sports activity. So each one should give only one preference for sports activity. Suppose there are five students in a class, each having a unique roll number. The class representative has prepared a list of sports preferences as shown below. Answer the following:

Table: Sports Preferences

Roll_no	Preference
9	Cricket
13	Football
17	Badminton
17	Football
21	Hockey
24	NULL
NULL	Kabaddi

(a) Roll no 24 may not be interested in sports. Can a NULL value be assigned to that student's preference field?

(b) Roll no 17 has given two preferences sports. Which property of relational DBMC is violated here? Can we use any constraint or key in the relational DBMS to check against such violation, if any?

(c) Kabaddi was not chosen by any student. Is it possible to have this tuple in the Sports Preferences relation?

Ans. (a) Yes, a NULL value can be assigned to roll number 24's preference field, as it indicates that the student has not chosen any sports activity. However, if participation is mandatory, this should be handled through constraints to ensure valid entries.

(b) Roll number 17 has two preferences, violating the uniqueness property of a Primary Key or Entity Integrity Constraint in a relational DBMS. To prevent this, we can use the Primary Key constraint on the Roll_no column or define a UNIQUE constraint on it to ensure that each student has only one sports preference.

(c) No, the tuple containing "Kabaddi" without a roll number should not be present, as every tuple in a relational database should have a unique identifier (Primary Key), and NULL in the primary key column is not allowed.

7. **In another class having 2 sections, the two respective class representatives have prepared 2 separate Sports Preferences tables, as shown below: Sports preference of section 1 (arranged on roll number column)**

Table: Sports Preferences

Roll_no	Preference
9	Cricket
13	Football
17	Badminton
21	Hockey
24	Cricket

Sports preference of section 2 (arranged on Sports name column, and column order is also different)

Table: Sports Preferences

Sports	Roll_no
Badminton	17
Cricket	9
Cricket	24
Football	13
Hockey	21

Are the states of both the relations equivalent? Justify.

Ans. Yes, both relations represent the same data but are arranged differently. The content remains the same; only the column order and sorting criteria differ. Since relations in a relational database are defined by the data they contain and not by the order of rows or columns, these two states are equivalent.

8. **The school canteen wants to maintain records of items available in the school canteen and generate bills when students purchase any item from the canteen. The school wants to create a canteen database to keep track of items in the canteen and the items purchased by students. Design a database by answering the following questions:**

(a) To store each item name along with its price, what relation should be used? Decide appropriate attribute names along with their data type. Each item and its price should be stored only once. What restriction should be used while defining the relation?

(b) In order to generate bill, we should know the quantity of an item purchased. Should this information be in a new relation or a part of the previous relation? If a new relation is required, decide appropriate name and data type for attributes. Also, identify appropriate primary key and foreign key so that the following two restrictions are satisfied:

(i) The same bill cannot be generated for different orders.

(ii) Bill can be generated only for available items in the canteen.

(c) The school wants to find out how many calories students intake when they order an item. In which relation should the attribute 'calories' be stored?

Ans. (a) To store item details we can create ITEMS table

Items_table	Code of Item
Item_No	Unique, Non-null value
Description	Description of Item
Price	Non-null price of the item

The restrictions and contraints are

- Item_no-must be unique and non-null for each row.
- Description and Price cannot be blank or null.

(b) Yes the Item Sale information should be stored in a separate relation say, saleorders

Orderno	Unique non-null order number	Primary Key
Itemno	Itemno from Items table	
Qty_purchased	Non-null value of qty sold of an item	
Order_Date	Date of the order	

(c) In ITEMS table.

9. **An organisation wants to create a database EMP-DEPENDENT to maintain following details about its employees and their dependent.**

EMPLOYEE(AadharNumber, Name, Address, Department,EmployeeID)

DEPENDENT(EmployeeID, DependentName, Relationship)

(a) Name the attributes of EMPLOYEE, which can be used as candidate keys.

(b) The company wants to retrieve details of dependent of a particular employee. Name the tables and the key which are required to retrieve this detail.

(c) What is the degree of EMPLOYEE and DEPENDENT relation?

Ans. (a) AadharNumber, EmployeeId

(b) Employee and Dependent tables linked via key EmployeeId

(c) Degree of Employee : 5 , Degree of Dependent :3

10. **School uniform is available at M/s Sheetal Private Limited. They have maintained SCHOOL_UNIFORM Database with two relations viz. UNIFORM and COST. The following figure shows database schema and its state.**

Attributes and Constraints

Table : UNIFORM

Attribute	UCode	Uname	UColor
Constraints	Primary Key	Not Null	–

Table : COST

Attribute	UCode	Size	Price
Constraints	Composite	Primary Key	>0

Table : UNIFORM

UCode	UName	UColor
1	Shirt	White
2	Pant	Grey
3	Skirt	Grey
4	Tie	Blue
5	Socks	Blue
6	Belt	Blue

Table :

UCode	Size	COST Price
1	M	500
1	L	580
1	XL	620
2	M	810
2	L	890
2	XL	940
3	M	770
3	L	830
3	XL	910
4	S	150
4	L	170
5	S	180
5	L	210
6	M	110
6	L	140
6	XL	160

(i) **Can they insert the following tuples to the UNIFORM Relation? Give reasons in support of your answer.**

(a) 7, Handkerchief, NULL

(b) 4, Ribbon, Red

(c) 8, NULL, White

(ii) **Can they insert the following tuples to the COST Relation? Give reasons in support of your answer.**

(a) 7, S, 0 (b) 9, XL, 100

Ans. (i) (a) Yes it can be inserted

(b) Yes it can be inserted

(c) No, it cannot be inserted as Uname cannot be NULL

(ii) (a) No , it cannot be inserted as price must be >0

(b) Yes it can be inserted.

11. **In a multiplex, movies are screened in different auditoriums. One movie can be shown in more than one auditorium. In order to maintain the record of movies, the multiplex maintains a relational database consisting of two relations viz. MOVIE and AUDI respectively as shown below:**

Movie(Movie_ID, MovieName, ReleaseDate)

Audi(AudiNo, Movie_ID, Seats, ScreenType, TicketPrice)

(a) **Is it correct to assign Movie_ID as the primary key in the MOVIE relation? If no, then suggest an appropriate primary key.**

(b) **Is it correct to assign AudiNo as the primary key in the AUDI relation? If no, then suggest appropriate primary key.**

(c) **Is there any foreign key in any of these relations?**

Ans. (a) Yes, it is correct to assign Movie_ID as primary key.

(b) No, AudiNo along with MovieID should be made the primary key . That is the relation should have composite primary key as AudiNo + Movie_ID

(c) MovieID

12.

Student Project Database

Table : Student

Roll No	Name	Class	Section	Registration_ID
11	Mohan	XI	1	IP-101-15
12	Sohan	XI	2	IP-104-15
21	John	XII	1	CS-103-14
22	Meena	XII	2	CS-101-14
23	Juhi	XII	2	CS-101-10

Table : PROJECT

ProjectNo	PName	Submission Data
101	Airline Database	12/01/2018
102	Library Database	12/01/2018
103	Employee Database	15/01/2018
104	Student Database	12/01/2018
105	Inventory Database	15/01/2018
106	Railway Database	15/01/2018

Table : PROJECT ASSIGNED

Registration_ID	ProjectNo
IP-101-15	101
IP-104-15	103
CS-101-14	102
CS-101-14	105
CS-101-10	104

For the above given database STUDENT-PROJECT, answer the following:

(a) **Name primary key of each table.**

(b) **Find foreign key(s) in table PROJECT-ASSIGNED.**

(c) **Is there any alternate key in table STUDENT? Give justification for your answer.**

(d) **Can a user assign duplicate value to the field RollNo of STUDENT table? Jusify.**

Ans. (a) Table : Student : RollNo

Table Project : ProjectNo

Table Project_Assigned : Registration_ID

(b) ProjectNo

(c) Name can be an alternate key as it stores unique values for each row.

(d) No, RollNo being the primary key must have unique values for each row.

13. **For the above given database STUDENT-PROJECT, can we perform the following operations?**

(a) **Insert a student record with missing roll number value.**

(b) Insert a student record with missing registration number value.

(c) Insert a project detail without submission-date.

(d) Insert a record with registration ID IP-101-19 and ProjectNo 206 in table PROJECT-ASSIGNED.

Ans. (a) No

(b) Yes

(c) Yes

(d) No, because RegistrationId IP-101-19 does not exist in the Student table, and ProjectNo 206 also does not exist in the Project Table.

EXAM PATTERN QUESTIONS

Objective Type Questions

Multiple Choice Questions

1. What is the full form of DBMS?

(a) Data of Binary Management System
(b) Database Management System
(c) Database Management Service
(d) Data Backup Management System

2. What is DBMS?

(a) DBMS is a collection of queries
(b) DBMS is a high-level language
(c) DBMS is a programming language
(d) DBMS stores, modifies and retrieves data

3. Who created the first DBMS?

(a) Edgar Frank Codd (b) Charles Bachman
(c) Charles Babbage (d) Sharon B. Codd

4. Which of the following is not a type of database?

(a) Hierarchical (b) Network
(c) Distributed (d) Decentralized

5. Which of the following is not a feature of DBMS?

(a) Minimum Duplication and Redundancy of Data
(b) High Level of Security
(c) Single-user Access only
(d) Support ACID Property

6. A university is using a database management system (DBMS) to handle student records, ensuring that data remains accurate, secure, and accessible to authorized users. Which of the following functions of DBMS helps achieve this? Competency Based Que.

(a) Storing data
(b) Providing multi-user access control
(c) Data Integrity
(d) All of the above

7. Which of the following is a component of the DBMS?

(a) Data (b) Data Languages
(c) Data Manager (d) All of these

8. Which of the following is not an example of DBMS?

(a) MySQL (b) Microsoft Acess
(c) IBM DB2 (d) Google

9. In which of the following formats data is stored in the database management system?

(a) Image (b) Text (c) Table (d) Graph

10. What is a database?

(a) Organized collection of information that cannot be accessed, updated, and managed
(b) Collection of data or information without organizing
(c) Organized collection of data or information that can be accessed, updated, and managed
(d) Organized collection of data that cannot be updated

11. A school is planning to store various types of student-related information, including text documents, student photos, and recorded lectures. Which type of data can be stored in a database to manage this information efficiently? Competency Based Que.

(a) Only text-based data
(b) Only image and audio files
(c) Only structured numeric data
(d) All of the above

12. A company wants to implement a system that allows multiple employees to securely access, update, and retrieve stored business data. Which of the following features of a database would support this requirement? Competency Based Que.

(a) No-backup for the data stored
(b) User interface provided
(c) Lack of authentication
(d) Store data in multiple locations

13. **Which of the following is not a function of the database?**
(a) Managing stored data (b) Manipulating data
(c) Security for stored data (d) Analysing code

14. **What is information about data called?**
(a) Hyper data (b) Tera data
(c) Meta data (d) Relations

15. **_____ is a hardware component that is most important for the operation of a database management system.**
(a) Microphone
(b) High speed, large capacity disk to store data
(c) High-resolution video display
(d) Printer

16. **Which of the following is known as a set of entities of the same type that share same properties, or attributes?**
(a) Relation set (b) Tuples
(c) Entity set (d) Entity Relation model

17. **What does an RDBMS consist of?**
(a) Collection of Records (b) Collection of Keys
(c) Collection of Tables (d) Collection of Fields

18. **Software that is used to create , manipulate , maintain a relational database management system is called**
(a) documentation software (b) spreadsheet software
(c) RDBMS (d) designing software

19. **The total number of columns in a table is called**
(a) cardinality (b) degree
(c) spreadsheet (d) relation

20. **The total number of rows in a table is called**
(a) domain (b) tuple
(c) field (d) cardinality

21. **A table can have .... primary key(s).**
(a) 1 (b) 2 (c) 3 (d) multiple

22. **Tables can be linked by**
(a) primary key (b) candidate key
(c) alternate key (d) foreign key

23. **The values appearing in given attributes of any tuple in the referencing relation must likewise occur in specified attributes of at least one tuple in the referenced relation, according to ______ integrity constraint.**
(a) Referential (b) Primary
(c) Referencing (d) Specific

24. **________ is a set of one or more attributes taken collectively to uniquely identify a record.**
(a) Primary Key (b) Foreign key
(c) Super key (d) Candidate key

Fill in the Blanks

25. A ________ is a software system that enables users to define, create, and maintain a database.

26. In a relational database, data is stored in different ________ with relationships to each other.

27. The ________ of a relational table uniquely identifies each record in the table.

28. The ________ level of data abstraction describes how data is physically stored on a storage medium.

29. In a hierarchical data model, the relationship between parent and child segments is ________ to ________.

State Whether True or False

30. A Database Management System (DBMS) eliminates data redundancy and inconsistency.

31. In the file processing system, handling new queries is easy and does not require changes in application programs.

32. A Foreign Key is a non-key attribute whose value is derived from the primary key of another table.

33. The conceptual level of data abstraction describes how data is physically stored.

34. Relational databases store data in tables called relations, where data can be reorganized and accessed flexibly.

35. The referential integrity rule states that a foreign key value must always reference a primary key value in another table or be null.

Assertion And Reason Questions

Assertion (A) and Reason (R) based questions. Mark the correct choice as

(a) Both (A) and (R) are true and (R) is the correct explanation for (A).
(b) Both (A) and (R) are true and (R) is not the correct explanation for (A).
(c) (A) is true and (R) is false.
(d) (A) is false but (R) is true.

36. **Assertion (A)** A relationship is a crucial part of the design of a database.
Reason (R) It is used to establish a connection between a pair of logically related entities.

37. **Assertion (A)** An attribute type is a property of an entity type.
Reason (R) A relationship may associate an entity with itself.

38. Assertion (A) A table is a set of rows and columns.

Reason (R) Attributes of the entity are represented as rows, and data about the entities as columns.

39. Assertion (A) Enforcing data integrity ensures that the data in the database is valid and correct.

Reason (R) Keys play an important role in maintaining data integrity.

40. Assertion (A) A data model refers to a set of concepts to describe the structure of a database and certain constraints that the database should obey.

Reason (R) In relational data models, data is organized into tables.

Answers

1. (b) Database Management System
2. (d) DBMS stores, modifies and retrieves data
3. (b) Charles Bachman
4. (d) Decentralized
5. (c) Single-user Access only
6. (d) All of the above
7. (d) All of these
8. (d) Google
9. (c) Table
10. (c) Organized collection of data or information that can be accessed, updated, and managed
11. (d) All of the above
12. (d) Store data in multiple locations
13. (d) Analysing code
14. (c) Meta data
15. (b) High speed, large capacity disk to store data
16. (c) Entity set
17. (c) Collection of Tables
18. (c) RDBMS
19. (b) degree
20. (d) cardinality
21. (a) 1
22. (d) foreign key
23. (a) Referential
24. (c) Super key
25. Database Management System (DBMS)
26. tables
27. primary key
28. physical
29. one to many
30. True
31. False
32. True
33. False
34. True
35. True
36. (a) Both (A) and (R) are true and (R) is the correct explanation for (A).
37. (b) Both (A) and (R) are true and (R) is not the correct explanation for (A).
38. (c) (A) is true and (R) is false.
39. (b) Both (A) and (R) are true and (R) is not the correct explanation for (A).
40. (b) Both (A) and (R) are true and (R) is not the correct explanation for (A).

Subjective Type Questions

Very Short Answer Type Questions

1. What is a database?

Ans. A database is a collection of data that is organized so that its contents can be easily accessed, managed, and updated.

2. Define the term DBMS.

Ans. DBMS stands for Database Management System. It refers to the software which is used for storing, maintaining and utilizing a database.

3. Ravi is assigned the task of managing a company's database. His team includes individuals responsible for designing, maintaining, and using the database efficiently. Who are the three key types of users in this scenario? **Competency Based Que.**

Ans. Database administrator, application programmers, end users.

4. List the major components of a database system.

Ans. The major components of a database system are

(i) User (ii) Hardware

(iii) Software (iv) Data

5. Who is called database administrator?

Ans. The person having the central control over the system is called database administrator.

6. Name the various types of data that a database can contain.

Ans. User Data, Meta Data, Application Data.

7. Define the term metadata.

Ans. Metadata is data that describes other data or we can say 'data about data'.

8. Which level of abstraction describes how the data is physically stored?

Ans. Internal or physical level.

9. If R1 is a relation with 8 rows and 5 colums, then what will be the cardinality of R1?

Ans. The cardinality of R1 will be 8.

10. Write one difference between degree and cardinality.

Ans. Degree refers to the number of columns and cardinality refers to the number of rows in a relation.

11. Who developed RDBMS?

Ans. The Relational Database Management System was created by Dr. E.F.Codd.

12. What do you mean by a key in DBMS?

Ans. It is defined as the column or attribute or a combination of attributes that is used to identify records of the database table.

13. List different types of keys used in a table in DBMS.

Ans. There are various types of keys used in a table in DBMS, such as

(i) Primary key (ii) Candidate key
(iii) Alternate key (iv) Foreign key

14. What is a foreign key?

Ans. A foreign key is a field or collection of fields in one table whose value is derived from the primary key of another table.

15. What are clients in a database system?

Ans. Clients are the programs that connect to the database server and issue queries in a pre-specified format.

16. Expand the following abbreviations.

(i) RDBMS

(ii) SQL

Ans. (i) Relational Database Management System.

(ii) Structured Query Language.

Short Answer Type I Questions

17. List some commonly used DBMS software packages.

Ans. Some commonly used DBMS software packages are

(i) MySQL (ii) Oracle
(iii) Postgre (iv) DB2
(v) MS-SQL (vi) Sybase

18. Write one difference between data and information with an example.

Ans. Data is raw, unorganized facts that need to be processed. Data can be something simple and seemingly random and useless until it is organized.

For example, each student's test score is one piece of data. When data is processed, organized, structured or presented in a given context so as to make it useful, it is called information.

For example, the class average score is the information that can be concluded from the given data.

19. Describe the following terms.

(i) Domain

(ii) DB2

Ans. (i) **Domain** It is a set of possible values for an attribute. A domain is said to be atomic if elements of the domain are considered as indivisible units.

(ii) **DB2** It is a Relational Database Management System (RDBMS), fully-featured, high performance database capable of handling large quantities of data and concurrently serving many users.

20. Differentiate between DBMS and RDBMS.

Ans. Differences between DBMS and RDBMS

DBMS	RDBMS
In DBMS, relationship between two tables or files are maintained programmatically.	In RDBMS, relationship between two tables or files can be specified at the time of table creation.
DBMS does not support client-server architecture.	Most of the RDBMS support client-server architecture.
DBMS does not support distributed databases.	Most of the RDBMS support distributed databases.
In DBMS, there is no security of data.	In RDBMS, there are multiple levels of security such as command level, object level.
Each table is given an extension in DBMS.	Many tables are grouped in one database in RDBMS.

21. Differentiate between an attribute and a tuple with an example.

Ans. The columns of a table are referred to as attributes. It is also known as field which is reserved for a specific piece of data. The rows of a table are referred to as tuples.

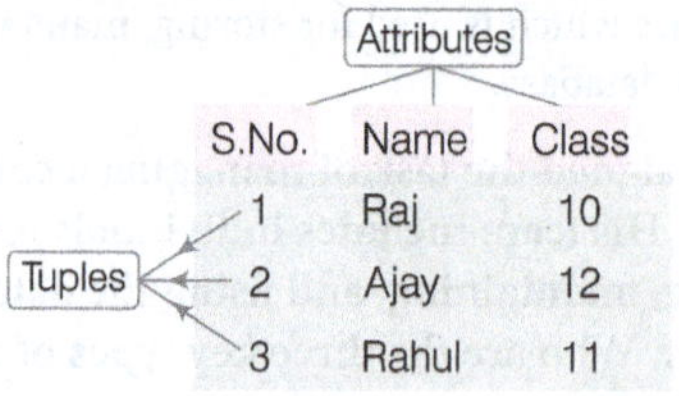

Short Answer Type II Questions

22. **Riya is working on a project where she stores student records in multiple text files. Over time, she notices that the same student data appears in different files, and when she updates one file, the changes are not reflected in others. She also finds it difficult to retrieve specific information quickly. Based on this scenario, explain why a database system would be a better choice than a traditional file processing system.**
Competency Based Que.

Ans. A database system is needed to overcome the limitations of the file processing system. In Riya's case, using a database system would help:

(i) **Reduce data redundancy** Avoids storing duplicate information.

(ii) **Ensure data consistency** Updates reflect across all records.

(iii) **Improve security** Controls access to sensitive data.

(iv) **Enable efficient queries** Allows easy retrieval of specific information.

By using a database, Riya can manage student records more effectively, ensuring accuracy and security.

23. **Describe the levels of abstraction.**

Ans. There are three levels of abstraction, which are described below

(i) **Internal level** It describes how the data are actually stored. This level is also known as physical level.

(ii) **Conceptual level** It describes what data are stored in the database, and what relationship exist among them. It is also known as logical level.

(iii) **External level** This level describes only part of the entire database. This level is also known as view level.

24. **Explain the following terms.**

(i) **Relation**

(ii) **Cardinality**

(iii) **Primary key**

(iv) **Alternate key**

Ans. (i) **Relation** All data items and relationships among them are represented in a two dimensional table known as a relation.

(ii) **Cardinality** The number of rows in a table is known as cardinality.

(iii) **Primary key** The key that uniquely identifies each record in a table is known as a primary key.

(iv) **Alternate key** From the set of candidate keys after selecting one of the key as primary key, all other remaining keys are known as alternate keys.

25. **Write down some differences between a primary and candidate key.**

Ans. Differences between candidate and primary keys are as follows.

Candidate Key	Primary Key
A candidate key can be any column or a combination of columns that can identify as unique key in database.	A primary key is a column or a combination of columns that uniquely identify a record.
A table can have multiple candidate keys.	A table cannot have more than one primary key.
Each candidate key can identify as primary key.	Only one candidate key can be primary key.

Long Answer Type Questions

26. **Explain database and DBMS in detail.**

Ans. **Database** The Database is a shared collection of logically related data, designed to meet the information needs of an organization.

A database is a computer based record keeping system whose over all purpose is to record and maintains information. The database holds not only the organization's operational data but also a description of this data. For this reason, a database is also defined as a self-describing collection of integrated records. The description of the data is known as the data dictionary or metadata (the 'data about data').

DBMS A Database Management System (DBMS) is a collection of programs that enables users to store, modify, and extract information from a database as per the requirements. It acts as an interface between the application programme and the operating system to access or manipulate the database. A database management system is a piece of software that provides services for accessing a database, while maintaining all the required features of the data. Commercially available database management systems in the market are dbase, FoxPro, Oracle, MySQL and DB2 etc.

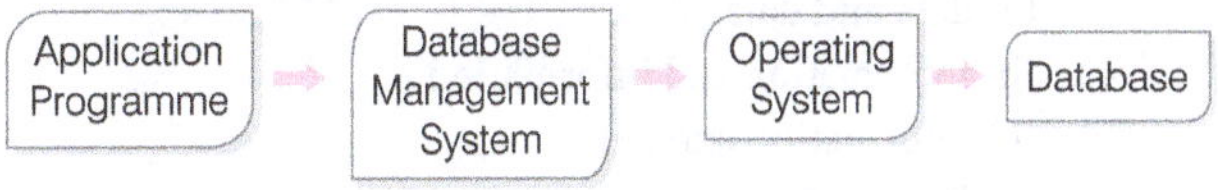

27. **What do you mean by data models? Explain various data models.**

Ans. Refer to text on page no. 178-179 (Data models).

28. **What is relational database? Also, define its terminology.**

Ans. Refer to text on page no. 179 (Relational database).

Case Study Based Questions

Case Study 1

A Database Management System is a software system that enables users to define, create, and maintain the database and provides controlled access to this database.The primary goal of a DBMS is to provide a way to store and retrieve database information that is both convenient and efficient. Data in a database can be added, deleted, changed, sorted or searched, all using a DBMS.

Application program accesses the data stored in the database by sending request to the DBMS. e.g. MySQL, INGRES, MS-ACCESS etc.

The purpose of a Database Management System is to bridge the gap between information and data. The data stored in memory or on disk must be converted to usable information.

Based on the above information, answer the following questions.

(i) DBMS stands for
(a) Database Management System
(b) Database Manage System
(c) Data Management System
(d) Data Manage System

(ii) Advantage(s) of DBMS is/are
(a) reduced data redundancy
(b) data integrity
(c) backup and recovery
(d) All of the above

(iii) It is a collection of data elements representing real world information.
(a) DBMS
(b) Database
(c) Relation
(d) Query

(iv) The purpose of DBMS is to bridge the gap between
(a) data and data
(b) information and information
(c) information and data
(d) information and database

Ans. (i) (a) Database Management System
(ii) (d) All of the above
(iii) (b) Database
(iv) (c) information and data

Case Study 2

Data model can be defined as an integrated collection of concepts for describing and manipulating data, relationship between data and constraints on the data in an organisation.

A data model provides a way to describe the design of a database at the internal, conceptual and external level.

A data model comprises of three components, which are given below:

- A structural part, consisting a set of rules according to which databases can be constructed.
- A manipulative part, defining the types of operations that are allowed on the data (this includes the operations that are used for updating or retrieving data from the database and for changing the structure of the database).
- Possibly a set of integrity rules, which ensures that the data is accurate.

Based on the above information, answer the following questions.

(i) The purpose of a data model is to represent data and to make the
(a) data understandable (b) data characterisation
(c) data outputting (d) None of these

(ii) How many types of data model are there in DBMS?
(a) 2 (b) 3
(c) 4 (d) 5

(iii) Which of the following ensures that the data is accurate?
(a) Structural part (b) Manipulative part
(c) Integrity rules (d) None of these

(iv) In which of the following data model, data is organised in a tree like structure?
(a) Hierarchical data model
(b) Network data model
(c) Relational data model
(d) All of the above

Ans. (i) (a) data understandable
(ii) (b) 3
(iii) (c) Integrity rules
(iv) (a) Hierarchical data model

SELF ASSESSMENT TEST

Multiple Choice Questions

1. The other name for a table is
(a) database
(b) relation
(c) domain
(d) degree

2. The foreign key of a table
(a) has unique values
(b) has integer type values
(c) has a linking column in another table
(d) None of the above

3. The number of rows of a table is
(a) limited
(b) not limited
(c) can be restricted while table creation
(d) None of the above

Fill in the Blanks

4. A ....describes the structure of the database, including how data is defined, represented, and the relationships among data.

5. The .... of a relation is determined by the number of .... it contains.

6. The number of .... in a relation is called its ....

7. A domain is a set of values from which an .... can take a value in each row.

State Whether True or False

8. The most commonly used data model is the Object-Oriented Data Model.

9. The number of attributes in a relation is called the Degree of the relation.

10. A candidate key is an attribute that is chosen as the primary key of a relation.

11. A composite primary key consists of more than one attribute to uniquely identify tuples in a relation.

12. A foreign key is an attribute in a relation that references the primary key of another relation.

Assertion and Reason Questions

Assertion (A) and Reason (R) based questions. Mark the correct choice as
(a) Both (A) and (R) are true and (R) is the correct explanation for (A).
(b) Both (A) and (R) are true and (R) is not the correct explanation for (A).
(c) (A) is true and (R) is false.
(d) (A) is false but (R) is true.

13. **Assertion (A)** The relational data model is the most commonly used data model in database management systems.
Reason (R) The relational data model defines the structure of the database, relationships among data, and constraints using tables.

14. **Assertion (A)** In a relational database, each relation must have at least one attribute that holds unique values.
Reason (R) A candidate key is an attribute or a set of attributes that can uniquely identify tuples in a relation.

15. **Assertion (A)** A foreign key in a relational database can take NULL values in all cases.
Reason (R) A foreign key is an attribute in one relation that refers to the primary key of another relation.

Very Short Answer Type Questions

16. Write any two properties of database.

17. Who is the application programmer in database?

18. How will you define the role of clients in a database system?

Short Answer Type Questions

19. What is degree and cardinality of relation and how are they linked to rows and columns?

20. Define the following:
(a) Data item (b) Record
(c) Table (d) Data redundancy

21. Define conceptual level.

22. Explain primary key with an example.

Long Answer Type Questions

23. Define the following terms.

(i) User data (ii) Application data

(iii) Meta data (iv) Data

(v) End user

24. Explain working of Database.

Case Study Based Question

25. ABC School maintains student records in a computerized system. The school uses a Database Management System (DBMS) to store and manage student details such as roll number, name, class, and contact information. The database is structured using the Relational Data Model, where student records are stored in a table (relation). Each record consists of multiple fields like Roll Number, Name, Class, and Phone Number.

To ensure uniqueness, the Roll Number is chosen as the Primary Key. Other unique attributes like Phone Number could be considered as an Alternate Key. The table follows the principles of domain, tuple, relation, and keys to maintain data consistency and organization.

Based on above information Answer the following Questions:

(i) What is the primary purpose of a Database Management System (DBMS) in ABC School?

(a) To manually store student data in files

(b) To manage and organize data efficiently

(c) To create only printed student records

(d) To replace computer networks

(ii) In the Relational Data Model, what does a tuple represent in a database table?

(a) A column in a table

(b) A relationship between two tables

(c) A single row or record in a table

(d) A unique identifier for a table

(iii) Which of the following attributes in the student database can be considered a Candidate Key?

(a) Roll Number (b) Name

(c) Class (d) Section

(iv) If Roll Number is the Primary Key, which of the following can be an Alternate Key?

(a) Student Name (b) Phone Number

(c) Class Name (d) Date of Birth

(v) In a relational database, what does the term domain refer to?

(a) The number of rows in a table

(b) The permissible values a column can have

(c) A unique key that identifies a row

(d) The total number of tables in a database

Answers

1. (b) 2. (c) 3. (b) 4. data model

5. degree, attributes 6. tuples, cardinality

7. attribute 8. False

9. True 10. False 11. True 12. True

13. (a) 14. (a) 15. (c)

25. (i) → (b), (ii) → (c), (iii) → (a), (iv) → (b), (v) → (b)

12

CHAPTER

This chapter introduces Structured Query Language (SQL), the standard language for managing and querying relational databases, covering its purpose, fundamental concepts, and common operations.

YOUR STUDY GOALS

12.1 MySQL
12.2 Tokens of MySQL
12.3 Table Constraints
12.4 Operators in MySQL
12.5 Structured Query Language (SQL)

YOUR PRACTICE GOAL

- Objective Type Questions (40 Qs ; MCQs, True or False, Fill in the Blanks, Assertion and Reason)
- Subjective Type Questions (47 Qs ; VSA, SA, LA)
- Case Study Based Questions-2

Structured Query Language

A query is a statement in the language of SQL that extracts either a set of data or makes certain changes to the data in a table. SQL is a 5th generation non procedural language that users can write easily to perform their desired operations on the data set present in a table.

It is an easy to use command based interaction where users can perform their work by issuing simple commands.

e.g.
```
SELECT DISTINCT Student_name
FROM STUDENT
ORDER BY Age;65
```

This query searches the 'Student_name' field from the STUDENT table and sorts the list by the age.

12.1 MySQL

Most organizations track different types of information, like; information about their employees, clients, projects and any other terms, which support or which might support their programs and services. Managing this information is crucial.

A DBMS (Database Management System) allows the user to manage and use a vast variety of information easily. DBMS also provides a centralized control of its operational data.

DBMS is easy to set-up, easy to manipulate and easy to use. There are many DBMSs available in the market such as MySQL, INGRES, POSTGRES, DB2, Oracle, etc, among them MySQL is very popular database management system.

MySQL is an open source Relational Database Management System(RDBMS) based on SQL(Structured Query Language).

In MySQL database, information is stored in tables and runs virtually on all platforms including Linux, Unix and Windows.

MySQL provides many features such as storing, maintaining and controlling data in a secured environment. It is a fast, reliable, scalable substitute to many of the commercial RDBMSs available today. MySQL works with many languages like PHP, Perl, C, C++, Java etc.

History of MySQL

MySQL was introduced by a software company MySQL AB, founded by **David Axmark**, **Allan Larsson** and **Michael Widenius** in the year 1994 in Sweden.

Sun Microsystems (a well known ZJava development company) acquired MySQL AB on 26-February-2008. MySQL was first released on 23-May-1995, for personal usage based on ISAM (Indexed Sequential Access Method).

It supports the basic principles of database and data manipulation used to retrieve, insert and update stored data. Being an open source anyone can use and change the software for their needs.

It supports the basic principles of database and data manipulation using SQL statements.

MySQL 8.0.16 was the latest version of MySQL and it is available free of cost on Internet.

Some of the MySQL versions are as follows

Versions	Released Date
MySQL 3.20.0	May 1997
MySQL 3.23.0	August 1999
MySQL 3.23.32	January 2001
MySQL 4.1	October 2004
MySQL 5.0	October 2005
MySQL 5.1	November 2008
MySQL 5.5	December 2010
MySQL 5.6	February 2013
MySQL 8.0.16	April 2018

Starting MySQL

MySQL also starts the same way like other application programs. Before starting you have to ensure that MySQL server is installed on your computer system.

- To install MySQL server follow the given steps

Step 1 Download the latest version of MySQL from the following available links and if you are not sure which version to select then download MySQL installer **for Windows.**
`www.filehippo.com/download-mysql/`
or `www.mysql.com`

Step 2 Login into your computer as an administrator because it will give you administrator rights which will make the installation smoother.

Step 3 Double click on the downloaded file (the installation file comes as a .zip format). You need to unzip this file.

Step 4 After unzip the file, double click on **Setup.exe** (single file inside the .zip format file). This will initialize the setup process.

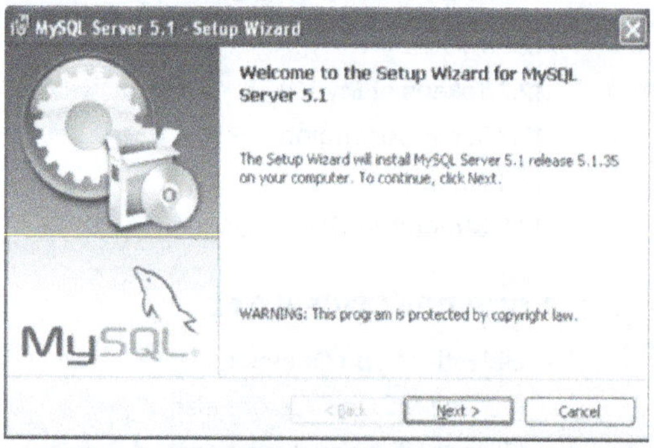

Step 5 Click **Next** to begin the setup.

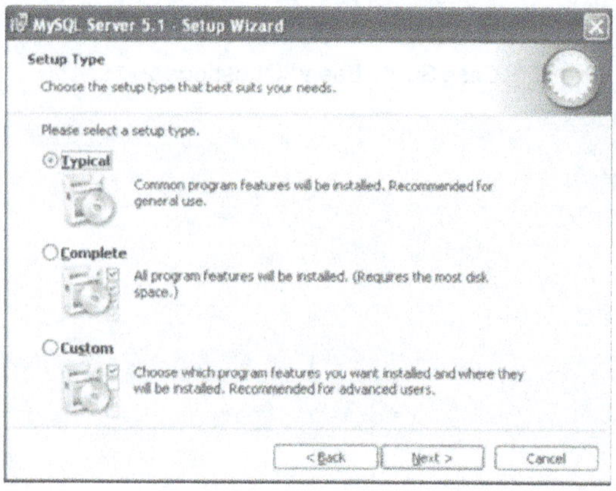

Step 6 Click Typical and then Next.

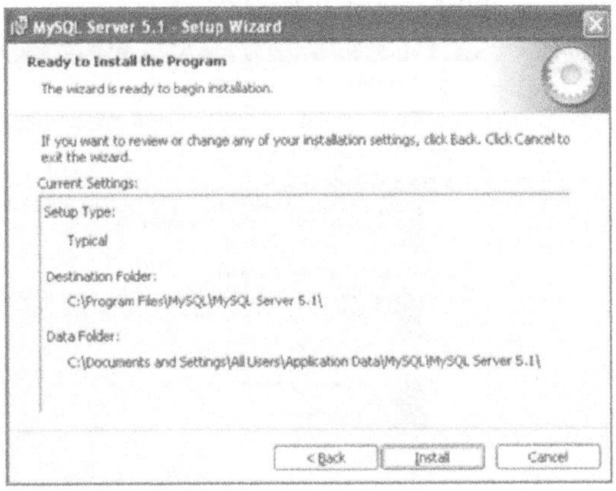

Step 7 Click **Install.**

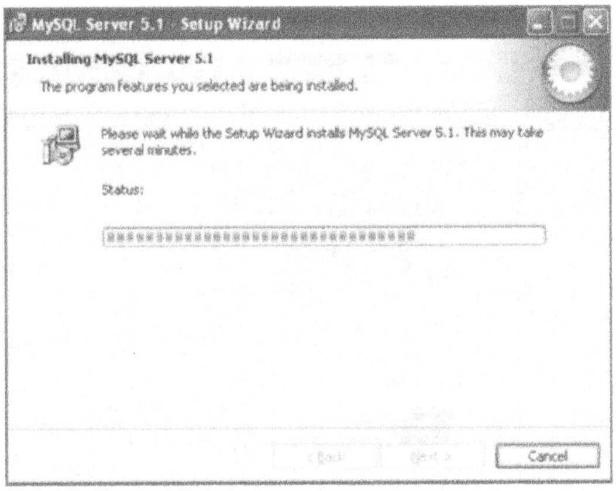

Step 8 Wait while the program self installs and then click Next. The MySQL enterprise window appears. It contains the features of MySQL enterprise.

Step 9 Click Next. A window appears which displays the MySQL Enterprise Monitor Service.

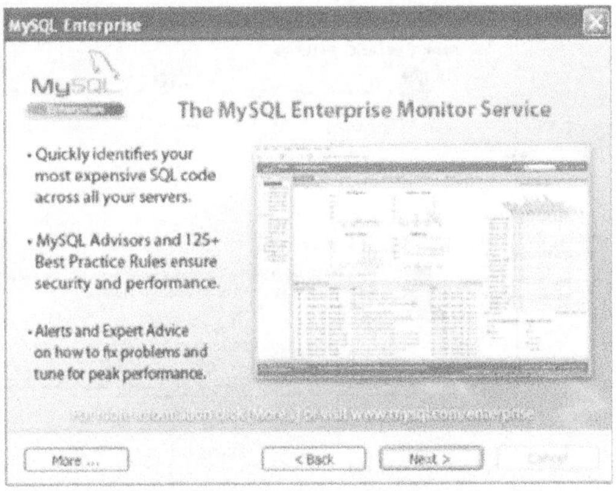

Step 10 Click Next, then the following window will appear.

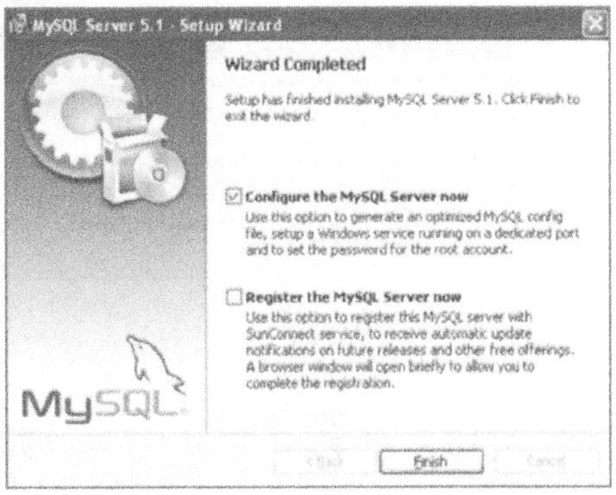

Step 11 If you checked the Configure the MySQL Server now check box on the final dialog of the MySQL server installation, then the MySQL Server Instance Configuration wizard will automatically start. Now click Finish and then click Next.

Step 12 Select Reconfigure Instance and then click Next.

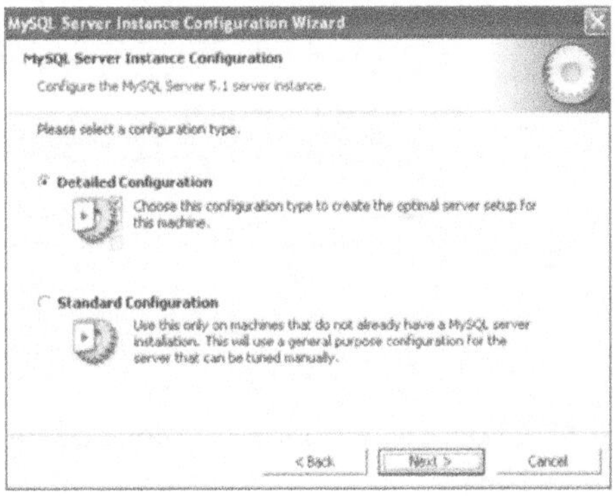

Step 13 Select Detailed Configuration and then click Next.

Step 14 Select server type in which you are interested and then click Next.

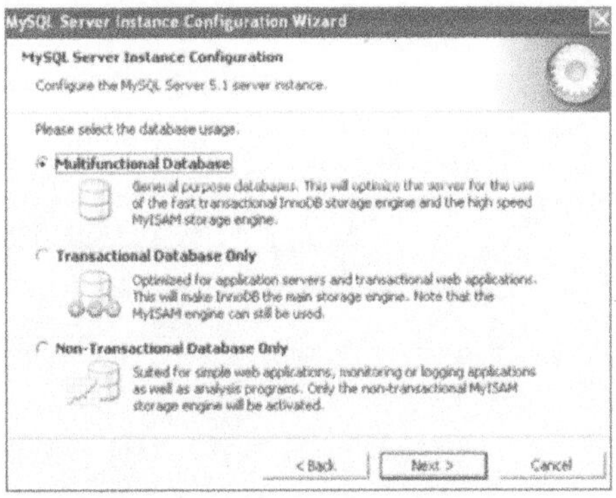

Step 15 Select the database which you want and then click Next.

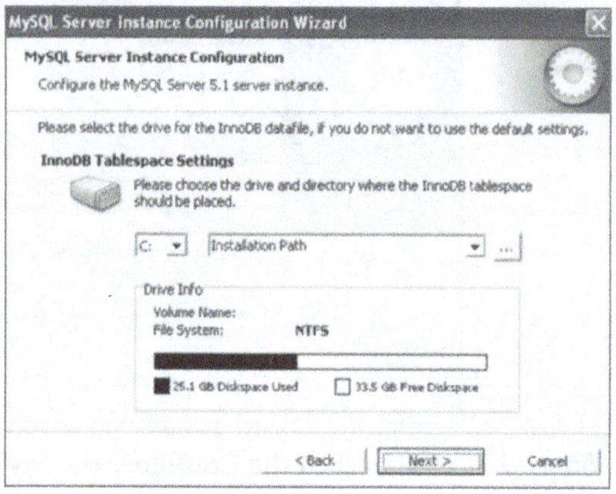

Step 16 Select the drive where the database files will be stored and then click Next.

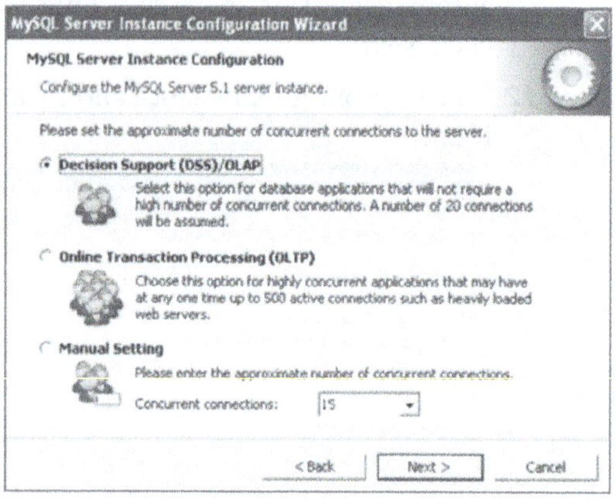

Step 17 Choose a appropriate option and then click Next.

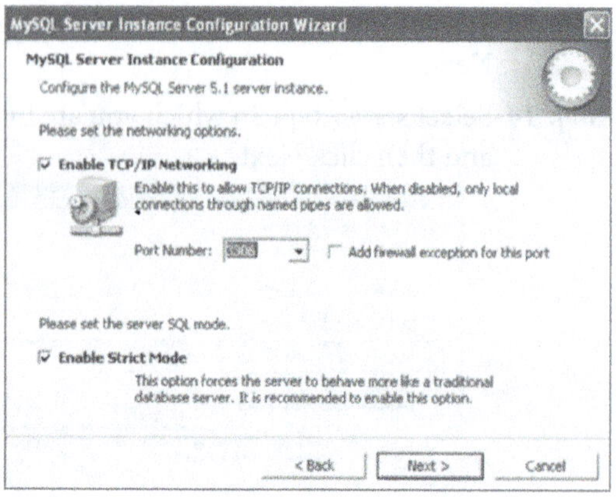

Step 18 It is recommended that you leave the default post 3306. Click Next.

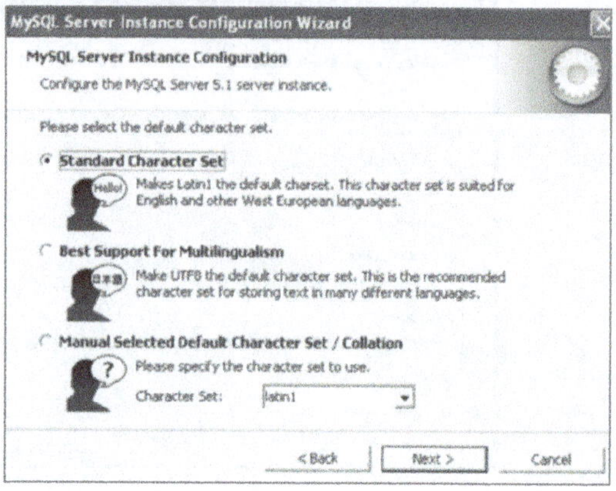

Step 19 Select the default character set and then click Next.

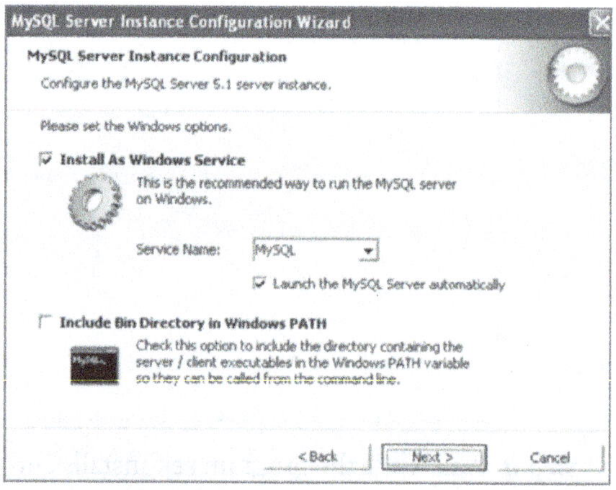

Step 20 It is highly recommended that you run the MySQL server as a window service. Click Next.

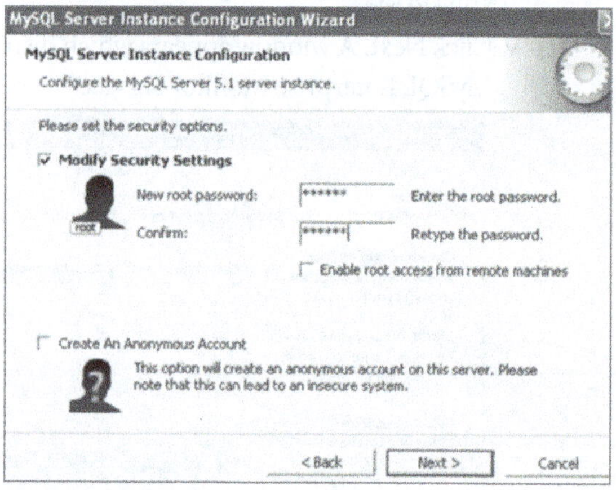

Step 21 Specify a secure root password and click Next.

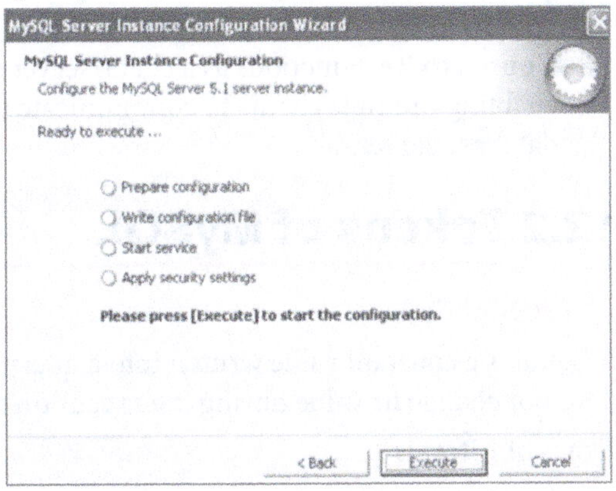

Step 22 Click Execute.

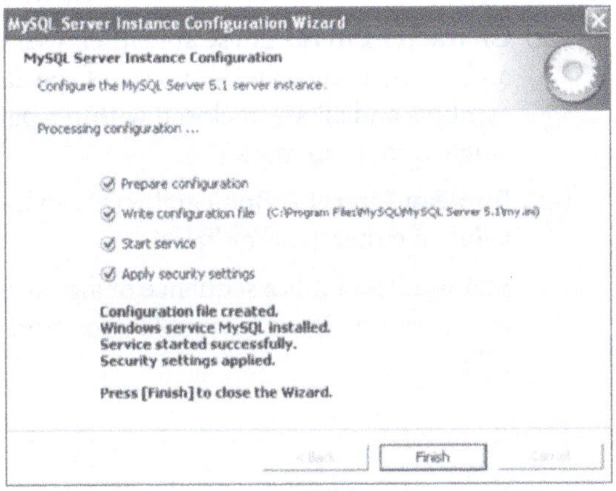

Step 23 Click Finish.

Once you installed the MySQL server program in your computer system then

Click Start → All Programs → MySQL → MySQL Server → MySQL Command Line client

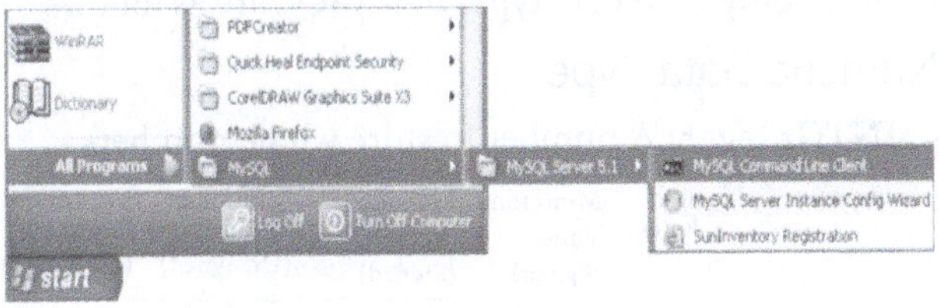

- MySQL command line client window appears.

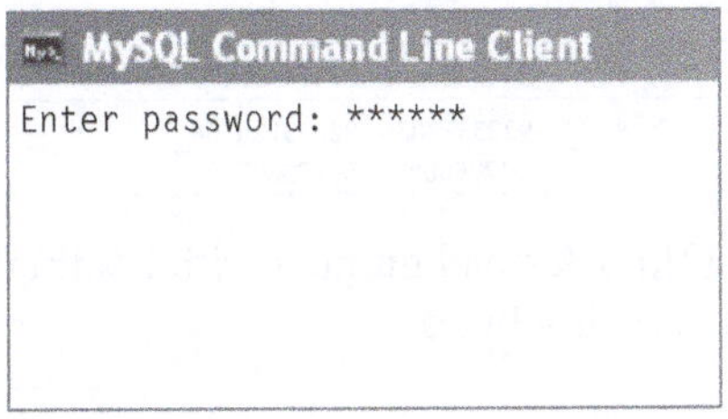

- Here, you need to enter the password (same password entered during initialisation).

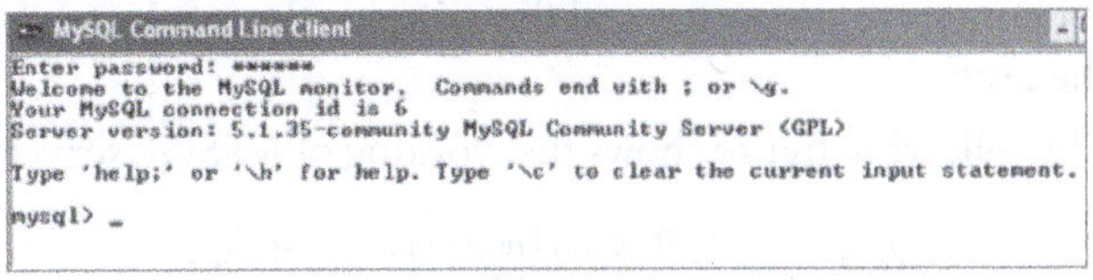

- Now, you can start working in MySQL.
- If you want to exit from MySQL command line client window, type quit in the command prompt and press enter.

```
mysql >quit; ↵
```

Components of MySQL

A database is a structured collection of data, the vast amount of information. To add, access, and process data stored in a computer database, you need a database management system such as MySQL server.

Information system is the key role of database management system and database server is the key to solve the problems of information management.

MySQL can be used for variety of applications but it is mostly used for the web applications on the Internet.

MySQL database system consists of the following three components

Server (MySQL server)

MySQL server is an engine which provides access to databases, responsible for creating, managing database, executing and returning queries and maintaining security together with additional tools to manage multiple MySQL servers.

Clients

A client is a program that connects to the database server and issue queries in a pre-specified format. In MySQL, you can enter command-line queries to manage user permissions and utilities to import and export MySQL database.

Client Library

A client library is an Application Programming Interface (API) where a client can write their own programs using a programming language like C, C++, Java, etc.

Working of MySQL

MySQL database works on client/server architecture. It is installed on a server (*i.e.*, single machine), but it can provide the database facility to a variety of clients at different locations. MySQL server can be accessed directly via various client interfaces, which send SQL statements to the server and then display the results to the user.

The following figure shows the working of MySQL server

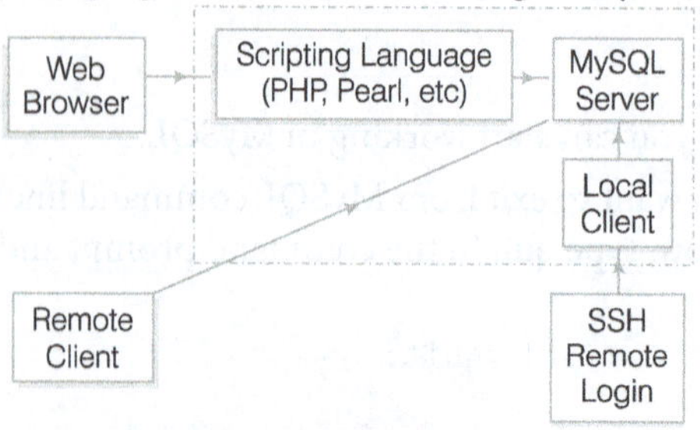

Working of MySQL Server

(a) **Local Client** It is a program on the same machine as the server. *For example*, Command Line MySQL client software.

(b) **Scripting Language** It can pass SQL queries to the server and display the result.

For example, PHP, Pearl, Python, etc.

(c) **Remote Client** It is a program on different machine that can be connected to the server and display the result.

(d) **Remote Login** It allows connecting to the server machine to run one of its local clients.

(e) **Web Browser** We can use a web browser and scipts that someone has written.

Features of MySQL

1. **Speed** MySQL is fast and reliable, supporting demanding applications with benchmark-backed performance.
2. **Open Source** It is free to use and customizable, allowing developers to modify the source code.
3. **Ease of Use** Simple to set up and manage compared to larger database systems.
4. **Query Language Support** Uses ANSI-standard SQL for querying and managing relational databases.
5. **Security** Encrypts passwords and transactions, preventing unauthorized access and data breaches.
6. **Cross-Platform Portability** Works on Linux, Windows, Solaris, and supports multiple programming languages like C, C++, PHP, Java, and Python.
7. **Licensing** Operates under the GPL, making it free for users.
8. **Connectivity** Functions as a client/server system, enabling multiple clients to communicate with the database server.

12.2 Tokens of MySQL

1. Literals

A literal is a constant value written into a query. A literal does not change its value during the execution of a query.

Types of Literals

(i) **Numeric Literal** These are the sequences of digits which may be positive or negative.

(ii) **Character Literal** These are either a set of alphabets, a set of digits or a set of special symbols and all are enclosed within a pair of single quotation mark (' ').

(iii) **Boolean Literal** A Boolean literal can have a value of either 'true' or 'false'.

(iv) **String Literal** It is a sequence of alpha-numeric characters enclosed in double quotation marks (" ").

2. Data Types

Data exists in various forms. It can be in the form of numbers, fractional numbers, characters, strings (groups of characters) , dates , sound , picture etc.

A table in a database stores data in each of these formats, like Name is a string, age is an integer, marks is float, date of birth is of type date etc.

Some mainly used data types in MySQL are as follows

Numeric Data Type

- **INT(Integer)** A number to store whole numbers

Types	Length in Bytes	Minimum Value (Signed)	Maximum Value (Signed)	Minimum Value (Unsigned)	Maximum Value (Unsigned)
TINYINT	1	-128	127	0	255
SMALLINT	2	-32768	32767	0	65535
MEDIUMINT	3	-8388608	8388607	0	16777215
INT	4	-2147483648	2147483647	0	4294967295
BIGINT	8	-9223372036 854775808	92233720368 54775807	0	18446744073 709551615

- **FLOAT** (N,D) A small number with floating decimal point. It's size is 4 bytes.

- **DOUBLE** (N,D) A large number with floating decimal point. It's size is 8 bytes.
- **DECIMAL** (N,D) An unpacked floating point number

String/Text Data Type

It allows the database server to store string values such as Name of the students, Address etc.

Types	Description	Display Format	Range in characters
CHAR	Contains non-binary strings. Length is fixed as you declare while creating a table. When stored, they are right-padded with spaces to the specified length.	Trailing spaces are removed.	The length can be any value from 0 to 255.
VARCHAR	Contains non-binary strings. Columns are variable length strings.	As stored.	A value from 0 to 255 before MySQL 5.0.3, and 0 to 65,535 in 5.0.3 and later versions.

Date and Time Data Type

It allows the database server to store a date using the fields YEAR, MONTH and DAY in the format YYYY-MM-DD.

For example, Date of admission, Date of birth etc.

Types	Description	Display Format	Range
TIME	Use when you need only time information	HH:MM:SS	–838:59:59 to 838:59:59
DATETIME	Use when you need values containing both date and time information.	YYYY-MM-DD HH:MM:SS	'1000-01-01 00:00:00' to '9999-12-31 23:59:59'
DATE	Use when you need only date information.	YYYY-MM-DD	'1000-01-01' to '9999-12-31'
TIMESTAMP	Values are converted from the current time zone to UTC (Co-ordinated Universal Time), while storing and converted back from UTC to the current time zone when retrieved.	YYYY-MM-DD HH:MM:SS	'1970-01-01 00:00:01' UTC to '2038-01-19 03:14:07' UTC
YEAR	The year type is a 1-byte type used to represent year values. It can be declared as year (2) or year (4) to specify a display width of two or four characters. If no width is given, the default is 4 characters.	4444	1901 to 2155

3. NULLs or Null Values

If a column in a table row has no value, then the column is said to be a null. Nulls can appear in columns of any data type provided they are not restricted by NOT NULL or PRIMARY KEY integrity constraints.

To test for NULL values, the IS NULL and IS NOT NULL operators are used.

(i) **IS NULL Operator** returns true if column value is NULL.

(ii) **IS NOT NULL Operator** returns true if column value is not NULL.

4. Comments

It is the text that is not executed and is used only for documentation purpose.

Comments are used to clarify the purpose or effect of particular SQL statements.

Comment Symbol	Description
Double Hyphen (followed by a space) "-- "	The double hyphen precedes a comment within a single line. To comment more than one line, put double hyphen symbols at the beginning of each comment line. In MySQL, the "-- " comment style requires the second dash to be followed by atleast one white space or control character (such as a space, tab, newline and so on).
slash and asterisk /*.....*/	C-language style slash and asterisk (/* */) paired delimeters enclose the comment. The /* precedes the comment, and the */ follows it. These can delimit single-line or multiple-line comments, but comments cannot be nested.
Hash #	Begin the comment with #. Proceed with the text of the comment. This text cannot be extended to a new line. End the comment with a line break.

Writing SQL Commands

<table>
<tr><th>Symbol</th><th>Description</th></tr>
<tr><td>|</td><td>Symbolic way of 'or' whatever precedes this symbol may optionally be replaced by whatever follows it.</td></tr>
<tr><td>[ ]</td><td>Everything enclosed in it is optional.</td></tr>
<tr><td>...</td><td>Whatever precedes, it may be repeated number of times.</td></tr>
<tr><td>.,..</td><td>Whatever precedes, it may be repeated number of times with individual occurrences of commas.</td></tr>
<tr><td>{ }</td><td>Everything enclosed in it, is evaluating different symbols (1., ... etc.).</td></tr>
<tr><td>< ></td><td>SQL and some other terms are enclosed by this angle brackets.</td></tr>
</table>

12.3 Table Constraints

Constraints are rules that may be applied to fields of a table, so that data entered in the table follows the rules to restrict entry of invalid data.

There are two types of constraints as follows.

(i) **Column Constraints** It applies only to individual columns.

(ii) **Table Constraints** It applies to groups of one or more columns.

Syntax

```
CREATE TABLE table_name
(
column_name1 data_type(size)
constraint_name,
column_name2 data_type(size)
constraint_name,
------
);
```

Integrity Constraints

(i) **Unique Constraints** It ensures distinct values in the specified columns.

For example,

```
CREATE TABLE Employee (ecode INTEGER
UNIQUE,
ename CHAR (20));
```

(ii) **Default Constraints** Used to provide a default value for a column without a value.

For example,

```
CREATE TABLE Employee (ecode INTEGER, ename
CHAR(20), salary INTEGER DEFAULT 10000);
```

(iii) **Primary Key Constraints** Ensures not null and distinct values for a column. This constraint can be applied to only one column

For example,

```
CREATE TABLE Employee (ecode INTEGER
PRIMARY KEY, enameCHAR(20));
```

(iv) **Foreign Key Constraints** It is a constraint that ensures that columns in one table match the primary key column of same or another table.

For example,

```
CREATE TABLE Items (Order_No INTEGER
PRIMARY KEY, Itemno INTEGER REFERENCES
Items (Order_No));
```

(v) **Check Constraints** Used to provide any other business condition.

For example,

```
CREATE TABLE Employee (ecode INTEGER
PRIMARY KEY, salary DECIMAL CHECK
(salary>5000));
```

(vi) **Not Null Constraints** This constraint ensures that a column carries non blank values.

For example,

```
CREATE TABLE Employee (ecode INTEGER NOT
NULL, ename CHAR (20));
```

12.4 Operators in MySQL

MySQL supports different types of operators, some of them are explained below

1. Arithmetic Operators

These operators are used to perform mathematical calculation.

OPERATOR	DESCRIPTION
+ (Addition)	Add the two arguments together
– (Subtraction)	Subtract the second argument from the first argument
* (Multiplication)	Multiplies the two arguments
/ (Division)	Divide the first argument by the second argument
% (Remainder)	Divide the first argument from the second argument and provides the remainder of that operation

2. Comparison Operators

These operators are used to test or compare the value of two operands i.e. between two variable.

OPERATOR	DESCRIPTION
=	Equal to
>	Greater than
<	Less than
>=	Greater than or equal to
<=	Less than or equal to
<> or !=	Not equal to (not ISO standard)
!<	Not less than (not ISO standard)
!>	Not greater than (not ISO standard)

3. Logical Operator

The logical operators compare two conditions at a time to determine whether a row can be selected for the output.

BETWEEN Operator

The BETWEEN operator is used in a WHERE clause to check that the field values are within a specified inclusive range. The values can be numbers, text or dates.

IN Operator

This operator checks a value within a set of values separated by commas and retrieve the rows from the table which are matching.

LIKE Operator

This operator is used to search a specified pattern in a column. It is useful when you want to search rows to match a specific pattern, or when you do not know the entire value.

Two special wildcard operators, are used to match patterns

(i) **The Percent Sign (%)** It is used to match any substring.

(ii) **TheUnderscore (_)** It is used tomatch any character.

The symbols can also be used in combinations.

Rule Write the characters that you know, replace unknown letters by % or _

Examples:

COMMAND	DESCRIPTION
WHERE SALARY LIKE '100%'	Find any values that start with 100
WHERE SALARY LIKE '%100%'	Find any values that have 100 in any position
WHERE SALARY LIKE '_00%'	Find any values that have 00 in the second and third positions
WHERE SALARY LIKE '1_%_%'	Find any values that start with 1 and are atleast 2 characters in length
WHERE SALARY LIKE '%2'	Find any values that end with 2
WHERE SALARY LIKE '_2%3'	Find any values that have a 2 in the second position and end with a 3
WHERE SALARY LIKE '2__3'	Find any values in a four-digit number that start with 2 and end with 3

For patterns to include the special pattern characters (that is, % and _), SQL allows the specification of an escape character.

To illustrate, consider the following patterns, which use a backslash (\ ) as the escape character.

- Like'ab\%cd%' escape '\' matches all strings beginning with "ab%cd".
- Like 'ab\\cd%' escape '\' matches all strings beginning with "ab\cd".

Quick Test 1

1. What is DBMS and why is it important?
2. Who introduced MySQL and in which year?
3. Which programming languages are supported by MySQL?
4. What is the latest version of MySQL mentioned in the content?
5. What is the purpose of the LIKE operator in MySQL?

12.5 Structured Query Language (SQL)

SQL is used by all programs and users to access data within the MySQL database. There is a structure to this language, it uses english phrases to define an action, but uses math-like symbols to make comparisons.

For example,

```
SELECT * FROM Table;
```

where, `'SELECT'` `'FROM'` and `'table'` are in english.

SQL was initially developed at IBM by **Donald D. Chamberlin** and **Raymond F. Boyce** in the early 1970s.

This version initially called SEQUEL (Structured English Query Language), was designed to manipulate and retrieve data stored in IBM's original RDBMS.

In the late 1970s, Oracle Corporation saw the potential of the concepts described by codd, Chamberlin and Boyce and developed their own SQL-based RDBMS with aspirations of selling it to the various U.S. government agencies. In June 1979, Oracle Corporation introduced the first commercially available implementation of SQL, Oracle V2 for VAX computers. The American National Standards Institute (ANSI) adopted SQL as the standard language for RDBMSs in 1986.

The International Standards Organization (ISO) has also adopted SQL as the standard language for RDBMSs.

Characteristics of SQL

Main characteristics of SQL are given below

- SQL is an ANSI and ISO standard computer language for creating and manipulating databases.
- SQL allows the user to create, update, delete and retrieve data from a database.

- SQL is very simple and easy to learn.
- SQL is used specifically for relational databases.
- SQL works with database programs like DB2, Oracle, MS Access, Sybase MS SQL Server, etc.

Advantages of SQL

SQL is an efficient language for database communication. It has various advantages, some of them are listed below:

1. **Ease of Use** SQL uses simple and readable commands like SELECT, INSERT, and UPDATE.
2. **Efficient Data Retrieval** SQL allows quick retrieval of large datasets using optimized queries.
3. **Scalability** Works well for small to large databases, supporting millions of records.
4. **Data Integrity** Enforces constraints like PRIMARY KEY, FOREIGN KEY, and NOT NULL to maintain consistency.
5. **Security** Provides access control using user permissions and authentication mechanisms.
6. **Portability** SQL is standardized and works across various database systems (MySQL, PostgreSQL, SQL Server, etc.).

Disadvantages of SQL

The disadvantages of SQL are as follows

1. **Complex for Beginners** Requires understanding of commands, joins, and normalization.
2. **Performance Issues** Poorly optimized queries can slow down large databases.
3. **Limited Procedural Capabilities** SQL lacks advanced programming constructs like loops and conditions, requiring procedural extensions.
4. **Costly for Large Enterprises** Some databases (e.g., Oracle, SQL Server) have high licensing costs.
5. **Data Security Risks** Improper configurations can lead to SQL injection attacks.
6. **Rigid Structure** Requires predefined schemas; changes can be complex and time-consuming.

SQL Commands

In order to access data from MySQL database, all applications, programmers and users must use Structured Query Language (SQL). SQL commands are the instructions used to communicate with the database to perform specific task that work with data.

SQL commands can be used not only for searching the database but also to perform various other functions like, create tables, add data to tables, modify data, drop the table, set permissions for users and many more.

SQL commands can be classified into following categories

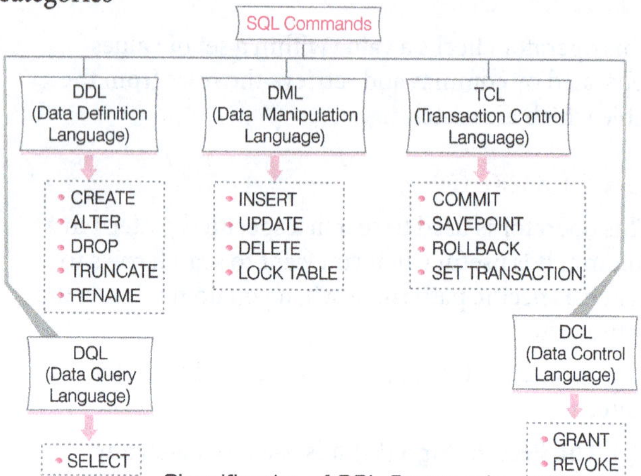

Classification of SQL Commands

Data Definition Language (DDL)

DDL is used to define and modify the structure of database objects such as tables, views, schemas, and indexes.

It specifies the database schema and allows the creation, alteration, and deletion of objects.

Common DDL Commands

- **CREATE** Creates database objects like tables and views.
- **ALTER** Modifies the structure of a table by adding, deleting, or modifying columns.
- **DROP** Deletes database objects permanently.
- **TRUNCATE** Removes all records from a table but retains its structure.
- **RENAME** Renames an existing database object.

Database in MySQL

A database is a container that stores a group of related tables of a domain together.

Creating a Database

Creating a database is an easier task. You need to just type the name of the database in a CREATE DATABASE command.

Syntax `CREATE DATABASE [IF NOT EXISTS] <database_name>;`

Selecting/Opening a Database

To work on a database , it must be opened first.

Syntax `USE <database_name>;`

Show Databases

To get the list of databases in your computer, the show databases command can be used.

Syntax `SHOW DATABASES;`

Dropping a Database

A database can be removed from the computer along with all its constituents

Syntax `DROP DATABASE <database_name>;`

Accessing Database

To access a database USE command is used.

Syntax `USE<database_name>;`

Table Creation

Tables are the main holder of data. Database is a collection of tables. Tables are created using CREATE TABLE command.

Example

```
mysql> CREATE TABLE STUDENT
(
  Student_Code INTEGER,
  Student_Name CHAR(20),
  Sex CHAR(1),
  Grade CHAR(2),
  Total_Marks DECIMAL
);
```

Things to remember before table creation

(i) The table and column names must start with a letter and can be followed by letters, numbers, or underscores.

(ii) Table or column names not to exceed a total of 30 characters in length and not use any SQL reserved keywords as names for tables or column names (such as 'select', 'create', 'insert', etc).

(iii) It is important to make sure that you are using an open parenthesis before the beginning of a table definition and a closing parenthesis after the end of the last column definition.

(iv) Separate each column definition with a comma (,).

(v) All SQL statements should end with a semi-colon (;).

Displaying the Table Structure

DESCRIBE or DESC command is used to display the table structure along with the data type, size and constraints.

Syntax `DESCRIBE <table_name>;`

Or `DESC <table_name>;`

Data Manipulation Language (DML)

DML consists of commands used to access and manipulate data in a database, including inserting, retrieving, updating, and deleting records. It enhances user interaction with the system and is a key part of SQL.

Types of DML

1. **Procedural DML** Specifies both what data is needed and how to retrieve it.
2. **Non-Procedural DML** Specifies only what data is needed without detailing how to retrieve it.

Common DML Commands

1. **INSERT** Adds new records to a table.
2. **UPDATE** Modifies existing records in a table.
3. **DELETE** Removes records from a table while retaining its structure.
4. **LOCK TABLE** Controls concurrent access to prevent conflicts.

A query language is a subset of DML used for retrieving information, often used interchangeably with DML.

Differences between DDL and DML

DDL	DML
DDL is the abbreviation of Data Definition Language.	DML is the abbreviation of Data Manipulation Language.
It is used to create and modify the structure of database objects in database.	It is used to retrieve, store, modify, delete, insert and update data in database.
DDL commands allow us to perform tasks related to data definition.	DML commands are used to manipulate data.
For example, CREATE, ALTER, and DROP commands.	*For example*, UPDATE, and INSERT commands.

Changing and Updating Data – DML Commands

(a) Inserting Data

The INSERT command is used to add a single record or multiple records into a table.

Syntax

```
INSERT INTO <table_name> (col_1, col_2,
col_3,..,col_n) VALUES(value_1,
value_2,... value_n);
```

(b) Inserting Null Values

For example,

```
mysql>INSERT INTO STUDENT(Roll_No, Name,
Subject) VALUES(107, 'Viku', NULL);
```

(c) Inserting Different Types of Values Together

For example,

```
mysql> INSERT INTO STUDENT1(Roll_No, Name,
Total, Percentage) VALUES (129,'Vinay',
1560, 70.5);
```

(d) Inserting Date Values

For example,

```
mysql> INSERT INTO STUDENT1(Roll_ No, Name,
Total, DOB) VALUES(129, 'Vinay', 1560,
'1984-12-29');
```

Modifying/Updating Data of a Table

(a) UPDATE Command

The UPDATE command is used to update a single record or multiple records in a table.

To update multiple fields, each field assignment is separated with a comma(,) symbol.

WHERE Clause

The WHERE clause in the UPDATE syntax specifies which record or records should be updated.

Syntax

```
UPDATE<table name > SET <column1>
= <value1>, [<column2> = <value2> ,.....]
WHERE <condition>;
```

(b) Using Expressions in Update

Expression are also used in the SET clause of the UPDATE command to manipulate the values.

You can use the WHERE command to update the salary of some employee's, as follows

Example

```
UPDATE COMPANY
SET EMP_SALARY = EMP_SALARY + 1000
WHERE EMP_DEPT_NO = 'D05';
```

(c) Updating to NULL Values

You can use UPDATE command to enter the NULL values just as other values.

Example

```
UPDATE COMPANY SET EMP_ADDRESS = NULL
WHERE EMP_NAME = 'Ravi Shukla';
```

DELETE Command

To remove unnecessary data from a table, the DELETE command can be used.

The DELETE command with where clause can be used to delete certain records.

The DELETE command without where will delete all records.

Syntax `DELETE FROM <table name>;`

Or

```
DELETE * FROM <table name>;
```

Changing structure of a table: Alter table command

The ALTER table command can be used to change the structure of a table by

(a) Adding a Column in a Table

Syntax

```
ALTER TABLE <table_name> ADD
<column_name>datatype<value>;
```

Example

```
ALTER TABLE COMPANY ADD EXPERIENCE INT(3);
```

(b) Deleting a Column from a Table

Syntax

```
ALTER TABLE<table_name> DROP
COLUMN<column_name>;
```

Or

```
ALTER TABLE<table_name> DROP
<column_name>;
```

Example

```
ALTER TABLE COMPANY DROP COLUMN EXPERIENCE;
```

(c) Modifying a column

Syntax

```
ALTER TABLE <table_name> MODIFY COLUMN
<column_name> datatype <value>;
```

Or

```
ALTER TABLE <table_name> MODIFY
<column_name> datatype <value>;
```

Example

```
ALTER TABLE COMPANY MODIFY COLUMN DOJ
VARCHAR (15);
```

(d) Adding and Dropping Constraints

Syntax

To ADD PRIMARY KEY or UNIQUE KEY constraint

```
ALTER TABLE table_name
ADD CONSTRAINT <constraint_name>
PRIMARY KEY/UNIQUE KEY <column_name>;
```

To ADD FOREIGN KEY constraint

```
ALTER TABLE table_name
ADD CONSTRAINT <constraint_name>
FOREIGN KEY(col1, col2,..., coln)
REFERENCES <parent_table>(col1,
col2,...,coln);
```

To ADD CHECK constraint

```
ALTER TABLE table_name
ADD CONSTRAINT <constraint_name> CHECK
(column_name condition);
```

To DROP constraints

```
ALTER TABLE table_name
DROP CONSTRAINT constraint_name;
```

(e) Disable and Enable Constraints

Syntax

To DISABLE constraints

```
ALTER TABLE table_name
DISABLE CONSTRAINT constraint_name;
```

To Enable constraints

```
ALTER TABLE table_name
ENABLE CONSTRAINT constraint_name;
```

To disable a foreign key constraint employee_fk from EMPLOYEE table.

RENAME Command

The RENAME command is used to change the name of the table or the database object.

Syntax

```
RENAME table oldtable_name TO
newtable_name;
```

DROP TABLE Command

SQL DROP TABLE statement is used to remove table in a database.

Syntax

```
DROP TABLE table_name;
```

Quick Test 2

1. What does SQL stand for?
2. Who developed SQL and when?
3. Which command is used to create a database in MySQL?
4. Which SQL command is used to display the structure of a table?
5. Name any two SQL commands classified under Data Definition Language (DDL).
6. What is the function of the DESC command in SQL?

Data Query Language (DQL)

These statements can be used in order to query the data and information contained in schema objects. It allows you to get and organise data from a database.

SELECT Command is used to extract data from a database in order to perform actions on it.

SQL SELECT Statement

The most commonly used SQL command is SELECT statement. The SQL SELECT statement is used to query or retrieve data from a table in the database.

Syntax `SELECT column_list FROM table_name;`

Here, table_name is the name of the table from which the information is retrieved and column_list includes one or more columns from which data is retrieved.

Terms to remember while understanding SQL Commands

Some terminologies used in SQL commands are given below

- **Keyword** A keyword refers to a special word that has a special meaning to SQL. Reserved keywords are part of the grammar of the SQL language that is used by SQL server to parse and understand the SQL statements.

  For example, SELECT, FROM, INSERT, etc, are keywords.
- **Commands or Statements** These are instructions given by you to a SQL database.

  For example, SELECT student_name FROM student; is a statement.
- **Clause** Commands consist of one or more logically distinct parts, called clauses. Clauses begin with a keyword for which they are generally named, and consist of keywords and arguments.

  For example, consider the statement SELECT student_name FROM student;

  Here, 'SELECT student_name' and 'FROM student' are clauses.
- **Arguments** Arguments complete or modify the meaning of a clause.

  For example, in the above example, 'student' is the argument and FROM is the keyword of FROM clause.

Displaying All columns

Syntax

```
SELECT<column_name1>,[<column_name2>,...,<column_nameN>]
FROM <table_name>;
```

column_name1,column_name2,......,column_name specifies the name of the columns.

Or

Select * from table_name; #Displays all the columns of the table.

Let us consider the following table COMPANY

EMP_ CODE	EMP_ NAME	EMP_AD DRESS	EMP_SA LARY	EMP_DE PT_NO	DOJ
100	Rahul Sharma	C-21, Arya Nagar	25600	D05	2012-02-06
101	Vikas Mittal	A/44, Mayur Vihar	26000	D03	2002-12-04
102	Puneet Jain	50-MIG, Rohini	21000	D05	2004-08-06
103	Sachin Vats	A-21, Ankur Vihar	23500	D02	2007-09-06
104	Uday Singh	D-34, Indraprasth	26000	D03	2001-07-06
105	Ravi Shukla	45/A, Vivek Nagar	23500	D01	2012-05-06
106	Vinay Rana	120, DDA Colony	24000	D03	2001-02-06

Examples:

(a) To display the salary and department number:

```
mysql>  SELECT EMP_SALARY, EMP_DEPT_NO
        FROM COMPANY;
```

Output

```
+------------+--------------+
| EMP_SALARY | EMP_DEPT_NO  |
+------------+--------------+
|   25600    |  D05         |
|   26000    |  D03         |
|   21000    |  D05         |
|   23500    |  D02         |
|   26000    |  D03         |
|   23500    |  D01         |
|   24000    |  D03         |
+------------+--------------+
7 rows in set (0.00 sec)
```

(b) To display all the columns

```
mysql>SELECT * FROM COMPANY;
```

Output

EMP_ CODE	EMP_ NAME	EMP_AD DRESS	EMP_SA LARY	EMP_DE PT_NO	DOJ
100	Rahul Sharma	C-21, Arya Nagar	25600	D05	2012-02-06
101	Vikas Mittal	A/44, Mayur Vihar	26000	D03	2002-12-04
102	Puneet Jain	50-MIG, Rohini	21000	D05	2004-08-06
103	Sachin Vats	A-21, Ankur Vihar	23500	D02	2007-09-06
104	Uday Singh	D-34, Indraprasth	26000	D03	2001-07-06
105	Ravi Shukla	45/A, Vivek Nagar	23500	D01	2012-05-06
106	Vinay Rana	120, DDA Colony	24000	D03	2001-02-06

Column Alias

May be used to give a temporary name to a column in the output.

Syntax

```
SELECT <column_name> AS <Alias_name> FROM <table_name>;
```

Example

```
mysql> SELECT DOJ AS Joining_Date
       FROM COMPANY;
```

Output

```
+--------------+
| Joining_Date |
+--------------+
| 2012-02-06   |
| 2002-12-04   |
| 2004-08-06   |
| 2007-09-06   |
| 2001-07-06   |
| 2012-05-06   |
| 2001-02-06   |
+--------------+
7 rows in set (0.00 sec)
```

Putting Text in the Query Output

It is possible to display some comments in each row of thequery output by using the SELECT statement.

```
mysql> SELECT EMP_NAME,' IS IN DEPARTMENT', EMP_DEPT_No
FROM COMPANY;
```

```
+--------------+-----------------------+--------------+
| EMP_NAME     | IS IN DEPARTMENT      | EMP_DEPT_NO  |
+--------------+-----------------------+--------------+
| Rahul Sharma | IS IN DEPARTMENT      |     D05      |
| Vikas Mittal | IS IN DEPARTMENT      |     D03      |
| Puneet Jain  | IS IN DEPARTMENT      |     D05      |
| Sachin Vats  | IS IN DEPARTMENT      |     D02      |
| Uday Singh   | IS IN DEPARTMENT      |     D03      |
| Ravi Shukla  | IS IN DEPARTMENT      |     D01      |
| Vinay Rana   | IS IN DEPARTMENT      |     D03      |
+--------------+-----------------------+--------------+
7 rows in set (0.05 sec)
```

SQL WHERE Clause

The WHERE clause is used to retrieve specific information from a table while excluding irrelevant data.

SQL offers a feature called the WHERE clause, which can be used to restrict the data retrieved from a table. The condition provided in the WHERE clause filters the rows that are retrieved.

The WHERE clause can be used with SELECT, DELETE, and UPDATE statements. When used with the SELECT statement, the WHERE clause retrieves records from a table based on specified conditions.

As the SELECT query executes, SQL processes one row at a time. Each time the condition specified in the WHERE clause is met (i.e., returns true), the corresponding row is included in the result set.

Syntax

```
SELECT <column_name>
FROM <table_name> WHERE <condition>;
```

Transaction Control Language (TCL)

TCL commands manage transactions in a database by controlling changes made by DML statements. Transactions group multiple operations into a single unit of work, ensuring data consistency.

If a transaction is successful, changes are permanently saved. If an error occurs, changes can be rolled back.

TCL Commands

1. **COMMIT** Saves all changes made in the transaction permanently.
2. **SAVEPOINT** Sets a point within a transaction to which you can later roll back.
3. **ROLLBACK** Reverts changes made since the last COMMIT or SAVEPOINT.
4. **SET TRANSACTION** Defines properties for the current transaction.

Data Control Language (DCL)

DCL commands are used to assign security levels in database which involves multiple user setups.

They are used to grant defined role and access privilages to the users.

There are two kinds of user in the schema

- **Users** They work with the data, but cannot change the structure of the schema. They write data manipulation language.
- **Admin** They can change the structure of the schema and control access to the schema objects. They write data definition language.

Basically, the DCL command of the SQL language is used to create privileges to allow users access to and manipulation of the database. Two types of DCL commands are

(i) **GRANT** Used to give user's access privileges to database.

(ii) **REVOKE** Used to withdraw access privileges given with the GRANT command.

Quick Test 3

1. What is the key difference between Procedural DML and Non-Procedural DML?
2. Which DML command can be used to prevent conflicts in concurrent access scenarios?
3. How can you update multiple fields in a table using the UPDATE command?
4. What will happen if the DELETE command is executed without a WHERE clause?
5. Which SQL clause is used to filter records while retrieving, updating, or deleting data?
6. What is the purpose of column aliases in SQL, and how are they used?

Mind Map

Operators

Arithmetic Operators
+, –, *, /, %

Comparison Operators
= , > , < , >=, <=, <> or != , !< , !>

Logical Operators
AND, OR, NOT

BETWEEN Operator
Used to check range

IN Operator
Check a value within a set of values.

LIKE Operator Used to search a specific pattern in a column.

Constraints

Unique Constraints No two rows have the same value in the specified columns

Default Constraints Default value is inserted in the field automatically.

Primary Key Constraints Unique identification of each rows and do not allow NULL value.

Foreign Key Constraints It ensures that values in one table match values in another table.

Check Constraints Used to limit the value range that can be placed in a column.

Not Null Constraints Enforces a column to NOT accept NULL values.

STRUCTURED QUERY LANGUAGE

MySQL

It is an open source Relational Database Management System (RDBMS) based on SQL (Structured Query Language).

Components

Server (MySQL Server) Manages the data

Client It connects to the database server and queries in a pre-specified format.

Client Library It is an Application Programming Interface where a client can write their own programs using a programming language

Tokens

Literals A constant value written into a query.

Data Types

Numeric Data Type Store numbers such as integers and real numbers in a column.
Types – INT, FLOAT, DOUBLE, DECIMAL

String/Text Data Type Store string values such as Name of the Students, Address, etc.
Types –CHAR, VARCHAR, TEXT

Date and Time Data Type Store a date using the fields YEAR, MONTH and DAY in the format YYYY-MM-DD.
Types – DATETIME, DATE, TIMESTAMP

NULLs or Null Values If a column in a table has no value, then the column is said to be a null.

Comments These statements do not affect the statement execution.

SQL Commands

Data Query Language (DQL)
It allows you to get and organise data from a database.
Command SELECT.

Data Definition Language (DDL)
Define the structure of your tables and other objects in the database.
Commands CREATE, ALTER, DROP, RENAME, TRUNCATE, COMMENT.

Data Manipulation Language (DML)
Access and manipulate data in existing database.
Commands SELECT, INSERT, UPDATE, DELETE.

Transaction Control Language (TCL)
Manage transactions in database.
Commands COMMIT, ROLLBACK and SAVEPOINT.

Data Control Language (DCL)
Assign security levels in database.
Commands GRANT and REVOKE.

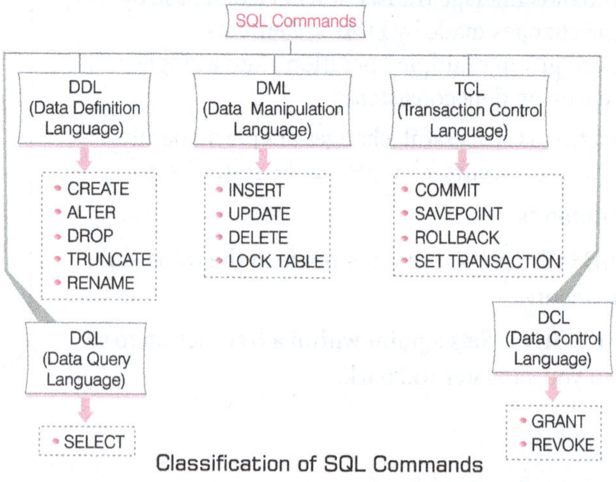

Classification of SQL Commands

NCERT Folder

In-text Questions

1. Match the following clauses with their respective functions.

ALTER	Insert the values in a table
UPDATE	Restrictions on columns
DELETE	Table definition
INSERT INTO	Change the name of a column
CONSTRAINTS	Update existing information in a table
DESC	Delete an existing row froma table
CREATE	Create a database

Ans.

Alter	Change the name of a column
Update	Update existing information in a table
Delete	Delete an existing row from a table
Insert into	Insert the values in a table
Constraints	Restrictions on columns
Desc	Table definition
Create	Create a database

2. Choose appropriate answer with respect to the following code snippet.

```
CREATE TABLE student (
                name CHAR(30),
student_id INT,
gender CHAR(1),
PRIMARY KEY (student_id)
);
```

(a) **What will be the degree of student table?**

(a) 30 (b) 1 (c) 3 (d) 4

(b) **What does 'name' represent in the above code snippet?**

(a) a table (b) a row (c) a column (d) a database

(c) **What is true about the following SQL statement?**

```
    Select * FROM student;
```

(a) Displays contents of table 'student'

(b) Displays column names and contents of table 'student'

(c) Results in error as improper case has been used

(d) Displays only the column names of table 'student'

(d) **What will be the output of following query?**

```
INSERT INTO student
VALUES ("Suhana",109,'F'),
VALUES ("Rivaan",102,'M'),
VALUES ("Atharv",103,'M'),
VALUES ("Rishika",105,'F'),
VALUES ("Garvit",104,'M'),
VALUES ("Shaurya",109,'M');
```

(a) Error

(b) No Error

(c) Depends on compiler

(d) Successful completion of the query

(e) **In the following query how many rows will be deleted?**

```
DELETE student
WHERE student_id =109;
```

(a) 1 row

(b) All the rows where student ID is equal to 109

(c) No row will be deleted

(d) 2 rows

Ans. (i) (c) 3 (ii) (c) A column

(iii) (b) Displays column names and contents of table 'student'

(iv) (a) Error (v) (a) 1 row

3. Fill in the blanks:

(a) **……………….declares that an index in one table is related to that in another table.**

(a) Primary Key (b) Foreign Key

(c) Composite Key (d) Secondary Key

(b) **The symbol Asterisk (*) in a select query retrieves ____________.**

(a) All data from the table

(b) Data of primary key only

(c) NULL data

(d) None of the mentioned

Ans. (i) (b) Foreign key

(ii) (a) All data from the table.

4. Consider the following MOVIE database and answer the SQL queries based on it.

MovieID	Movie Name	Category	RelaseDate	Production Cost	Business Cost
001	Hindi_ Movie	Misical	2018-04-23	124500	130000
002	Tamil_ Movie	Action	2016-05-17	112000	118000
003	English _Movie	Horror	2017-08-06	245000	360000
004	Bengali _Movie	Adventure	2017-01-04	72000	100000
005	Telugu _Movie	Action	-	100000	-
006	Punjabi _Movie	Comedy	-	30500	-

(a) Retrieve movies information without mentioning their column names.

(b) List business done by the movies showing only MovieID, MovieName and BusinessCost.

(c) List the different categories of movies.

(d) Find the net profit of each movie showing its ID, Name and Net Profit.

Hint Net Profit = BusinessCost – ProductionCost

Make sure that the new column name is labelled as NetProfit. Is this column now a part of the MOVIE relation. If no, then what name is coined for such columns? What can you say about the profit of a movie which has not yet released? Does your query result show profit as zero?

(e) List all movies with ProductionCost greater than 80,000 and less than 1,25,000 showing ID, Name and ProductionCost.

(f) List all movies which fall in the category of Comedy or Action.

(g) List the movies which have not been released yet.

Ans. (a) Select * from Movie;

(b) Select MovieID, MovieName, BusinessCost from Movie where Businesscost <> 0;

(c) Select distinct category from movie;

(d) Select MovieID,MovieName, Businesscost-ProductionCost as NetProfit from Movie where ReleaseDate IS NOT NULL;

(e) Select MovieID, MovieName, ProductionCost from Movie where ProductionCost between 80000 and 125000;

(f) Select * fromMovie where category IN ('Action', 'Comedy');

(g) Select * from Movie where ReleaseDate IS NULL;

5. Suppose your school management has decided to conduct cricket matches between students of class XI and Class XII. Students of each class are asked to join any one of the four teams — Team Titan, Team Rockers, Team Magnet and Team Hurricane. During summer vacations, various matches will be conducted between these teams. Help your sports teacher to do the following:

(a) Create a database "Sports".

(b) Create a table "TEAM" with following considerations:

(i) It should have a column TeamID for storing an integer value between 1 to 9, which refers to unique identification of a team.

(ii) Each TeamID should have its associated name (TeamName), which should be a string of length not less than 10 characters.

(c) Using table level constraint, make TeamID as primary key.

(d) Show the structure of the table TEAM using SQL command.

(e) As per the preferences of the students four teams were formed as given below.

Insert these four rows in TEAM table:

Row 1: (1, Team Titan)

Row 2: (2, Team Rockers)

Row 3: (3, Team Magnet)

Row 4: (4, Team Hurricane)

(f) Show the contents of the table TEAM.

(g) Now create another table below. MATCH_DETAILS and insert data as shown in table. Choose appropriate domains and constraints for each attribute.

MatchID	Match Date	FirstTeamID	SecondTeamID	FirstTeamScore	SecondTeamScore
M1	2018-07-17	1	2	90	86
M2	2018-07-18	3	4	45	48
M3	2018-07-19	1	3	78	56
M4	2018-07-19	2	4	56	67
M5	2018-07-20	1	4	32	87
M6	2018-07-21	2	3	67	51

(h) Use the foreign key constraint in the MATCH_DETAILS table with reference to TEAM table so that MATCH_DETAILS table records score of teams existing in the TEAM table only.

Ans. (a) Create database Sports;

(b) Create table Team(TeamID int check(TeamID between 1 and 9), Teamname varchar(20) check(length(Teamname)>10));

(c) Alter table Team ADD Primary key(TeamID);

(d) Describe Team;

(e) Insert into team values((1,"Team Titan"),(2,"Team Rockers"),(3,"eam Magnet"),(4,"Team Hurricane"));

(f) Select * from Team;

(g) Create table Match_Detais(MatchID char(2) Primary key, MAtchDate Date, FirstTeamID INT,SecondTeamID Int,FirstTeamScore int, SecondTeamScore int);

(h) Alter table MATCH_Details ADD Foreign Key(FirstTeamID) References Team(TeamID),ADD Foreign key (SecondTeamID) References Team(TeamID);

6. Using the sports database containing two relations (TEAM, MATCH_DETAILS), answer the following relational algebra queries.

(a) Retrieve the MatchID of all those matches where both the teams have scored > 70.

(b) Retrieve the MatchID of all those matches where FirstTeam has scored < 70 but SecondTeam has scored > 70.

(c) Find out the MatchID and date of matches played by Team 1 and won by it.

(d) Find out the MatchID of matches played by Team 2 and not won by it.

(e) In the TEAM relation, change the name of the relation to T_DATA. Also change the attributes TeamID and TeamName to T_ID and T_NAME respectively.

Ans. (a) Select MatchID from MATCH_DETAILS where FirstTeamScore> 70 and SecondTeamScore>70;

(b) Select MatchID from MATCH_DETAILS where FirstTeamScore< 70 and SecondTeamScore>70;

(c) Select MatchID, MatchDate from MATCH_DETAILS where FirstTeamScore > SecondTeamScore;

(d) Select MatchID from MATCH_DETAILS where FirstTeamScore > SecondTeamScore;

(e) Rename TEAM To T_Data;

Alter table TEAM Change TeamID T_ID INT;

Alter table TEAM Change TeamName T_NAME varchar(30);

7. Differentiate between the following commands:

(a) ALTER and UPDATE

(b) DELETE and DROP

Ans. (a) ALTER and UPDATE

3 Alter	Update
DDL	DML
Used to make changes to the structure of the table	Used to make changes to the data of the table
4	5

(b) DELETE and DROP

Delete	Drop
DML	DDL
Used to remove rows of a table	Used to remove table or database.

8. Create a database called STUDENT_PROJECT having the following tables. Choose appropriate data type and apply necessary constraints.

Table : PROJECT_STUDENT

RollNo	Name	Stream	Section	RegistrationID

- The values in Stream column can be either Science, Commerce, or Humanities.
- The values in Section column can be either I or II.

Table PROJECT_ASSIGNED

RegistrationID	ProjectID	AssignDate

Table PROJECT

Project ID	Project Name	SubmissionDate	TeamSize	GuideTeacher

(a) Populate these tables with appropriate data.

(b) Write SQL queries for the following.

(i) Find the names of students in Science Stream.

(ii) What will be the primary keys of the three tables?

(iii) What are the foreign keys of the three relations?

(iv) Finds names of all the students studying in class 'Commerce stream' and are guided by same teacher, even if they are assigned different projects.

Ans. (a) Create table Project_Student (RollNo int not null Unique, name varchar(20) not null , stream varchar(20) check (stream in ('Science', 'Commerce', 'Humanities')), Section varchar(2) check section IN ('I', 'II')), Registration int Primary Key);

Create table Project_Assigned(RegistrationID int, ProjectID int, AssignDate date, constraint FK_Student Foreign Key(RegistrationID) References Student(RegistrationID),

Constraint FK_Project Foreign key(ProjectID) References Project(ProjectID));

Create table Project(ProjectID int Primary key , ProjectNAme varchar(20) not null, Submissiondate Date, Teamsize int, GuideTeacher varchar(30));

(b) (i) Select Name from Student where Stream="Science";

(ii) Primary keys

Project_Student Table: RollNo

Project_Assigned Table: RegistrationID

Project Table: ProjectID

(iii) Foreign keys

Project_Student Table: RegistrationID

Project_Assigned Table: ProjectID

(iv) Select t.Name from Student t, Project_Assigned pa, Project p where t.stream="Commerce" Group by p.GuideTeacher where t.RegistrationID= pa.RegistrationID and pa.ProjectID=p.ProjectID;

9. An organization ABC maintains a database EMP-DEPENDENT to record the following details about its employees and their dependents.

EMPLOYEE(AadhaarNo, Name, Address, Department, EmpID)

DEPENDENT(EmpID, DependentName, Relationship)

Use the EMP-DEPENDENT database to answer the following SQL queries:

(a) Find the names of employees with their dependent names.

(b) Find employee details working in a department, say, 'PRODUCTION'.

(c) Find employee names having no dependent

(d) Find names of employees working in a department, say, 'SALES' and having exactly two dependents.

Ans. (a) Select A.Name, B.DependentName from Employee A , Dependent B where A.EmpID = B.EmpID;

(b) Select * from Employee where Department="Production";

(c) Select A.Name from Employee A , Dependent B where A.EmpID=B.EmpID Group by A.EmpID where count(EmpID)=0;

(d) Select A.Name from Employee A , Dependent B where A.EmpID=B.EmpID and A.Department="Sales" Group by A.EmpID where count(EmpID)=0;

10. A shop called Wonderful Garments that sells school uniforms maintain a database SCHOOL_UNIFORM as shown below. It consisted of two relations — UNIFORM and PRICE. They made UniformCode as the primary key for UNIFORM relation. Further, they used UniformCode and Size as composite keys for PRICE relation. By analysing the database schema and database state, specify SQL queries to rectify the following anomalies.

(a) The PRICE relation has an attribute named Price. In order to avoid confusion, write SQL query to change the name of the relation PRICE to COST.

UNIFORM

UCode	Uname	UColor
1	Shirt	White
2	Pant	Grey
3	Skirt	grey
4	Tie	Blue
5	Socks	Blue
6	Belt	Blue

Price

UCode	Size	Price
1	M	500
1	L	580
1	XL	620
2	M	810
2	L	890
2	XL	940
3	M	770
3	L	830
3	XL	910
4	S	150
4	L	170
5	S	180
5	L	210
6	M	110
6	L	140
6	XL	160

(b) M/S Wonderful Garments also keeps handkerchiefs of red color, medium size of ` 100 each. Insert this record in COST table.

(c) When you used the above query to insert data, you were able to enter the values for handkerchief without entering its details in the UNIFORM relation. Make a provision so that the data can be entered in COST table only if it is already there in UNIFROM table.

(d) Further, you should be able to assign a new UCode to an item only if it has a valid UName. Write a query to add appropriate constraint to the SCHOOL_ UNIFORM database.

(e) ALTER table to add the constraint that price of an item is always greater than zero.

Ans. (a) Alter table Price Rename to Cost;

b) Insert into cost values(7,"M",100);

(c) Alter table cost add foreign key(Ucode) references Uniform(Ucode);

(d) Alter table Uniform modify column Uname char(50) Not Null;

(e) Alter table Cost modify Price int check (price>0);

EXAM PATTERN QUESTIONS

Objective Type Questions

Multiple Choice Questions

1. **Which of the following is not a feature of MySQL?**
(a) Cross platform
(b) User friendly
(c) Open source
(d) License fee is to be paid for use

2. **Which of the following is not a MySQL data type:**
(a) int (b) float
(c) date (d) complex

3. **The .... data type can be used to store the date of joining of an employee.**
(a) varchar (b) char
(c) int (d) date

4. **Which of the following is not a valid keyword in SQL?**
(a) Select (b) Delete
(c) where (d) Include

5. **Which of the following operators is used to compare two values in SQL?**
(a) + (b) = (c)<> (d) &

6. **Which are the two wildcard characters used with Like clause?**
(a) _ and & (b) _ and %
(c) * and // (d) * and /

7. **The .... Clause matches a range of values in SQL**
(a) range (b) between
(c) order (d) between values

8. **MySQL is**
(a) Cross platform (b) Open source
(c) Easy to use (d) All of these

9. **There are .... categories of SQL commands.**
(a) 2 (b) 3 (c) 1 (d) 4

10. **The SQL Like operator is used in which of the following clause?**
(a) having (b) select
(c) where (d) group by

11. **Which of the following command opens a database?**
(a) open (b) create
(c) use (d) set

12. **The .... command shows the fields and their data types in SQL.**
(a) Structure (b) Show create table
(c) Describe (d) Both (b) and (c)

13. **The command CREATE belongs to**
(a) DDL (b) DML
(c) TCL (d) DCL

14. **The command to change a column name in SQL is:**
(a) Change (b) Drop
(c) Alter table (d) Rename column

15. **The command to modify data in SQL**
(a) ALTER (b) UPDATE
(c) CREATE (d) None of these

16. **The command used to remove objects from a database is**
(a) DELETE (b) DROP
(c) REMOVE (d) CLEAR

Fill in the Blanks

17. A database is a __________ that stores a group of related tables together.

18. SQL stands for __________ Query Language.

19. __________ operator is used in the WHERE clause to check that the field values are within a specified inclusive range.

20. The __________ operator is used to check whether a value exists within a set of values.

21. __________ values are used to represent a field with no value.

22. In MySQL, __________ command is used to display the structure of a table.

23. The __________ command is used to add new columns to an existing table.

24. The __________ command is used to query or retrieve data from a table in a database.

State Weather True or False

25. SQL is a 4th generation procedural language.

26. NULL values cannot appear in columns with a UNIQUE constraint.

27. The BETWEEN operator is inclusive of the specified range.

28. A column alias is a permanent renaming of a column in the database.

29. The WHERE clause is mandatory for the DELETE command to work.

30. The UPDATE command can only modify one record at a time.

31. The RENAME command can rename both tables and databases.

32. The DROP TABLE command removes both table structure and data from the database.

Assertion and Reason Questions

Assertion and Reason based questions. Mark the correct choice as

(a) Both A and R are true, and R is the correct explanation of A.
(b) Both A and R are true, but R is not the correct explanation of A.
(c) A is true, but R is false.
(d) A is false, but R is true.

33. Assertion (A) Constraints like UNIQUE and PRIMARY KEY ensure data integrity.

Reason (R) UNIQUE allows duplicate values, while PRIMARY KEY enforces uniqueness.

34. Assertion (A) Logical operators in SQL can combine multiple conditions in a query.

Reason (R) Logical operators include AND, OR, and NOT for conditional evaluation.

35. Assertion (A) The LIKE operator uses wildcards to match patterns in data.

Reason (R) The percent sign (%) is used in LIKE to match any substring.

36. Assertion (A) The WHERE clause can only be used with SELECT statements.

Reason (R) The WHERE clause filters rows based on specified conditions.

37. Assertion (A) The DESC command is used to display the structure of a table.

Reason (R) DESC shows columns, data types, sizes, and constraints of a table.

38. Assertion (A) The INSERT command allows adding multiple rows into a table.

Reason (R) The INSERT command requires specifying values for all columns in the table.

39. Assertion (A) The RENAME command can rename a table in MySQL.

Reason (R) The syntax for renaming is RENAME table <old_name> TO <new_name>.

40. Assertion (A) The DROP TABLE command permanently deletes a table along with its data.

Reason (R) The DROP TABLE command removes the structure and constraints of the table.

Answers

1. (d) License fee is to be paid for use
2. (d) Complex
3. (d) date
4. (d) Include
5. (c) <>
6. (b) _ and %
7. (b) between
8. (d) All of these
9. (d) 4
10. (c) where
11. (c) use
12. (d) Both (b) and (c)
13. (a) DDL
14. (c) Alter table
15. (b) UPDATE
16. (b) DROP
17. container
18. Structured
19. BETWEEN
20. IN
21. NULL
22. DESCRIBE
23. ALTER TABLE
24. SELECT
25. False
26. False
27. True
28. False
29. False
30. False
31. True
32. True
33. (c) A is true, but R is false.
34. (a) Both A and R are true, and R is the correct explanation of A.
35. (a) Both A and R are true, and R is the correct explanation of A.
36. (d) A is false, but R is true.
37. (a) Both A and R are true, and R is the correct explanation of A.
38. (c) A is true, but R is false.
39. (a) Both A and R are true, and R is the correct explanation of A.
40. (a) Both A and R are true, and R is the correct explanation of A.

Subjective Type Questions

Very Short Answer Type Questions

1. List some basic elements of MySQL.

Ans. *The basic elements of MySQL are*

(i) Literals (ii) Data types

(iii) Nulls (iv) Comments

2. How many types of constraints are available in SQL?

Ans. *Constraints are of two types*

(i) Column constraints (ii) Table constraints

3. What do you mean by constraints?

Ans. Constraints are the rules enforced on data columns on table.

4. Give the syntax of unique constraints.

Ans. CREATE TABLE Employee (ecode INTEGER UNIQUE ename CHAR (20));

5. A company maintains an employee database where each employee has a unique employee ID. To prevent duplicate entries, the database administrator applies a rule that ensures no two employees have the same ID. What rule should be applied to ensure that no two employees have the same ID? **Competency Based Que.**

Ans. A unique constraint should be applied to prevent duplicate values in the specified column(s).

6. What is the use of Check constraints?

Ans. Check constraint is used to limit the value range that can be placed in a column.

7. Name the various components of MySQL expression.

Ans. (i) Column names (ii) Literal value

(iii) Function (iv) Operator

8. Write the syntax to create a database.

Ans.
```
CREATE DATABASE [IF NOT
EXISTS]<database_name>;
```

9. Which command is used to select a database?

Ans. USE command.

10. Write the use of DROP DATABASE command.

Ans. The DROP DATABASE command is used to delete the database permanently.

11. Name the command which is used to create a table in SQL?

Ans. CREATE TABLE command is used to create the table in SQL.

12. A school maintains a database to store student records. Each student has a unique admission number, name, class, and section. The principal wants to ensure that all student records are organized systematically. Why is it important to create tables in a database for storing student records? **Competency Based Que.**

Ans. Tables help store data in an orderly fashion, making it easy to organize and retrieve information.

13. Which command is used to display the structure of the table?

Ans. DESCRIBE or DESC command is used to display the structure of the table.

14. Write a MySQL command to display the structure of a table DEPARTMENT.

Ans.
```
MySQL>DESCRIBE DEPARTMENT;
```

15. Explain column alias with an example.

Ans. Column alias is used to temporarily rename a table's column for the purpose of a particular query.

```
mysql>SELECT DOJ AS Joining_Date FROM
Company;
```

16. What is the use of WHERE clause in SELECT query?

Ans. WHERE clause in SELECT query is used to specify conditions for retrieving only the required data.

17. Write SQL statement to display the result of arithmetic expression 5 * 12 + 4 on screen.

Ans.
```
mysql> SELECT 5 * 12 + 4;
```

18. How would you store an apostrophe in a character literal?

Ans. By using \' (backslash followed by apostrophe).

19. What does asterisk (*) mean in SQL?

Ans. Asterisk (*) in SQL command is denoted to retrieve all the columns of a table.

20. Is there any difference in the output of following statements?

```
Select * From Item;
SELECT * FROM Item;
```

Ans. No, because SQL is not case-sensitive.

21. Write a sample query to display E_name and E_Sal of employees from table Employee, whose salary is greater than or equal to 9000.

Ans.
```
mysql>SELECT E_name,E_Sal FROM Employee
WHERE E_Sal >= 9000;
```

22. What does a SELECT command returns without a WHERE clause?

Ans. The SELECT command would return all the records from a table when a WHERE clause is not specified.

23. **Write a query to display the name of students from table STUDENT whose father's name is Rakesh.**

Ans.
```
mysql>SELECT Student_Name FROM STUDENT
WHERE Father_Name = 'Rakesh';
```

Short Answer Type I Questions

24. **Raj is working on a school project where he needs to store student information, such as names, roll numbers, and marks. His teacher suggests using a database with tables to organize the data efficiently. How do tables help Raj manage and retrieve student information in the database?** **Competency Based Que.**

Ans. Tables store related data items of an entity in an organized manner. They help in efficient data manipulation and retrieval, making it easier and faster to fetch required information.

25. **What is foreign key constraints?**

Or

Which command is used to display the table structure and how?

Ans. Foreign key constraint is a constraint that ensures that columns in one table match the primary key column of same or another table.

For example,
```
CREATE TABLE Items(Order_No INTEGER
PRIMARY KEY,Itemno INTEGER REFERENCES
Items (Order_No));
```

Or

DESCRIBE or DESC command displays the column names, available data items with their data types.

Syntax `DESCRIBE<table_name>;`
or `DESC<table_name>;`

26. **How can you create database in SQL?**

Ans. Creating a database is an easier task. You need to just type the name of the database in a CREATE DATABASE command.

Syntax
```
CREATE DATABASE [IF NOT
EXIST]<database_name>;
```

27. **Write a command to create the table VEHICLE with given constraint.**

Table: VEHICLE

Column_Name	Data Type (SIZE)	Constraint
Reg. No.	Char (10)	Primary Key
Regdate	Date	
Owner	Varchar (30)	
Address	Varchar (40)	

Ans
```
CREATE TABLE VEHICLE (Reg.No CHAR(10)
PRIMARY KEY, Regdate DATE, Owner VARCHAR
(30), Address VARCHAR(40));
```

28. **Given a statement as follows:**
```
CREATE TABLE EMPLOYEE
(Emp_id INT NOT NULL,
OrderNo INT NOT NULL,
Emp_rank INT,
PRIMARY KEY(Emp_id),
FOREIGN KEY(Emp_rank) REFERENCES
PERSONS (Emp_rank));
```
Identify the number and types of constraints in the table EMPLOYEE.

Ans There are total three different types of constraints defined in EMPLOYEE table:

(i) Two NOT NULL constraints for column Emp_id and OrderNo.

(ii) One PRIMARY KEY constraint for column Emp_id.

(iii) One FOREIGN KEY constraint for column Emp_rank.

29. **Write MySQL command to create the table STOCK including its constraints.**

Table: STOCK

Name_of_Column	Type	Size	Constraint
ID	Decimal	4	Primary Key
Name	Varchar	20	
Company	Varchar	20	
Price	Decimal	8	Not Null

Ans The MySQL command to create a table as per given structure is as follows:
```
CREATE TABLE STOCK
(ID DECIMAL(4) PRIMARY KEY,
Name VARCHAR(20),
Company VARCHAR(20),
Price DECIMAL(8) NOT NULL);
```

30. **Write MySQL command to create the Table PAYMENT whose structure is given below:**

Table: PAYMENT

Field_Name	Type	Size	Constraint
Loan_Number	Integer	4	Primary Key
Payment_Number	Varchar	3	
Payment_Date	Date		
Payment_Amount	Integer	8	Not Null

Ans The MySQL command to create a table as per given structure is as follows:

```
CREATE TABLE PAYMENT
(Loan_Number INTEGER(4) PRIMARY KEY,
Payment_Number VARCHAR(3),
Payment_Date DATE,
Payment_Amount INTEGER(8) NOT NULL);
```

31. Consider the following table Employee and write the MySQL command to insert the value (105, Vanshika, Programmer, 35000).

Emp_Id	Name	Designation	Salary
101	Abhimaan	Manager	40000
102	Aman	Project Leader	35000
103	Shreya	HOD	38000
104	Tushar	Programmer	32000

Ans.
```
mysql>INSERT INTO Exmployee (Emp_Id, Name,
Designation, Salary) VALUES (105,
'Vanshika', 'Programmer', 35000);
```

32. Insert some information into a table COLLEGE, whose structure is given below.

ROLL_NO	NAME	CLASS	BRANCH

Ans. (i)
```
mysql>INSERT INTO COLLEGE (ROLL_NO,
NAME, CLASS, BRANCH) VALUES(2,'VIKAS',
12, 'SCIENCE');
```
(ii)
```
mysql>INSERT INTO COLLEGE (ROLL_NO,
NAME, CLASS, BRANCH) VALUES(3, 'RAJ',
10,'SCIENCE');
```

33. What do you mean by SELECT command? Write its syntax.

Ans. The SQL SELECT command is used to perform query from the database and to retrieve the selected data that match the criteria, specified by the user.

Syntax

```
SELECT <column_name> FROM <table_name>
WHERE <condition>;
```

34. What is the use of AS keyword with SELECT statement?

Ans. In MySQL, the AS keyword is used to temporarily rename the column's name, *i.e.* the AS keyword is used to define column alias.

This renaming is a temporary change and the actual column name does not change in the database.

The syntax of using the AS keyword is given below

```
SELECT <column_name1> AS <Alias_Name>
FROM <table_name>;
```

35. What will be the output of the following queries on the basis of EMPLOYEE table?

Table: EMPLOYEE

Emp_Id	Name	Salary
E01	Siya	54000
E02	Joy	NULL
E03	Allen	32000
E04	Neev	42000

(i)
```
SELECT Salary + 100 FROM EMPLOYEE
WHERE Emp_Id = 'E02';
```
(ii)
```
SELECT Name FROM EMPLOYEE
WHERE Emp_Id = 'E04';
```

Ans The output of the following queries:

(i)

Salary+100
NULL

(ii)

Name
Neev

36. Consider the table CUSTOMER

C_ID	C_Name	C_City	C_Salary
100	DUSHYANT	MEERUT	15000
101	RAJ	DELHI	12000
102	VIKAS	GOA	10000

(i) Write a MySQL query to display the names of all customers from Meerut.

(ii) Name the data type used for C_City field.

Ans. (i)
```
mysql>SELECT C_Name FROM CUSTOMER WHERE
C_City='MEERUT';
```
(ii) varchar.

37. Read the following data

Item_Code	Item_Name	Price
100	Refrigerator	9000
101	Television	8000
102	Computer	12000
103	Washing Machine	7000

Write MySQL queries for the following (table name is PRODUCT)

(i) Use column alias on Price column.

(ii) Select those items whose price is greater than 7000.

Ans. (i)
```
mysql> SELECT Price AS Item_Price FROM
PRODUCT;
```
(ii)
```
mysql> SELECT Item_Code, Item_Name FROM
PRODUCT WHERE Price>7000;
```

38. **Write the queries for the following questions using the table Item with the following fields. (Item_ Code, Item_Name, Quantity, Price)**

(i) **Display the price of item having code as I06.**

(ii) **Display the name of all items with quantity greater than 50 and price less than 500.**

Ans. (i)
```
mysql>SELECT Price FROM Item
      WHERE Item_Code = 'I06';
```
(ii)
```
mysql>SELECT Item_Name
      FROM Item
WHERE (Quantity > 50) AND (Price < 500);
```

Short Answer Type II Questions

39. **Define the generally used data types in SQL.**

Ans. SQL provides several data types to define the kind of data a column can store. Here are some commonly used data types:

- **VARCHAR2 (size)** A variable-length character string, can hold up to 4000 bytes of characters.
- **CHAR (size)** A fixed-length character string, with a maximum size of 255 characters.
- **VARCHAR (size)** This data type is often used interchangeably with VARCHAR2.
- **NUMERIC (P,S)** A numeric data type used to store fixed or floating point numbers.
  - P represents the precision (the total number of digits).
  - S represents the scale (the number of digits to the right of the decimal point).
- **LONG** Used to store variable-length character strings up to 2 gigabytes in size.
- **DATE** Used to store date and time information, typically in the format YYYY-MM-DD.

40. **Define the LIKE operator of SQL with an example.**

Ans. The LIKE operator in SQL is used in a WHERE clause to search for a specified pattern within a column. Patterns are defined using wildcard characters:

- **Percent (%)** Matches zero or more characters.
- **Underscore (_)** Matches exactly one character.

Example of pattern matching:

- **"abc%"** Matches any string that starts with 'abc'.
- **"%abc%"** Matches any string that contains 'abc' anywhere.
- **"___"** Matches any string of exactly three characters.
- **"a%"** Matches any string that starts with 'a' and is at least one-character long.

SQL Query Example:
```
SELECT Emp_Code, Emp_Name
FROM Employee
WHERE Emp_Name LIKE "%00%";
```
This query will return the employees whose names contain the substring "00".

41. **What is the original purpose of SQL?**

Ans. The original purpose of SQL (Structured Query Language) is to define, manipulate, and manage data within relational database systems. SQL serves various purposes, including:

(a) To specify the syntax and semantics of data definition language: This refers to defining the structure of the database itself, such as creating, altering, or deleting tables and other database objects.

(b) To specify the syntax and semantics of data manipulation language: This refers to querying and manipulating the data in the database, such as inserting, updating, or deleting records.

(c) To define the data structures: SQL helps in creating the structures for storing data, but its primary function is more aligned with defining and manipulating data rather than defining data structures directly.

42. **Amit is learning MySQL for his computer science project. His teacher explains that MySQL uses different types of SQL commands to manage and retrieve data efficiently. Amit wants to create a database, define tables, insert records, and retrieve specific information.** **Competence Based Que.**

Which categories of SQL commands will Amit use for:

(a) **Creating a database and tables**

(b) **Inserting and updating records**

(c) **Retrieving specific data**

Ans. (a) Data Definition Language (DDL) – CREATE DATABASE, CREATE TABLE, ALTER, DROP

(b) Data Manipulation Language (DML) – INSERT, UPDATE, DELETE

(c) Data Query Language (DQL) – SELECT, FROM, WHERE, BETWEEN, IS NULL, IS NOT NULL

Long Answer Type Questions

43. **Discuss various types of SQL integrity constraint.**

Ans. Integrity constraints are the rules and regulations that you specify to guarantee the accuracy, completeness and consistency of data in tables.

There are various types of integrity constraints in SQL

(i) **Primary Key Constraint** This constraint defines a single column or group of columns which uniquely identifies each row in the table.

(ii) **Foreign Key Constraint** This constraint identifies any column referencing the PRIMARY KEY in another table. It establishes a relationship between the two columns of some table or between different tables.

(iii) **Unique Constraint** This constraint ensures that a column or a group of columns in each row have a unique value.

(iv) **Check Constraint** This constraint enforce the domain integrity by limiting the values that are accepted by a column.

(v) **Default Constraint** This constraint is used to insert a default value into a column that is left blank at the time of input data.

44. Write SQL commands for the questions from (a) to (d) on the basis of table SHOP.

S_No	P_Name	S_Name	Qty	Cost	City
S1	Biscuit	Priyagold	120	12.00	Delhi
S2	Bread	Britannia	200	25.00	Mumbai
S3	Chocolate	Cadbury	350	40.00	Mumbai
S4	Sauce	Kissan	400	45.00	Chennai

(a) Display all products whose quantity is 200.

(b) Display data for all products whose cost is more than 40.

(c) To list S_Name, P_Name, Cost for all the products whose quantity is less than 300.

(d) To display S_No, P_Name, S_Name, Qty for Mumbai city from the SHOP table.

Ans. (a) `mysql> SELECT * FROM SHOP WHERE Qty = 200;`

(b) `mysql> SELECT * FROM Cost > 40;`

(c) `mysql> SELECT S_Name, P_Name, Cost FROM SHOP WHERE Qty<300;`

(d) `mysql> SELECT S_No, P_Name, S_Name, Qty FROM SHOP WHERE City = “Mumbai”;`

45. Consider the table STUDENT given below and write SQL commands for (i) to (iv).

Student_No	Class	Name	Game	G_Grade	Section	Marks
01	7	Rahul	Swimming	B	A	99
02	8	Sameer	Tenis	A	B	20
03	10	Dushyant	FootBall	C	C	87
04	12	Kapil	Tennis	D	C	90
05	6	Ravinder	Cricket	A	B	97

(i) Display Student_No and G_Grade of all students from table STUDENT.

(ii) List the Name from table STUDENT whose Student _No is 04.

(iii) Display Game and Marks for those students whose name is Kapil.

(iv) Write a query to display Name and Section for those students whose Marks more than 85.

Ans. (i) `mysql>SELECT Student_No, G_Grade FROM STUDENT;`

(ii) `mysql>SELECT Name FROM STUDENT WHERE Student _No = 04;`

(iii) `mysql>SELECT Game, Marks FROM STUDENT WHERE Name = “Kapil”;`

(iv) `mysql>SELECT Name, Section FROM STUDENT WHERE Marks > 85;`

46. Write the SQL commands for the questions from (a) to (d) on the basis of table Employee?

Emp_no	E_name	Profile	Manager	Hire_date	Salary	Commission	Dept_no
8369	SMITH	CLERK	8902	1990-12-18	8000	NULL	20
8499	ANYA	SALESMAN	8698	1991-02-20	16000	300.00	30
8521	SETH	SALESMAN	8698	1991-02-22	12500	500.00	30
8566	MAHADEVAN	MANAGER	8839	1991-04-02	29850	NULL	20
8654	MOMIN	SALESMAN	8698	1991-09-28	12500	1400.00	30
8698	BINA	MANAGER	8839	1991-05-01	28500	NULL	30
8882	SHIVANSH	MANAGER	8839	1991-06-09	24500	NULL	10

Emp_no	E_name	Profile	Manager	Hire_date	Salary	Commission	Dept_no
8888	SCOTT	ANALYST	8566	1992-12-09	30000	NULL	20
8839	AMIR	PRESIDENT	NULL	1991-11-18	50000	NULL	10
8844	KULDEEP	SALESMAN	8698	1991-09-08	15000	0.00	30

(a) **Display Employee Name and Salary of those employees whose salary is greater than or equal to 22000?**

(b) **Display the name of employee whose Emp_no is 8521.**

(c) **Display the Profile of employee whose employee name is ANYA.**

(d) **Display the Salary of those employees whose Hire_date is less than 1991-04-02.**

Ans. (a) mysql>SELECT E_name, Salary FROM Employee WHERE Salary>=22000;

(b) mysql>SELECT E_name FROM Employee WHERE Emp_no = 8521;

(c) mysql>SELECT Profile FROM Employee WHERE E_name = 'ANYA';

(d) mysql>SELECT Salary FROM Employee WHERE Hire_date < '1991-04-02'>;

47. **Consider the table DOCTOR given below. Write commands in SQL for (i) to (iii) and output of (iv).**

Table: DOCTOR

ID	DocName	Department	DOJ	Gender	Salary
1	Amit Kumar	Orthopaedics	1993-02-12	M	35000
2	Anita Hans	Paediatrics	1998-10-16	F	30000
3	Sunita Maini	Gynaecology	1991-08-23	F	40000
4	Joe Thomas	Surgery	1994-10-20	M	55000
5	Gurpreet Kaur	Paediatrics	1999-11-24	F	52000
6	Anandini Burman	Oncology	1994-03-16	F	31000
7	Siddharth Dang	Surgery	1995-09-08	M	47000
8	Rama Mukherjee	Oncology	2000-06-27	F	54500

(i) **Display the names and dates of joining of doctors of Oncology department.**

(ii) **Display the names and salaries of all the female doctors who are getting salary above 50000.**

(iii) **Insert the record (9, Arnav Sharma, Surgery, 1995-07-21, M, 60000)**

(iv) SELECT Department FROM DOCTOR WHERE Salary >= 55000;

Ans (i) SELECT DocName, DOJ FROM DOCTOR WHERE Department = 'Oncology';

(ii) SELECT DocName, Salary FROM DOCTOR WHERE Gender = 'F' AND Salary > 50000;

(iii) INSERT INTO DOCTOR (ID, DocName, Department, DOJ, Gender, Salary)
VALUES (9, "Arnav Sharma", "Surgery", "1995-07-21", "M", 60000);

(iv)

Department
Surgery

Case Study Based Questions

1. **Consider the following table Employee :**

EMP_CODE	EMP_NAME	EMP_ADDRESS	EMP_SALARY	EMP_DEPT_NO	DOJ
100	Rahul Sharma	C-21, Arya Nagar	30000	D05	2012-02-06
101	Vikas Mittal	A/44, Mayur Vihar	27000	D03	2002-12-04
103	Sachin Vats	A-21, Ankur Vihar	24500	D02	2007-09-06
104	Uday Singh	D-34, Indraprasth	27000	D03	2001-07-06
105	Ravi Shukla	45/A, Vivek Nagar	24500	D01	2012-05-06
106	Vinay Rana	120, DDA Colony	25000	D03	2001-02-06

Based on the above table, answer the following questions.

(i) Find the output of following statement.

```
SELECT EMP_CODE, EMP_SALARY FROM
Employee WHERE EMP_DEPT_NO = D03;
```

(a)

EMP_CODE	EMP_SALARY
101	27000
104	27000
106	27000

(b)

EMP_CODE	EMP_SALARY
101	27000
104	27000
106	25000

(c)

EMP_CODE	
101	
101	

(d)

EMP_CODE	
101	
104	

(ii) Which statement is best suited for following output?

EMP_NAME	EMP_SALARY
Sachin Vats	27000
Ravi Shukla	27000

(a) `SELECT EMP_NAME, EMP_SALARY FROM Employee WHERE EMP_DEPT_NO < D03;`
(b) `SELECT EMP_NAME, EMP_SALARY FROM Employee WHERE EMP_SALARY = 24500;`
(c) Either (a) or (b)
(d) None of the above

(iii) Which column will be use for primary key?

(a) EMP_DEPT_NO (b) EMP_CODE (c) EMP_SALARY (d) DOJ

(iv) Which of the following is used for foreign key of table Employee?

(a) EMP_DEPT_NO (b) EMP_CODE (c) EMP_SALARY (d) DOJ

(v) Find the correct statement for given output.

EMP_CODE	EMP_NAME
100	Rahul Sharma

(a) `SELECT EMP_CODE, EMP_NAME FROM Employee WHERE NAME = Rahul;`

(b) `SELECT EMP_CODE, NAME FROM Employee WHERE NAME = "Rahul Sharma";`

(c) `SELECT EMP_CODE, EMP_NAME FROM Employee WHERE NAME = "Rahul Sharma";`

(d) `SELECT * FROM Employee WHERE NAME = "Rahul Sharma";`

Ans. (i) (*b*)

```
+----------+------------+
| EMP_CODE | EMP_SALARY |
+----------+------------+
|   101    |   27000    |
|   104    |   27000    |
|   106    |   25000    |
+----------+------------+
```

(ii) (*c*) Either (a) or (b)

(ii) (*b*) EMP_CODE

(iii) (*a*) EMP_DEPT_NO

(iv) (*c*) `SELECT EMP_CODE, EMP_NAME FROM Employee WHERE NAME = "Rahul Sharma";`

2. **Ronita wants to store the data of some products in a table as follows**

PNo	PName	Qty	Date_Of_Mfg
P01	Pencil	20	2020-09-01
P02	Eraser	5	1990-09-11
P03	Book	16	2000-04-03
P04	Notebook	15	2016-12-11
P05	Color	10	2015-02-04

She also wants to perform some operations and manipulations on the table .

Help her to find the solutions of following questions.

(i) **A command that displays the details of all the products will be**

(a) `SELECT * FROM Product;` (b) `SHOW * FROM Product;`

(c) `DISPLAY * FROM Product;` (d) `SELECT ALL details FROM Product;`

(ii) **The default date format in which date has to be stored in MySQL is**

(a) DD-MM-YYYY (b) DD-YY-MM (c) MM-YY-DD (d) YYYY-MM-DD

(iii) **Which command she can use to add a new record to the table?**

(a) INSERT (b) UPDATE (c) ADD COLUMN (d) ALTER

(iv) **Suggest her a proper data type for the "PName" column.**

(a) Varchar (b) Double (c) Float (d) Integer

Ans. (i) (*a*) `SELECT * FROM Product;`

(ii) (*d*) By default, MySQL stores date in YYYY-MM-DD format.

(iii) (*a*) The INSERT command can be used to add a new record to the table.

(iv) (*a*) The varchar is a variable length data type that can used for columns storing string/character type of data.

SELF ASSESSMENT TEST

Multiple Choice Questions

1. .... **commands work with entire database objects.**

(a) DML (b) DDL
(c) TCL (d) DCL

2. The time format used in MySQL is

(a) MM:HH:SS (b) HH:MM:SS
(c) SS:MM:HH (d) None of these

3. What is the maximum number of characters that can be specified for a varchar field?

(a) 10 (b) 200
(c) 100 (d) 255

State Whether True or False

4. Duplication of data is known as Data Redundancy.

5. An attribute is a set of values of a dissimilar type of data.

6. MySQL supports different platforms like UNIX and Windows.

7. Null (Unavailable and unknown) values are entered by the following command:

```
INSERT INTO TABLE NAME VALUES ("NULL") ;
```

8. ALTER TABLE command is used to modify the structure of the table.

Fill in the Blanks

9. The .... allows you to perform tasks related to data definition.

10. The .... allows you to perform tasks related to data manipulation.

11. A .... is a text that is not executed.

12. .... are words that have a special meaning in SQL.

13. .... command helps to open the database for use.

14. .... command helps to fetch data from a relation.

15. .... command helps to see the structure of a table/relation.

Assertion and Reason Based Questions

Assertion (A) and Reason (R) Type questions. Choose the correct option as:

(a) Both Assertion (A) and Reason (R) are true, and Reason (R) is the correct explanation of Assertion (A).
(b) Both Assertion (A) and Reason (R) are true, but Reason (R) is not the correct explanation of Assertion (A).
(c) Assertion (A) is true, but Reason (R) is false.
(d) Assertion (A) is false, but Reason (R) is true.

16. Assertion (A) MySQL is an open-source database system.

Reason (R) Anyone can use MySQL without incurring any cost.

17. Assertion (A) A MySQL server acts as an engine for managing databases.

Reason (R) It is responsible for creating, managing databases, executing queries, and ensuring security.

18. Assertion (A) SQL is used to operate databases.

Reason (R) SQL allows users to query, create, update, and manage data in relational databases.

19. Assertion (A) DML commands are categorized as procedural and non-procedural.

Reason (R) Procedural DML requires specifying both what data is needed and how to retrieve it, while non-procedural DML only specifies what is needed.

20. Assertion (A) SQL commands include DDL, DML, DQL, TCL, and DCL categories.

Reason (R) These categories allow users to define, manipulate, query, control, and manage transactions in the database.

21. Assertion (A) The REVOKE command grants access privileges to users.

Reason (R) The GRANT command is used to assign privileges, and REVOKE removes them.

Very Short Answer Type Questions

22. Give a note on column alias.

23. Can multiple conditions be used in WHERE clause?

24. Name the command which is used to access the path of data from a database table.

25. Explain the use of check constraint with an example.

Short Answer Type Questions

26. What do you mean by data integrity through constraints?

27. How can you show the database?

28. What do you mean by constraints and unique constraint?

29. How does DDL effects the structure of database objects? Explain.

Long Answer Type Questions

30. Explain the data types in MySQL.

31. Consider the table TEACHER given below. Write commands in SQL for (i) to (iii) and output for (iv).

Table: TEACHER

Id	NAME	Department	Hiredate	Category	Gender	Salary
1	James Kaur	Art	1994-03-17	TGT	M	25000
2	Richa Nanda	English	1995-02-12	PRT	F	27000
3	Sumesh Roy	English	1989-10-16	TGT	M	28000
4	Akhilesh Madan	Math	1991-03-14	PGT	M	30000
5	Kirti Pathak	Science	1994-09-02	TGT	F	27000

(i) To display all information about teacher of PGT category.

(ii) To list the name of female teachers of English department.

(iii) Insert the new record whose detail is (6, Kiyaan Verma, Science, 1995-10-3, TGF, M, 25000)

(iv) `SELECT Name, Gender FROM TEACHER WHERE Department = "Math";`

Answers

1. (b) 2. (b) 3. (d) 4. True 5. False 6. True 7. False 8. True 9. DDL 10. DML
11. Comment 12. Keywords 13. USE 14. SELECT 15. DESC 16. (a) 17. (a)
18. (a) 19. (a) 20. (a) 21. (d)

13

CHAPTER

This chapter explores the dynamic landscape of "emerging trends," focusing on the latest innovations and shifts that are reshaping industries and societies across various sectors, from technology to healthcare and beyond.

Emerging Trends

▼ **YOUR STUDY GOALS**

13.1 Artificial Intelligence (AI)
13.2 Big Data
13.3 Internet of Things (IoT)
13.4 Smart Cities
13.5 Cloud Computing
13.6 Grid Computing
13.7 Blockchain Technology

▼ **YOUR PRACTICE GOAL**

- Objective Type Questions (43 Qs ; MCQs, True or False, Fill in the Blanks, Assertion and Reason)
- Subjective Type Questions (38 Qs ; VSA, SA, LA)
- Case Study Based Questions-4

Computers have been an integral part of our lives for a long time. With each passing day, new technologies and innovations continue to emerge, shaping the way we interact with the digital world. To stay informed and understand ongoing advancements, it is essential to keep track of emerging trends.

While many new technologies are introduced frequently, not all of them succeed. Some fade away over time, while others thrive, gaining widespread adoption and transforming the digital landscape.

Emerging trends refer to cutting-edge technologies that gain popularity and influence user behavior. In this chapter, we will explore some of these trends that are set to make a significant impact on the digital economy and modern society.

13.1 Artificial Intelligence (AI)

Artificial Intelligence (AI) is an area of computer science that emphasizes the creation of intelligent machines that work and react like humans.

The term may also be applied to any machine that exhibits traits associated with a human mind such as learning and problem-solving.

Knowledge engineering is a core part of AI research. Machines can often act and react like humans only if they have abundant information relating to the world. Artificial intelligence must have access to objects, categories, properties and relations between all of them to implement knowledge engineering.

Types of Artificial Intelligence

Artificial intelligence can be categorized into two parts, which as follows :

1. **Weak AI** It embodies a system designed to carry out one particular job. Weak AI systems include video games and personal assistants such as the chess and Amazon's Alexa respectively.
2. **Strong AI** These systems are systems that carry on the tasks considered to be human like. Strong AI tend to be more complex and complicated systems. These kinds of systems can be found in applications like self-driving cars, in hospital operating rooms etc.

Applications of Artificial Intelligence

There are some applications of artificial intelligence as follows :

1. **In Business** Robotic process automation is being applied to highly repetitive tasks normally performed by humans. Machine learning algorithms are being integrated into analytics and CRM (Customer Relationship Management) platforms to uncover information on how to better serve customers.
2. **In Gaming** Over the past few years, AI has become an integral part of the gaming industry. In fact, one of the biggest accomplishment of AI is in the gaming industry.
3. **In Healthcare** Companies are applying machine learning to make better and faster diagnoses than humans. One of the best known technologies is IBM's Watson. It understands natural language and can respond to questions asked it.
4. **In Banking** A lot of banks have already adopted AI-based systems to provide customer support, detect anomalies and credit card frauds. AI solutions can be used to enhance security across a number of business sector, including retail and finance.
5. **In Autonomous Vehicles** Just like humans, self driving cars need to have sensors to understand the world around them and a brain to collect, processes and choose specific actions based on information gathered. Autonomous vehicles are with advanced tool to gather information, including long range radar, cameras and LIDAR (Light Detection and Ranging).
6. **In Social Media** In social media platforms like facebook, AI is used for face verification wherein machine learning and deep learning concepts are used to detect facial features and tag your friends.

Machine Learning

It is a subsystem of Artificial Intelligence, wherein computers have the ability to learn from data using statistical techniques, without being explicitly programmed by a human being. It comprises algorithms that use data to learn on their own and make predictions.

These algorithms called models, are first trained and tested using a training data and testing data, respectively. After successive trainings, once these models are able to give results to an acceptable level of accuracy, they are used to make predictions about new and unknown data.

Natural Language Processing (NLP)

Natural language processing is a field of Computer Science, artificial intelligence and linguistic dealing with the interactions between computers and human languages.

It gives machines the ability to read and understand the language that humans speak such as Hindi and English. The natural language processing system would enable natural language user interfaces and the acquisition of knowledge directly from human written sources, such as news and other unstructured texts.

The predictive typing feature of search engine that helps us by suggesting the next word in the sentence while typing keywords and the spell checking features are examples of natural language processing. In fact, it is possible to search the web or operate or control our devices using our voice. All this has been possible by NLP. An NLP system can perform text to speech and speech to text conversion.

Machine translation is a rapidly emerging field where machines are able to translate texts from one language to another with fair amount of correctness. Another emerging application area is automated customer service where a computer software can interact with customers to serve their queries or complaints.

Immersive Experiences

With the three dimensional (3D) videography, the joy of watching movies in theaters have reached to a new level video games are also being developed to provide immersive experiences to the player.

Immersive experiences allow us to visualise, feel and react by stimulating over senses. It enhances our interaction and involvement, making them more realistic and engaging.

Immersive experiences have been used in the field of training, such as driving simulators, flight simulator and so on. Immersive experiences can be achieved using virtual reality and augmented reality.

1. Virtual Reality

Virtual Reality (VR) is a computer interface which tries to mimic real world beyond the flat monitor to give an immersive 3D visual experiences. It is an artificial environment that is created with software and presented to the user in such a way that the user suspends belief and accepts it as a real environment. On a computer, virtural reality is primarily experienced through two of the five senses i.e., sight and sound.

Virtual reality technology is applied to advance fields of medicine, engineering, education, design, training and entertainment.

Applications of Virtual Reality

Virtual reality (VR) has a wide range of applications across numerous industries. Here are some of the key areas where VR is making a significant impact:

- **Healthcare** Used for surgical training, pain management, therapy, rehabilitation, and medical training through realistic simulations.
- **Education & Training** Enhances learning, vocational training, and military simulations with interactive experiences.
- **Entertainment & Gaming** Enables immersive gaming, virtual concerts, and interactive entertainment experiences.
- **Architecture & Design** Facilitates virtual walkthroughs and product visualization before actual construction.
- **Automotive Industry** Assists in vehicle design, virtual showrooms, and training for technicians.
- **Retail & Marketing** Powers virtual shopping and product visualization for engaging customer experiences.
- **Tourism & Hospitality** Offers virtual tours and hotel previews, allowing users to explore destinations remotely.

Augmented Reality

Augmented Reality (AR) is a technology that enhances the real-world environment by overlaying digital information in real time. Unlike Virtual Reality (VR), which creates a completely artificial environment, AR integrates computer-generated elements into the physical world, allowing users to interact with both simultaneously.

AR has diverse applications, ranging from decision-making support to entertainment. It can modify real-world surroundings visually or provide additional data to users, enhancing their experience. The key advantage of AR is its ability to seamlessly blend digital and three-dimensional (3D) elements with real-world perception.

AR delivers visual effects, sound, and other sensory inputs through devices such as smartphones, AR glasses, or headsets, making it an essential tool in fields like education, healthcare, gaming, and industrial design.

With the help of location based AR apps, travellers can access real time information of historical places just by pointing their camera viewfinder to subjects. Location based AR apps are major forms of AR apps.

Applications of Augmented Reality

There are few applications of augmented reality:

(i) **In Surgery** Augmented reality and the healthcare industry seem like the perfect match. Complicated medical procedures could be massively improved using AR technology surgery can be risky, and even seasoned surgeons can make mistakes. However, Cambridge consultants have found a potential solution by combining MRI and CT scans to build up a 3D image of a patient's body.

The image is then projected onto the patient themselves when the surgeon puts on an AR headset. In future, it could be combined with alerts to tell surgeons when they are close to a nerve for example. In this way, the technology could be incredibly helpful for trainee or less experienced surgeons too. However, it won't be used on humans until it's completely accurate which could take years.

(ii) **In Engineering** Production and manufacturing have been disrupted by innovative technology. Augmented Reality has provided another tool for the creation and maintenance of complicated and expensive machines, making it easier for engineers to carry out repairs.

NGRAIN, a Canadian 3D imaging company, uses 3D scans and analytics to detect minor aircraft damage and improve Maintenance and Repair Operations (MRO). In collaboration with Lockheed Martin, engineers use Epson Moverio BT-200 AR glasses with motion and depth sensors to overlay images onto the workspace. This technology enables engineers to work up to 30 times faster with 96% accuracy. Augmented reality repairs are now widely adopted, with companies like Hyundai introducing AR apps to assist car owners with basic maintenance.

(iii) **In Military** Despite seeming like a relatively new application of Augmented reality, the first fully functioning. AR system was developed at the US Air Force Research Laboratory back in 1992. Since then, the US military has had a desires interest in the technology.

At the Natick Soldier Research Development and Engineering Center (NSRDEC), a team is carrying out research on the interactions soldiers have with AR. Eventually, this information will inform AR applications within the military.

Dr Tad Brunye, a senior research psychologist at NSRDEC, suggests that augmented reality tech could be used in high fidelity visualisation, improving situation awareness and therefore mission planning. 3D models of environments could also be vitally important to carrying out successful operations.

Robotics

A robot is basically a machine capable of carrying out one or more tasks automatically with accuracy and precision. Unlike other machines, a robot is programmable, which means it can follow the instructions given through computer programs. Robots were initially conceptualised for doing repetitive industrial tasks that are boring or stressful for humans or were labour intensive.

Sensors are one of the prime components of a robot. Robot can be of many types, such as wheeled robots, legged robots, manipulators and humanoids. Robots that resemble humans are known as humanoids. Robots are being used in industries medical science, bionics, scientific research, military etc. Some examples are :

- NASA's Mars Exploration Rover (MER) mission is a robotic space mission to study about a planet mars.

- Sophia is a humanoid that uses artificial intelligence, visual data processing, facial recognition and also imitates human gestures and facial expressions.

- A drone is an unmanned aircraft which can be remotely controlled or can fly autonomously through software controlled flight plans in their embedded systems. Drones are being used in many fields, such as journalism, filming and aerial photography, shipping or delivery at short distances, disaster management, search and rescue operations, healthcare, geographic mapping and structural safety inspections, agriculture, wildlife monitoring, besides law enforcement.

13.2 Big Data

It is a phrase used to mean a massive volume of both structured and unstructured data that is so large. It is difficult to process using traditional database and software techniques.

Big data has the potential to help companies, improve operations and make faster more intelligent decisions.

The data is collected from a number of sources including emails, mobile devices, applications, databases, servers and other means. This data, when captured, formatted, manipulated, stored and then analyzed, can help a company to gain useful insight to increase revenues, get or retain customers and improve operations.

Characteristics of Big Data

Big data has five key characteristics that differentiate it from traditional data:

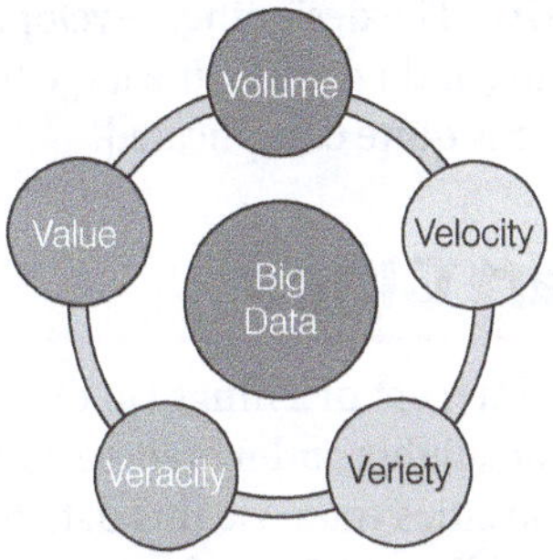

1. **Volume** Big data is massive in size and cannot be processed efficiently using traditional DBMS tools.
2. **Velocity** It is generated and stored at an exceptionally high speed compared to conventional data sets.
3. **Variety** It includes different types of data such as structured, semi-structured, and unstructured formats like text, images, and videos.
4. **Veracity** It refers to the trustworthiness of data, as big data can sometimes be inconsistent, biased, or noisy.
5. **Value** Big data contains hidden patterns and valuable insights, but analyzing it requires careful evaluation to ensure meaningful results.

Applications of Big Data

Many applications of big data are as follows :

(i) **In Government** When government agencies are harnessing and applying analytics to their big data, they have improvised a lot in terms of managing utilities, running agencies, dealing with traffic congestion or preventing the crimes.

(ii) **In Healthcare** Big data had already started to create a huge difference in the healthcare sector. With the help of predictive analytics, medical professionals can now able to provide personalized healthcare services to individual patient.

(iii) **In Banking** The banking sector relies on big data for fraud detection. Big data tools can efficiently detect fraudulent acts in real time such as misuse of credit/debit cards etc.

(iv) **In Manufacturing** Using big data manufacturing industry can improve product quality and output while minimizing waste.

Data Analytics

Data analytics is the process of examining data sets to extract meaningful insights using specialized tools and software.

With growing popularity, data analytics helps businesses make informed decisions and assists researchers in validating scientific models and theories. In programming, the Python library Pandas simplifies data analysis, making it more efficient and accessible.

13.3 Internet of Things (IoT)

IoT is a network in which all physical objects are connected to the Internet through network devices and exchange data. IoT allows objects to be controlled remotely across existing network infrastructure. The goal of IoT is to extend to Internet connectivity from standard devices like computer, mobile, tablet to relatively dumb devices like a toaster.

Advancements in medicine, power, gene therapies, agriculture, smart cities and smart homes are few examples where IoT is strongly established.

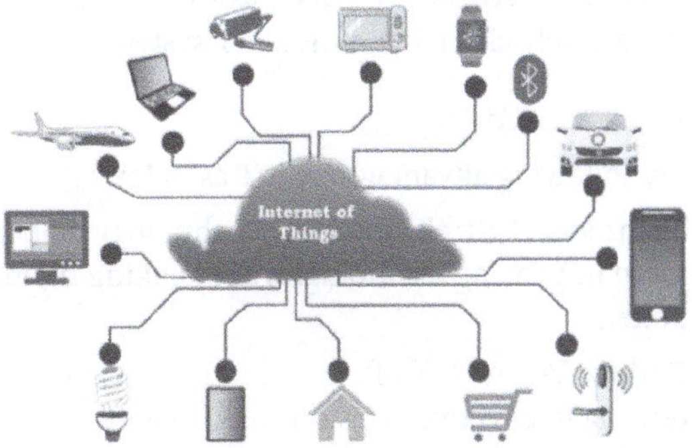

Components of IoT

There are four fundamental components of IoT system as follows :

1. **Sensors/Devices** These are key components that help you to collect live data from the surrounding

environment. All this data may have various levels of complexities. It could be a simple temperature monitoring sensor or it may be in the form of the video feed.

The display also changes to vertical or horizontal with respect to the way we hold our mobile. This is possible with the help of two sensors, namely accelerometer and gyroscope. The accelerometer sensor in the mobile phones detects the orientation of the phone. The gyroscope sensors track rotation or twist of your hand and add to the information supplied by the accelerometer.

2. **Connectivity** All the collected data is sent to a cloud infrastructure. The sensors should be connected to the cloud using various media of communication. These communication media include Mobile or Satellite networks, Bluetooth, Wi-Fi, WAN, etc.
3. **Data Processing** Once the data is collected and it gets to the cloud, the software performs processing on the gathered data.

   This process can be just checking the temperature, reading on devices like AC or heaters. However, it can sometimes also be very complex like identifying objects using computer vision on video.
4. **User Interface** The information made available to the end user in some ways. This can achieve by triggering alarms on their phones or notifying through text or E-mails. Also, a user sometimes might also have an interface through which they can actively check in on their IoT system.

Advantages of IoT

There are following advantages of IoT as follows :

(i) **Technical Optimization** IoT technology helps a lot in improving technologies and making them better.

(ii) **Reduce Waste** IoT offers real time information leading to effective decision-making and management of resources.

(iii) **Improved Customer Engagement** IoT allows you to improve customer experience by detecting problems and improving the process.

(iv) **Improved Data Collection** Traditional data collection has its limitations and its design for passive use.

Disadvantages of IoT

There are following disadvantages of IoT as follows :

(i) **Security** As the IoT systems are interconnected and communicate over networks, the system offers little control despite any security measures. It can lead the various kinds of network attacks.

(ii) **Privacy** Even without the active participation of the user, IoT system provides substantial personal data in maximum detail.

(iii) **Complexity** The designing, developing, maintaining and enabling the large technology to IoT system is quite complicated.

13.4 Smart Cities

Smart cities use Internet of Things (IoT) devices such as connected sensors, lights and meters to collect and analyze data. The cities then use this data to improve infrastructure, public utilities and services and more. The smart city concept integrates Information and Communication Technology (ICT) and various physical devices connected to the IoT network to optimize the efficiency of city operations and services and connect to citizens.

Smart city technology allows city officials to interact directly with both community and city infrastructure and to monitor what is happening in the city and how the city is evolving.

ICT is used to enhance quality, performance and interactivity of urban services, to reduce costs and resource consumption and to increase contact between citizens and government.

How Does a Smart City Work?

A smart city collects and analyzes data from IoT sensors and video cameras. In essence, it senses the environment so that the city operator can decide how and when to take action.

Some actions can be performed automatically. *For example*, a public waste bin can contact the city for service when it is near capacity instead of waiting for a scheduled pickup.

Benefits of a Smart City

(i) **For City Agencies** Gain more citizen engagement and optimize operations through real-time data intelligence and intra-agency collaboration.

(ii) **For Citizens** Improve daily life through city service. Smart cities offer visibility into real time city data for improving mobility, connectivity and safety services.

(iii) **For Businesses** Drive new revenue stream and economic development by enhancing awareness of customer activity and behaviour.

(iv) **For Development and Vendors** Fuel application development of city data. Help the city improve operational efficiences, engage citizens and boost economic viability.

13.5 Cloud Computing

It provides computing and storage capacity services to heterogeneous community of end recipients. Cloud computing is an emerging trend in the field of information technology, where computer based services are delivered over the Internet or the cloud, for the case of their accessibility from any where using any smart device.

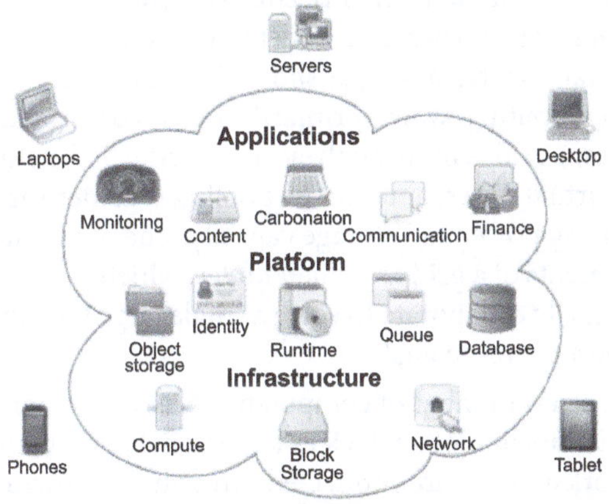

Cloud Computing

The services comprise software, hardware, databases, storage etc. These resources are provided by companies called cloud service providers and usually charge on pay per use basis, like the way we pay for electricity usage.

We already use cloud services while storing our pictures and files as backup on Internet, or host a website on the Internet.

Through cloud computing, a user can run a bigger application or process a large amount of data without having the required storage or processing power on their personal computer as long as they are connected to the Internet.

Characteristics of Cloud Computing

Some essential characteristics of cloud computing are as follows :

(i) **On Demand Self Services** Computer services such as E-mail, applications, network or server service can be provided without requiring human interaction with each service provider.

(ii) **Broad Network Access** Cloud capabilities are available over the network and accessed through standard mechanisms that promote use by heterogeneous thin or thick client platforms such as mobile phones, laptops, PDAs, etc.

(iii) **Resource Pooling** The provider's computing resources are pooled together to serve multiple consumers using multiple-tenant model with different physical and virtual resources dynamically assigned and reassigned according to consumer demand.

(iv) **Rapid Elasticity** Cloud services can be rapidly and elastically provisioned, in some cases automatically, to quickly scale IN/OUT and rapidly released to quickly scale in.

(v) **Measured Service** Cloud computing resource usage can be measured, controlled and reported providing transparency for both the provider and consumer of the utilised service.

(vi) **Multi Tenacity** It refers to the need for policy-driven enforcement, segmentation, isolation, governance, service levels and chargeback/billing models for different consumer constituencies.

Types of Cloud Deployments

There are three types of cloud deployments categorized based on an organization's ability to manage and secure assets as follows :

1. **Public Cloud** It is managed by third party which provides cloud services over the Internet to public. They offer solutions for minimizing IT infrastructure costs and act as a good option for handling peak loads on the local infrastructure. A public cloud is meant to serve multiple users, not a single customer.
2. **Private Cloud** It is distributed system that works on a private infrastructure and providing the users

with dynamic provisioning of computing resources.

3. **Hybrid Cloud** It is a heterogeneous distributed system resulted by combining facilities of public cloud and private cloud. For this reason, they are also called heterogeneous clouds.

Cloud Computing Services

The most common and widely used cloud computing services are :

1. **Infrastructure as a Service** (IaaS) It is a cloud computing model where virtualized infrastructure is offered to and managed for business by external cloud providers. Some examples of the wide usage of IaaS are automated, policy-driven operations such as backup, recovery, etc.
2. **Software as a Service (SaaS)** It is a method for delivering software applications over the Internet as per the demand and on a subscription basis. Most common examples of SaaS are MicrosoftOffice 360, Oracle CRM, Marketo, etc.
3. **Platform as a Service (PaaS)** It refers to the supply on-demand environment for developing, testing, delivering and managing software applications. Some key players offering PaaS are Bluemix, CloudBees, Salesforce.com, etc.

Applications of Cloud Computing

The applications of cloud computing are limitless. With the right middleware, a cloud computing system could execute all the programs a normal computer could run.

Potentially, everything from generic word processing software to customized computer programs designed for a specific company could work on a cloud computing system.

There are some applications of cloud computing as follows :

(i) Clients would be able to access their applications and data from anywhere at any time.

(ii) It could bring hardware costs down. You would not need a large hard drive because you'd store all your information on a remote computer.

(iii) Corporations that rely on computers have to make sure they have the right software in place to achieve goals. Cloud computing systems give these organisations company-wide access to computer applications.

The companies do not have to buy a set of softwares or software licenses for every employee.

Instead, the company could pay a metered fee to a cloud computing company.

(iv) Servers and digital storage devices take up space. Some companies rent physical space to store servers and databases because they do not have it available on site. Cloud computing gives these companies the option for storing data on someone else's hardware, removing the need for physical space on the front end.

(v) Corporations might save money on IT support. Streamlined hardware would, in theory, have fewer problems than a network of heterogeneous machines and operating systems.

13.6 Grid Computing

A grid is a computer network consisting of geographically dispersed and heterogeneous computational resources, as shown in Figure 2.13. Unlike cloud computing, which primarily focuses on providing services, a grid is more application-specific. It functions like a virtual supercomputer by pooling together vast processing power and storage capacity. The individual components of a grid are called nodes, which temporarily collaborate to solve a single large task and achieve a common goal.

Today, a vast number of computational nodes, ranging from handheld mobile devices to personal computers and workstations, are connected through Local Area Networks (LANs) or the Internet. This makes it economically viable to reuse and utilize their resources, such as memory and processing power. Grid computing enables the resolution of computationally intensive scientific and research problems without the need for expensive hardware.

Grids are broadly classified into two types:

1. **Data Grid** Used for managing large, distributed datasets with multi-user access capabilities.
2. **CPU or Processor Grid** Involves distributing processing tasks across multiple PCs. Large tasks are broken into subtasks and assigned to different nodes for parallel execution.

Difference Between Grid Computing and IaaS Cloud Computing

Grid computing differs from Infrastructure as a Service (IaaS) cloud computing. In IaaS, a service provider rents computing infrastructure to users on demand. In contrast, grid computing brings together multiple independent computing nodes to work collectively on a shared computational problem.

To establish a grid, nodes must be interconnected at both the data and CPU levels, requiring middleware to implement the distributed processing architecture. One widely used software toolkit for building grids is the Globus Toolkit (http://toolkit.globus.org/toolkit). It is an open-source solution that provides essential services such as security, resource management, data management, communication, and fault detection.

How Does Grid Computing Work?

Grid computing works by running specialized software on every computer that participates in the data grid. The software acts as the manager of the entire system and coordinates various tasks across the grid.

Specifically, the software assigns subtasks to each computer so they can work simultaneously on their respective subtasks. After the completion of subtasks, the outputs are gathered and aggregated to complete a large scale task.

The software lets each computer communicates over the network with the other computers so they can share information on what portion of the subtasks each computer is running, and how to consolidate and deliver outputs.

13.7 Blockchain Technology

The blockchain is an encrypted, distributed database that records data. It is a digital ledger of any transactions, contracts that need to be independently recorded. In financial sector, with blockchain technology the participants can interact directly and can make transactions across the Internet without the interference of a third party.

With all the fraud resistant features, the blockchain technology holds the potential to revolutionize various business sectors and make processes smarter, secure, transparent, and more efficient compared to the traditional business processes.

How Blockchains Work?

When a new transaction or an edit to an existing transaction comes into a blockchain, generally a majority of the nodes within a blockchain implementation must execute algorithms to evaluate and verify the history of the individual blockchain block that is proposed.

If a majority of the nodes come to a consensus that the history and signature is valid, the new block of transactions is accepted into the ledger and a new block is added to the chain of transactions. If a majority does not concede to the addition or modification of the ledger entry, it is denied and not added to the chain.

This distributed consensus model is what allows blockchain to run as a distributed ledger without the need for some central, unifying authority saying that transactions are valid and which ones are not.

Advantages of Blockchain Technology

There are some advantages of blockchain technology as follows :

(i) It allows smart devices to speak to each other better and faster.

(ii) It allows the removal of intermediaries that are involved in record keeping and transfer of assets.

(iii) It provides durability, reliability and longevity with decentralized network.

(iv) The data that are entered in blockchain based systems are immutable which prevents against fraud through manipulating transactions and the history of data.

(v) It brings everyone to the highest degree of accountability.

Challenges of Blockchain Technology

Some challenges of blockchain technology are as follows

(i) To verify all the transactions huge power, i.e. electricity is required.

(ii) Blocks in a chain must be verified by the distributed network and it can take time. So, transaction speed can be an issue.

Mind Map

Emerging Trends

Artificial Intelligence (AI)

Artificial Intelligence (AI) is an area of computer science that emphasizes the creation of intelligent machines that work and react like humans.

Weak AI

Weak AI systems include video games and personal assistants such as the chess and Amazon's Alexa respectively.

Strong AI

These kinds of systems can be found in applications like self-driving cars, in hospital operating rooms etc.

Machine Learning

It is a subsystem of Artificial Intelligence, wherein computers have the ability to learn from data using statistical techniques, without being explicitly programmed by a human being.

Natural Language Processing (NLP)

Natural language processing is a field of Computer Science, artificial intelligence and linguistic dealing with the interactions between computers and human languages.

Immersive experiences

Immersive experiences have been used in the field of training, such as driving simulators, flight simulator and so on. Immersive experiences can be achieved using virtual reality and augmented reality.

Virtual Reality

Virtual Reality (VR) is a computer interface which tries to mimic real world beyond the flat monitor to give an immersive 3D visual experiences.

Augmented Reality

Augmented Reality (AR) is a type of interactive, reality based display environment that takes the capabilities of computer generated display, sound, text and effects to enhance the user's real world experience.

Cloud Computing

Cloud computing is an emerging trend in the field of information technology, where computer based services are delivered over the Internet or the cloud, for the case of their accessibility from any where using any smart device.

Blockchain Technology

The blockchain is an encrypted, distributed database that records data. It is a digital ledger of any transactions, contracts that need to be independently recorded.

Cloud Computing Services

The most common and widely used cloud computing services are :

Infrastructure as a Service (IaaS)Some examples of the wide usage of IaaS are automated, policy-driven operations such as backup, recovery, etc.

Software as a Service (SaaS) Most common examples of SaaS are MicrosoftOffice 360, Oracle CRM, Marketo, etc.

Platformas a Service (PaaS) Some key players offering PaaS are Bluemix, CloudBees, Salesforce.com, etc.

Grid Computing

Grid computing is a group of networked computers which work together as a virtual super computer to perform large tasks, such as analysing huge sets of data or weather modeling.

01 Data grid   02 CPU or Processor grid

Robotics

A robot is basically a machine capable of carrying out one or more tasks automatically with accuracy and precision. Unlike other machines, a robot is programmable, which means it can follow the instructions given through computer programs.

Big Data

Big data has the potential to help companies, improve operations and make faster more intelligent decisions.

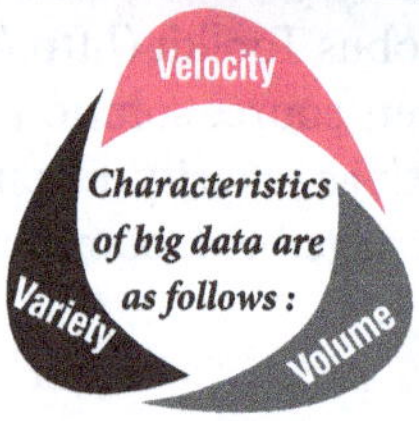

Internet of Things (IOT)

IoT is a network in which all physical objects are connected to the Internet through network devices and exchange data. IoT allows objects to be controlled remotely across existing network infrastructure.

Components of IoT

Sensors/Devices

These are key components that help you to collect live data from the surrounding environment.

Connectivity

The sensors should be connected to the cloud using various media of communication. These communication media includeMobile or Satellite networks, Bluetooth, Wi-Fi,WAN, etc.

Data Processing

Once the data is collected and it gets to the cloud, the software performs processing on the gathered data.

User Interface

The information made available to the end user in some ways.

Smart Cities

The smart city concept integrates Information and Communication Technology (ICT) and various physical devices connected to the IoT network to optimize the efficiency of city operations and services and connect to citizens.

NCERT Folder

Intext Questions

1. Can a drone be helpful in the event of a natural calamity?

Ans. Yes, drones can be highly useful after a disaster. They help relief workers by providing an aerial view of affected areas, locating survivors faster, assessing structural damage, delivering essential supplies, and even assisting in firefighting efforts. Additionally, drones improve the safety of recovery workers by monitoring hazardous zones that are too dangerous to enter.

2. What are your ideas for transforming your city into a smart city?

Ans. A smart city should focus on efficient public transport, reduced dependence on private vehicles, and enhanced infrastructure.

(i) Wide roads should ensure smooth traffic flow, with designated footpaths for pedestrians.

(ii) Well-lit streets with underground electric cables for safety.

(iii) Shopping complexes should have multi-level parking facilities.

(iv) Use of e-services to save citizens' time by reducing the need for in-person visits for bill payments and other services.

3. Name any two areas other than those mentioned where blockchain technology can be useful.

Ans. (i) **Insurance** Blockchain can help in fraud prevention and transparent claims processing.

(ii) **Supply Chain** It ensures secure and transparent tracking of goods from manufacturer to consumer.

(iii) **Banking and Transactions** It provides enhanced security and faster cross-border payments.

4. How are your digital activities contributing to the generation of Big Data?

Ans. Every digital activity contributes to Big Data. When we create a social media account, browse the internet, watch videos, listen to music, or search for topics, all this data is collected. Even actions like checking in at locations or frequently reading specific types of news add to Big Data, helping companies analyze user behavior and preferences.

5. How can some of the emerging trends discussed in this chapter be used as assistive tools for people with disabilities?

Ans. Emerging technologies can greatly assist people with disabilities:

(i) **Natural Language Processing (NLP)** Helps visually impaired individuals interact with computers through voice commands.

(ii) **Virtual Reality (VR)** Allows people with mobility disabilities to experience places virtually.

(iii) **Robotics** Assists individuals with disabilities in performing daily tasks.

Exercise Questions

1. List some of the cloud-based services that you are using at present.

Ans.
- Google drive
- Play Store
- YouTube
- social media like: - Facebook, Instagram, WhatsApp etc.

2. What do you understand by the Internet of Things? List some of its potential applications.

Ans. **IOT** Internet of Things (IOT) is a phenomenon that connects the things (the smart devices) to the internet over wired or wireless connections.

Some of its potential applications:-

- Home appliances:- fridges, cookers, coffee makers, heaters, HVAC, TVs, DVD players, lights, doors, windows etc.
- **Wearables** Clothes, shoes, hats, watches, heart monitors etc.
- **Vehicles** Cars, buses, bicycles, trains etc.
- **Factories** Machines, robots, warehouse shelves, parts within machines, tools etc.
- **Agriculture** Bio-chip transponders on farm animals and plants, farm humidity and temperature sensors etc.
- **Food** Sensors for monitoring the condition of food.

3. Write a short note on the following:

(a) Cloud computing

(b) Big data and its characteristics

Ans. (a) **Cloud computing** Cloud computing is Internet-based computing, whereby shared resources, software, and information are provided to computers and other devices on demand, like the electricity grid) A basic definition of cloud computing is the use of the Internet for the tasks you perform on your computer for storage, retrieval and access. The "cloud" represents the Internet. Cloud computing is a new name for an old concept: the delivery of computing services from a remote location. Cloud computing services are delivered through a network, usually the Internet.

(b) **Big data** The generation of data sets of enormous volume and complexity called Big Data.

(c) **Characteristics of Big Data**

- **Volume** The most prominent characteristic of big data is its enormous size. If a particular data set is of such large size that it is difficult to process it with traditional DBMS tools, it can be termed as big data.
- **Velocity** It represents the rate at which the data under consideration is being generated and stored. Big data has an exponentially higher rate of generation than traditional data sets.
- **Variety** It asserts that a data set has varied data, such as structured, semi-structured and unstructured data. Some examples are text, images, videos, web pages and so on.
- **Veracity** Big data can be sometimes inconsistent, biased, and noisy or there can be abnormality in the data or issues with the data collection methods. Veracity refers to the trustworthiness of the data because processing such incorrect data can give wrong results or mislead the interpretations.
- **Value** Big data is not only just a big pile of data, but also possess to have hidden patterns and useful knowledge which can be of high business value.

4. Explain the following along with their applications.

(a) Artificial Intelligence

(b) Machine Learning

Ans. (a) **Artificial Intelligence** Artificial Intelligence endeavours to simulate the natural intelligence of human beings into machines, thus making them behave intelligently. An intelligent machine is supposed to imitate some of the cognitive functions of humans like learning, decision-making and problem solving. AI system can also learn from past experiences or outcomes to make new decisions.

Applications of Artificial Intelligence:-

- Artificial Intelligence in Navigation like:- Google map
- Artificial Intelligence powered Assistants like:- Google Assistant, Siri
- Artificial Intelligence in Robotics
- Artificial Intelligence in Healthcare
- Artificial Intelligence in Gaming
- Artificial Intelligence in Social Media

(b) **Machine Learning** Machine Learning is a subsystem of Artificial Intelligence, wherein computers have the ability to learn from data using statistical techniques, without being explicitly programmed by a human being.

Applications of Machine Learning:-

- Image Recognition
- Speech Recognition
- Traffic prediction
- Product recommendation
- Self-driving cars
- Email Spam and Malware Filtering.

5. Differentiate between cloud computing and grid computing with suitable examples.

Ans. The differentiation between Cloud Computing and Grid Computing:

Cloud Computing	Grid Computing
Follows a client-server computing architecture.	Follows a distributed computing architecture.
More flexible in terms of scalability and resource allocation.	Less flexible compared to cloud computing.
Operates as a centralized management system.	Operates as a decentralized management system.
Cloud servers are owned by infrastructure providers.	Grids are owned and managed by the organization.
Uses services like IaaS, PaaS, and SaaS.	Uses systems like distributed computing, distributed information, and distributed pervasive.
Service-oriented computing model.	Application-oriented computing model.
Example: Google Drive, AWS, Microsoft Azure.	Example: SETI@home, Large Hadron Collider Grid (LHC Grid).

6. Justify the following statement-
'Storage of data is cost effective and time saving in cloud computing.'

Ans. Now, a days a single person produced more data like video, photo and many more. These data's need storage device but these devices are more costly then cloud computing. And also need extra care of devices. So far cloud computing is cost effective.

If a person put these data's in storage device then there is need to handle this data and also need care for device which take a lot of time. So if person use cloud computing then they need only internet to upload data on cloud. So we can say that cloud computing is saving the time of person.

7. What is on-demand service? How it is provided in cloud computing?

Ans. On-demand computing is a business computing model in which computing resources are made available to the user on an "as needed" basis.

Rather than all at once, on-demand computing allows cloud hosting companies to provide their clients with access to computing resources as they become necessary.

8. **Write examples of the following:**

(a) **Government provided cloud computing platform**

(b) **Large scale private cloud service providers and the services they provide**

Ans. (a) 'GI Cloud' which has been named as 'MeghRaj' (https://cloud.gov.in).

(b) Google drive, Amazon Web Services (AWS), Microsoft Azure, media fire etc.

9. **A company interested in cloud computing is looking for a provider who offers a set of basic services such as virtual server provisioning and on-demand storage that can be combined into a platform for deploying and running customised applications. What type of cloud computing model fits these requirements?**

(a) **Platform as a Service**

(b) **Software as a Service**

(c) **Infrastructure as a Service**

Ans. (c) Infrastructure as a Service

10. **Which is not one of the features of IoT devices?**

(a) **Remotely controllable**

(b) **Programmable**

(c) **Can turn themselves off if necessary**

(d) **All of the above**

Ans. (a) Remotely controllable

11. **If Government plans to make a smart school by applying IoT concepts, how can each of the following be implemented in order to transform a school into IoT enabled smart school?**

(a) **e-textbooks**

(b) **Smart boards**

(c) **Online tests**

(d) **Wifi sensors on classrooms doors**

(e) **Sensors in buses to monitor their location**

(f) **Wearables (watches or smart belts) for attendance monitoring**

Ans. (a) **e-textbooks** e-textbooks can be provided e-library or web services.

(b) **Smart Boards** Smart boards can be used by computer or mobile.

(c) **Online Tests** Students can give these tests from home.

(d) **Wi-Fi sensors and classrooms doors** Wi-Fi sensors and classroom doors can be used to lock and unlock them. These sensors also provides security to students and other stakeholders.

(e) **Sensors in buses to monitor their location** These sensors enables quick reporting and monitoring to the coordinates and parents to know the status of child and bus after leaving the school.

(f) **Wearables (watches or smart belts) for attendance monitoring** These devices can be used or implemented for students in such a way that identifies a student and marks the attendance accordingly.

12. **Five friends plan to try a startup. However, they have a limited budget and limited computer infrastructure. How can they avail the benefits of cloud services to launch their startup?**

Ans. They can purchase cloud computing services either government or private. In this they need not take maintenance of computer and also they can save money.

13. **How IoT and WoT are related?**

Ans. Internet of Things allows us to interact with different devices through Internet with the help of smartphones or computers, But to interact with 'n' number of different devices, we need to install 'n' different apps.

Web of Things (WoT) allows the use of web services to connect anything in the physical world, besides human identities on web. IoT along with WoT helps to create smart homes, smart offices, smart cities and so on.

14. **Match the following:**

Column A	Column B
You got a reminder to take medication	Smart Parking
You got a sms alert that you forgot to lock the door	Smart Wearable
You got the sms alert that parking space is available near your block	Home Automation
You turned off your LED TV from your wrist watch	Smart Health

Ans.

Column B	Column A
Smart Parking	You got an SMS alert that parking space is available near your block
Smart Wearable	You turned off your LED TV from your wrist watch
Home Automation	You got an SMS alert that you forgot to lock the door
Smart Health	You got a reminder to take medication

EXAM PATTERN QUESTIONS

Objective Type Questions

Multiple Choice Questions

1. Which of the following is not a emerging trend in technology?

(a) Sensors (b) Smart cities
(c) Blockchains (d) Fax machines

2. Which of the following is not a service in cloud computing?

(a) IaaS (b) SaaS (c) PaaS (d) NaaS

3. Which of the following function(s) is/are possible by a robot?

(a) Helping in daily activities
(b) Helping in computation
(c) Helping in industries
(d) All of the above

4. Which of the following is/are an advantage(s) of blockchain technology?

(a) It allows smart devices to speak to each other better and faste.
(b) It provides durability.
(c) It provides reliability.
(d) All of the above

5. Mohan found that he could search for a product in a shopping site using voice search. This is an instance of

Competency Based Que.

(a) Natural language processing
(b) Immersive experience
(c) Grid computing
(d) Block chain technology

6. IoT stands for ....

(a) Industry of Things
(b) Internet of Things
(c) Intelligence of Things
(d) Internal. Internet of Things

7. Which one of these is not an area of AI?

(a) Computer vision/Image recognition
(b) Voice recognition
(c) Web design
(d) Robotics

8. "Virtual Reality" is:

(a) Where parts of a person's body are used for identification purposes. They are unique.
(b) A software environment that recreates a real world or imaginary scenario like a game.
(c) The use of computers to encrypt data so that messages can be sent with complete privacy.
(d) Where images are made to appear three-dimensional and have 'depth'.

9. Where is artificial intelligence used?

(a) Training soldiers in combat using battlefield simulations
(b) In self-driving cars that do not require a driver
(c) To allow access to buildings
(d) To create prototypes of cars or any other object

10. Where is virtual reality used?

(a) Training soldiers in combat using battlefield simulations
(b) In three-dimensional (3D) films
(c) To allow access to buildings
(d) To create prototypes of cars or any other object

11. Where is computer-assisted translation used in everyday life?

(a) Training TV hosts
(b) Spellcheckers used in word processing software
(c) Dictation tests
(d) Recording weather conditions

12. Which of the following is a positive impact of artificial intelligence in self-driving cars?

(a) An immersive video experience for the viewer using special glasses.
(b) Data is completely secure and cannot be tampered with.
(c) Only authorized people can travel in the car.
(d) Safer transport as there are fewer road accidents.

13. What hardware is typically used for virtual reality?

(a) A powerful computer, headset with a screen to see, headphones to hear and sometimes gloves
(b) Keyboard, mouse, printer and plotter
(c) Smartphone, mic and tablet
(d) Plotters, mouse, speakers and tablet

14. A company interested in cloud computing is looking for a provider who offers a set of basic services such as virtual server provisioning and on-demand storage that can be combined into a platform for deploying and running customized applications. What type of cloud computing model would fit these requirements? Competency Based Que.

(a) Platform as a Service
(b) Software as a Service
(c) Infrastructure as a Service
(d) None of these

15. Which of the following is not a feature of IoT devices?

(a) Remotely controllable
(b) Security
(c) Can turn themselves off, if necessary
(d) Wearables

16. Consider the figure given aside and identify the missing characteristic of big data.

(a) Veracity (b) Vivacity
(c) Voracity (d) Venality

17. Ms. Dhriti is really impressed by the predictive typing feature of search engine that helps us by suggesting the next word in the sentence while typing keywords. Suggest the feature of Artificial Intelligence by which she was impressed. Competency Based Que.

(a) Computer Vision
(b) Data Analysis
(c) Natural Language Processing (NLP)
(d) None of these

18. A company interested in cloud computing is looking for a provider who offers to outsource the hardware and software on demand basis and pay as per the usage, thereby saving the cost of software, hardware and other things as well as the cost of setting up, maintenance and security. What type of cloud computing model fits these requirements? Competency Based Que.

(a) IaaS (b) PaaS
(c) DaaS (d) SaaS

19. In IoT, T stands for :

(a) Technology (b) Things
(c) Technical (d) Traffic

Fill in the Blanks

20. Artificial Intelligence (AI) emphasizes embedding human __________ into machines.

21. __________ AI is designed to carry out one particular job, such as video games or personal assistants.

22. Machine Learning is a subsystem of AI that allows computers to learn from __________.

23. Predictive typing and spell-checking features are examples of __________.

24. In a smart city, __________ is used to enhance quality, performance, and interactivity of urban services.

25. Cloud computing delivers computer-based services over the __________.

26. Blockchain technology is an encrypted, distributed database that serves as a digital __________.

27. __________ computing involves splitting tasks over multiple computers to reduce processing time.

State Whether True or False

28. Artificial Intelligence reduces human involvement in tasks by automating them.

29. Machine Learning requires explicit programming by a human for every task it performs.

30. Natural Language Processing (NLP) helps machines understand and process human languages like English and Hindi.

31. Augmented Reality completely replaces the real world with a digital environment.

32. Virtual reality is being used in healthcare for training and treatment of mental health issues.

33. Big data refers to a small, manageable volume of structured data.

34. Grid computing uses a group of networked computers to act as a virtual supercomputer.

35. IoT increases privacy and security without any potential risks.

Assertion and Reason Based Questions

Assertion and Reason based questions. Mark the correct choice as

(a) Both A and R are true, and R is the correct explanation of A.
(b) Both A and R are true, but R is not the correct explanation of A.
(c) A is true, but R is false.
(d) A is false, but R is true.

36. Assertion (A) Artificial Intelligence (AI) can perform tasks with higher accuracy and speed than human in many cases.

Reason (R) AI is an area of computer science that emphasizes embedding human intelligence into machines.

37. Assertion (A) Weak AI is capable of performing multiple tasks like humans.

Reason (R) Weak AI systems are designed to carry out one particular job, such as personal assistants or video games.

38. Assertion (A) Virtual Reality improves teaching and learning experiences.

Reason (R) Virtual Reality creates a simulated 3D environment where a large group of students can interact and learn.

39. Assertion (A) Augmented Reality can be used in surgery for complicated medical procedures.

Reason (R) Augmented Reality integrates computer-generated visuals into the physical world, enhancing the real-world experience.

40. Assertion (A) Natural Language Processing (NLP) enables machines to understand human languages.

Reason (R) Predictive typing and spell-checking are examples of NLP applications.

41. Assertion (A) Blockchain technology ensures data entered into the system is immutable.

Reason (R) Blockchain technology prevents fraud by making data tamper-proof.

42. Assertion (A) Smart cities improve communication between citizens and government.

Reason (R) Smart cities use IoT to collect data and optimize city services for better efficiency.

43. Assertion (A) SaaS eliminates the need for software installation on user devices.

Reason (R) SaaS applications like Google Docs are accessed via the Internet and require only a subscription or license.

Answers

1. (d) Fax machines
2. (d) NaaS
3. (d) All of the above
4. (d) All of the above
5. (a) Natural language processing
6. (b) Internet of Things
7. (c) Web design
8. (b) A software environment that recreates a real world or imaginary scenario like a game.
9. (b) In self-driving cars that do not require a driver
10. (a) Training soldiers in combat using battlefield simulations
11. (b) Spellcheckers used in word processing software
12. (d) Safer transport as there are fewer road accidents.
13. (a) A powerful computer, headset with a screen to see, headphones to hear and sometimes gloves
14. (c) Infrastructure as a Service
15. (b) Security
16. (a) Veracity
17. (c)Natural Language Processing (NLP)
18. (a) IaaS
19. (b) Things
20. intelligence
21. Weak
22. data
23. Natural Language Processing (NLP)
24. ICT (Information and Communication Technology)
25. Internet
26. ledger
27. Grid
28. True
29. False
30. True
31. False
32. True
33. False
34. True
35. False
36. (b) Both A and R are true, and R is not the correct explanation of A.
37. (d) A is false, but R is true.
38. (a) Both A and R are true, and R is the correct explanation of A.
39. (a) Both A and R are true, and R is the correct explanation of A.
40. (a) Both A and R are true, and R is the correct explanation of A.
41. (a) Both A and R are true, and R is the correct explanation of A.
42. (a) Both A and R are true, and R is the correct explanation of A.
43. (a) Both A and R are true, and R is the correct explanation of A.

Subjective Type Questions

Very Short Answer Type Questions

1. Write the names of the artificial intelligence.

Ans. Artificial intelligence can be categorized into two parts

(i) Weak artificial intelligence

(ii) Strong artificial intelligence

2. What is the use of artificial intelligence in banking?

Ans. A lot of banks have already adopted AI-based system to provide customer support, detect anomalies and credit card frauds.

3. What is the meaning of NLP?

Ans. NLP (Natural Language Processing) is a field of computer science, artificial intelligence and linguistic dealing with the interactions between computers and human languages.

4. Rahul is a medical student who is learning complex surgical procedures. His university has introduced a new technology that allows him to practice surgeries in a simulated environment before performing them on real patients.

Similarly, his friend Aisha, an engineering student, uses the same technology to visualize and test designs before building them.Which technology is being used by Rahul and Aisha, and in which fields can it be applied?

Ans. Rahul and Aisha are using Virtual Reality (VR) technology. VR is applied in advanced fields such as medicine, engineering, education, design, training, and entertainment.

5. Write the names of application of augmented reality.

Ans. There are few applications of augmented reality

(i) In surgery

(ii) In engineering

(iii) In military

6. Aryan visits a manufacturing plant where he sees a machine assembling products without human intervention. The machine follows precise instructions and performs repetitive tasks with high accuracy. What is the machine that Aryan saw, and what is its function?

Ans. The machine Aryan saw is a robot. A robot is a machine capable of carrying out one or more tasks automatically with accuracy and precision.

7. What is meant by variety of big data?

Ans. Variety of big data refers to structured, unstructured and semi-structured data i.e. gathered from multiple sources.

8. Write any two advantages of Internet of things.

Ans. (i) Technical optimization

(ii) Reduce cost

9. What is the role of smart cities?

Ans. Smart cities use Internet of Things (IoT) devices such as connected sensors, lights and meters to collect and analyze data. The cities then use this data to improve infrastructure, public utilities, services and more.

10. Write the names of most common cloud computing services.

Ans. The most common and widely used cloud computing services are

(i) Infrastructure as a Service (IaaS)

(ii) Software as a Service (SaaS)

(iii) Platform as a Service (PaaS)

11. Give few examples of public cloud?

Ans. Microsoft Azure, Google driver, Amazon cloud Drive, icloud.

12. What is a private cloud?

Ans. A private cloud consists of computing resources exclusively Owned by one business or organization.

13. What are the characteristics of Big Data?

Ans. Volume, Variety, Veracity and Value.

14. What is a grid in grid computing?

Ans. A grid is a computer network of geographically dispersed and heterogeneous computational resources that work together to solve a single large task.

15. What is required to set up a grid?

Ans. A middleware is required to connect multiple nodes and implement the distributed processor architecture.

16. What is blockchain technology based on?

Ans. Blockchain technology is based on a decentralized and shared database, where each computer has a copy of the database.

17. What is a block in a blockchain?

Ans. A block is a secured chunk of data or a valid transaction that contains some data called its header, visible to all nodes, while the private data is accessible only to its owner.

18. What is the Globus toolkit?

Ans. It includes tools for security, resource management, data management, communication, and fault detection.

Short Answer Type I Questions

19. What is the use of artificial intelligence?

Ans. Artificial Intelligence (AI) is an area of computer science that emphasizes the creation of intelligent machines that work and react like humans. The term may also be applied to any machine that exhibits traits associated with a human mind such as learning and problem solving.

20. Write a short note on machine learning.

Ans. Refer to text on page no. 226 (Machine learning).

21. Give some examples of robotics.

Ans. Refer to text on page no. 228 (Robotics).

22. What do you understand by big data analytics?

Ans. Big data analytics is the process of collecting organizing and analysing large sets of data to discover patterns and other useful information. Big data analytics can help organisations to better understand the information contained within the data that is most important to the business and future business decisions.

23. Rahul is working on a smart home project that adjusts the room temperature based on environmental conditions. He wants to ensure that the system can collect real-time temperature data and make automatic adjustments. Which IoT component will help Rahul collect live temperature data, and how does it function in an IoT system? Competency Based Que.

Ans. Sensors or devices are key components that help collect live data from the surrounding environment. In Rahul's case, a temperature monitoring sensor will continuously track temperature changes and send the data to the IoT system. These sensors can range from simple temperature detectors to more complex devices like video feed sensors, depending on the application's requirements.

24. Explain the augmented reality in brief.

Ans. Refer to text on page no. 227 (Augmented reality).

25. Priya is working on a research project that requires high computational power to analyze large datasets. She is exploring different technologies and comes across grid computing and cloud computing. However, she is unsure which one would be more suitable for her needs. How is grid computing different from cloud computing, and which one would be more suitable for Priya's research project? Competency Based Que.

Ans. Unlike cloud computing, which primarily provides on-demand services like storage, computing, and networking, grid computing is more application-specific and combines multiple computers to create a virtual supercomputer with enormous processing power. Since Priya requires high computational power for data analysis, grid computing would be a better choice, as it distributes complex tasks across multiple systems, speeding up the processing time.

26. What are the two types of grids?

Ans. The two types of grids are:

(i) **Data grid** used for managing large and distributed data with multi-user access.

(ii) **CPU or Processor grid** where processing is moved between computers or divided into subtasks for parallel processing.

27. Mention two real-world applications of blockchain technology apart from digital currency.

Ans. Blockchain technology can be used in:

- **Healthcare** For better data sharing among healthcare providers, leading to accurate diagnosis and effective treatments.
- **Land registration records** To prevent disputes related to land ownership claims and encroachments.

Short Answer Type II Questions

28. What is the role of immersive experiences in artificial intelligence?

Ans. With the three dimensional (3D) videography, the joy of watching movies in theatres has reached to a new level. Video games are also being developed to provide immersive experiences to the player.

Immersive experience allows us to visualise, feel and react by stimulating over senses. It enhances our interaction and involvement, making them more realistic and engaging. Immersive experiences have been used in the field of training such as driving simulators, flight simulator and so on.

29. Write the use of virtual reality in gaming.

Ans. Virtual Reality (VR) is a computer interface which tries to mimic real world beyond the flat monitor to give an immersive 3D visual experiences.

Virtual technology's devices are used for virtual gaming experiences. Along with this, devices such as Wi-Fi Remote, Playstation Move/Eye, kinect are based on virtual reality which track and send input of the players to the game.

30. What is the use of big data?

Ans. Big data is a phrase used to mean a massive volume of both structured and unstructured data that is so large, it is difficult to process using traditional database and software techniques. Big data has the potential to help companies improve operations and make faster more intelligent decisions.

The data is collected from a number of sources including e-mails, mobile devices, applications, databases, servers and other means.

31. **How does a smart city work?**

Ans. Refer to text on page no. 230 (How does a smart city work).

32. **What is blockchain technology and how does it ensure data security?**

Ans. Blockchain technology is a decentralized and shared database system where each computer (node) has a copy of the database.

It ensures data security by maintaining an "append-only" open ledger, which is updated only after authentication by all nodes in the network. Since all members keep a copy, no single member can alter the data, making it secure and tamper-proof.

33. **What do you meant by virtual reality?**

Ans. Virtual reality is a computer interface which tries to mimic real world beyond the flat monitor to give an immersive 3D visual experiences.

It is an artificial environment that is created with software and presented to the user in such a way that the user suspends belief and accepts it as a real environment. On a computer, virtual reality is primarily experienced through two of the five senses i.e. sight and sound. Virtual reality is one of the offshoots of mobile technology and it has impacted on human lives in many ways.

Long Answer Type Questions

34. **Write the introduction to artificial intelligence and its also write its applications..**

Ans. Refer to text on page no. 226-227 (Artificial intelligence, Applications of artificial intelligence).

35. **What is the use of augmented reality in engineering?**

Ans. Refer to text on page no. 227-228 (Applications of augmented reality).

36. **Explain the cloud computing services in brief.**

Ans. The most common and widely used cloud computing services are:

(i) **Infrastructure as a Service (IaaS)** It is a cloud computing model where virtualized infrastructure is offered to and managed for business by external cloud providers. Some examples of the wide usage of IaaS are automated, policy driven operations such as backup, recovery etc.

(ii) **Software as a Service (SaaS)** It is a method for delivering software applications over the Internet as per the demand and on a subscription basis. Most common examples of SaaS are microsoft office 360, Oracle CRM, Marketo etc.

(iii) **Platform as a Service (PasS)** It refers to the supply on-demand environment for developing, testing, delivering and managing software applications. Some key players offering PaaS are Bluemix, Cloudbees etc.

37. **What do you understand by grid computing? Explain its categories.**

Ans. A grid is a computer network consisting of geographically dispersed and heterogeneous computational resources. Unlike cloud computing, which primarily focuses on providing services, a grid is more application-specific.

It functions like a virtual supercomputer by pooling together vast processing power and storage capacity. The individual components of a grid are called nodes, which temporarily collaborate to solve a single large task and achieve a common goal.

Today, a vast number of computational nodes, ranging from handheld mobile devices to personal computers and workstations, are connected through Local Area Networks (LANs) or the Internet.

This makes it economically viable to reuse and utilize their resources, such as memory and processing power. Grid computing enables the resolution of computationally intensive scientific and research problems without the need for expensive hardware.

Grids are broadly classified into two types:

1. **Data Grid** Used for managing large, distributed datasets with multi-user access capabilities.
2. **CPU or Processor Grid** Involves distributing processing tasks across multiple PCs. Large tasks are broken into subtasks and assigned to different nodes for parallel execution.

38. **How does blockchain technology work? Explain advantages and challenges of blockchain technology.**

Ans. Refer to text on page no. 233 (Block chain technology).

Case Study Based Questions

Case Study 1

Natural language processing is a field of computer science, artificial intelligence and linguistic dealing with the interactions between computers and human languages. It gives machines the ability to read and understand the language that humans speak such as Hindi and English.

The natural language processing system would enable natural language user interfaces and the acquisition of knowledge directly from human written sources, such as news and other unstructured texts.

The predictive typing feature of search engine that helps us by suggesting the next word in the sentence while typing keywords and the spell checking features are examples of natural language processing.

In fact, it is possible to search the web or operate or control our devices using our voice. All this has been possible by NLP. An NLP system can perform text to speech and speech to text conversion.

Based on the above information, answer the following questions.

(i) The full form of NLP is
(a) Natural Language Processing
(b) Nature Language Processing
(c) Natural Language Process
(d) None of the above

(ii) NLP is a field of computer dealing with interaction between
(a) computer and computer
(b) hardware and software
(c) software and human
(d) computers and human languages

(iii) NLP gives machines the ability to read and understand the language that human
(a) input (b) speak
(c) output (d) None of these

(iv) ...... is a rapidly emerging field where machines are able to translate texts from one language to another.
(a) Machine translation
(b) NLP
(c) NLP translation
(d) None of the above

(v) Another emerging application area is .... where a computer software can interact with customers.
(a) NLP
(b) Machine translation
(c) Automated customer service
(d) Customer service machine

Ans. (i) (a) Natural Language Processing
(ii) (d) computers and human languages
(iii) (b) speak
(iv) (a) Machine translation
(v) (c) Automated customer service

Case Study 2

A robot is basically a machine capable of carrying out one or more tasks automatically with accuracy and precision. Unlike other machines, a robot is programmable, which means it can follow the instructions given through computer programs.

Robots were initially conceptualised for doing repetitive industrial tasks that are boring or stressful for humans or were labour intensive.

Sensors are one of the prime components of a robot. Robot can be of many types, such as wheeled robots, legged robots, manipulators and humanoids. Robots that resemble humans are known as humanoids. Robots are being used in industries, medical science, bionics, scientific research, military etc.

Based on the above information, answer the following questions.

(i) .... are one of the prime components of a robot.
(a) Sensors (b) Manipulators
(c) Humanoids (d) All of these

(ii) In which field(s), robots are used?
(a) Medical science (b) Bionics
(c) Scientific research (d) All of these

(iii) Robots that resemble humans are known as
(a) human robots (b) humanoids
(c) robot humans (d) None of these

(iv) Which of the following is an unmanned aircraft which can be remotely controlled through software controlled flight plans?
(a) Sophia humanoid (b) Drone
(c) MER (d) All of these

(v) Sophia is a humanoid that uses
(a) artificial intelligence (b) visual data processing
(c) facial recognition (d) All of the above

Ans. (i) (a) Sensors
(ii) (d) All of the above
(iii) (b) humanoids
(iv) (b) Drone
(v) (d) All of the above

Case Study 3

Big data is a phrase used to mean a massive volume of both structured and unstructured data that is so large. It is difficult to process using traditional database and software techniques.

Big data has the potential to help companies, improve operations and make faster more intelligent decisions. The data is collected from a number of sources including emails, mobile devices, applications, databases, servers and , manipulated, stored and then analysed, can help a company to gain useful other means.

This data, when captured, formatted insight to increase revenues, get or retain customers and improve operations.

Based on the above information, answer the following questions.

(i) **It is a collection of data that is huge in volume, yet growing exponentially with time.**
(a) Robotic (b) Big data
(c) Cloud computing (d) Grid computing

(ii) **.................. of big data refers to structured, unstructured and semi-structured data, i.e. gathered from multiple sources.**
(a) Variety (b) Velocity
(c) Volume (d) None of these

(iii) **Big data is used in field(s)**
(a) government (b) healthcare
(c) banking (d) All of these

(iv) **In big data, it essentially refers to the speed at which data is being created in real time.**
(a) Variety (b) Velocity
(c) Volume (d) None of these

(v) **Big data has the potential to help companies**
(a) improve operations
(b) make faster more intelligent decision
(c) Both (a) and (b)
(d) None of the above

Ans. (i) (b) Big data
(ii) (a) Variety
(iii) (d) All of these
(iv) (b) Velocity
(v) (c) Both (a) and (b)

Case Study 4

Cloud computing provides computing and storage capacity services to heterogeneous community of end recipients. Cloud computing is an emerging trend in the field of information technology, where computer based services are delivered over the Internet or the cloud, for the case of their accessibility from any where using any smart device.

We already use cloud services while storing our pictures and files as backup on Internet, or host a website on the Internet. Through cloud computing, a user can run a bigger application or process a large amount of data without having the required storage or processing power on their personal computer as long as they are connected to the Internet.

Based on the above information, answer the following questions.

(i) **Essential characteristic(s) of cloud computing is/are**
(a) on demand self services
(b) resource pooling
(c) rapid elasticity
(d) All of the above

(ii) **How many types of cloud deployment are there?**
(a) 2 (b) 3
(c) 4 (d) 5

(iii) **This cloud is managed by third party which provides cloud services over the Internet to public.**
(a) Public (b) Private
(c) Hybrid (d) None of these

(iv) **Which of the following service is not used by cloud computing?**
(a) IaaS (b) SaaS
(c) NaaS (d) PaaS

(v) **Most common example(s) of SaaS is/are**
(a) Microsoft Office 360 (b) Oracle CRM
(c) Marketo (d) All of these

Ans. (i) (d) All of the above
(ii) (c) 4
(iii) (a) Public
(iv) (c) NaaS
(v) (d) All of these

SELF ASSESSMENT TEST

Multiple Choice Questions

1. .... allows users to have access to their digital resources from any part of the world.

(a) Phone
(b) Tablet
(c) Computer
(d) Cloud computing

2. Google drive is a .... area in the cloud.

(a) personal
(b) special
(c) public
(d) None of these

3. .... is an application area of voice / speech recognition.

(a) Playing back simple information
(b) Call steering
(c) Automated identification of caller
(d) All of these

Fill in the Blanks

4. Virtual Reality is an artificial environment created with ___________.

5. ___________ Reality integrates digital components into the physical world to enhance real-world experiences.

6. A ___________ is a machine capable of carrying out one or more tasks automatically with accuracy and precision.

7. Big Data has three main characteristics: variety, __________, and volume.

8. IoT stands for ___________ of Things.

State whether True or False

9. Drones are an example of IoT devices.

10. Smart cities use IoT sensors and video cameras to collect and analyze data.

11. Cloud computing eliminates the need for physical storage by using remote servers.

12. Public cloud systems are exclusively used by private organizations.

13. The main characteristic of block chain technology is that its data can be easily modified by any user.

Assertion and Reason Based Questions

Assertion and Reason based questions. Mark the correct choice as

(a) Both A and R are true, and R is the correct explanation of A.
(b) Both A and R are true, but R is not the correct explanation of A.
(c) A is true, but R is false.
(d) A is false, but R is true.

14. Assertion (A) Big Data can help improve decision-making processes in companies.

Reason (R) Big Data combines structured and unstructured data collected from multiple sources.

15. Assertion (A) Internet of Things (IoT) can reduce waste effectively.

Reason (R) IoT provides real-time information, enabling better decision-making and management of resources.

16. Assertion (A) Cloud computing allows users to access their data from anywhere.

Reason (R) Cloud computing services are accessible via the Internet and eliminate the need for physical storage.

17. Assertion (A) Public clouds are private infrastructures for exclusive use by organizations.

Reason (R) Public clouds are managed by third-party providers and are available to the general public.

18. Assertion (A) Grid computing solves complex problems faster by splitting tasks across multiple machines.

Reason (R) Grid computing operates as a virtual supercomputer to increase efficiency and minimize wasted resources.

Very Short Answer Type Questions

19. What is the role of artificial intelligence in social media?

20. Write the example of volume characteristic of big data.

21. Write the names of component of IoT.

22. What is the use of private cloud.

23. Write any one challenge of blockchain technology.

Short Answer Type Questions

24. What is the use of virtual reality in engineering and architecture?

25. Explain the disadvantages of IoT.

26. Explain the benefits of a smart city in brief.

27. Describe the applications of cloud computing.

28. How does a grid computing work?

Long Answer Type Questions

29. Describe the type of artificial intelligence.

30. What is the use of augmented reality in military?

31. Explain the characteristics of cloud computing.

32. What do you mean by Internet of Things? Explain its advantages.

33. Explain the term big data along with its applications in detail.

Case Study Based Questions

34. The city of Metropolia is implementing a Smart City initiative using IoT (Internet of Things) technology. The city has deployed smart traffic lights, connected sensors, and AI-powered surveillance systems to improve urban mobility and safety.

Additionally, automated waste management systems have been installed to monitor and optimize garbage collection. The government is also using cloud computing to store and analyze vast amounts of data generated by these smart systems.

Based on given information Answer the following Questions:

(i) What role do IoT sensors play in the smart traffic lights of Metropolia?

(a) They help control streetlights based on daylight availability.

(b) They collect real-time traffic data to optimize signal timings.

(c) They provide free Wi-Fi to pedestrians.

(d) They monitor air quality only.

(ii) Which of the following technologies is most useful for storing and processing large amounts of city data in the cloud?

(a) Blockchain technology

(b) Augmented Reality (AR)

(c) Cloud Computing

(d) Virtual Reality (VR)

(iii) How does the automated waste management system improve garbage collection in a smart city?

(a) By predicting weather patterns to adjust collection schedules

(b) By notifying authorities only when bins are full

(c) By randomly collecting waste from different locations

(d) By reducing the use of garbage trucks completely

(iv) Which of the following is a major benefit of using AI-powered surveillance in smart cities?

(a) It completely replaces human law enforcement.

(b) It helps in real-time threat detection and security monitoring.

(c) It allows users to edit images in real-time.

(d) It increases the number of security cameras installed.

(v) Which of the following is NOT an application of IoT in smart cities?

(a) Smart parking systems

(b) Wearable fitness trackers

(c) Intelligent street lighting

(d) Environmental monitoring sensors

Answers

1. (d) 2. (a) 3. (d)
4. Computer technology 5. Augmented
6. Robot 7. Velocity 8. Internet 9. False
10. True 11. True 12. False 13. False
14. (a) 15. (a) 16. (a) 17. (d) 18. (a)
34. (i) → (b), (ii) → (c), (iii) → (b), (iv) → (b), (v) → (b)

Practical List of Python Programming

AIM 1. **To find average and grade for given marks.**

Procedure

```
n = int(input("Enter the number of subjects: "))
marks = []
for i in range(n):
    mark = float(input(f"Enter marks for subject {i+1}: "))
    marks.append(mark)
average = sum(marks) / n
if average >= 90:
    grade = "A"
elif average >= 80:
    grade = "B"
elif average >= 70:
    grade = "C"
elif average >= 60:
    grade = "D"
else:
    grade = "F"
print("\nAverage Marks:", average)
print("Grade:", grade)
```

Output   Clear

```
Enter the number of subjects: 3
Enter marks for subject 1: 50
Enter marks for subject 2: 60
Enter marks for subject 3: 10

Average Marks: 40.0
Grade: F

=== Code Execution Successful ===
```

AIM 2. **To find sale price of an item with given cost and discount (%).**

Procedure

```
cost_price = float(input("Enter the cost price of the item: "))
discount = float(input("Enter the discount percentage: "))
discount_amount = (discount / 100) * cost_price
sale_price = cost_price - discount_amount
print("\nDiscount Amount:", discount_amount)
print("Sale Price:", sale_price)
```

Output   Clear

```
Enter the cost price of the item: 100
Enter the discount percentage: 10

Discount Amount: 10.0
Sale Price: 90.0

=== Code Execution Successful ===
```

AIM 3. To calculate perimeter/circumference and area of shapes such as triangle, rectangle, square and circle.

Procedure

```
import math
shape = input("Enter the shape (triangle, rectangle, square, circle): ").lower()
if shape == "triangle":
    a = float(input("Enter side a: "))
    b = float(input("Enter side b: "))
    c = float(input("Enter side c: "))
    perimeter = a + b + c
    s = perimeter / 2
    area = math.sqrt(s * (s - a) * (s - b) * (s - c))
    print("Perimeter:", perimeter)
    print("Area:", area)
elif shape == "rectangle":
    length = float(input("Enter length: "))
    width = float(input("Enter width: "))
    perimeter = 2 * (length + width)
    area = length * width
    print("Perimeter:", perimeter)
    print("Area:", area)
elif shape == "square":
    side = float(input("Enter side: "))
    perimeter = 4 * side
    area = side * side
    print("Perimeter:", perimeter)
    print("Area:", area)
elif shape == "circle":
    radius = float(input("Enter radius: "))
    perimeter = 2 * math.pi * radius
    area = math.pi * radius * radius
    print("Circumference:", perimeter)
    print("Area:", area)
else:
    print("Invalid shape.")
```

Output Clear

```
Enter the shape (triangle, rectangle, square, circle): square
Enter side: 4
Perimeter: 16.0
Area: 16.0

=== Code Execution Successful ===
```

AIM 4. To calculate Simple and Compound interest.

Procedure

```
principal = float(input("Enter the principal amount: "))
rate = float(input("Enter the annual interest rate (percentage): "))
time = float(input("Enter the time period in years: "))
# Simple Interest Calculation
```

```
simple_interest = (principal * rate * time) / 100
print(f"Simple Interest: {simple_interest:.2f}")
# Compound Interest Calculation
compounding_frequency = int(input("Enter compounding frequency per year (1 for annually, 12 for monthly, etc.): "))
amount = principal * (1 + (rate / (100 * compounding_frequency)))**(compounding_frequency * time)
compound_interest = amount - principal
print(f"Compound Interest: {compound_interest:.2f}")
```

```
Output                                                        Clear
Enter the principal amount: 2200
Enter the annual interest rate (percentage): 110
Enter the time period in years: 2
Simple Interest: 4840.00
Enter compounding frequency per year (1 for annually, 12 for monthly, etc.):
```

AIM 5. To calculate Profit - Loss for given cost and Sell Price.

Procedure

```
# Profit or Loss Calculation
cost_price = float(input("Enter Cost Price: "))
selling_price = float(input("Enter Selling Price: "))
if selling_price > cost_price:
    profit = selling_price - cost_price
    print("Profit:", profit)
elif selling_price < cost_price:
    loss = cost_price - selling_price
    print("Loss:", loss)
else:
    print("No Profit, No Loss.")
```

```
Output                                                        Clear
Enter Cost Price: 50000
Enter Selling Price: 20000
Loss: 30000.0

=== Code Execution Successful ===
```

AIM 6. To calculate EMI for Amount, period and interest.

Procedure

```
principal = float(input("Enter the loan amount (principal): "))
rate = float(input("Enter the annual interest rate (percentage): "))
time = float(input("Enter the loan period in years: "))
# Convert annual interest rate to monthly rate
monthly_rate = (rate / 12) / 100
# Convert loan period to months
months = time * 12
# Calculate EMI
```

```
emi = (principal * monthly_rate * (1 + monthly_rate)**months) / ((1 +
monthly_rate)**months - 1)
print(f"The EMI is: {emi:.2f}")
```

```
Output                                                    Clear
Enter the loan amount (principal): 4000
Enter the annual interest rate (percentage): 20
Enter the loan period in years: 10
The EMI is: 77.30

=== Code Execution Successful ===
```

AIM 7. **To calculate tax-GST/ Income Tax.**

Procedure

```
income = float(input("Enter your income: "))
tax_type = input("Enter tax type (GST or Income Tax): ").lower()
if tax_type == "gst":
    gst_rate = float(input("Enter GST rate (percentage): "))
    gst_amount = (income * gst_rate) / 100
    print(f"GST Amount: {gst_amount:.2f}")
elif tax_type == "income tax":
    # Example Income Tax Calculation (Replace with actual tax brackets)
    if income <= 250000:
        tax_amount = 0
    elif income <= 500000:
        tax_amount = (income - 250000) * 0.05
    elif income <= 1000000:
        tax_amount = 12500 + (income - 500000) * 0.20
    else:
        tax_amount = 112500 + (income - 1000000) * 0.30
    print(f"Income Tax Amount: {tax_amount:.2f}")
else:
    print("Invalid tax type.")
```

```
Output                                                    Clear
Enter your income: 25000
Enter tax type (GST or Income Tax): GST
Enter GST rate (percentage): 18
GST Amount: 4500.00

=== Code Execution Successful ===
```

AIM 8. **To find the sum of squares of the first 100 natural numbers.**

Procedure

```
sum_of_squares = 0
for i in range(1, 101):
    sum_of_squares += i * i
print("Sum of squares of first 100 natural numbers:", sum_of_squares)
```

```
Output                                                    Clear
Sum of squares of first 100 natural numbers: 338350

=== Code Execution Successful ===
```

AIM 9. To find the largest/smallest number in a list.

Procedure

```
numbers = [12, 45, 1, 89, 34, 7, 96, 5]
largest = numbers[0]
smallest = numbers[0]
for num in numbers:
    if num > largest:
        largest = num
    if num < smallest:
        smallest = num
print("Largest number:", largest)
print("Smallest number:", smallest)
```

Output

Clear

```
Largest number: 96
Smallest number: 1

=== Code Execution Successful ===
```

AIM 10. To find the third largest/smallest number in a list

Procedure

```
numbers = [12, 45, 2, 89, 34, 7, 99, 5]
numbers.sort()
third_smallest = numbers[2]
third_largest = numbers[-3]
print("Third smallest number:", third_smallest)
print("Third largest number:", third_largest)
```

Output

Clear

```
Third smallest number: 7
Third largest number: 45

=== Code Execution Successful ===
```

AIM 11. To count the number of vowels in a user entered string.

Procedure

```
text = input("Enter a string: ")
vowels = "aeiouAEIOU"
vowel_count = 0
for char in text:
    if char in vowels:
        vowel_count += 1
print("Number of vowels:", vowel_count)
```

Output

Clear

```
Enter a string: ARIHANT
Number of vowels: 3

=== Code Execution Successful ===
```

AIM 12. To print the first n multiples of a given number.

Procedure
```
num = int(input("Enter the number: "))
n = int(input("Enter how many multiples to print: "))
for i in range(1, n + 1):
    print(num * i)
```

```
Output                                        Clear
Enter the number: 23
Enter how many multiples to print: 7
23
46
69
92
115
138
161

=== Code Execution Successful ===
```

AIM 13. To print the words starting with a alphabet in a user entered string.

Procedure
```
text = input("Enter a string: ")
words = text.split()
for word in words:
    if word[0] == 'A' or word[0] == 'a':
        print(word)
```

```
Output                                        Clear
Enter a string: ARIHANT PUBLICATION
ARIHANT

=== Code Execution Successful ===
```

AIM 14. Create a dictionary to store names of states and their capitals.

Procedure
```
states = {}
n = int(input("Enter the number of states: "))
for i in range(n):
    state = input("Enter state name: ")
    capital = input("Enter capital name: ")
    states[state] = capital
print("\nState-Capital Dictionary:")
print(states)
```

```
Output                                        Clear
Enter the number of states: 1
Enter state name: MP
Enter capital name: MUMBAI

State-Capital Dictionary:
{'MP': 'MUMBAI'}

=== Code Execution Successful ===
```

AIM 15. To print number of occurrences of a given alphabet in each string

Procedure

```
text = input("Enter a string: ")
char = input("Enter the alphabet to count: ")
count = 0
for letter in text:
    if letter == char:
        count += 1
print(f"Occurrences of '{char}' in the string:", count)
```

Output Clear

```
Enter a string: SHRUTI
Enter the alphabet to count: T
Occurrences of 'T' in the string: 1

=== Code Execution Successful ===
```

AIM 16. Create a dictionary of students to store names and marks obtained in 5 subjects.

Procedure

```
students = {}
n = int(input("Enter the number of students: "))
for i in range(n):
    name = input("Enter student name: ")
    marks = []
    for j in range(5):
        mark = int(input(f"Enter marks for subject {j+1}: "))
        marks.append(mark)
    students[name] = marks
print("\nStudent Records:")
print(students)
```

Output Clear

```
Enter the number of students: 1
Enter student name: PRIYANKA
Enter marks for subject 1: 20
Enter marks for subject 2: 23
Enter marks for subject 3: 24
Enter marks for subject 4: 25
Enter marks for subject 5: 26

Student Records:
{'PRIYANKA': [20, 23, 24, 25, 26]}

=== Code Execution Successful ===
```

AIM 17. To print the highest and lowest values in the dictionary.

Procedure

```
students = {"Alice": 85, "Bob": 92, "Charlie": 78, "David": 95, "Eve": 88}
values = list(students.values())
highest = values[0]
lowest = values[0]
for value in values:
    if value > highest:
        highest = value
```

```
    if value < lowest:
        lowest = value
print("Highest value:", highest)
print("Lowest value:", lowest)
```

```
Output                                                    Clear

Highest value: 95
Lowest value: 78

=== Code Execution Successful ===
```

Data Management: SQL Commands

AIM 1. To create a database

Procedure To create a database in SQL, the command is:

```
CREATE DATABASE database_name;
```

Example

```
CREATE DATABASE SchoolDB;
```

AIM 2. To create a student table with the student id, class, section, gender, name, dob, and marks as attributes where the student id is the primary key.

Procedure

```
CREATE TABLE Student (
    student_id INT PRIMARY KEY,
    class VARCHAR(10),
    section VARCHAR(5),
    gender VARCHAR(10),
    name VARCHAR(100),
    dob DATE,
    marks DECIMAL(5,2)
);
```

AIM 3. To insert the details of at least 10 students in the above table.

Procedure

```
INSERT INTO Student (student_id, class, section, gender, name, dob, marks)
VALUES
(1, '10th', 'A', 'Male', 'Arjun Sharma', '2005-03-15', 88.50),
(2, '10th', 'A', 'Female', 'Priya Patel', '2005-04-10', 92.00),
(3, '10th', 'B', 'Male', 'Amit Kumar', '2005-05-20', 75.50),
(4, '12th', 'C', 'Female', 'Sanya Gupta', '2003-12-25', 85.00),
(5, '12th', 'C', 'Male', 'Ravi Singh', '2004-01-18', 78.00),
(6, '11th', 'A', 'Female', 'Neha Reddy', '2004-08-30', 90.25),
(7, '11th', 'B', 'Male', 'Vikram Iyer', '2004-02-14', 84.75),
(8, '10th', 'C', 'Female', 'Anjali Mehta', '2005-07-05', 92.50),
(9, '12th', 'A', 'Male', 'Karan Joshi', '2003-11-12', 80.00),
```

```
(10, '10th', 'B', 'Female', 'Simran Kapoor', '2005-09-22', 86.75);
```

AIM 4. To display the entire content of the table.

Procedure To display the entire content of a table in SQL, the command is:

```
SELECT * FROM table_name;
```

Example

```
SELECT * FROM Student;
```

AIM 5. To display Rno, Name and Marks of those students who are scoring marks more than 75.

Procedure

```
SELECT student_id AS Rno, name, marks
FROM Student
WHERE marks > 75;
```

AIM 6. To display Rno, Name, DOB of those students who are born between '2005-01-01' and '2005-12-31'.

Procedure

```
SELECT student_id AS Rno, name, dob
FROM Student
WHERE dob BETWEEN '2005-01-01' AND '2005-12-31';
```

SAMPLE QUESTION PAPER 1

A Highly Simulated Sample Question Paper for CBSE Class XI Examination

INFORMATICS PRACTICES

Time : 3 Hours **Max. Marks : 70**

General Instructions

1. Please check this question paper contains 37 questions.
2. All questions are compulsory. However, internal choices have been provided in some questions. Attempt only one of the choices in such questions.
3. The paper is divided into 5 Sections- A, B, C, D and E.
4. Section A consists of 21 questions (1 to 21). Each question carries 1 Mark.
5. Section B consists of 7 questions (22 to 28). Each question carries 2 Marks.
6. Section C consists of 4 questions (29 to 32). Each question carries 3 Marks.
7. Section D consists of 2 case study type questions (33 to 34). Each question carries 4 Marks.
8. Section E consists of 3 questions (35 to 37). Each question carries 5 Marks.
9. All programming questions are to be answered using Python Language only.
10. In case of MCQ, text of the correct answer should also be written.

SECTION A

$21 \times 1 = 21$

1. State whether the following statement is True or False:

NULL values cannot appear in columns with a UNIQUE constraint.

2. In order for a peripheral to operate correctly, its ...... must be installed.

(a) device driver (b) user interface
(c) internet connection (d) operating system

3. Which of the following is NOT a Data Definition Language (DDL) command in SQL?

(a) CREATE TABLE (b) ALTER TABLE
(c) INSERT INTO (d) DROP DATABASE

4. System software

(a) allows the user to diagnose and troubleshoot the device
(b) is a programming language
(c) is a part of productivity suite
(d) helps the computer manage internal resources

5. In a relational database, a candidate key is:

(a) A column that uniquely identifies each row in a table.
(b) A column that is chosen to be the primary key.
(c) A column that is used to establish relationships between tables.
(d) A column that is automatically generated by the database system.

6. Write the output of `Num = (2 + 3) * 3.`

(a) 10 (b) 11 (c) 15 (d) 18

7. Find the output

```
L=[3,4,53,4,0,2,4,7,29]
L[:6]
```

(a) [3, 4, 53, 4, 0, 2] (b) [4, 0, 2, 4, 7, 29]
(c) [3, 4, 53, 4, 0, 2, 4] (d) [53, 4, 0, 2, 4, 7, 29]

8. What will be the output?

```
dicl=.["Rahul":234,"Shrey":250]
dicl["Shrey"]
```

(a) 250 (b) 251
(c) 234 (d) 235

9. System software also provides the interface between .... and components of the computer.

(a) software (b) user
(c) hardware (d) None of these

10. State whether the following statement is True or False:

The WHERE clause is mandatory for the DELETE command to work.

11. Fill in the Blank

In the relational data model, a ________ is a single row in a table.

(a) Tuple (b) Domain
(c) Attribute (d) Column

12. What is the purpose of the BETWEEN operator in SQL?

(a) To check if a value is within a specified range.

(b) To compare two values for equality.

(c) To combine results from multiple tables.

(d) To sort the result set in ascending or descending order.

13. Which of the following is an advantage of using SQL?

(a) It is procedural. (b) It is standardized.

(c) It is proprietary. (d) It is low-level.

14. In which data model, data is organised in a tree-like structure?

(a) Hierarchical data model

(b) Network data model

(c) Relational data model

(d) None of the above

15. ...... refers to the number of tuples in a relation.

(a) Degree (b) Attribute

(c) Cardinality (d) Tuple

16. Match SQL Functions with Their Descriptions

SQL Function		Description
P. COUNT()	1.	Returns the number of rows in a result set
Q. LOWER()	2.	Converts a string to lowercase
R. ROUND()	3.	Rounds a number to the nearest integer or decimal places
S. DISTINCT	4.	Returns unique values from a column

(a) P-1, Q-2, R-3, S-4 (b) P-4, Q-3, R-1, S-2

(c) P-2, Q-1, R-4, S-3 (d) P-3, Q-4, R-2, S-1

17. Fill in the blanks:

In Python, an identifier cannot start with a _______.

(a) Letter (b) Underscore

(c) Number (d) Special character (@, #, $, etc.)

18. Which of the following is not a service in cloud computing?

(a) IaaS (b) SaaS (c) PaaS (d) NaaS

19. ...... is a distributed architecture of large number of computers connected to solve a complex problem.

(a) Cloud computing (b) Big data

(c) Blockchain (d) Grid computing

Directions (Q. Nos. 20 and 21) *are Assertion (A) and Reason (R) Type questions. Choose the correct option as*

(a) Both Assertion (A) and Reason (R) are true, and Reason (R) is the correct explanation of Assertion (A)

(b) Both Assertion (A) and Reason (R) are true, but Reason (R) is not the correct explanation of Assertion (A)

(c) Assertion (A) is True, but Reason (R) is False

(d) Assertion (A) is False, but Reason (R) is True

20. Assertion (A) Python supports both ASCII and Unicode characters.

Reason (R) Unicode allows representing characters from multiple languages.

21. Assertion (A) Logical operators in SQL can combine multiple conditions in a query.

Reason (R) Logical operators include AND, OR, and NOT for conditional evaluation.

SECTION B

7 × 2 = 14

22. What is a Python character set? Explain briefly.

Or Explain the concept of constants in Python.

23. What is the role of I/O devices? Give two examples and their functions.

24. Write an SQL query to add a new column PublicationYear (INTEGER) to the Books table.

25. State two things which are done by an operating system.

Or **Secondary storage is also known as auxiliary memory. Explain it.**

26. Shreya is programming in Python and writing a following code. But she found an error, what is the reason?

```
a = 10
b = 20
c = a + b
    print ("The output is :", c)
```

27. What is foreign key constraints?

28. Find the output.

```
dic = {'data1' : 200, 'data2' : 56, 'data3': 47}
result = 1
for key in dic:
  result = result*dic[key]
print(result)
```

Or **Find the output of the given Python program.**

```
key1 = ["Data 1", "Data 2"]
name = ["Manish", "Nitin"]
marks = [480, 465]
print ("The original key list : " +
str(key1))
print ("The original nested name list : " +
str(name))
print ("The original nested marks list : " +
str(marks))
output = {key : {'Name' : name, 'Marks' :
marks} for key, name, marks in zip(key1,
name, marks)}
print("The dictionary after creation :",
str(output))
```

SECTION C

4 × 3 = 12

29. Natural language processing is a field of computer science, artificial intelligence and linguistic dealing with the interactions between computers and human languages. It gives machines the ability to read and understand the language that humans speak such as Hindi and English.

The natural language processing system would enable natural language user interfaces and the acquisition of knowledge directly from human written sources, such as news and other unstructured texts.

The predictive typing feature of search engine that helps us by suggesting the next word in the sentence while typing keywords and the spell checking features are examples of natural language processing.

In fact, it is possible to search the web or operate or control our devices using our voice. All this has been possible by NLP. An NLP system can perform text to speech and speech to text conversion.

Based on the above information, answer the following questions.

(i) Write the full form of NLP.

(ii) What is a rapidly emerging field where machines are able to translate texts from one language to another?

(iii) Another emerging application area is .... where a computer software can interact with customers.

30. Write a Python program to split dictionary keys and values into separate lists.

Or

Write the output of the following program.

```
a = float(input("Enter first angle: "))
b = float(input("Enter second angle: "))
c = float(input("Enter third angle: "))
sum_of_angles = a + b + c
if sum_of_angles == 180:
    print("These angles will make a triangle")
else:
    print("These angles will not make a triangle")
```

31. Create and Insert into the EMPLOYEES Table

I. Write an SQL statement to create a table named EMPLOYEES with the following specifications:

Column Name	Data Type	Key
EmpID	Numeric	Primary Key
FirstName	Varchar(20)	
LastName	Varchar(15)	
HireDate	Date	
Salary	Float(10,2)	

II. Write an SQL query to insert the following data into the EMPLOYEES table:

101, Arjun, Sharma, 2015-06-25, 50000.75

32. Consider the table 'PERSONS' given below. Write commands in SQL for (i) to (iii).

Table: PERSONS

PId	Sur Name	First Name	Gender	City	Pin Code	Basic Salary
1	Sharma	Geet	F	Udhamwara	182141	50000
2	Singh	Surinder	M	Kupwara Nagar	193222	75000
3	Jcob	Peter	M	Bhawani	185155	45000
4	Alvis	Thomas	M	Ahmed Nagar	380025	50000
5	Mohan	Garima	M	Nagar Coolangatta	390026	33000
6	Azmi	Simi	F	New Delhi	110021	40000
7	Kaur	Manpreet	F	Udhamwara	182141	42000

(i) Display the SurName, FirstName and City of people residing in Udhamwara city.

(ii) Display the Person Id(PId), City and PinCode of PERSONS whose salary is 75000.

(iii) Display the FirstName and City of all the females getting BasicSalary above 40000.

Or Write SQL commands for the questions from (i) to (iii) on the basis of table SHOP.

S_No	P_Name	S_Name	Qty	Cost	City
S1	Biscuit	Priyagold	120	12.00	Delhi
S2	Bread	Britannia	200	25.00	Mumbai
S3	Chocolate	Cadbury	350	40.00	Mumbai
S4	Sauce	Kissan	400	45.00	Chennai

(i) Display all products whose quantity is 400.

(ii) Display data for all products.

(iii) To list S_Name, P_Name, Cost for all the products whose quantity is less than 300.

SECTION D

2 × 4 = 8

33. Rohan is developing a program to manage a list of student scores. Assist him by writing the following Python code snippets:

scores = [85, 92, 78, 95, 88, 78, 90]

(i) Write a Python statement to find the highest score from the scores list.

(ii) Write a Python statement to count how many times the score 78 appears in the scores list.

(iii) Write a Python statement to add a new score of 89 to the end of the scores list.

(iv) Write a Python statement to remove the first occurrence of the score 78 from the scores list.

34. Write SQL commands for the questions from (i) to (iv) on the basis of table SHOP.

S_No	P_Name	S_Name	Qty	Cost	City
S1	Biscuit	Priyagold	120	12.00	Delhi
S2	Bread	Britannia	200	25.00	Mumbai
S3	Chocolate	Cadbury	350	40.00	Mumbai
S4	Sauce	Kissan	400	45.00	Chennai

(i) Display all products whose quantity is 200.

(ii) Display data for all products whose cost is more than 40.

(iii) To list S_Name, P_Name, Cost for all the products whose quantity is less than 300.

(iv) To display S_No, P_Name, S_Name, Qty for Mumbai city from the SHOP table.

Or Consider the table STUDENT given below and write SQL commands for (i) to (iv).

Student_No	Class	Name	Game	G_Grade	Section	Marks
01	7	Rahul	Swimming	B	A	99
02	8	Sameer	Tennis	A	B	20
03	10	Dushyant	FootBall	C	C	87
04	12	Kapil	Tennis	D	C	90
05	6	Ravinder	Cricket	A	B	97

(i) Display Student_No and G_Grade of all students from table STUDENT.

(ii) List the Name from table STUDENT whose Student _No is 04.

(iii) Display Game and Marks for those students whose name is Kapil.

(iv) Write a query to display Name and Section for those students whose Marks more than 85.

SECTION E

3 × 5 = 15

35. Ronita wants to store the data of some products in a table as follows:

PNo	PName	Qty	Date_Of_Mfg
P01	Pencil	20	2020-09-01
P02	Eraser	5	1990-09-11
P03	Book	16	2000-04-03
P04	Notebook	15	2016-12-11
P05	Color	10	2015-02-04

She also wants to perform some operations and manipulations on the table.

Help her to find the solutions of the following questions.

(i) Write a command that displays the details of all the products.

(ii) Write the default date format in which the date has to be stored in MySQL.

(iii) Which command can she use to add a new record to the table?

(iv) Suggest a proper data type for the "PName" column.

(v) Write a command to display the product names and quantities of all products manufactured after the year 2000.

36. Consider the following Python list:

```
fruits = ['Apple', 'Banana', 'Mango',
'Grapes', 'Orange']
```

Write Python statements to:

I. Add 'Pineapple' at the end of the list.

II. Insert 'Cherry' at the second position.

III. Remove 'Banana' from the list.

IV. Reverse the order of the list.

V. Sort the list in alphabetical order.

37. Write suitable SQL query for the following:

I. Write an SQL query to display the total number of records in the Customers table.

II. Write an SQL query to display the name column from the Students table, ensuring that all characters are in uppercase.

III. Write an SQL query to retrieve all rows from the Orders table where the order_date falls between '2024-01-01' and '2024-06-30'.

IV. Write an SQL query to remove all records from the Products table where the stock_quantity is NULL.

V. Write an SQL query to update the price column in the Items table by increasing all values by 10%.

Or I. Create a new database named 'SchoolDB'.

II. Insert a new record into the 'Students' table with the following values:

RollNo = 101

Name = 'Amit Kumar'

Age = 16

Class = '10A'

III. Update the age of the student with RollNo 101 to 17.

IV. Delete the record of the student whose RollNo is 101.

V. Display all records from the 'Students' table where the age is between 15 and 18.

Answers

1. False
2. (a)
3. (c)
4. (d)
5. (a)
6. (c)
7. (a)
8. (a)
9. (b)
10. False
11. (a)
12. (a)
13. (b)
14. (a)
15. (c)
16. (a)
17. (c)
18. (d)
19. (d)
20. (a)
21. (a)

22. A character set is a collection of valid characters that a programming language can recognize and process. It includes letters, digits, symbols, and special characters used in coding.

Or

Constants are fixed values in a program that do not change during execution. In Python, constants are typically written in uppercase letters (e.g., PI = 3.14159) by convention, although Python does not enforce immutability.

23. Input/Output (I/O) devices are essential components that allow a computer to communicate with the user and other devices.

They act as a bridge, handling the flow of information both into and out of the computer system.

Examples:

Mouse An input device that allows users to control a cursor on the screen and interact with graphical elements.

Printer An output device that produces hard copies of documents and images stored in the computer.

24. ALTER TABLE Books ADD COLUMN PublicationYear INT;

25. At the simplest level, an operating system does two things

(i) It manages the hardware and software resources of the system. In a desktop computer, these resources include the processor, memory, disk space, etc.

(ii) It provides a stable, consistent way for applications to deal with the hardware without having to know all the details of the hardware.

Or

Secondary storage is also known as auxiliary memory because it is a part of external memory and used to store a large amount of data at less cost per-byte than primary memory.
The secondary storage devices were used to overcome the problems with primary memory.

26. The given code is identation error and correct code is

```
a = 10
b = 20
c = a + b
print ("The output is :", c)
```

27. Foreign key constraint is a constraint that ensures that columns in one table match the primary key column of same or another table.

For example,

```
CREATE TABLE Items(Order_No INTEGER
PRIMARY KEY,Itemno INTEGER REFERENCES
Items (Order_No));
```

28. 526400

Or **Output**

The original key list : ['Data 1', 'Data 2']

The original nested name list : ['Manish', 'Nitin']

The original nested marks list : [480, 465]

The dictionary after creation : {'Data 2' : {'Name' : 'Nitin', 'Marks' : 465}, 'Data 1' : {'Name' : 'Manish', 'Marks' : 480}}

29. (i) Natural Language Processing

(ii) Machine translation

(iii) Automated customer service

30.
```
dic = {'A' : 'Apple', 'B' : 'Ball', 'C' :
'Cat', 'D' : 'Dog', 'E' : 'Elephant'}
print("Original Dictionary:",str(dic))
# split dictionary into keys and values
keys = dic.keys()
values = dic.values()
#printing keys and values seperately
print ("keys : ", str(keys))
print ("values : ", str(values))
```

Or

Enter first angle: 45.6

Enter second angle: 44.4

Enter third angle: 90.0

These angles will make a triangle

31.
```
CREATE TABLE EMPLOYEES (
    EmpID NUMERIC PRIMARY KEY,
    FirstName VARCHAR(20),
    LastName VARCHAR(15),
    HireDate DATE,
    Salary FLOAT(10,2)
);
INSERT INTO EMPLOYEES (EmpID, FirstName, LastName,
                       HireDate, Salary)
VALUES (101, 'Arjun', 'Sharma', '2015-06-25', 50000.75);
```

32. (i) `SELECT SurName, FirstName, City FROM PERSONS WHERE City = 'Udhamwara';`

(ii) `SELECT PId, City, PinCode FROM PERSONS WHERE BasicSalary = 75000;`

(iii) `SELECT FirstName, City FROM PERSONS WHERE Gender = 'F' AND BasicSalary > 40000;`

Or

(i) `SELECT * FROM SHOP WHERE Qty = 400;`

(ii) `SELECT * FROM SHOP;`

(iii)
```
SELECT S_Name, P_Name, Cost FROM SHOP
WHERE Qty<300;
```

33. (i)
```
highest_score = max(scores)
print(highest_score)
```
Output 95

(ii)
```
count_78 = scores.count(78)
print(count_78)
```
Output 2

(iii)
```
scores.append(89)
print(scores)
```
Output [85, 92, 78, 95, 88, 78, 90, 89]

(iv)
```
scores.remove(78)
print(scores)
```
Output [85, 92, 95, 88, 78, 90, 89]

34. (i) `mysql> SELECT * FROM SHOP WHERE Qty = 200;`

(ii) `mysql> SELECT * FROM Cost > 40;`

(iii)
```
mysql> SELECT S_Name, P_Name, Cost FROM SHOP
WHERE Qty<300;
```

(iv)
```
mysql> SELECT S_No, P_Name, S_Name, Qty FROM
SHOP WHERE City = "Mumbai";
```

Or

(i) `mysql>SELECT Student_No, G_Grade FROM STUDENT;`

(ii)
```
mysql>SELECT Name FROM STUDENT WHERE Student
_No = 04;
```

(iii)
```
mysql>SELECT Game, Marks FROM STUDENT WHERE
Name = "Kapil";
```

(iv)
```
mysql>SELECT Name, Section FROM STUDENT WHERE
Marks > 85;
```

35. (i) `SELECT * FROM products;`

(ii) The default date format in MySQL is: YYYY-MM-DD

(iii) The Alter command can be used to make any changes to the structure of a table.

(iv) A proper data type for the "PName" column would be: VARCHAR(length).

(v)
```
SELECT PName, Qty
FROM products
WHERE Date_Of_Mfg > '2000-12-31';
```

36. I. fruits.append('Pineapple')

II. fruits.insert(1, 'Cherry')

III. fruits.remove('Banana')

IV. fruits.reverse()

V. fruits.sort()

37. I. SELECT COUNT(*) FROM Customers;

II. SELECT UPPER(name) FROM Students;

III. SELECT * FROM Orders WHERE order_date BETWEEN '2024-01-01' AND '2024-06-30';

IV. DELETE FROM Products WHERE stock_quantity IS NULL;

V. UPDATE Items SET price = price * 1.10;

Or

I. CREATE DATABASE SchoolDB;

II. INSERT INTO Students (RollNo, Name, Age, Class) VALUES (101, 'Amit Kumar', 16, '10A');

III. UPDATE Students
SET Age = 17
WHERE RollNo = 101;

IV. DELETE FROM Students WHERE RollNo = 101

V. SELECT * FROM Students WHERE Age BETWEEN 15 AND 18;

SAMPLE QUESTION PAPER 2

A Highly Simulated Sample Question Paper for CBSE Class XI Examination

INFORMATICS PRACTICES

Time : 3 Hours **Max. Marks : 70**

General Instructions

1. Please check this question paper contains 37 questions.
2. All questions are compulsory. However, internal choices have been provided in some questions. Attempt only one of the choices in such questions.
3. The paper is divided into 5 Sections- A, B, C, D and E.
4. Section A consists of 21 questions (1 to 21). Each question carries 1 Mark.
5. Section B consists of 7 questions (22 to 28). Each question carries 2 Marks.
6. Section C consists of 4 questions (29 to 32). Each question carries 3 Marks.
7. Section D consists of 2 case study type questions (33 to 34). Each question carries 4 Marks.
8. Section E consists of 3 questions (35 to 37). Each question carries 5 Marks.
9. All programming questions are to be answered using Python Language only.
10. In case of MCQ, text of the correct answer should also be written.

SECTION A

21 × 1 = 21

1. **State whether the following statement is True or False:**
The BETWEEN operator is inclusive of the specified range.

2. **A disc's content that is recorded at the time of manufacture and that cannot be changed or erased by the user is**

(a) memory only (b) write only
(c) once only (d) read only

3. **Which of the following is used to modify the structure of an existing table in SQL?**

(a) CREATE TABLE (b) UPDATE TABLE
(c) ALTER TABLE (d) MODIFY TABLE

4. **In a relational database, what is a "tuple"?**

(a) A column in a table.
(b) A row in a table.
(c) The relationship between two tables.
(d) The name of a table.

5. **The .... clause matches a range of values in SQL.**

(a) range (b) between
(c) order (d) between values

6. **Which of the following expression is invalid?**

(a) $p / q + a - c$ (b) $p / q + a + c$
(c) $x / y + p * a / b$ (d) $a * + b$

7. **Find the output.**

```
x = 1
while (x < 5):
  print(x)
  x = x * 2
```

(a) 1 2 3 4 (b) 1 2 4
(c) 1 2 3 4 5 (d) 0 1 2 3 4

8. **Fill in the blanks:**
The function used to remove an element from a list at a specific index is ________.

(a) pop() (b) delete()
(c) remove() (d) discard()

9. **........... is a set of valid characters that a language can recognise.**

(a) Variable
(b) Datatype
(c) Character set
(d) Token

10. **It is the type of memory which is very nearest to the CPU and all the recent instructions are stored in it.**

(a) Primary memory (b) Cache memory
(c) Secondary memory (d) None of these

11. **Fill in the Blank**

In SQL, the __________ clause is used to filter records based on a specified condition.

(a) FROM (b) SELECT
(c) WHERE (d) ORDER BY

12. **What is the purpose of using aggregate functions in SQL, such as COUNT(), SUM(), AVG(), etc.?**

(a) To retrieve individual data entries from a table.
(b) To perform calculations on multiple rows of a single column and return a single summary value.
(c) To filter data based on specific conditions.
(d) To sort the result set in ascending or descending order.

13. **State whether the following statement is True or False:**

A column alias is a permanent renaming of a column in the database.

14. **The primary purpose of the Windows operating system is**

(a) to make the most efficient use of the computer hardware
(b) to allow people to use the computer
(c) to keep systems programmer's employed
(d) to make computers easier to use

15. **The person who has such central control over the system is called ....**

(a) DBA (b) System analysts
(c) Database designer (d) None of these

16. **...... refers to the number of attributes in each tuple.**

(a) Cardinality (b) Degree
(c) Both (a) and (b) (d) None of these

17. **Match SQL Clauses with Their Uses**

SQL Clause	Use
P. WHERE	1. Filters records based on a condition
Q. GROUP BY	2. Groups data for aggregate functions
R. ORDER BY	3. Sorts the query result
S. HAVING	4. Filters grouped data

18. **It is the highest level of database abstraction and also known as view level.**

(a) Internal level (b) Conceptual level
(c) External level (d) None of these

19. **...... is an encrypted and a distributed database that records data.**

(a) Cloud computing (b) Big data
(c) Block chain (d) Grid computing

Directions (Q. Nos. 20 and 21) *are Assertion (A) and Reason (R) Type questions. Choose the correct option as*

(a) Both Assertion (A) and Reason (R) are true, and Reason (R) is the correct explanation of Assertion (A)
(b) Both Assertion (A) and Reason (R) are true, but Reason (R) is not the correct explanation of Assertion (A)
(c) Assertion (A) is True, but Reason (R) is False
(d) Assertion (A) is False, but Reason (R) is True

20. **Assertion (A)** Lists in Python are mutable.

Reason (R) Elements of a list can be changed after the list is created.

21. **Assertion (A)** The DROP TABLE command permanently deletes a table along with its data.

Reason (R) The DROP TABLE command removes the structure and constraints of the table.

SECTION B

7×2=14

22. **What is the data type?**

Or **What are some examples of mutable data types in Python?**

23. **How has the evolution of computers affected software? Give one example.**

24. **Explain column alias with an example.**

25. **Differentiate between hardware and software.**

Or

Why are hard disk drives so popular?

26. **Rewrite the following code in python after removing all syntax errors.**

```
A = int(input("enter any numbeer:"))
Ar = 0
for x in range(0,A,2)
    Ar+=x
    if x%2=0:
        Print (x*10)
    Else:
        print(C)
 print(Ar)
```

27. **Given a statement as follows:**

```
CREATE TABLE EMPLOYEE
(Emp_id INT NOT NULL,
OrderNo INT NOT NULL,
Emp_rank INT,
PRIMARY KEY(Emp_id),
FOREIGN KEY(Emp_rank) REFERENCES
PERSONS (Emp_rank));
```

Identify the number and types of constraints in the table EMPLOYEE.

28. Predict the output.

```
dic = {1 : [45, 89, 65], 'A' : (23, 45, 6)}
print(dic.keys())
print(dic.values())
```

Or

Find the output.

(i)
```
n = {'a' : [2, 3, 1], 'b' : [5, 2, 1], 'c'
: [2, 3, 4]}
sorted_dic = {i : sorted(j) for i, j in
n.items ()}
print(sorted_dic)
```

(ii)
```
dict = {'c' : 789, 'a' : 796, 'b' : 908}
for i in sorted(dict):
    print(dict[i])
```

SECTION C

4 × 3 = 12

29. A robot is basically a machine capable of carrying out one or more tasks automatically with accuracy and precision. Unlike other machines, a robot is programmable, which means it can follow the instructions given through computer programs.

Robots were initially conceptualised for doing repetitive industrial tasks that are boring or stressful for humans or were labour intensive.

Sensors are one of the prime components of a robot. Robot can be of many types, such as wheeled robots, legged robots, manipulators and humanoids.

Robots that resemble humans are known as humanoids. Robots are being used in industries, medical science, bionics, scientific research, military etc.

Based on the above information, answer the following questions.

(i) .... are one of the prime components of a robot.

(ii) In which field(s), robots are used?

(iii) Robots that resemble humans are known as

30. What is the relationship between system and application software? Provide an example of each type of software to illustrate their relationship.

Or

To enter a character and print whether a given character is an alphabet, digit or any character.

31. Consider the table CUSTOMER

C_ID	C_Name	C_City	C_Salary
100	DUSHYANT	MEERUT	15000
101	RAJ	DELHI	12000
102	VIKAS	GOA	10000

(i) Write a MySQL query to display the names of all customers from Meerut.

(ii) Name the data type used for C_City field.

32. Consider the table Doctor given below. Write commands in SQL for (i) to (iii).

ID	DocName	Department	DOJ	Gender	Salary
1	Amit Kumar	Orthopaedics	1993-02-12	M	35000
2	Anita Hans	Paediatrics	1998-10-16	F	30000
3	Sunita Maini	Gynaecology	1991-08-23	F	40000
4	Joe Thomas	Surgery	1994-10-20	M	55000
5	Gurpreet Kaur	Paediatrics	1999-11-24	F	52000
6	Anandini Burman	Oncology	1994-03-16	F	31000
7	Siddharth Dang	Surgery	1995-09-08	M	47000
8	Rama Mukherjee	Oncology	2000-06-27	F	54500

(i) Display the names and dates of joining of doctors of Oncology department.

(ii) Display the names and salaries of female doctors.

(iii) Display the names and salaries of all the female doctors who are getting salary above 50000.

Or

Consider the table Student given below and write SQL commands for (i) to (iii).

Student_No	Class	Name	Game	G_Grade	Section	Marks
01	7	Rahul	Swimming	B	A	99
02	8	Sameer	Tennis	A	B	20
03	10	Dushyant	FootBall	C	C	87
04	12	Kapil	Tennis	D	C	90
05	6	Racinder	Cricket	A	B	97

(i) Display Student_No and G_Grade of all students from table Student.

(ii) List the Name from table Student whose Student_No is 05.

(iii) Display Game and Marks for those students whose name is Rahul.

SECTION D

2 × 4 = 8

33. A student is writing a program to process a list of numbers. Help them by writing the following Python code snippets:

```
numbers = [12, 5, 20, 9, 25, 2, 18]
```

(i) Write a Python for loop that iterates through the numbers list and prints each number.

(ii) Write a Python for loop that iterates through the numbers list and prints only the even numbers.

(iii) Write a Python while loop that prints numbers from 1 to 5.

(iv) Write a Python for loop that calculates the sum of all the numbers in the numbers list and prints the sum.

34. Write the SQL commands for the questions from (i) to (iv) on the basis of table Employee?

Emp_no	E_name	Profile	Manager	Hire_date	Salary	Commission	Dept_no
8369	SMITH	CLERK	8902	1990-12-18	8000	NULL	20
8499	ANYA	SALESMAN	8698	1991-02-20	16000	300.00	30
8521	SETH	SALESMAN	8698	1991-02-22	12500	500.00	30
8566	MAHADEVAN	MANAGER	8839	1991-04-02	29850	NULL	20
8654	MOMIN	SALESMAN	8698	1991-09-28	12500	1400.00	30
8698	BINA	MANAGER	8839	1991-05-01	28500	NULL	30
8882	SHIVANSH	MANAGER	8839	1991-06-09	24500	NULL	10
8888	SCOTT	ANALYST	8566	1992-12-09	30000	NULL	20
8839	AMIR	PRESIDENT	NULL	1991-11-18	50000	NULL	10
8844	KULDEEP	SALESMAN	8698	1991-09-08	15000	0.00	30

(i) Display Employee Name and Salary of those employees whose salary is greater than or equal to 22000?

(ii) Display the name of employee whose Emp_no is 8521.

(iii) Display the Profile of employee whose employee name is ANYA.

(iv) Display the Salary of those employees whose Hire_date is less than 1991-04-02.

Or

Consider the table DOCTOR given below. Write commands in SQL for (i) to (iii) and output of (iv).

Table: DOCTOR

ID	DocName	Department	DOJ	Gender	Salary
1	Amit Kumar	Orthopaedics	1993-02-12	M	35000
2	Anita Hans	Paediatrics	1998-10-16	F	30000
3	Sunita Maini	Gynaecology	1991-08-23	F	40000
4	Joe Thomas	Surgery	1994-10-20	M	55000
5	Gurpreet Kaur	Paediatrics	1999-11-24	F	52000
6	Anandini Burman	Oncology	1994-03-16	F	31000
7	Siddharth Dang	Surgery	1995-09-08	M	47000
8	Rama Mukherjee	Oncology	2000-06-27	F	54500

(i) Display the names and dates of joining of doctors of Oncology department.

(ii) Display the names and salaries of all the female doctors who are getting salary above 50000.

(iii) Insert the record (9, Arnav Sharma, Surgery, 1995-07-21, M, 60000)

(iv) `SELECT Department FROM DOCTOR WHERE Salary >= 55000;`

SECTION E

3×5=15

35. Given the following Employee Form

No.	Name	Age	Department	Dateofrtd	Salary	Sex
1	Pankaj	54	Engg.	10/01/97	1200	M
2	Shalini	41	Estb	24/03/98	2000	F
3	Sanjay	32	Engg.	12/12/96	3500	M
4	Sudha	25	Science	01/07/99	4700	F
5	Rakesh	32	Engg.	05/09/97	2500	M
6	Shakeel	40	Language	27/06/98	3000	M
7	Surya	44	Estb	25/02/97	2100	M
8	Shikha	33	Science	31/07/97	2600	F

Write SQL queries for the following:

(i) To show all information about the employees of the Engg. Branch.

(ii) To list the names of female employees who are in the Science branch.

(iii) To list the names of all employees with their date of retirement in ascending order.

(iv) To list the names and departments of employees who joined before the year 1998.

(v) To display the names and salaries of employees who earn more than 2000 in descending order of salary.

36. Consider the following string:

```
sentence = "Python programming is fun and powerful"
```

Write Python statements to:

I. Convert the string into a list of words.

II. Convert the string to uppercase.

III. Find the index of the word 'fun'.

IV. Replace 'fun' with 'awesome'.

V. Count the occurrences of the letter 'o'.

37. Write suitable SQL queries for the following:

I. To create a database named SchoolDB.

II. To create a table Students with columns: StudentID (integer, primary key), Name (varchar(50)), Class (integer), and Marks (integer).

III. To display the names of students who have scored more than 75 marks from the Students table.

IV. To update the Marks of a student with StudentID 101 to 90 in the Students table.

V. To delete the records of students from the Students table where Class is 12.

Answers

1. True	2. (d)	3. (c)	4. (b)	5. (b)	6. (d)	7. (b)	8. (a)	9. (c)	10. (b)
11. (c)	12. (b)	13. (*)	14. (a)	15. (a)	16. (b)	17. (a)	18. (c)	19. (c)	20. (a)
21. (a)									

SAMPLE QUESTION PAPER 3

A Highly Simulated Sample Question Paper for CBSE Class XI Examination

INFORMATICS PRACTICES

Time : 3 Hours **Max. Marks : 70**

General Instructions

1. Please check this question paper contains 37 questions.
2. All questions are compulsory. However, internal choices have been provided in some questions. Attempt only one of the choices in such questions.
3. The paper is divided into 5 Sections- A, B, C, D and E.
4. Section A consists of 21 questions (1 to 21). Each question carries 1 Mark.
5. Section B consists of 7 questions (22 to 28). Each question carries 2 Marks.
6. Section C consists of 4 questions (29 to 32). Each question carries 3 Marks.
7. Section D consists of 2 case study type questions (33 to 34). Each question carries 4 Marks.
8. Section E consists of 3 questions (35 to 37). Each question carries 5 Marks.
9. All programming questions are to be answered using Python Language only.
10. In case of MCQ, text of the correct answer should also be written.

SECTION A

21 × 1 = 21

1. State whether the following statement is True or False:

The RENAME command can rename both tables and databases.

2. Which unit of computer helps in communication between the memory and the arithmetic logical unit?

(a) CMU (b) CU

(c) UPS (d) CPU

3. Which of the following best defines a Database Management System (DBMS)?

(a) A system that only stores data

(b) A software that manages and organizes data efficiently

(c) A hardware device for storing data

(d) A programming language for writing scripts

4. In the relational data model, which term refers to a single row in a table?

(a) Attribute (b) Domain

(c) Tuple (d) Relation

5. Which of the following is NOT a type of key in the relational data model?

(a) Candidate Key (b) Foreign Key

(c) Primary Key (d) Virtual Key

6. Which component of a relational data model defines the set of possible values an attribute can have?

(a) Relation

(b) Tuple

(c) Domain

(d) Candidate Key

7. Find the output.

```
L = [89, 45, "Taj", "Qutub", 93, 42,
    "Minar", "Delhi", "Agra"]
L [ 2 : 5]
```

(a) ['Taj', 'Qutub', 93]

(b) [45, 'Taj', 'Qutub', 93]

(c) ['Taj', 'Qutub', 93, 42]

(d) [45, 'Taj', 'Qutub', 93, 42]

8. Which type of error occurs when statements are not meaningful?

(a) Syntax error

(b) Logical error

(c) Semantic error

(d) Run time error

9. State whether the following statement is True or False:

The DROP TABLE command removes both table structure and data from the database.

10. Which SQL command is used to remove an entire database named 'CompanyDB'?

(a) DELETE DATABASE CompanyDB;
(b) REMOVE DATABASE CompanyDB;
(c) DROP DATABASE CompanyDB;
(d) ERASE DATABASE CompanyDB;

11. Fill in the Blank

The _______ operator is used to retrieve records within a specific range of values.

(a) BETWEEN (b) IN
(c) LIKE (d) DISTINCT

12. Which of the following statements about candidate keys and primary keys is MOST accurate?

(a) A candidate key can be null, while a primary key cannot.
(b) A table can have multiple primary keys but only one candidate key.
(c) A table can have multiple candidate keys, but only one primary key.
(d) A primary key is always a foreign key in another table.

13. Data capturing refers to

(a) Collecting data from different sources in printed form
(b) Collecting data from different sources in digital form
(c) Billing data at shopping outlet using bar code reader
(d) Commenting data on social media

14. Which SQL data type is best suited for storing a true/false value?

(a) VARCHAR (b) INTEGER
(c) BOOLEAN (d) DATE

15. Fill in the blanks:

The statement used to terminate a loop before its normal execution is _______.

(a) pass (b) break
(c) continue (d) return

16. Match SQL Aggregate Functions with Their Use

Function	Use
P. SUM()	1. Adds all values in a column
Q. AVG()	2. Calculates the average value
R. COUNT()	3. Counts the number of records
S. MIN()	4. Finds the smallest value

(a) P-1, Q-2, R-3, S-4 (b) P-4, Q-3, R-1, S-2
(c) P-2, Q-1, R-4, S-3 (d) P-3, Q-4, R-2, S-1

17. Which technology is crucial for analyzing vast datasets to find patterns in smart city traffic management?

(a) Robotics (b) Machine Learning
(c) Virtual Reality (VR) (d) Grid Computing

18. The relationship between two tables is established with the help of which type of key?

(a) Primary key
(b) Candidate key
(c) Foreign key
(d) Alternate key

19. It is a phrase used to mean a massive volume of both structured and unstructured data that is so large.

(a) Cloud computing
(b) Big data
(c) Block chain
(d) Grid computing

Directions (Q. Nos. 20 and 21) ***are Assertion (A) and Reason (R) Type questions. Choose the correct option as***

(a) Both Assertion (A) and Reason (R) are true, and Reason (R) is the correct explanation of Assertion (A)
(b) Both Assertion (A) and Reason (R) are true, but Reason (R) is not the correct explanation of Assertion (A)
(c) Assertion (A) is True, but Reason (R) is False
(d) Assertion (A) is False, but Reason (R) is True

20. Assertion (A) The % operator is used to calculate the remainder of a division operation.

Reason (R) It's known as the modulo operator.

21. Assertion (A) The INSERT command allows adding multiple rows into a table.

Reason (R) The INSERT command requires specifying values for all columns in the table.

SECTION B

7 × 2 = 14

22. What will be the result of the following expression?

-a < = 5

(i) if a = 5 **(ii) if a = -5**

Or

Convert the equation into corresponding Python statement y = a3 + b2 + c 2bc

23. List two components of a computer system and briefly explain the difference between system and application software.

24. What does a SELECT command returns without a WHERE clause?

25. Differentiate between system software and application software? Give examples of each type of software.

Or

Differentiate between volatile and non-volatile memory.

26. Rewrite the following code in Python after removing all syntax errors.

```
fee=250
0=i
while fee=<2000:
  if fee<=750:
       print(fee)
       fee=+250
  else:
       print("fee"*i)
       i=i+1
       fee=Fee+250
```

27. What is the use of AS keyword with SELECT statement?

28. Predict the output.

```
dic = {'a' : 1, 'b' : 2, 'c' : 3, 'd' : 4}
print(dic)
if 'a' in dic :
      del dic['a']
print(dic)
```

Or Find the output of the given Python program to swap keys and values in dictionary.

```
old_dict = {'One' : 742, 'Two':145, 'Three' :
654, 'Four' : 321, 'Five' : 120, 'Six': 365,
'Seven':459, 'Eight': 449}
new_dict = dict([(value, key)for key, value
in old_dict.items()])
print("Original dictonary is :")
print (old_dict)
print()
print("Dictionary after swapping is:")
print("Keys:Values")
for i in new_dict:
      print(i, " : ", new_dict[i])
```

SECTION C

4 × 3 = 12

29. Big data is a phrase used to mean a massive volume of both structured and unstructured data that is so large. It is difficult to process using traditional database and software techniques.

Big data has the potential to help companies, improve operations and make faster more intelligent decisions. The data is collected from a number of sources including emails, mobile devices, applications, databases, servers and other means. This data, when captured, formatted, manipulated, stored and then analysed, can help a company to gain useful insight to increase revenues, get or retain customers and improve operations.

Based on the above information, answer the following questions.

(i) .... is a collection of data that is huge in volume, yet growing exponentially with time.

(ii) .... of big data refers to structured, unstructured and semi-structured data, i.e. gathered from multiple sources.

(iii) Big data is used in field(s) ....

30. Explain system vs. application software with examples. Briefly define data deletion and why recovery matters.

Or

Write the output of the following program.

```
i = int(input("Enter first number: "))
j = int(input("Enter second number: "))
k = int(input("Enter third number: "))
print("i =", i)
print("j =", j)
print("k =", k)
largest = i
if j > largest:
    largest = j
if k > largest:
    largest = k
print("The largest number is", largest)
```

31. Read the following data

Item_Code	Item_Name	Price
100	Refrigerator	9000
101	Television	8000
102	Computer	12000
103	Washing Machine	7000

Write MySQL queries for the following (table name is PRODUCT)

(i) Use column alias on Price column.

(ii) Select those items whose price is greater than 7000.

32. Consider the table Shopee given below. Write commands in MySQL for (i) to (iii).

Scode	Pname	Supname	Qty	City	Price
102	Biscuit	Hide and Seek	100	Delhi	10.00
103	Jam	Kissan	110	Kolkata	25.00
101	Coffee	Nestle	200	Kolkata	55.00
106	Sauce	Maggi	56	Mumbai	55.00
107	Cake	Britannia	72	Delhi	10.00
104	Maggi	Nestle	150	Mumbai	10.00
105	Chocolate	Cadboury	170	Delhi	25.00

(i) To display names of the product, whose name is Cake.

(ii) To display code, product name and city of the product whose quantity is less than 100.

(iii) To display Supname in the table.

Or

Consider the table Exam given below. Write commands in MySQL for (i) to (iii).

SNo	Name	Stipend	Subject	Average	Division
1	Karan	400	English	68	FIRST
2	Aman	680	Mathematics	72	FIRST
3	Javed	500	Accounts	67	FIRST
4	Bishakh	200	Informatics	55	SECOND
5	Sugandha	400	History	35	THIRD
6	Suparna	550	Geography	45	THIRD

(i) To list the names of those students, who have obtained Division as FIRST.

(ii) To display a report listing Name, Subject and annual Stipend received assuming that the Stipend column has monthly stipend.

(iii) To display students, who have Accounts as Subject.

SECTION D

2×4=8

33. A student is working on a program to manage a dictionary of student names and their corresponding grades. Assist them by writing the following Python code snippets:

```
grades = {
    "Alice": 85,
    "Bob": 92,
    "Charlie": 78,
    "David": 95
}
```

(i) Write a Python statement to print the grade of "Charlie" from the grades dictionary.

(ii) Write a Python statement to add a new student named "Eve" with a grade of 88 to the grades dictionary.

(iii) Write a Python statement to remove "Bob" from the grades dictionary.

(iv) Write a Python statement to print all the student names (keys) and their corresponding grades (values) from the grades dictionary.

34. Consider the table TEACHER given below. Write commands in SQL for (i) to (iii) and output for (iv).

Table: TEACHER

Id	NAME	Department	Hiredate	Category	Gender	Salary
1	James Kaur	Art	1994-03-17	TGT	M	25000
2	Richa Nanda	English	1995-02-12	PRT	F	27000
3	Sumesh Roy	English	1989-10-16	TGT	M	28000
4	Akhilesh Madan	Math	1991-03-14	PGT	M	30000
5	Kirti Pathak	Science	1994-09-02	TGT	F	27000

(i) To display all information about teacher of PGT category.

(ii) To list the name of female teachers of English department.

(iii) Insert the new record whose detail is (6, Kiyaan Verma, Science, 1995-10-3, TGF, M, 25000)

(iv) `SELECT Name, Gender FROM TEACHER WHERE Department = "Math";`

Or

Consider the table given below and write SQL commands for (i) to (iv).

Table: STUDENT

StudentNo.	Class	Name	Game	GGrade	SupW
10	7	Sameer	Cricket	B	Photography
11	8	Sujit	Tennis	A	Gardening
12	7	Kamal	Swimming	B	Photography
13	7	Veerna	Tennis	C	Cooking
14	9	Archana	Basket Ball	A	Literature

(i) Display the number of students getting Grade 'A' in Cricket.

(ii) Display the name and class of students who play Tennis.

(iii) Display the record of student whose name is Veerna.

(iv) Insert the record as
15, 8, Akshat, Cricket, A, Photography

SECTION E

3×5=15

35. A database manager is working with an 'Employees' table and a 'Departments' table. Help them by writing the following SQL queries:

Given Tables:

Employees (EmployeeID, EmployeeName, DepartmentID, Salary)

Departments (DepartmentID, DepartmentName)

(i) Write an SQL query to display the names of all employees and their corresponding department names.

(ii) Write an SQL query to display the names of employees who have a salary greater than 50,000.

(iii) Write an SQL query to calculate the average salary of employees in each department.

(iv) Write an SQL query to display the name of the department with the highest average salary.

(v) Write an SQL query to delete the department named 'Sales' from the Departments table.

36. Consider the following dictionary:

employee = {'ID': 101, 'Name': 'Amit', 'Department': 'HR', 'Salary': 50000}

Write Python statements to:

I. Display only the keys of the dictionary.

II. Display only the values of the dictionary.

III. Add a new key-value pair 'Experience': 5 to the dictionary.

IV. Remove the key 'Salary' from the dictionary.

V. Update the value of 'Department' to 'Finance'.

37. Write suitable SQL queries for the following:

I. To create a database named SchoolDB.

II. To create a table named Students with the following attributes:

StudentID (Integer, Primary Key)

Name (VARCHAR with a maximum length of 50 characters)

Class (Integer)

Marks (Decimal with 5 digits in total and 2 after the decimal)

III. To insert a record into the Students table with the following details:

StudentID: 101

Name: 'Amit Sharma'

Class: 10

Marks: 87.50

IV. To update the Marks column of the student with StudentID = 101, setting it to 90.00.

V. To delete all records from the Students table where Marks is less than 33.00.

Or

I. Create a table named Employee with columns EmpID (integer, primary key), Name (varchar(50)), and Salary (decimal(10,2)).

II. Insert a record into the Employee table with EmpID = 101, Name = 'John Doe', and Salary = 50000.

III. Retrieve all details from the Employee table where Salary is greater than 40000.

IV. Update the Salary of the employee with EmpID 101 to 55000.

V. Delete the record of the employee whose EmpID is 101.

Answers

1. True	**2.** (b)	**3.** (b)	**4.** (c)	**5.** (d)	**6.** (c)	**7.** (a)	**8.** (c)	**9.** True	**10.** (c)
11. (a)	**12.** (c)	**13.** (b)	**14.** (c)	**15.** (b)	**16.** (a)	**17.** (b)	**18.** (c)	**19.** (b)	**20.** (a)
21. (c)									